GREGG

College Document Processing

OBER
JOHNSON
ZIMMERLY

MAP

enter

Lessons 61-120

10th Edition

Scot Ober
Ball State University

Jack E. Johnson
State University of West Georgia

Arlene Zimmerly
Los Angeles City College

Visit the *College Keyboarding* Web site at **www.mhhe.com/gdp**

**McGraw-Hill
Irwin**

Boston   Burr Ridge, IL   Dubuque, IA   Madison, WI   New York   San Francisco   St. Louis
Bangkok   Bogotá   Caracas   Kuala Lumpur   Lisbon   London   Madrid   Mexico City
Milan   Montreal   New Delhi   Santiago   Seoul   Singapore   Sydney   Taipei   Toronto

McGraw-Hill
Irwin

GREGG COLLEGE DOCUMENT PROCESSING, LESSONS 61-120

Published by McGraw-Hill/Irwin, a business unit of The McGraw-Hill Companies, Inc., 1221 Avenue of the Americas, New York, NY, 10020. Copyright © 2006, 2002, 1997, 1994, 1989, 1984, 1979, 1970, 1964, 1957 by The McGraw-Hill Companies, Inc. All

This book is printed on acid-free paper.

1 2 3 4 5 6 7 8 9 0 QPD/QPD 0 9 8 7 6 5 4

ISBN   0-07-296342-5

Editorial director: *John E. Biernat*
Publisher: *Linda Schreiber*
Sponsoring editor: *Doug Hughes*
Developmental editor: *Tammy Higham*
Developmental editor: *Megan Gates*
Marketing manager: *Keari Bedford*
Lead producer, Media technology: *Victoria Bryant*
Lead project manager: *Pat Frederickson*
Freelance project manager: *Rich Wright*
Senior production supervisor: *Michael R. McCormick*
Lead designer: *Matthew Baldwin*
Photo research coordinator: *Lori Kramer*
Senior supplement producer: *Susan Lombardi*
Senior digital content specialist: *Brian Nacik*
Cover design: *Subtle Intensity*
Interior design: *Matthew Baldwin*
Typeface: *11/12 Times Roman*
Compositor: *Seven Worldwide Publishing Solutions*
Printer: *Quebecor World Dubuque Inc.*

www.mhhe.com

CONTENTS

PART FOUR: Advanced Formatting

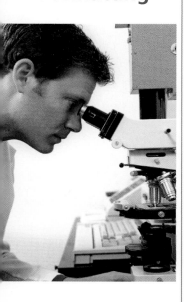

PART SIX:
Using and
Designing
Business
Documents

TEST 6 SKILLS ASSESSMENT ON PART 6 490

SKILLBUILDING

APPENDIX

INDEX

PREFACE

Gregg College Keyboarding & Document Processing Lessons 1–120, 10th Edition, is a multi-component instructional program designed to give the student and the instructor a high degree of flexibility and a high degree of success in meeting their respective goals. For student and instructor convenience, the core components of this instructional system are available in either a kit format or a book format. *Gregg College Keyboarding Lessons 1–20, 10th Edition,* is also available for the development of touch-typing skills for use in shorter computer keyboarding classes.

The Kit Format

Gregg College Keyboarding & Document Processing Lessons 1–120, 10th Edition, provides a complete kit of materials for both courses in the keyboarding curriculum generally offered by colleges. Each kit, which is briefly described below, contains a softcover textbook and a student word processing manual.

Kit 1: Lessons 1–60. This kit provides the text and word processing manual for the first course. Since this kit is designed for the beginning student, its major objectives are to develop touch control of the keyboard and proper typing techniques, to build basic speed and accuracy, and to provide practice in applying those basic skills to the formatting of reports, letters, memos, tables, and other kinds of personal and business communications.

Kit 2: Lessons 61–120. This kit provides the text and word processing manual for the second course. This course continues developing of basic typing skills and emphasizes the formatting of various kinds of business correspondence, reports, tables, electronic forms, and desktop publishing projects from arranged, unarranged, and rough-draft sources.

The Book Format

For the convenience of those who wish to obtain the core instructional materials in separate volumes, *Gregg College Keyboarding & Document Processing Lessons 1–120, 10th Edition,* offers textbooks for the first course: *Gregg College Keyboarding & Document Processing Lessons 1–60, 10th Edition,* or *Gregg College Keyboarding Lessons 1–20, 10th Edition.* For the second course, *Gregg College Document Processing Lessons 61–120* is offered, and for the two-semester course, *Gregg College Keyboarding & Document Processing Lessons 1–120* is available. In each instance, the content of the textbooks is identical to that of the corresponding textbooks in kit format. Third semester instruction is available in *Gregg College Document Processing Lessons 121–180.*

Supporting Materials

Gregg College Keyboarding & Document Processing Lessons 1–120, 10th Edition, includes the following additional components:

Instructional Materials. Supporting materials are provided for instructor use with either the kits or the textbooks. The special Instructor Wraparound Edition (IWE) offers lesson plans and reduced-size student pages to enhance classroom instruction. Distance-learning tips, instructional methodology, adult learner strategies, and special needs features are also included in this wraparound edition. Solution keys for all of the formatting exercises in Lessons 1–180 are contained in separate booklets used with this program. Finally, test booklets are available with the objective tests and alternative document processing tests for each part.

Computer Software. PC-compatible computer software is available for the entire program. The computer software provides complete lesson-by-lesson instruction for the entire 120 lessons.

Structure

Gregg College Keyboarding & Document Processing, 10th Edition, opens with a two-page part opener that introduces students to the focus of the instruction. Objectives are presented, and opportunities within career clusters are highlighted. The unit opener familiarizes students with the lesson content to be presented in the five lessons in the unit.

Every lesson begins with a Warmup that should be typed as soon as students are settled at the keyboard. In the New Keys Section, all alphabet, number, and symbol keys are introduced in the first 20 lessons. Drill lines in this section provide the practice necessary to achieve keyboarding skills.

An easily identifiable Skillbuilding section can be found in every lesson. Each drill presents to the student a variety of different activities designed to improve speed and accuracy. Skillbuilding exercises include Technique Timings, Diagnostic Practice, Paced Practice, Progressive Practice, MAP (Misstroke Analysis and Prescription), and Timed Writings, which progress from 1 to 5 minutes in length.

Many of the Skillbuilding sections also include a Pretest/Practice/Posttest routine. This routine is designed to build speed and accuracy skills as well as confidence. The Pretest helps identify speed and accuracy needs. The Practice activities consist of a variety of intensive enrichment drills. Finally, the Posttest measures improvement.

Goals

- Type at least 30wpm/3'/5e
- Format one-page business reports

Starting a Lesson

Each lesson begins with the goals for that lesson. Read the goals carefully so that you understand the purpose of your practice. In the example at the left (from Lesson 26), the goals for the lesson are to type 30wpm (words per minute) on a 3-minute timed writing with no more than 5 errors and to format one-page business reports.

Building Straight-Copy Skill

Warmups. Each lesson begins with a Warmup that reinforces learned alphabet, number, and/or symbol keys.

Skillbuilding. The Skillbuilding portion of each lesson includes a variety of drills to individualize your keyboarding speed and accuracy development. Instructions for completing the drills are always provided beside each activity.

Additional Skillbuilding drills are included in the back of the textbook. These drills are intended to help you meet your individual goals.

Measuring Straight-Copy Skill

Straight-copy skill is measured in wpm. All timed writings are the exact length needed to meet the speed goal for the lesson. If you finish a timed writing before time is up, you have automatically reached your speed goal for the lesson.

Counting Errors. Specific criteria are used for counting errors. Count an error when:

1. Any stroke is incorrect.
2. Any punctuation after a word is incorrect or omitted. Count the word before the punctuation as incorrect.
3. The spacing after a word or after its punctuation is incorrect. Count the word as incorrect.
4. A letter or word is omitted.
5. A letter or word is repeated.
6. A direction about spacing, indenting, and so on, is violated.
7. Words are transposed.

(**Note:** Only one error is counted for each word, no matter how many errors it may contain.)

Determining Speed. Typing speed is measured in wpm. To compute wpm, count every 5 strokes, including spaces, as 1 "word." Horizontal word scales below an activity divide lines into 5-stroke words. Vertical word scales beside an activity show the number of words in each line cumulatively totaled. For example, in the illustration below, if you complete a line, you have typed 8 words. If you complete 2 lines, you have typed 16 words. Use the bottom word scale to determine the word count of a partial line. Add that number to the cumulative total for the last complete line.

```
23  Ada lost her letter; Dee lost her card.        8
24  Dave sold some of the food to a market.        16
25  Alva asked Walt for three more matches.        24
26  Dale asked Seth to watch the last show.        32
     |  1  |  2  |  3  |  4  |  5  |  6  |  7  |  8  |
```

Correcting Errors

As you learn to type, you will probably make some errors. To correct an error, press BACKSPACE (shown as ← on some keyboards) to delete the incorrect character. Then type the correct character.

If you notice an error on a different line, use the up, down, left, or right arrows to move the insertion point immediately to the left or right of the error. Press BACKSPACE to delete a character to the left of the insertion point, or DELETE to delete a character to the right of the insertion point. Error-correction settings in the GDP software determine whether you can correct errors in timed writings and drills. Consult your instructor for error-correction guidelines.

Typing Technique

Correct position at the keyboard enables you to type with greater speed and accuracy and with less fatigue. When typing for a long period, rest your eyes occasionally by looking away from the screen. Change position, walk around, or stretch when your muscles feel tired. Making such movements and adjustments may help prevent your body from becoming too tired. In addition, long-term bodily damage, such as carpal tunnel syndrome, can be prevented.

If possible, adjust your workstation as follows:

Chair. Adjust the height so that your upper and lower legs form a 90-degree angle and your lower back is supported by the back of the chair.
Keyboard. Center your body opposite the J key, and lean forward slightly. Keep your forearms horizontal to the keyboard.
Screen. Position the monitor so that the top of the screen is just below eye level and about 18 to 26 inches away.
Text. Position your textbook or other copy on either side of the monitor as close to it as vertically and horizontally possible to minimize head and eye movement and to avoid neck strain.

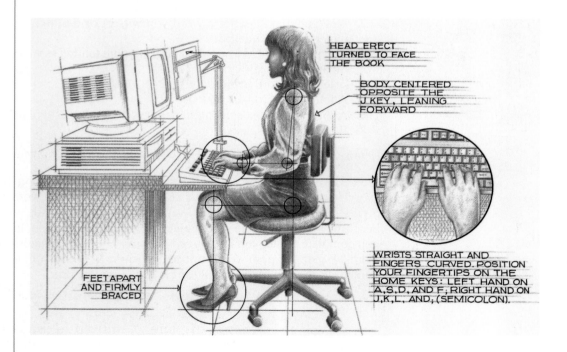

HEAD ERECT TURNED TO FACE THE BOOK

BODY CENTERED OPPOSITE THE J KEY, LEANING FORWARD

FEET APART AND FIRMLY BRACED

WRISTS STRAIGHT AND FINGERS CURVED. POSITION YOUR FINGERTIPS ON THE HOME KEYS: LEFT HAND ON A, S, D, AND F; RIGHT HAND ON J, K, L, AND ; (SEMICOLON).

ABOUT YOUR BOOK

Part 4

Advanced Formatting

Each **Part Opener** is a two-page spread that provides a list of the part objectives and a special feature that focuses on the use of your keyboarding skills in various career clusters.

Keyboarding in Health Services

Within the health services job cluster, there is an enormous range of job opportunities in the medical and health care industry. Hundreds of different occupations exist in health care practice, including business-oriented positions. In fact, career opportunities within this cluster are among the fastest growing in the national marketplace. The current job outlook is quite positive because the growth in managed care has significantly increased opportunities for doctors and other health professionals, particularly in the area of preventive care. In addition, the aging population requires more highly skilled medical workers.

Opportunities in Health Careers

Consider health care jobs, medical careers, health care management, and medical management. Various job possibilities exist in these areas, and work as a medical transcriber, clinical technician, nurse, medical analyst, surgical technician or surgeon, physical therapist, orderly, pharmacist, or medical researcher can most likely be easily found. Interestingly, keyboarding skill is important for all of these positions.

Objectives

KEYBOARDING

- Type at least 43 words per minute on a 5-minute timed writing with no more than 5 errors.

LANGUAGE ARTS

- Refine proofreading skills and correctly use proofreaders' marks.
- Use capitals, punctuation, and grammar correctly.
- Improve composing and spelling skills.
- Recognize subject/verb agreement.

WORD PROCESSING

- Use the word processing commands necessary to complete the document processing activities.

DOCUMENT PROCESSING

- Format reports, multipage letters, multipage memos, and tables.

TECHNICAL

- Answer at least 90 percent of the questions correctly on an objective test.

213

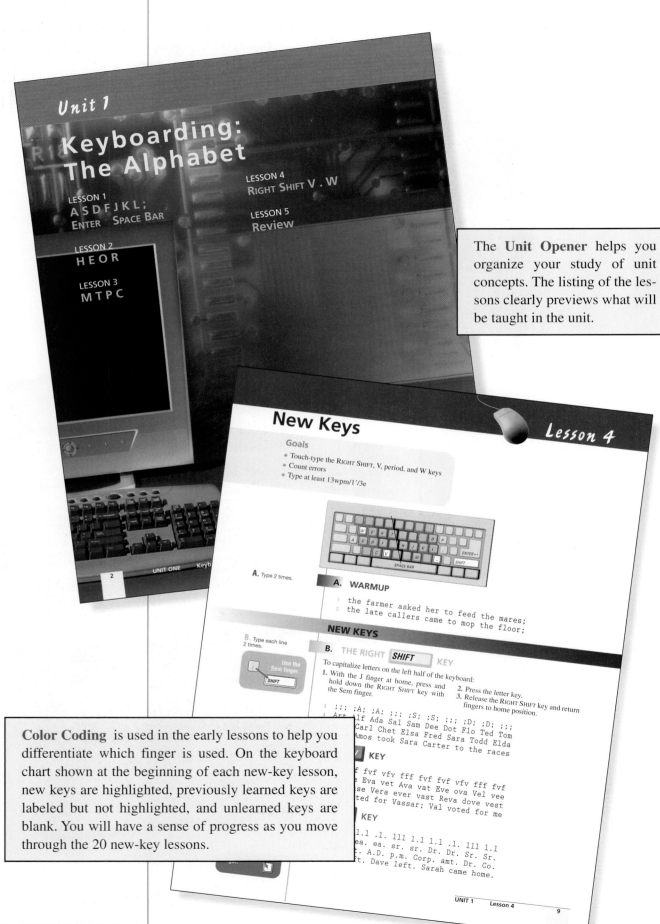

Unit 1

Keyboarding: The Alphabet

LESSON 1
ASDFJKL;
ENTER SPACE BAR

LESSON 2
H E O R

LESSON 3
M T P C

LESSON 4
RIGHT SHIFT V . W

LESSON 5
Review

The **Unit Opener** helps you organize your study of unit concepts. The listing of the lessons clearly previews what will be taught in the unit.

New Keys

Lesson 4

Goals

* Touch-type the RIGHT SHIFT, V, period, and W keys
* Count errors
* Type at least 13wpm/1'/3e

A. Type 2 times.

A. WARMUP

1 the farmer asked her to feed the mares;
2 the late callers came to mop the floor;

NEW KEYS

B. Type each line 2 times.

Use the Sem finger.

SHIFT

B. THE RIGHT **SHIFT** KEY

To capitalize letters on the left half of the keyboard:

1. With the J finger at home, press and hold down the RIGHT SHIFT key with the Sem finger.

2. Press the letter key.

3. Release the RIGHT SHIFT key and return fingers to home position.

3 ;;; ;A; ;A; ;;; ;S; ;S; ;;; ;D; ;D; ;;;
4 Art Alf Ada Sal Sam Dee Dot Flo Ted Tom
 Carl Chet Elsa Fred Sara Todd Elda
 Amos took Sara Carter to the races

KEY

f fvf vfv fff fvf fvf vfv fff fvf
 Eva vet Ava vat Eve ova Vel vee
 se Vera ever vast Reva dove vest
 ted for Vassar; Val voted for me

KEY

1.1 .1. lll 1.1 1.1 .1. lll 1.1
 ea. ea. sr. sr. Dr. Dr. Sr. Sr.
 t. A.D. p.m. Corp. amt. Dr. Co.
 t. Dave left. Sarah came home.

Color Coding is used in the early lessons to help you differentiate which finger is used. On the keyboard chart shown at the beginning of each new-key lesson, new keys are highlighted, previously learned keys are labeled but not highlighted, and unlearned keys are blank. You will have a sense of progress as you move through the 20 new-key lessons.

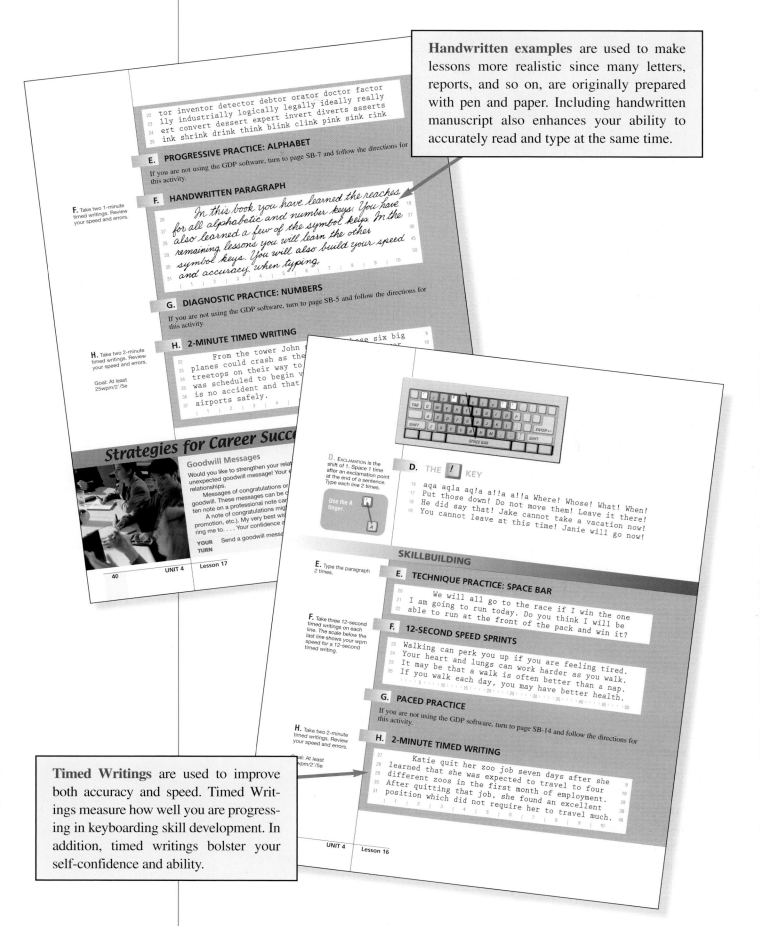

Handwritten examples are used to make lessons more realistic since many letters, reports, and so on, are originally prepared with pen and paper. Including handwritten manuscript also enhances your ability to accurately read and type at the same time.

```
22  tor inventor detector debtor orator doctor factor
23  lly industrially logically legally ideally really
24  ert convert dessert expert invert diverts asserts
25  ink shrink drink think blink clink pink sink rink
```

E. PROGRESSIVE PRACTICE: ALPHABET

If you are not using the GDP software, turn to page SB-7 and follow the directions for this activity.

F. HANDWRITTEN PARAGRAPH

In this book you have learned the reaches for all alphabetic and number keys. You have also learned a few of the symbol keys. In the remaining lessons you will learn the other symbol keys. You will also build your speed and accuracy when typing.

F. Take two 1-minute timed writings. Review your speed and errors.

G. DIAGNOSTIC PRACTICE: NUMBERS

If you are not using the GDP software, turn to page SB-5 and follow the directions for this activity.

H. 2-MINUTE TIMED WRITING

H. Take two 2-minute timed writings. Review your speed and errors.

Goal: At least 25wpm/2'/5e

```
32      From the tower John s        ose six big
33  planes could crash as the            er
34  treetops on their way to
35  was scheduled to begin v
36  is no accident and that
37  airports safely.
```

Strategies for Career Success

Goodwill Messages

Would you like to strengthen your relat...
unexpected goodwill message? Your e...
relationships.

Messages of congratulations or...
goodwill. These messages can be c...
ten note on a professional note car...

A note of congratulations migh...
promotion, etc.). My very best wis...
ring me to. . . . Your confidence a...

YOUR TURN Send a goodwill messa...

40   UNIT 4   Lesson 17

D. EXCLAMATION is the shift of 1. Space 1 time after an exclamation point at the end of a sentence. Type each line 2 times.

Use the A finger.

D. THE [!] KEY

```
16  aqa aqla aq!a a!!a a!!a Where! Whose! What! When!
17  Put those down! Do not move them! Leave it there!
18  He did say that! Jake cannot take a vacation now!
19  You cannot leave at this time! Janie will go now!
```

SKILLBUILDING

E. Type the paragraph 2 times.

E. TECHNIQUE PRACTICE: SPACE BAR

```
20      We will all go to the race if I win the one
21  I am going to run today. Do you think I will be
22  able to run at the front of the pack and win it?
```

F. Take three 12-second timed writings on each line. The scale below the last line shows your wpm speed for a 12-second timed writing.

F. 12-SECOND SPEED SPRINTS

```
23  Walking can perk you up if you are feeling tired.
24  Your heart and lungs can work harder as you walk.
25  It may be that a walk is often better than a nap.
26  If you walk each day, you may have better health.
     |  '  5 |  ' 10 |  ' 15 |  ' 20 |  ' 25 |  ' 30 |  ' 35 |  ' 40 |  ' 45 |  ' 50
```

G. PACED PRACTICE

If you are not using the GDP software, turn to page SB-14 and follow the directions for this activity.

H. Take two 2-minute timed writings. Review your speed and errors.

Goal: At least ...wpm/2'/5e

H. 2-MINUTE TIMED WRITING

```
27      Katie quit her zoo job seven days after she       9
28  learned that she was expected to travel to four
29  different zoos in the first month of employment.   19
30  After quitting that job, she found an excellent    28
31  position which did not require her to travel much. 48
     | 1 | 2 | 3 | 4 | 5 | 6 | 7 | 8 | 9 | 10 |
```

UNIT 4 | Lesson 16

Timed Writings are used to improve both accuracy and speed. Timed Writings measure how well you are progressing in keyboarding skill development. In addition, timed writings bolster your self-confidence and ability.

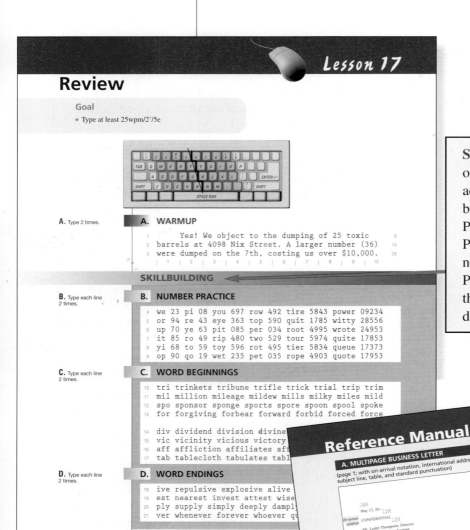

Review

Lesson 17

Goal
- Type at least 25wpm/2'/5e

A. Type 2 times.

A. WARMUP

```
1        Yes! We object to the dumping of 25 toxic     9
2 barrels at 4098 Nix Street. A larger number (36)    19
3 were dumped on the 7th, costing us over $10,000.    28
  | 1 | 2 | 3 | 4 | 5 | 6 | 7 | 8 | 9 | 10
```

SKILLBUILDING

B. Type each line 2 times.

B. NUMBER PRACTICE

```
4 we 23 pi 08 you 697 row 492 tire 5843 power 09234
5 or 94 re 43 eye 363 top 590 quit 1785 witty 28556
6 up 70 ye 63 pit 085 per 034 root 4995 wrote 24953
7 it 85 ro 49 rip 480 two 529 tour 5974 quite 17853
8 yi 68 to 59 toy 596 rot 495 tier 5834 queue 17373
9 op 90 qo 19 wet 235 pet 035 rope 4903 quote 17953
```

C. Type each line 2 times.

C. WORD BEGINNINGS

```
10 tri trinkets tribune trifle trick trial trip trim
11 mil million mileage mildew mills milky miles mild
12 spo sponsor sponge sports spore spoon spool spoke
13 for forgiving forbear forward forbid forced force

14 div dividend division divine
15 vic vicinity vicious victory
16 aff affliction affiliates aff
17 tab tablecloth tabulates tabl
```

D. Type each line 2 times.

D. WORD ENDINGS

```
18 ive repulsive explosive alive
19 est nearest invest attest wise
20 ply supply simply deeply dampl
21 ver whenever forever whoever qu
```

Skillbuilding practice in every lesson offers an individualized plan for speed and accuracy development. A variety of skill-building exercises, including Technique Practice, Pretest/Practice/Posttest, Sustained Practice, 12-Second Speed Sprints, Diagnostic Practice, Progressive Practice, Paced Practice, and Number Practice, provide the foundation for progress in your skill development.

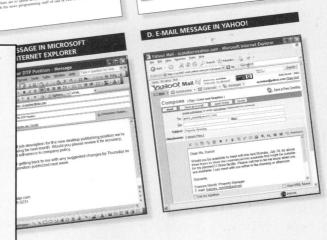

The Reference Manual material found in the front of the book and in the Word manual enables you to easily locate information regarding the proper way to format business letters, reports, e-mail messages, memoranda, and other forms of written communication. Elements such as line spacing and the placement of letterhead and body text are all illustrated in detail for your instructional support. In addition, 50 "must-know" rules for language arts in business contexts are included with examples in the Reference Manual to help improve writing skills.

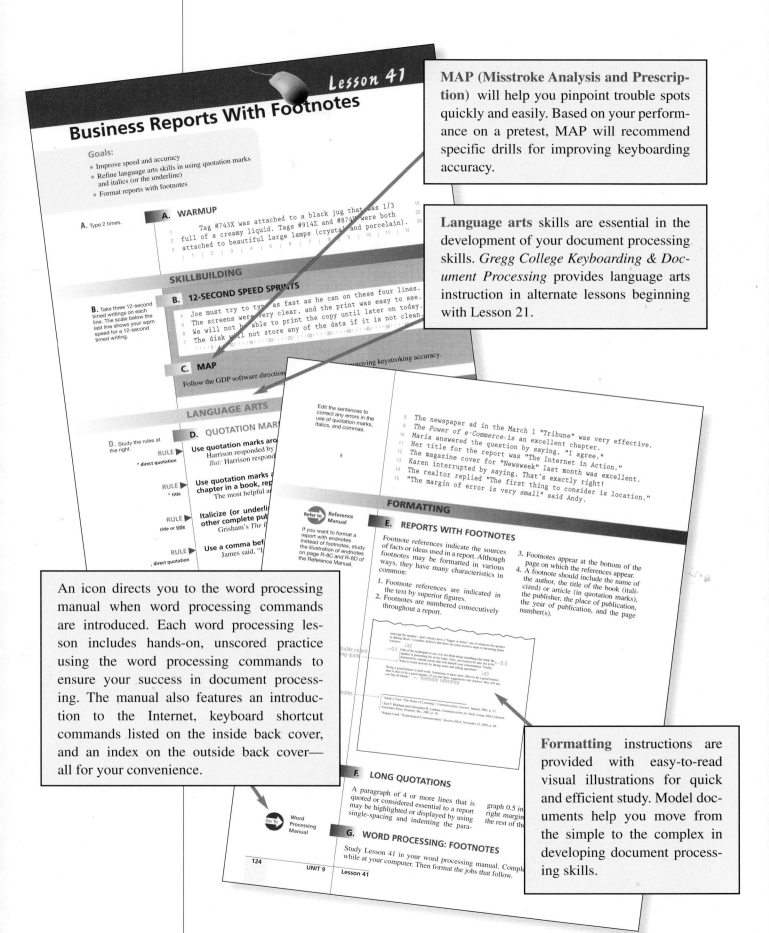

MAP (Misstroke Analysis and Prescription) will help you pinpoint trouble spots quickly and easily. Based on your performance on a pretest, MAP will recommend specific drills for improving keyboarding accuracy.

Language arts skills are essential in the development of your document processing skills. *Gregg College Keyboarding & Document Processing* provides language arts instruction in alternate lessons beginning with Lesson 21.

An icon directs you to the word processing manual when word processing commands are introduced. Each word processing lesson includes hands-on, unscored practice using the word processing commands to ensure your success in document processing. The manual also features an introduction to the Internet, keyboard shortcut commands listed on the inside back cover, and an index on the outside back cover—all for your convenience.

Formatting instructions are provided with easy-to-read visual illustrations for quick and efficient study. Model documents help you move from the simple to the complex in developing document processing skills.

Lesson 41

Business Reports With Footnotes

Goals:
- Improve speed and accuracy
- Refine language arts skills in using quotation marks and italics (or the underline)
- Format reports with footnotes

A. WARMUP

A. Type 2 times.

Tag #743X was attached to a black jug that was 1/3 full of a creamy liquid. Tags #914Z and #874Y were both attached to beautiful large lamps (crystal and porcelain).

SKILLBUILDING

B. 12-SECOND SPEED SPRINTS

B. Take three 12-second timed writings on each line. The scale below the last line shows your wpm speed for a 12-second timed writing.

Joe must try to type as fast as he can on these four lines. The screens were very clear, and the print was easy to see. We will not be able to print the copy until later on today. The disk will not store any of the data if it is not clean.

C. MAP

Follow the GDP software directions ... improving keystroking accuracy.

LANGUAGE ARTS

D. QUOTATION MARKS

D. Study the rules at the right.

RULE ▶ " direct quotation
Use quotation marks around ...
Harrison responded by ...
But: Harrison respond...

RULE ▶ " title
Use quotation marks ... chapter in a book, rep...
The most helpful a...

RULE ▶ title or *title*
Italicize (or underli... other complete pub...
Grisham's *The F*...

RULE ▶ , direct quotation
Use a comma bef...
James said, "I...

Edit the sentences to correct any errors in the use of quotation marks, italics, and commas.

8 The newspaper ad in the March 1 "Tribune" was very effective.
9 *The Power of e-Commerce* is an excellent chapter.
10 Maria answered the question by saying, "I agree."
11 Her title for the report was "The Internet in Action."
12 The magazine cover for "Newsweek" last month was excellent.
13 Karen interrupted by saying, That's exactly right!
14 The realtor replied "The first thing to consider is location."
15 "The margin of error is very small" said Andy.

FORMATTING

Refer to Reference Manual

If you want to format a report with endnotes instead of footnotes, study the illustration of endnotes on page R-8C and R-8D of the Reference Manual.

E. REPORTS WITH FOOTNOTES

Footnote references indicate the sources of facts or ideas used in a report. Although footnotes may be formatted in various ways, they have many characteristics in common:

1. Footnote references are indicated in the text by superior figures.
2. Footnotes are numbered consecutively throughout a report.

3. Footnotes appear at the bottom of the page on which the references appear.
4. A footnote should include the name of the author, the title of the book (italicized) or article (in quotation marks), the publisher, the place of publication, the year of publication, and the page number(s).

F. LONG QUOTATIONS

A paragraph of 4 or more lines that is quoted or considered essential to a report may be highlighted or displayed by using single-spacing and indenting the para-graph 0.5 in... right margin... the rest of the...

G. WORD PROCESSING: FOOTNOTES

Study Lesson 41 in your word processing manual. Comple... while at your computer. Then format the jobs that follow.

Go To Word Processing Manual

124   UNIT 9   Lesson 41

The last document processing exercise in most units is designated as a Progress Check/Proofreading Check. Make it your goal is to have zero typographical errors when the GDP software first scores the document.

Special features are designed to enhance your study of keyboarding. The *Keyboarding Connection* features illustrate the importance of keyboarding skills outside of the classroom. The *Strategies for Career Success* features offer an employment-related narrative, including useful hints for succeeding in any career.

The Appendix contains instructions for the Ten-Key Numeric Keypad. Students practice entering numerical data using touch-typing techniques.

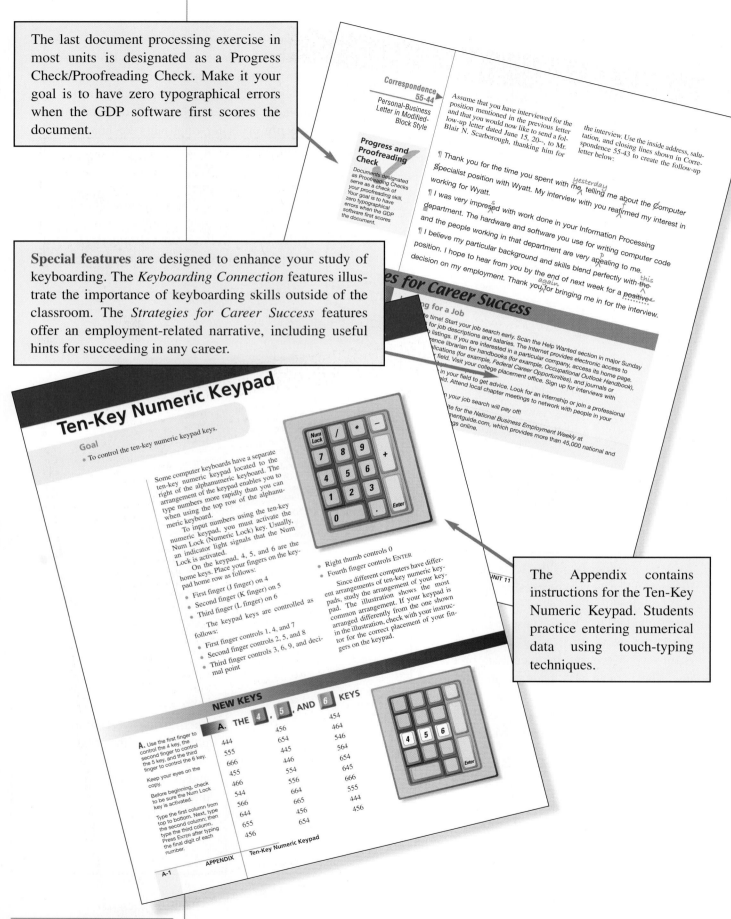

Correspondence
55-44
Personal-Business
Letter in Modified-
Block Style

Progress and Proofreading Check

Documents designated as Proofreading Checks serve as a check of your proofreading skill. Your goal is to have zero typographical errors when the GDP software first scores the document.

Assume that you have interviewed for the position mentioned in the previous letter and that you would now like to send a follow-up letter dated June 15, 20--, to Mr. Blair N. Scarborough, thanking him for the interview. Use the inside address, salutation, and closing lines shown in Correspondence 55-43 to create the follow-up letter below:

¶ Thank you for the time you spent with me, telling me about the Computer Specialist position with Wyatt. My interview with you reaffirmed my interest in working for Wyatt.

¶ I was very impressed with work done in your Information Processing department. The hardware and software you use for writing computer code and the people working in that department are very appealing to me.

¶ I believe my particular background and skills blend perfectly with the position. I hope to hear from you by the end of next week for a positive decision on my employment. Thank you for bringing me in for the interview.

Strategies for Career Success

Looking for a Job

... time! Start your job search early. Scan the Help Wanted section in major Sunday ... for job descriptions and salaries. The Internet provides electronic access to ... listings. If you are interested in a particular company, access its home page. ... ence librarian for handbooks (for example, *Occupational Outlook Handbook*), ... ications (for example, *Federal Career Opportunities*), and journals or ... field. Visit your college placement office. Sign up for interviews with ...

... in your field to get advice. Look for an internship or join a professional ... ld. Attend local chapter meetings to network with people in your ...

... on your job search will pay off!

... te for the *National Business Employment Weekly* at ... mentguide.com, which provides more than 45,000 national and ... gs online.

Ten-Key Numeric Keypad

Goal
- To control the ten-key numeric keypad keys.

Some computer keyboards have a separate ten-key numeric keypad located to the right of the alphanumeric keyboard. The arrangement of the keypad enables you to type numbers more rapidly than you can when using the top row of the alphanumeric keyboard.

To input numbers using the ten-key numeric keypad, you must activate the Num Lock (Numeric Lock) key. Usually, an indicator light signals that the Num Lock is activated.

On the keypad, 4, 5, and 6 are the home keys. Place your fingers on the keypad home row as follows:

- First finger (J finger) on 4
- Second finger (K finger) on 5
- Third finger (L finger) on 6

The keypad keys are controlled as follows:

- First finger controls 1, 4, and 7
- First finger controls 1, 2, 5, and 8
- Second finger controls 2, 5, and 8
- Second finger controls 3, 6, 9, and decimal point
- Third finger controls 3, 6, 9, and decimal point

- Right thumb controls 0
- Fourth finger controls ENTER

Since different computers have different arrangements of ten-key numeric keypads, study the arrangement of your keypad. The illustration shows the most common arrangement. If your keypad is arranged differently from the one shown in the illustration, check with your instructor for the correct placement of your fingers on the keypad.

NEW KEYS

A. THE 4, 5, AND 6 KEYS

A. Use the first finger to control the 4 key, the second finger to control the 5 key, and the third finger to control the 6 key.

Keep your eyes on the copy.

Before beginning, check to be sure the Num Lock key is activated.

Type the first column from top to bottom. Next, type the second column; then type the third column. Press ENTER after typing the final digit of each number.

	456	454
444	654	464
555	445	546
666	446	564
455	554	654
466	556	645
544	664	666
566	665	555
644	456	444
655	654	456
456		

APPENDIX   Ten-Key Numeric Keypad

A-1

70wpm

Indexing is the ability of a word processor to accumulate a list of words that appear in a document, including page numbers, and then print a revised list in alphabetic order.

72wpm

When a program needs information from you, a dialog box will appear on the desktop. Once the dialog box appears, you must identify the option you desire and then choose that option.

74wpm

A facsimile is an exact copy of a document, and it is also a process by which images, such as typed letters, graphs, and signatures, are scanned, transmitted, and then printed on paper.

76wpm

Compatibility refers to the ability of a computer to share information with another computer or to communicate with some other apparatus. It can be accomplished by using hardware or software.

78wpm

Some operators like to personalize their desktops when they use Windows by making various changes. For example, they can change their screen colors and the pointer so that they will have more fun.

80wpm

Wraparound is the ability of a word processor to move words from one line to another line and from one page to the next page as a result of inserting and deleting text or changing the size of margins.

82wpm

It is possible when using Windows to evaluate the contents of different directories o~ ~creen at the very same time. You can then choose to ~ ~rticular file from one directory to anoth~

84wpm

List processing is a ~ lists of data that c~ numeric order. A li~ is stored in one's ~

86wpm

A computer is a wo~ input and then pr~ computer perform~ programs, which ~

88wpm

The configurati~ processing sys~ used for enter~ one disk driv~

The back-of-the book skillbuilding routines are designed with YOU in mind. The Paced Practice skillbuilding paragraphs use an upbeat, motivational storyline with guidance in career choices. The Supplementary Timed Writings relate critical thinking skills to careers.

Supplementary Timed Writing 3

Office employees perform a variety of tasks during their workday. These tasks vary from handling telephone calls to forwarding personal messages, from sending short e-mail messages to compiling complex office reports, and from writing simple letters to assembling detailed letters with tables, graphics, and imported data. Office workers are a fundamental part of a company's structure.

The office worker uses critical thinking in order to accomplish a wide array of daily tasks. Some of the tasks are more urgent than other tasks and should be completed first. Some tasks take only a short time, while others take a lot more time. Some tasks demand a quick response, while others may be taken up as time permits or even postponed until the future. Some of the tasks require input from coworkers or managers. Whether a job is simple or complex, big or small, the office worker must decide what is to be tackled first by determining the priority of each task.

When setting priorities, critical thinking skills are essential. The office worker evaluates each aspect of the task. It is a good idea to identify the size of the task, determine its complexity, estimate its effort, judge its importance, and set its deadline. Once the office worker assesses each task that is to be finished within a certain period of time, then the priority for completing all tasks can be set. Critical thinking skills, if applied well, can save the employer money or, if executed poorly, can cost the employer.

| 1 | 2 | 3 | 4 | 5 | 6 | 7 | 8 | 9 | 10 | 11 | 12 |

10
21
33
44
56
67
77
88
100
111
123
135
147
158
170
182
193
204
216
228
239
250
262
274
285
296
300

Reference Manual

COMPUTER SYSTEM

keyboard, R-2B
parts of, R-2A

CORRESPONDENCE

application letter, R-12B
attachment notation, R-4D
blind copy notation, R-5B
block style, R-3A
body, R-3A
company name, R-5B
complimentary closing, R-3A
copy notation, R-3C, R-5B
date line, R-3A
delivery notation, R-4A, R-5B
e-mail, R-5C-D
enclosure notation, R-3B, R-5B
envelope formatting, R-6A
executive stationery, R-4A
half-page stationery, R-4B
inside address, R-3A
international address, R-3D
letter folding, R-6B
letterhead, R-3A
lists, R-3B-C, R-12C-D
memo, R-4D
modified-block style, R-3B
multipage, R-5A-B
on-arrival notation, R-5A
open punctuation, R-3B
page number, R-5B
personal-business, R-3D
postscript notation, R-5B
reference initials, R-3A, R-5B
return address, R-3D
salutation, R-3A
simplified style, R-3C
standard punctuation, R-3A, R-3D
subject line, R-3C, R-5A, R-7C
table, R-4D
window envelope, folding for, R-6B
window envelope, formatted for, R-4C
writer's identification, R-3A

EMPLOYMENT DOCUMENTS

application letter, R-12B
resume, R-12A

FORMS

R-14A

LANGUAGE ARTS

abbreviations, R-22
adjectives and adverbs, R-20
agreement, R-19
apostrophes, R-17
capitalization, R-21
colons, R-18
commas, R-15 to R-16
grammar, R-19 to R-20
hyphens, R-17
italics (or underline), R-18
mechanics, R-21 to R-22
number expression, R-21 to R-22
periods, R-18
pronouns, R-20
punctuation, R-15 to R-18
quotation marks, R-18
semicolons, R-16
sentences, R-19
underline (or italics), R-18
word usage, R-20

PROOFREADERS' MARKS

R-14C

REPORTS

academic style, R-8C-D
agenda, R-11A
APA style, R-10A-B
author/year citations, R-10A
bibliography, R-9B
business style, R-8A-B, R-9A
byline, R-8A
citations, R-9D
date, R-8A
endnotes, R-8C-D
footnotes, R-8A-B
headings, R-9D
headings, paragraph, R-8A
headings, side, R-8A
itinerary, R-11C
left-bound, R-9A
legal document, R-11D
lists, R-8A, R-8C, R-12D
margins, R-9D
memo report, R-9C
minutes of a meeting, R-11B
MLA style, R-10C-D
outline, R-7A
quotation, long, R-8B, R-8D
references page, R-10B
resume, R-12A
spacing, R-9D
subtitle, R-8A
table, R-8B
table of contents, R-7D
title, R-8A
title page, R-7B
transmittal memo, R-7C
works-cited page, R-10D

TABLES

2-line column heading, R-13B
body, R-13A
boxed, R-13A
capitalization in columns, R-13D
column headings, R-13A-D
in correspondence, R-4D, R-5A
dollar signs, R-13D
heading block, R-13D
note, R-13A
open, R-13B
percent signs, R-13D
in reports, R-8B, R-13C
ruled, R-13C
subtitle, R-13A, R-13D
table number, R-13C
table source, R-8B
title, R-13A
total line, R-13A, R13-D
vertical placement, R-13D

U.S. POSTAL SERVICE STATE ABBREVIATIONS

R-14B

A. MAJOR PARTS OF A MICROCOMPUTER SYSTEM

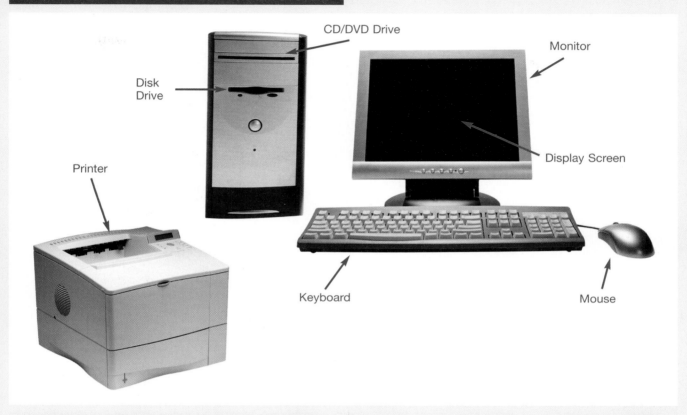

CD/DVD Drive

Disk Drive

Monitor

Printer

Display Screen

Keyboard

Mouse

B. THE COMPUTER KEYBOARD

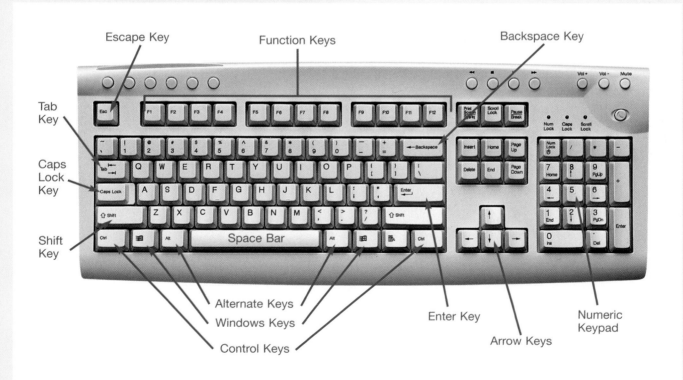

Escape Key

Function Keys

Backspace Key

Tab Key

Caps Lock Key

Shift Key

Alternate Keys

Windows Keys

Control Keys

Enter Key

Arrow Keys

Numeric Keypad

A. BUSINESS LETTER IN BLOCK STYLE
(with standard punctuation)

Date line September 5, 20-- ↓4X
↓6X

Inside address Ms. Joan R. Hunter
Bolwater Associates
One Parklands Drive
Darien, CT 06820 ↓2X

Salutation Dear Ms. Hunter: ↓2X

Body You will soon receive the signed contract to have your organization conduct a one-day workshop for our employees on eliminating repetitive-motion injuries in the workplace. As we agreed, this workshop will apply to both our office and factory workers and you will conduct separate sessions for each group.

We revised Paragraph 4b to require the instructor of this workshop to be a full-time employee of Bolwater Associates. In addition, we made changes to Paragraph 10-c to require our prior approval of the agenda for the workshop.

If these revisions are satisfactory, please sign and return one copy of the contract for our files. We look forward to this opportunity to enhance the health of our employees. I know that all of us will enjoy this workshop. ↓2X

Complimentary closing Sincerely, ↓4X

Writer's identification John L. Merritt
John L. Merritt, Director ↓2X

Reference initials fej

B. BUSINESS LETTER IN MODIFIED-BLOCK STYLE
(with open punctuation, multiline list, and enclosure notation)

Left tab: 3"
↓6X
→tab to centerpoint   May 15, 20-- ↓4X

Mr. Ichiro Xie
Bolwater Associates
One Parklands Drive
Darien, CT 06820 ↓2X

Dear Mr. Xie ↓2X

I am returning a signed contract to have your organization conduct a one-day workshop for our employees on eliminating repetitive-motion injuries in the workplace. We have made the following changes to the contract:

Multiline list 1. We revised Paragraph 4b to require the instructor of this workshop to be a full-time employee of Bolwater Associates.

2. We made changes to Paragraph 10-c to require our prior approval of the agenda for the workshop.

If these revisions are satisfactory, please sign and return one copy of the contract for our files. We look forward to this opportunity to enhance the health of our employees. I know that all of us will enjoy this workshop. ↓2X

→tab to centerpoint   Sincerely ↓4X
Reinalda Guerrero
Reinalda Guerrero, Director ↓2X

Enclosure notation pec
Enclosure

C. BUSINESS LETTER IN SIMPLIFIED STYLE
(with single-line list, enclosure notation, and copy notation)

↓6X
October 5, 20-- ↓4X

Mr. Dale P. Griffin
Bolwater Associates
One Parklands Drive
Darien, CT 06820 ↓3X

Subject line WORKSHOP CONTRACT ↓3X

I am returning the signed contract, Ms. Hunter, to have your organization conduct a one-day workshop for our employees on eliminating repetitive-motion injuries in the workplace. We have amended the following sections of the contract:

Single-line list • Paragraph 4b
• Table 3
• Attachment 2

If these revisions are satisfactory, please sign and return one copy of the contract for our files. We look forward to this opportunity to enhance the health of our employees. I know that all of us will enjoy this workshop. ↓4X

Kachina Haddad

KACHINA HADDAD, DIRECTOR ↓2X

iww
Enclosure
Copy notation c: Legal Department

D. PERSONAL-BUSINESS LETTER IN MODIFIED-BLOCK STYLE
(with international address and standard punctuation)

Left tab: 3"
↓6X
→tab to centerpoint   July 15, 20-- ↓4X

Mr. Luis Fernandez, President
Arvon Industries, Inc.
21 St. Claire Avenue East
International Address Toronto, ON M4T IL9
CANADA ↓2X

Dear Mr. Fernandez: ↓2X

As a former employee and present stockholder of Arvon Industries, I wish to protest the planned sale of the Consumer Products Division.

According to published reports, consumer products accounted for 19 percent of last year's corporate profits, and they are expected to account for even more this year. In addition, Dun & Bradstreet predicts that consumer products nationwide will outpace the general economy for the next five years.

I am concerned about the effect that this planned sale will have on overall corporate profits, on cash dividends for investors, and on the economy of Melbourne, where the two consumer-products plants are located. Please ask your board of directors to reconsider this matter. ↓2X

→tab to centerpoint   Sincerely, ↓4X
Roger J. Michaelson

Return address Roger J. Michaelson
901 East Benson, Apt. 3
Fort Lauderdale, FL 33301

Reference Manual

A. BUSINESS LETTER ON EXECUTIVE STATIONERY

(7.25" x 10.5"; 1" side margins; with delivery notation and standard punctuation.)

↓6X

July 18, 20-- ↓4X

Mr. Rodney Eastwood
BBL Resources
52A Northern Ridge
Fayetteville, PA 17222 ↓2X

Dear Rodney: ↓2X

I see no reason why we should continue to consider the locality around Geraldton for our new plant. Even though the desirability of this site from an economic view is undeniable, there is insufficient housing readily available for our workers.

In trying to control urban growth, the city has been turning down the building permits for new housing or placing so many restrictions on foreign investment as to make it too expensive.

Please continue to seek out other areas of exploration where we might form a joint partnership. ↓2X

Sincerely, ↓4X

Dalit Chande

Dalit Chande
Vice President for Operations ↓2X

mme
Delivery notation By Fax

B. BUSINESS LETTER ON HALF-PAGE STATIONERY

(5.5" x 8.5"; 0.75" side margins and standard punctuation)

↓4X

July 18, 20-- ↓4X

Mr. Aristeo Olivas
BBL Resources
52A Northern Ridge
Fayetteville, PA 17222 ↓2X

Dear Aristeo: ↓2X

We should continue considering Geraldton for our new plant. Even though the desirability of this site from an economic view is undeniable, there is insufficient housing readily available.

Please continue to search out other areas of new exploration where we might someday form a joint partnership. ↓2X

Sincerely, ↓4X

Mieko Nakamura

Mieko Nakamura
Vice President for Operations ↓2X

adk

C. BUSINESS LETTER FORMATTED FOR A WINDOW ENVELOPE

(with standard punctuation)

↓6X

July 18, 20-- ↓3X

Ms. Reinalda Guerrero
BBL Resources
52A Northern Ridge
Fayetteville, PA 17222 ↓3X

Dear Ms. Guerrero: ↓2X

I see no reason why we should continue to consider the locality around Geraldton for our new plant. Even though the desirability of this site from an economic view is undeniable, there is insufficient housing readily available for our workers.

In trying to control urban growth, the city has been turning down the building permits for new housing or placing so many restrictions on foreign investment as to make it too expensive.

Please continue to seek out other areas of exploration where we might form a joint partnership. ↓2X

Sincerely, ↓4X

Arlyn J. Bunch

Arlyn J. Bunch
Vice President for Operations ↓2X

woc

D. MEMO

(with table and attachment notation)

↓6X →tab

MEMO TO: Nancy Price, Executive Vice President ↓2X

FROM: Arlyn J. Bunch, Operations ajb ↓2X

DATE: July 18, 20-- ↓2X

SUBJECT: New Plant Site ↓2X

As you can see from the attached letter, I've informed BBL Resources that I see no reason why we should continue to consider the locality around Geraldton for our new plant. Even though the desirability of this site from an economic standpoint is undeniable, there is insufficient housing available. In fact, as of June 25, the number of appropriate single-family houses listed for sale within a 25-mile radius of Geraldton was as follows: ↓2X

Agent	Units
Belle Real Estate	123
Castleton Homes	11
Red Carpet	9
Geraldton Homes	5

↓1X

In addition, in trying to control urban growth, Geraldton has been either turning down building permits for new housing or placing excessive restrictions on them.

Because of this deficiency of housing for our employees, we have no choice but to look elsewhere. ↓2X

woc
Attachment notation Attachment

A. MULTIPAGE BUSINESS LETTER

(page 1; with on-arrival notation, international address, subject line, table, and standard punctuation)

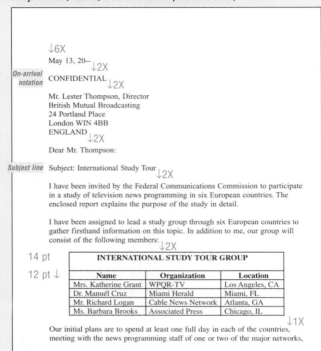

B. MULTIPAGE BUSINESS LETTER

(page 2; with company name; multiline list; enclosure, delivery, copy, postscript, blind copy notations; and standard punctuation)

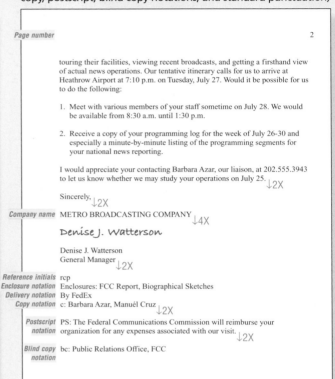

C. E-MAIL MESSAGE IN MICROSOFT OUTLOOK/ INTERNET EXPLORER

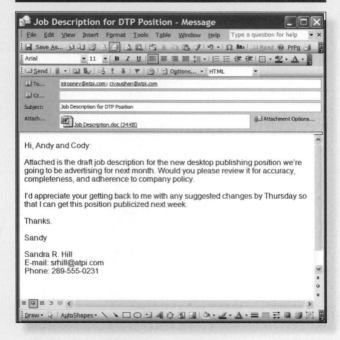

D. E-MAIL MESSAGE IN YAHOO!

A. FORMATTING ENVELOPES

A standard large (No. 10) envelope is 9.5 by 4.125 inches. A standard small (No. 6¼) envelope is 6.5 by 3.625 inches. Although either address format shown below is acceptable, the format shown for the large envelope (all caps and no punctuation) is recommended by the U.S. Postal Service for mail that will be sorted by an electronic scanning device.

Window envelopes are often used in a word processing environment because of the difficulty of aligning envelopes correctly in some printers. A window envelope requires no formatting, since the letter is formatted and folded so that the inside address is visible through the window.

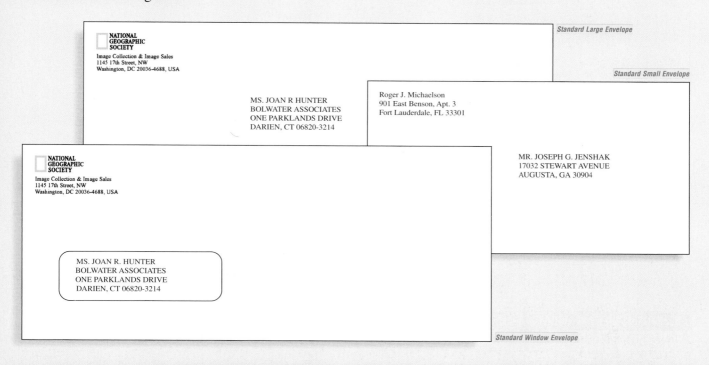

B. FOLDING LETTERS

To fold a letter for a large envelope:

1. Place the letter *face up* and fold up the bottom third.
2. Fold the top third down to 0.5 inch from the bottom edge.
3. Insert the last crease into the envelope first, with the flap facing up.

To fold a letter for a small envelope:

1. Place the letter *face up* and fold up the bottom half to 0.5 inch from the top.
2. Fold the right third over to the left.
3. Fold the left third over to 0.5 inch from the right edge.
4. Insert the last crease into the envelope first, with the flap facing up.

To fold a letter for a window envelope:

1. Place the letter *face down* with the letterhead at the top and fold the bottom third of the letter up.
2. Fold the top third down so that the address shows.
3. Insert the letter into the envelope so that the address shows through the window.

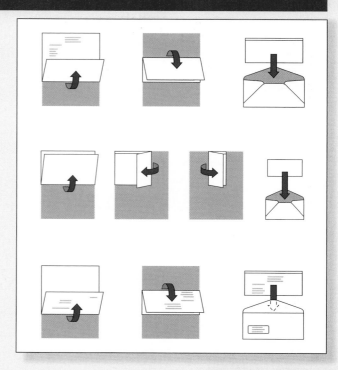

Reference Manual

A. OUTLINE

Right tab: 0.3"; left tabs: 0.4", 0.7"

↓6X

14 pt **AN ANALYSIS OF THE SCOPE AND EFFECTIVENESS**
OF ONLINE ADVERTISING ↓2X

12 pt↓ **The Status of Point-and-Click Selling** ↓2X

tab **Jonathan R. Evans** ↓2X

January 19, 20-- ↓2X

I. INTRODUCTION ↓2X

II. SCOPE AND TRENDS IN INTERNET ADVERTISING
   A. Internet Advertising
   B. Major Online Advertisers
   C. Positioning and Pricing
   D. Types of Advertising ↓2X

III. ADVERTISING EFFECTIVENESS
   A. The Banner Debate
   B. Increasing Advertising Effectiveness
   C. Measuring ROI ↓2X

IV. CONCLUSION

B. TITLE PAGE

center page↓

14 pt **AN ANALYSIS OF THE SCOPE AND EFFECTIVENESS**
OF ONLINE ADVERTISING ↓2X

12 pt↓ **The Status of Point-and-Click Selling** ↓12X

Submitted to ↓2X

Luis Torres
General Manager
ViaWorld, International ↓12X

Prepared by ↓2X

Jonathan R. Evans
Assistant Marketing Manager
ViaWorld, International ↓2X

January 19, 20--

C. TRANSMITTAL MEMO

(with 2-line subject line and attachment notation)

↓6X

→ tab

MEMO TO: Luis Torres, General Manager ↓2X

FROM: Jonathan R. Evans, Assistant Marketing Manager *jre* ↓2X

DATE: January 19, 20-- ↓2X

SUBJECT: An Analysis of the Scope and Effectiveness of Online
Advertising ↓2X

Here is the report analyzing the scope and effectiveness of Internet
advertising that you requested on January 5, 20--.

The report predicts that the total value of the business-to-business e-commerce
market will reach $1.3 trillion by 2003, up from $190 billion in 1999. New
technologies aimed at increasing Internet ad interactivity and the adoption of
standards for advertising response measurement and tracking will contribute to
this increase. Unfortunately, as discussed in this report, the use of "rich media"
and interactivity in Web advertising will create its own set of problems.

I enjoyed working on this assignment, Luis, and learned quite a bit from my
analysis of the situation. Please let me know if you have any questions about
the report. ↓2X

plw
Attachment

D. TABLE OF CONTENTS

Left tab: 0.5"; right dot-leader tab: 6".

↓6X

14 pt **CONTENTS** ↓2X

Reference Manual

A. BUSINESS REPORT

(page 1; with footnotes and multiline list)

↓6X

Title 14 pt **AN ANALYSIS OF THE SCOPE AND EFFECTIVENESS OF ONLINE ADVERTISING**
↓2X

Subtitle 12 pt↓ **The Status of Point-and-Click Selling**
↓2X

Byline **Jonathan R. Evans**
↓2X

Date **January 19, 20--**
↓2X

Over the past three years, the number of American households online has tripled, from an estimated 15 million in 1996 to 45 million in 1999. Jupiter Communications, predicts that by the year 2003, 70 million households, representing about 62 percent of all U.S. households, will be online. ↓2X

Side head **GROWTH FACTORS**
↓2X

Online business has grown in tandem with the expanding number of Internet users. Forrester Research Inc. predicts that the total value of business-to-business e-commerce will reach $109 billion in 1999 and is likely to reach $1.3 trillion by 2003.[1] ↓2X

Paragraph head **Uncertainty.** The uncertainties surrounding advertising on the Internet remain one of the major impediments to the expansion. The Internet advertising industry is today in a state of flux. ↓2X

Reasons for Not Advertising Online. A recent Association of National Advertisers survey found two main reasons cited for not advertising online:[2] ↓2X

1. The difficulty of determining return on investment, especially in terms of repeat business

2. The lack of reliable tracking and measurement data

Footnotes
[1] George Anders, "Buying Frenzy," *The Wall Street Journal*, July 12, 1999, p. R6.
[2] "eStats: Advertising Revenues and Trends," *eMarketer*, August 11, 1999, <http:www.emarketer.com/estats/ad>, accessed on January 7, 2000.

B. BUSINESS REPORT

(page 3; with long quotation and table)

3

who argue that banners have a strong potential for advertising effectiveness point out that it is not the banner format itself which presents a problem to advertising effectiveness, but rather the quality of the banner and the attention to its placement. According to Mike Windsor, president of Ogilvy Interactive: ↓2X

indent 0.5" Long quotation It's more a case of bad banner ads, just like there are bad TV ads. The space itself has huge potential. As important as using the space within the banner creatively is to aim it effectively. Unlike broadcast media, the Web offers advertisers the opportunity to reach a specific audience based on data gathered about who is surfing at a site and what their interests are[1] ← indent 0.5"

Thus, while some analysts continue to argue that the banner advertisement is passé, there is little evidence of its abandonment. Instead, ad agencies are focusing on increasing the banner's effectiveness. ↓2X

SCOPE AND TRENDS IN ONLINE ADVERTISING
↓2X

Starting from zero in 1994, analysts agree that the volume of Internet advertising spending has risen rapidly. However, as indicated in Table 3, analysts provide a wide range of the exact amount of such advertising. ↓2X

14 pt
12 pt↓

TABLE 3. INTERNET ADVERTISING
1998 Estimates

Source	Estimate
Internet Advertising Board	$1.92 billion
Forester	1.30 billion
IDC	1.20 billion
Burst! Media	560 million

Table source Source: "Advertising Age Teams with eMarketer for Research Report," *Advertising Age*, May 3, 1999, p. 24. ↓1X

The differences in estimates of total Web advertising spending is generally attributed to the different methodologies used by the research agencies to

[1] Lisa Napoli, "Banner Ads Are Under the Gun—And On the Move," *The New York Times*, June 17, 1999, p. D1.

C. ACADEMIC REPORT

(page 1; with endnotes and multiline list)

↓3DS

14 pt **AN ANALYSIS OF THE SCOPE AND EFFECTIVENESS OF ONLINE ADVERTISING** ↓1DS

12 pt↓ **The Status of Point-and-Click Selling** ↓1DS

Jonathan R. Evans ↓1DS

January 19, 20-- ↓1DS

Over the past three years, the number of American households online has tripled, from an estimated 15 million in 1996 to 45 million in 1999. Jupiter Communications, predicts that by the year 2003, 70 million households, representing about 62 percent of all U.S. households, will be online. ↓1DS

GROWTH FACTORS ↓1DS

Online business has grown in tandem with the expanding number of Internet users. Forrester Research Inc. predicts that the total value of business-to-business e-commerce will reach $109 billion in 1999.[1]

Reasons for Not Advertising Online. A recent Association of National Advertisers survey found two main reasons cited for not advertising online:[2]

1. The difficulty of determining return on investment, especially in terms of repeat business.

2. The lack of reliable tracking and measurement data.

Some analysts argue that advertising on the Internet can and should follow the same principles as advertising on television.[3] Other visual media

D. ACADEMIC REPORT

(last page; with long quotation and endnotes)

14

advertising effectiveness, but rather the quality of the banner and the attention to its placement. According to Mike Windsor, president of Ogilvy Interactive: ↓1DS

indent 0.5" Long quotation It's more a case of bad banner ads, just like there are bad TV ads. The space itself has huge potential. As important as using the space within the banner creatively is to aim it effectively. Unlike broadcast media, the Web offers advertisers the opportunity to reach a specific audience based on data gathered about who is surfing at a site and what their interests are.[7] ← indent 0.5" ↓1SS

From the advertiser's perspective, the most effective Internet ads do more than just deliver information to the consumer and grab the consumer's attention—they also gather information about consumers (e.g., through "cookies" and other methodologies). From the consumer's perspective, this type of interactivity may represent an intrusion and an invasion of privacy. There appears to be a shift away from the ad-supported model and toward the transaction model, wherein users pay for the content they want and the specific transactions they perform.

Endnotes
[i] George Anders, "Buying Frenzy," *The Wall Street Journal*, July 12, 1999, p. R6.
[ii] "eStats: Advertising Revenues and Trends," *eMarketer*, August 11, 1999, <http:www.emarketer.com/estats/ad>, accessed on August 11, 1999.
[iii] Bradley Johnson, "Nielsen/NetRatings Index Shows 4% Rise in Web Ads," *Advertising Age*, July 19, 2003, p. 18.
[iv] Tom Hyland, "Web Advertising: A Year of Growth," *Internet Advertising Board*, November 13, 1999, <http:www.iab.net/advertise>, accessed on January 8, 2000.
[v] Adrian Mand, "Click Here: Free Ride Doles Out Freebies to Ad Surfers," *Brandweek*, March 8, 1999, p. 30.
[vi] Andrea Petersen, "High Price of Internet Banner Ads Slips Amid Increase in Web Sites," *The Wall Street Journal*, March 2, 1999, p. B20.
[vii] Lisa Napoli, "Banner Ads Are Under the Gun—And On the Move," *The New York Times*, June 17, 1999, p. D1.

Reference Manual

A. LEFT-BOUND BUSINESS REPORT

(page 1; with endnotes and single-line list)

Left margin: 1.75"   Right margin: *default* (1.25")

↓6X

14 pt

AN ANALYSIS OF THE SCOPE AND EFFECTIVENESS OF ONLINE ADVERTISING ↓2X

12 pt↓

The Status of Point-and-Click Selling ↓2X

Jonathan R. Evans ↓2X

January 19, 20-- ↓2X

Over the past three years, the number of American households online has tripled, from an estimated 15 million in 1996 to 45 million in 1999. Jupiter Communications predicts that by the year 2003, 70 million households will be online. ↓2X

GROWTH FACTORS ↓2X

Online business has grown in tandem with the expanding number of Internet users. Forrester Research Inc. predicts that the total value of business-to-business e-commerce will reach $109 billion in 1999 and is likely to reach $1.3 trillion by 2003.[1]

ᶦ ↓2X

Uncertainty. The uncertainties surrounding advertising on the Internet remain one of the major impediments to the expansion. Dating from just 1994, when the first banner ads appeared on the Hotwired home page, the Internet advertising industry is today in a state of flux. ↓2X

Some analysts argue that advertising on the Internet can and should follow the same principles as advertising on television and other visual media. Others contend that advertising on the Internet should reflect the unique characteristics of this new medium. ↓2X

Reasons for Not Advertising Online. A recent Association of National Advertisers survey found two main reasons cited for not advertising online:[ii] ↓2X

1. The difficulty of determining return on investment
2. The lack of reliable tracking and measurement data

B. BIBLIOGRAPHY

(for business or academic style using either endnotes or footnotes)

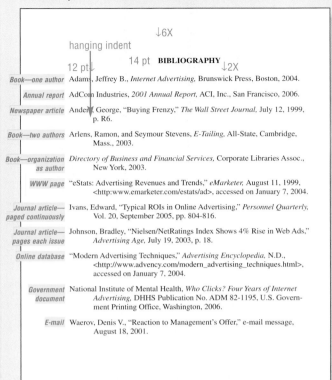

↓6X

hanging indent

12 pt↓   14 pt   **BIBLIOGRAPHY** ↓2X

Book—one author   Adams, Jeffrey B., *Internet Advertising*, Brunswick Press, Boston, 2004.

Annual report   AdCom Industries, *2001 Annual Report*, ACI, Inc., San Francisco, 2006.

Newspaper article   Anders, George, "Buying Frenzy," *The Wall Street Journal*, July 12, 1999, p. R6.

Book—two authors   Arlens, Ramon, and Seymour Stevens, *E-Tailing*, All-State, Cambridge, Mass., 2003.

Book—organization as author   *Directory of Business and Financial Services*, Corporate Libraries Assoc., New York, 2003.

WWW page   "eStats: Advertising Revenues and Trends," *eMarketer*, August 11, 1999, <http:www.emarketer.com/estats/ad>, accessed on January 7, 2004.

Journal article— paged continuously   Ivans, Edward, "Typical ROIs in Online Advertising," *Personnel Quarterly*, Vol. 20, September 2005, pp. 804-816.

Journal article— pages each issue   Johnson, Bradley, "Nielsen/NetRatings Index Shows 4% Rise in Web Ads," *Advertising Age*, July 19, 2003, p. 18.

Online database   "Modern Advertising Techniques," *Advertising Encyclopedia*, N.D., <http://www.advency.com/modern_advertising_techniques.html>, accessed on January 7, 2004.

Government document   National Institute of Mental Health, *Who Clicks? Four Years of Internet Advertising*, DHHS Publication No. ADM 82-1195, U.S. Government Printing Office, Washington, 2006.

E-mail   Waerov, Denis V., "Reaction to Management's Offer," e-mail message, August 18, 2001.

C. MEMO REPORT

(page 1, with single-line list)

↓6X

→tab

MEMO TO: Luis Torres, General Manager ↓2X

FROM: Jonathan R. Evans, Assistant Marketing Manager *jre* ↓2X

DATE: January 19, 20-- ↓2X

SUBJECT: An Analysis of the Scope and Effectiveness of Online Advertising ↓2X

According to a July 12, 1999, Wall Street Journal article, over the past three years, the number of American households online has tripled, from an estimated 15 million in 1996 to 45 million in 1999. Jupiter Communications, predicts that by the year 2003, 70 million households, representing 62 percent of all U.S. households, will be online. Online business has grown in tandem with the expanding number of Internet users. Forrester Research Inc. predicts that the total value of business-to-business e-commerce will reach $109 billion in 1999 and is likely to reach $1.3 trillion by 2003. ↓2X

UNCERTAINTY ↓2X

The uncertainties surrounding advertising on the Internet remain one of the major impediments to the expansion. Dating from just 1994, when the first banner ads appeared on the Hotwired home page, the Internet advertising industry is today in a state of flux.

Some analysts argue that advertising on the Internet can and should follow the same principles as advertising on television and other visual media. Others contend that all of the advertising on the Internet should reflect the unique characteristics of this new medium.

A recent Association of National Advertisers survey found two main reasons cited for not advertising online:

1. The difficulty of determining return on investment
2. The lack of reliable tracking and measurement data

D. REPORTS: SPECIAL FEATURES

Margins and Spacing. Use a 2-inch top margin for the first page of each section of a report (for example, the table of contents, first page of the body, and bibliography page) and a 1-inch top margin for other pages. Use default side margins (1.25 inches) and bottom margins (1 inch) for all pages. If the report is going to be bound on the left, add 0.5 inch to the left margin. Single-space business reports and double-space academic reports.

Headings. Center the report title in 14-point font (press ENTER to space down before switching to 12-point font). Single-space multiline report titles in a single-spaced report and double-space multiline titles in a double-spaced report. Insert 1 blank line before and after all parts of a heading block (consisting of the title, subtitle, author, and/or date) and format all lines in bold.

Insert 1 blank line before and after side headings and format in bold, beginning at the left margin. Format paragraph headings in bold; begin at the left margin for single-spaced reports and indent for double-spaced reports. The text follows on the same line, preceded by a period and 1 space.

Citations. For business and academic reports, format citations using your word processor's footnote (or endnote) feature. For reports formatted in APA or MLA style, use the format shown on page R-10.

Reference Manual

A. REPORT IN APA STYLE

(page 1; with author/year citations)

Top, bottom, and side margins: 1"

An Analysis of the Scope and Effectiveness

of Online Advertising

Jonathan R. Evans

Over the past three years, the number of American households online has tripled, from an estimated 15 million in 1996 to 45 million in 1999. Jupiter Communications predicts that by the year 2003, 70 million households, which represent 62 percent of all U.S. households, will be online (Napoli, 2003).

main head
Growth Factors

Online business has grown in tandem with the expanding number of Internet users. Forrester Research Inc. predicts that the total value of business-to-business e-commerce will reach $109 billion in 2003 (Arlens & Stevens, 2003).

subhead *Uncertainty*

The uncertainties surrounding advertising on the Internet remain one of the major impediments to the expansion. Dating from just 1994. when the first banner ads appeared on the Hotwired home page, the Internet advertising industry is today in a state of flux.

Some analysts argue that advertising on the Internet can and should follow the same principles as advertising on television and other visual media ("eStats," 2004). Others contend that advertising on the Internet should reflect

B. REFERENCES IN APA STYLE

Top, bottom, and side margins: 1"
Double-space throughout.
hanging indent

References

Book—one author Adams, J. B. (2004). *Internet advertising*. Boston: Brunswick Press.

Annual report AdCom Industries. (2006). 2005 *annual report*. San Francisco: ACI, Inc.

Newspaper article Anders, G. (2003, July 12). Buying frenzy. *The Wall Street Journal,* p. R6.

Book—two authors Arlens, R., & Stevens, S. (2003). *E-tailing*. Cambridge, MA: All-State.

Book—organization as author *Directory of business and financial services*. (2003). New York: Corporate Libraries Association.

WWW page eStats: Advertising revenues and trends. (n.d.). New York: eMarketer. Retrieved August 11, 2004, from the World Wide Web: http://www.emarketer.com/estats/ad

Journal article— paged continuously Ivans, E. (2005). Typical ROIs in online advertising. *Personnel Quarterly,* 20, 804-816.

Journal article— paged each issue Johnson, B. (2003, July 19). Nielsen/NetRatings Index shows 4% rise in Web ads. Advertising Age, 39, 18.

Online database *Modern advertising techniques*. (1998, January). *Advertising Encyclopedia*. Retrieved January 7, 2004, from http://www.advency.com/ads.html

Government document National Institute of Mental Health *Who clicks? Four years of Internet advertising* (DHHS Publication No. ADM 82-1195). Washington, DC. (2006).

C. REPORT IN MLA STYLE

(page 1; with author/page citations)

Top, bottom, and side margins: 1"
Double-space throughout.

Jonathan R. Evans

Professor Inman

Management 302

19 January 20--

An Analysis of the Scope and Effectiveness

of Online Advertising

Over the past three years, the number of American households online has tripled, from an estimated 15 million in 1996 to 45 million in 1999. Jupiter Communications predicts that by the year 2003, 70 million households, representing about 62% of all U.S. households, will be online (Napoli D1). Online business has grown in tandem with the expanding number of Internet users. Forrester Research Inc. predicts that the total value of business-to-business e-commerce will reach $109 billion in 1999 and is likely to reach $1.3 trillion by 2003 (Arlens & Stevens 376-379).

The uncertainties surrounding advertising on the Internet remain one of the major impediments to the expansion. Dating from just 1994, when the first banner ads appeared on the Hotwired home page, the Internet advertising industry is today in a state of flux.

Some analysts argue that advertising on the Internet can and should follow the same principles as advertising on television and other visual media ("eStats"). Others contend that advertising on the Internet should reflect the

D. WORKS CITED IN MLA STYLE

Top, bottom, and side margins: 1"
Double-space throughout.
hanging indent

Works Cited

Book—one author Adams, Jeffrey B. *Internet Advertising*. Boston: Brunswick Press, 2004.

Annual report AdCom Industries. *2006 Annual Report*. San Francisco: ACI, Inc., 2005.

Newspaper article Anders, George. "Buying Frenzy," *Wall Street Journal,* July 12, 2003, p. R6.

Book—two authors Arlens, Ramon, and Seymour Stevens. *E-Tailing*. Cambridge, MA: All-State, 2003.

Book—organization as author Corporate Libraries Association. *Directory of Business and Financial Services*. New York: Corporate Libraries Association, 2003.

WWW page "eStats: Advertising Revenues and Trends." *eMarketer,* 11 Aug. 1999. 7 Jan. 2004. <http:www.emarketer.com/estats/ad>.

Journal article— paged continuously Ivans, Edward. "Typical ROIs in Online Advertising." *Personnel Quarterly* Sep. 2005: 804-816.

Journal article— paged each issue Johnson, Bradley. "Nielsen/NetRatings Index Shows 4% Rise in Web Ads." *Advertising Age* 19 July 2003: 18.

Online database *Modern Advertising Techniques*. 2003. Advertising Encyclopedia. 7 Jan. 2004 <http://www.advency.com/modern_advertising_techniques.html>.

Government document National Institute of Mental Health. *Who Clicks? Four Years of Internet Advertising*. DHHS Publication No. ADM 82-1195. Washington, DC: GPO, 2006.

E-mail Richards, Denis V. E-mail to the author. 18 Dec. 2005.

A. MEETING AGENDA

↓6X

14 pt   **MILES HARDWARE EXECUTIVE COMMITTEE** ↓2X

12 pt↓   Meeting Agenda ↓2X

                 June 7, 20--, 3 p.m. ↓2X

1. Call to order ↓2X

2. Approval of minutes of May 5 meeting

3. Progress report on building addition and parking lot restrictions (Norman Hodges and Anthony Pascarelli)

4. May 15 draft of Five-Year Plan

5. Review of National Hardware Association annual convention

6. Employee grievance filed by Ellen Burrows (John Landstrom)

7. New expense-report forms (Anne Richards)

8. Announcements

9. Adjournment

B. MINUTES OF A MEETING

↓6X

	14 pt **RESOURCE COMMITTEE** ↓2X	
	12 pt↓ **Minutes of the Meeting** ↓2X	
	March 13, 20-- ↓1X	
ATTENDANCE	The Resource Committee met on March 13, 20--, at the Airport Sheraton in Portland, Oregon, with all members present. Michael Davis, chairperson, called the meeting to order at 2:30 p.m. ↓1X	
APPROVAL OF MINUTES	The minutes of the January 27 meeting were read and approved. ↓1X	
OLD BUSINESS	The members of the committee reviewed the sales brochure on electronic copyboards and agreed to purchase one for the conference room. Cynthia Giovanni will secure quotations from at least two suppliers. ↓1X	
NEW BUSINESS	The committee reviewed a request from the Purchasing Department for three new computers. After extensive discussion regarding the appropriate use of the computers and software to be purchased, the committee approved the request. ↓1X	
ADJOURNMENT	The meeting was adjourned at 4:45 p.m. ↓2X Respectfully submitted, ↓4X *D. S. Madsen* D. S. Madsen, Secretary	

(Note: Table shown with "Show Gridlines" active.)

C. ITINERARY

↓6X

	14 pt **ITINERARY** ↓2X	
	12 pt↓ **For Arlene Gilsdorf** ↓2X	
	March 12-15, 20-- ↓1X	
THURSDAY, MARCH 12 ↓1X		
5:10 p.m.-7:06 p.m.	Flight from Detroit to Portland; Northwest 83 (Phone: 800-555-1212); e-ticket; Seat 8D; nonstop; dinner ↓2X Jack Weatherford (Home: 503-555-8029; Office: 503-555-7631) will meet your flight on Thursday, provide transportation during your visit, and return you to the airport on Saturday morning. ↓2X Airport Sheraton (503-555-4032) King-sized bed, nonsmoking room; late arrival guaranteed (Reservation No. 30ZM6-02) ↓1X	
FRIDAY, MARCH 13		
9 a.m.-5:30 p.m.	Portland Sales Meeting 1931 Executive Way, Suite 10 Portland (503-555-7631)	
Evening	On your own	
SATURDAY, MARCH 14		
7:30 a.m.-2:47 p.m.	Flight from Portland to Detroit; Northwest 360; e-ticket; Seat 9a; nonstop; breakfast	

(Note: Table shown with "Show Gridlines" active.)

D. LEGAL DOCUMENT

Left tabs: 1", 3"

↓6X

12 pt↓   POWER OF ATTORNEY ↓2X

KNOW ALL MEN BY THESE PRESENTS that I, ATTORNEY LEE FERNANDEZ, of the City of Tulia, County of Swisher, State of Texas, do hereby appoint my son, Robert Fernandez, of this City, County, and State as my attorney-in-fact to act in my name, place, and stead as my agent in the management of my business operating transactions.

I give and grant unto my said attorney full power and authority to do and perform every act and thing requisite and necessary to be done in the said management as fully, to all intents and purposes, as I might or could do if personally present, with full power of revocation, hereby ratifying all that my said attorney shall lawfully do.

IN WITNESS WHEREOF, I have hereunto set my hand and seal this _____ day of _____, 20--. ↓2X

5 underscores ↑   20 underscores ↑

→tab to centerpoint   _____ ↓2X

SIGNED and affirmed in the presence of: ↓4X

_____ ↓4X

_____

A. RESUME

↓6X

14 pt **TERRY M. MARTINA** ↓2X

12 pt ↓ **250 Maxwell Avenue, Boulder, CO 80305**
Phone: 303-555-9311; e-mail: tmartina@ecc.edu ↓1X

↓1X

OBJECTIVE	Position in resort management anywhere in Colorado or the Southwest. ↓1X
EDUCATION	A.A. in hotel management to be awarded May 2005 Edgewood Community College, Boulder, Colorado. ↓1X
EXPERIENCE	*Assistant Manager, Burger King Restaurant* Boulder, Colorado: 2003-Present • Achieved grade point average of 3.1 (on 4.0 scale). • Received Board of Regents tuition scholarship. • Financed all college expenses. ↓2X *Student Intern, Ski Valley Haven* Aspen, Colorado: September-December 2004 • Worked as an assistant to the night manager. • Gained experience in operating First-Guest software. • Was in charge of producing daily occupancy reports. • Received Employee-of-the-Month award. ↓1X
PERSONAL	• Speak and write fluent Spanish. • Competent in Microsoft Office 2003. • Secretary of ECC Hospitality Services Association. • Special Olympics volunteer: Summer 2004. ↓1X
REFERENCES	Available upon request

(Note: Table shown with "Show Gridlines" active.)

B. APPLICATION LETTER IN BLOCK STYLE

(with standard punctuation)

↓6X

March 1, 20-- ↓4X

Mr. Lou Mansfield, Director
Human Resources Department
Rocky Resorts International
P.O. Box 1412
Denver, CO 80214 ↓2X

Dear Mr. Mansfield: ↓2X

Please consider me an applicant for the position of concierge for Suite Retreat, as advertised in last Sunday's *Denver Times*.

I will receive my A.A. degree in hotel administration from Edgewood Community College in May and will be available for full-time employment immediately. In addition to my extensive coursework in hospitality services and business, I've had experience in working for a ski lodge similar to Suite Retreats in Aspen. As a lifelong resident of Colorado and an avid skier, I would be able to provide your guests with any information they request.

After you've reviewed my enclosed resume, I would appreciate having an opportunity to discuss with you why I believe I have the right qualifications and personality to serve as your concierge. I can be reached at 303-555-9311. ↓2X

Sincerely, ↓4X

Terry M. Martina

Terry M. Martina
250 Maxwell Avenue, Apt. 8
Boulder, CO 80305 ↓2X

Enclosure

C. FORMATTING LISTS

Numbers or bullets may be used in letters, memos, and reports to call attention to items in a list. If the sequence of the items is important, use numbers rather than bullets.

❑ Begin the number or bullet at the paragraph point, that is, at the left margin for blocked paragraphs and indented 0.5 inch for indented paragraphs.

❑ Insert 1 blank line before and after the list.

❑ Within the list, use the same spacing (single or double) as is used in the rest of the document.

❑ For single-spaced documents, if all items require no more than 1 line, single-space the items in the list. If any item requires more than 1 line, single-space each item and insert 1 blank line between each item.

To format a list:

1. Type the list unformatted.
2. Select the items in the list.
3. Apply the number or bullet feature.
4. If necessary, use the Decrease Indent or Increase Indent button in Microsoft Word to adjust the position of the list.

The three bulleted and numbered lists shown at the right are all formatted correctly.

D. EXAMPLES OF DIFFERENT TYPES OF LISTS

According to PricewaterhouseCoopers and the Internet Advertising Bureau, the following are the most common types of advertising on the Internet:

• Banner ads that feature some type of animation to attract the viewer's attention.

• Sponsorship, in which an advertiser sponsors a content-based Web site.

• Interstitials, ads that flash up while a page downloads.

There is now considerable controversy about the effectiveness of banner ads. As previously noted, a central goal of banner advertisements is to increase the

* * *

According to PricewaterhouseCoopers, the following are the most common types of advertising on the Internet, shown in order of popularity:

1. Banner ads
2. Sponsorship
3. Interstitials

There is now considerable controversy about the effectiveness of banner ads. As previously noted, a central goal of banner advertisements is to increase the

* * *

According to PricewaterhouseCoopers, the following are the most common types of advertising on the Internet:

• Banner ads that feature some type of animation to attract the viewer's attention.

• Sponsorship, in which an advertiser sponsors a Web site.

• Interstitials, ads that flash up while a page downloads.

There is now considerable controversy about the effectiveness of banner advertising. As previously noted, a central goal of banner advertisements is to

Reference Manual

A. BOXED TABLE (DEFAULT STYLE)

(with subtitle, braced headings, total line, and table note.)

center page ↓

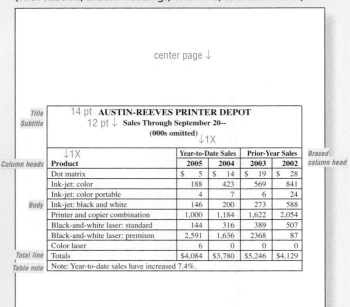

Title — 14 pt **AUSTIN-REEVES PRINTER DEPOT**
Subtitle — 12 pt ↓ **Sales Through September 20--**
(000s omitted)
↓1X

Column heads
↓1X
Body
Total line
Table note

Product	Year-to-Date Sales		Prior-Year Sales	
	2005	2004	2003	2002
Dot matrix	$ 5	$ 14	$ 19	$ 28
Ink-jet: color	188	423	569	841
Ink-jet: color portable	4	7	6	24
Ink-jet: black and white	146	200	273	588
Printer and copier combination	1,000	1,184	1,622	2,054
Black-and-white laser: standard	144	316	389	507
Black-and-white laser: premium	2,591	1,636	2368	87
Color laser	6	0	0	0
Totals	$4,084	$3,780	$5,246	$4,129
Note: Year-to-date sales have increased 7.4%.				

Braced column head

B. OPEN TABLE

(with subtitle, blocked column headings, and 2-line heading)

center page ↓

14 pt **SUITE RETREAT**
12 pt ↓ **New Lodging Rates**
↓1X

Location	Rack Rate	Discount Rate	Saving
Bozeman, Montana	$ 95.75	$ 91.50	4.4%
Chicago, Illinois	159.00	139.50	12.3%
Dallas, Texas	249.50	219.00	12.2%
Las Vegas, Nevada	98.50	89.95	8.7%
Los Angeles, California	179.00	139.00	22.3%
Minneapolis, Minnesota	115.00	95.00	17.4%
New York, New York	227.50	175.00	23.1%
Orlando, Florida	105.75	98.50	6.3%
Portland, Maine	93.50	93.50	0.0%
Seattle, Washington	143.75	125.75	12.5%

C. RULED TABLE

(with table number and centered column headings)

2

an effort to reduce errors and provide increased customer support, we have recently added numerous additional telephone support services, some of which are available 24 hours a day and others available during the workday. These are shown in Table 2.
↓2X

14 pt **Table 2. COMPUTER SUPPLIES SUPPORT SERVICES**
↓1X

12 pt↓

Support Service	Telephone	Hours
Product literature	800-555-3867	6 a.m. to 5 p.m.
Replacement parts	303-555-3388	24 hours a day
Technical documentation	408-555-3309	24 hours a day
Troubleshooting	800-555-8277	10 a.m. to 5 p.m.
Printer drivers	800-555-2377	6 a.m. to 5 p.m.
Software notes	800-555-3496	24 hours a day
Technical support	800-555-1205	24 hours a day
Hardware information	303-555-4289	6 a.m. to 5 p.m.

↓1X

We hope you will take advantage of these additional services to ensure that the computer hardware and software you purchase from Computer Supplies continues to provide you the quality and service you have come to expect from our company.

Sincerely,

Douglas Pullis

Douglas Pullis
General Manager

cds

D. TABLES: SPECIAL FEATURES

Vertical Placement. Vertically center a table that appears on a page by itself. Insert 1 blank line before and after a table appearing with other text.

Heading Block. Center and bold all lines of the heading, typing the title in all caps and 14-point font and the subtitle in upper- and lowercase and in 12-point font. If a table has a number, type the word *Table* in upper- and lowercase. Follow the table number with a period and 1 space.

Column Headings. If *all* columns in the table consist of text (such as words, phone numbers, or years), center all column headings and left-align all column entries. In all other situations, left-align all text column headings and text column entries and right-align all quantity column headings and quantity column entries. Regardless of the type of column, center braced headings. Use bold upper- and lowercase.

Column Capitalization. Capitalize only the first word and proper nouns in column entries.

Percentages and Dollars. Repeat the % sign for each number in a column (unless the heading identifies the data as percentages). Insert the $ sign only before the first amount and before a total amount. Align the $ sign with the longest amount in the column, inserting spaces after the $ sign as needed (leaving 2 spaces for each digit and 1 space for each comma).

Total Line. Add a border above a total line. Use the word *Total* or *Totals* as appropriate.

A. FORMATTING BUSINESS FORMS

Many business forms can be created and filled in by using templates that are provided within commercial word processing software. Template forms can be used "as is" or they can be edited. Templates can also be used to create customized forms for any business.

When a template is opened, the form is displayed on screen. The user can then fill in the necessary information, including personalized company information. Data are entered into cells or fields, and you can move quickly from field to field with a single keystroke—usually by pressing TAB or ENTER.

B. U.S. POSTAL SERVICE ABBREVIATIONS

(for States, Territories, and Canadian Provinces)

States and Territories

Alabama	AL	North Carolina	NC
Alaska	AK	North Dakota	ND
Arizona	AZ	Ohio	OH
Arkansas	AR	Oklahoma	OK
California	CA	Oregon	OR
Colorado	CO	Pennsylvania	PA
Connecticut	CT	Puerto Rico	PR
Delaware	DE	Rhode Island	RI
District of Columbia	DC	South Carolina	SC
Florida	FL	South Dakota	SD
Georgia	GA	Tennessee	TN
Guam	GU	Texas	TX
Hawaii	HI	Utah	UT
Idaho	ID	Vermont	VT
Illinois	IL	Virgin Islands	VI
Indiana	IN	Virginia	VA
Iowa	IA	Washington	WA
Kansas	KS	West Virginia	WV
Kentucky	KY	Wisconsin	WI
Louisiana	LA	Wyoming	WY
Maine	ME		
Maryland	MD	**Canadian Provinces**	
Massachusetts	MA	Alberta	AB
Michigan	MI	British Columbia	BC
Minnesota	MN	Labrador	LB
Mississippi	MS	Manitoba	MB
Missouri	MO	New Brunswick	NB
Montana	MT	Newfoundland	NF
Nebraska	NE	Northwest Territories	NT
Nevada	NV	Nova Scotia	NS
New Hampshire	NH	Ontario	ON
New Jersey	NJ	Prince Edward Island	PE
New Mexico	NM	Quebec	PQ
New York	NY	Saskatchewan	SK
		Yukon Territory	YT

C. PROOFREADERS' MARKS

Proofreaders' Marks		Draft	Final Copy
⌒	Omit space	data base	database
v or ∧	Insert	if he's going	if he's not going,
≡	Capitalize	Maple street	Maple Street
✗	Delete	a final draft	a draft
#	Insert space	allready to	all ready to
when / if	Change word	and if you	and when you
/	Use lowercase letter	our President	our president
¶	Paragraph	… to use it.¶We can	… to use it. We can
⋯	Don't delete	a true story	a true story
O	Spell out	the only ①	the only one
∽	Transpose	they all see	they see all

Proofreaders' Marks		Draft	Final Copy
SS	Single-space	first line / second line	first line / second line
ds	Double-space	first line / second line	first line / second line
⌐	Move right	Please send	Please send
⌐	Move left	May I	May I
∿	Bold	Column Heading	**Column Heading**
ital	Italic	Time magazine	*Time* magazine
u/l	Underline	Time magazine	Time magazine readers
♂	Move as shown	readers will see	will see

Language Arts for Business
(50 "must-know" rules)

PUNCTUATION

COMMAS

RULE 1
, direct address
(L. 21)

Use commas before and after a name used in direct address.

Thank you, John, for responding to my e-mail so quickly.

Ladies and gentlemen, the program has been canceled.

RULE 2
, independent clause
(L. 27)

Use a comma between independent clauses joined by a coordinate conjunction (unless both clauses are short).

Ellen left her job with IBM, and she and her sister went to Paris.

But: Ellen left her job with IBM and went to Paris with her sister.

But: John drove and I navigated.

Note: An independent clause is one that can stand alone as a complete sentence. The most common coordinate conjunctions are *and, but, or,* and *nor.*

RULE 3
, introductory expression
(L. 27)

Use a comma after an introductory expression (unless it is a short prepositional phrase).

Before we can make a decision, we must have all the facts.

But: In 2004 our nation elected a new president.

Note: An introductory expression is a group of words that come before the subject and verb of the independent clause. Common prepositions are *to, in, on, of, at, by, for,* and *with.*

RULE 4
, direct quotation
(L. 41)

Use a comma before and after a direct quotation.

James said, "I shall return," and then left.

RULE 5
, date
(L. 57)

Use a comma before and after the year in a complete date.

We will arrive on June 2, 2006, for the conference.

But: We will arrive on June 2 for the conference.

RULE 6
, place
(L. 57)

Use a comma before and after a state or country that follows a city (but not before a ZIP Code).

Joan moved to Vancouver, British Columbia, in May.

Send the package to Douglasville, GA 30135, by Express Mail.

But: Send the package to Georgia by Express Mail.

Reference Manual

RULE 7 ▶
, series
(L. 61)

Use a comma between each item in a series of three or more.

We need to order paper, toner, and font cartridges for the printer.

They saved their work, exited their program, and turned off their computers when they finished.

Note: Do not use a comma after the last item in a series.

RULE 8 ▶
, transitional expression
(L. 61)

Use a comma before and after a transitional expression or independent comment.

It is critical, therefore, that we finish the project on time.

Our present projections, you must admit, are inadequate.

But: You must admit our present projections are inadequate.

Note: Examples of transitional expressions and independent comments are *in addition to, therefore, however, on the other hand, as a matter of fact,* and *unfortunately.*

RULE 9 ▶
, nonessential expression
(L. 71)

Use a comma before and after a nonessential expression.

Andre, who was there, can verify the statement.

But: Anyone who was there can verify the statement.

Van's first book, *Crisis of Management,* was not discussed.

Van's book *Crisis of Management* was not discussed.

Note: A nonessential expression is a group of words that may be omitted without changing the basic meaning of the sentence. Always examine the noun or pronoun that comes before the expression to determine whether the noun needs the expression to complete its meaning. If it does, the expression is *essential* and does *not* take a comma.

RULE 10 ▶
, adjacent adjectives
(L. 71)

Use a comma between two adjacent adjectives that modify the same noun.

We need an intelligent, enthusiastic individual for this job.

But: Please order a new bulletin board for our main conference room.

Note: Do not use a comma after the second adjective. Also, do not use a comma if the first adjective modifies the combined idea of the second adjective and the noun (for example, *bulletin board* and *conference room* in the second example above).

SEMICOLONS

RULE 11 ▶
; no conjunction
(L. 97)

Use a semicolon to separate two closely related independent clauses that are *not* joined by a conjunction (such as *and, but, or,* or *nor*).

Management favored the vote; stockholders did not.

But: Management favored the vote, but stockholders did not.

RULE 12 ▶
; series
(L. 97)

Use a semicolon to separate three or more items in a series if any of the items already contain commas.

Staff meetings were held on Thursday, May 7; Monday, June 7; and Friday, June 12.

Note: Be sure to insert the semicolon *between* (not within) the items in a series.

Reference Manual

HYPHENS

RULE 13 ▶
- number
(L. 57)

Hyphenate compound numbers between twenty-one and ninety-nine and fractions that are expressed as words.

Twenty-nine recommendations were approved by at least three-fourths of the members.

RULE 14 ▶
- compound adjective
(L. 67)

Hyphenate compound adjectives that come before a noun (unless the first word is an adverb ending in -ly).

We reviewed an up-to-date report on Wednesday.

But: The report was up to date.

But: We reviewed the highly rated report.

Note: A compound adjective is two or more words that function as a unit to describe a noun.

APOSTROPHES

RULE 15 ▶
' singular noun
(L. 37)

Use 's to form the possessive of singular nouns.

The hurricane's force caused major damage to North Carolina's coastline.

RULE 16 ▶
' plural noun
(L. 37)

Use only an apostrophe to form the possessive of plural nouns that end in *s*.

The investors' goals were outlined in the stockholders' report.

But: The investors outlined their goals in the report to the stockholders.

But: The women's and children's clothing was on sale.

RULE 17 ▶
' pronoun
(L. 37)

Use 's to form the possessive of indefinite pronouns (such as *someone's* or *anybody's*); do not use an apostrophe with personal pronouns (such as *hers, his, its, ours, theirs,* and *yours*).

She could select anybody's paper for a sample.

It's time to put the file back into its cabinet.

Reference Manual

COLONS

RULE 18 ▶
: explanatory material
(L. 91)

Use a colon to introduce explanatory material that follows an independent clause.

The computer satisfies three criteria: speed, cost, and power.

But: The computer satisfies the three criteria of speed, cost, and power.

Remember this: <u>o</u>nly one coupon is allowed per customer.

Note: An independent clause can stand alone as a complete sentence. Do not capitalize the word following the colon.

PERIODS

RULE 19 ▶
. polite request
(L. 91)

Use a period to end a sentence that is a polite request.

Will you please call me if I can be of further assistance.

Note: Consider a sentence a polite request if you expect the reader to respond by doing as you ask rather than by giving a yes-or-no answer.

QUOTATION MARKS

RULE 20 ▶
" quotation
(L. 41)

Use quotation marks around a direct quotation.

Harrison responded by saying, "Their decision does not affect us."

But: Harrison responded by saying that their decision does not affect us.

RULE 21 ▶
" title
(L. 41)

Use quotation marks around the title of a newspaper or magazine article, chapter in a book, report, and similar terms.

The most helpful article I found was "Multimedia for All."

ITALICS (OR UNDERLINE)

RULE 22 ▶
title
(L. 41)

Italicize (or underline) the titles of books, magazines, newspapers, and other complete published works.

Grisham's *The Brethren* was reviewed in a recent *USA Today* article.

Reference Manual

GRAMMAR

SENTENCES

RULE 23 ▶
fragment
(L. 21)

Avoid sentence fragments.

Not: She had always wanted to be a financial manager. But had not had the needed education.

But: She had always wanted to be a financial manager but had not had the needed education.

Note: A fragment is a part of a sentence that is incorrectly punctuated as a complete sentence. In the first example above, "but had not had the needed education" is not a complete sentence because it does not contain a subject.

RULE 24 ▶
run-on
(L. 21)

Avoid run-on sentences.

Not: Mohamed is a competent worker he has even passed the MOS exam.

Not: Mohamed is a competent worker, he has even passed the MOS exam.

But: Mohamed is a competent worker; he has even passed the MOS exam.

Or: Mohamed is a competent worker. He has even passed the MOS exam.

Note: A run-on sentence is two independent clauses that run together without any punctuation between them or with only a comma between them.

AGREEMENT

RULE 25 ▶
agreement singular
agreement plural
(L. 67)

Use singular verbs and pronouns with singular subjects; use plural verbs and pronouns with plural subjects.

I <u>was</u> happy with <u>my</u> performance.

<u>Janet and Phoenix</u> <u>were</u> happy with <u>their</u> performance.

Among the items discussed <u>were</u> our <u>raises and benefits</u>.

RULE 26 ▶
agreement pronoun
(L. 81)

Some pronouns (*anybody, each, either, everybody, everyone, much, neither, no one, nobody,* and *one*) are always singular and take a singular verb. Other pronouns (*all, any, more, most, none,* and *some*) may be singular or plural, depending on the noun to which they refer.

<u>Each</u> of the employees <u>has</u> finished <u>his or her</u> task.

<u>Much</u> <u>remains</u> to be done.

<u>Most</u> of the pie <u>was</u> eaten, but <u>most</u> of the cookies <u>were</u> left.

RULE 27 ▶
agreement intervening words
(L. 81)

Disregard any intervening words that come between the subject and verb when establishing agreement.

The <u>box</u> containing the books and pencils <u>has</u> not been found.

<u>Alex</u>, accompanied by Tricia, <u>is</u> attending the conference and taking <u>his</u> computer.

RULE 28 ▶
agreement nearer noun
(L. 101)

If two subjects are joined by *or, either/or, neither/nor,* or *not only/but also,* make the verb agree with the subject nearer to the verb.

Neither the coach nor the <u>players</u> <u>are</u> at home.

Not only the coach but also the <u>referee</u> <u>is</u> at home.

But: <u>Both</u> the coach and the referee <u>are</u> at home.

Reference Manual

RULE 29 ▶

nominative pronoun

(L. 107)

Use nominative pronouns (such as *I, he, she, we, they,* and *who*) as subjects of a sentence or clause.

The programmer and <u>he</u> are reviewing the code.

Barb is a person <u>who</u> can do the job.

RULE 30 ▶

objective pronoun

(L. 107)

Use objective pronouns (such as *me, him, her, us, them,* and *whom*) as objects of a verb, preposition, or infinitive.

The code was reviewed by the programmer and <u>him</u>.

Barb is the type of person <u>whom</u> we can trust.

ADJECTIVES AND ADVERBS

RULE 31 ▶

adjective/adverb

(L. 101)

Use comparative adjectives and adverbs (*-er, more,* and *less*) when referring to two nouns or pronouns; use superlative adjectives and adverbs (*-est, most,* and *least*) when referring to more than two.

The <u>shorter</u> of the <u>two</u> training sessions is the <u>more</u> helpful one.

The <u>longest</u> of the <u>three</u> training sessions is the <u>least</u> helpful one.

WORD USAGE

RULE 32 ▶

accept/except

(L. 117)

***Accept* means "to agree to"; *except* means "to leave out."**

All employees <u>except</u> the maintenance staff should <u>accept</u> the agreement.

RULE 33 ▶

affect/effect

(L. 117)

***Affect* is most often used as a verb meaning "to influence"; *effect* is most often used as a noun meaning "result."**

The ruling will <u>affect</u> our domestic operations but will have no <u>effect</u> on our Asian operations.

RULE 34 ▶

farther/further

(L. 117)

***Farther* refers to distance; *further* refers to extent or degree.**

The <u>farther</u> we drove, the <u>further</u> agitated he became.

RULE 35 ▶

personal/personnel

(L. 117)

***Personal* means "private"; *personnel* means "employees."**

All <u>personnel</u> agreed not to use e-mail for <u>personal</u> business.

RULE 36 ▶

principal/principle

(L. 117)

***Principal* means "primary"; *principle* means "rule."**

The <u>principle</u> of fairness is our <u>principal</u> means of dealing with customers.

Reference Manual

MECHANICS

RULE 37 ▶
≡ sentence
(L. 31)

Capitalize the first word of a sentence.

Please prepare a summary of your activities.

RULE 38 ▶
≡ proper noun
(L. 31)

Capitalize proper nouns and adjectives derived from proper nouns.

Judy Hendrix drove to Albuquerque in her new Pontiac convertible.

Note: A proper noun is the official name of a particular person, place, or thing.

RULE 39 ▶
≡ time
(L. 31)

Capitalize the names of the days of the week, months, holidays, and religious days (but do not capitalize the names of the seasons).

On Thursday, November 25, we will celebrate Thanksgiving, the most popular holiday in the fall.

RULE 40 ▶
≡ noun #
(L. 77)

Capitalize nouns followed by a number or letter (except for the nouns *line, note, page, paragraph,* and *size*).

Please read Chapter 5, which begins on page 94.

RULE 41 ▶
≡ compass point
(L. 77)

Capitalize compass points (such as *north, south,* or *northeast*) only when they designate definite regions.

From Montana we drove south to reach the Southwest.

RULE 42 ▶
≡ organization
(L. 111)

Capitalize common organizational terms (such as *advertising department* and *finance committee*) only when they are the actual names of the units in the writer's own organization and when they are preceded by the word *the*.

The report from the Advertising Department is due today.

But: Our advertising department will submit its report today.

RULE 43 ▶
≡ course
(L. 111)

Capitalize the names of specific course titles but not the names of subjects or areas of study.

I have enrolled in Accounting 201 and will also take a marketing course.

RULE 44 ▶
general
(L. 41)

In general, spell out numbers zero through ten, and use figures for numbers above ten.

We rented two movies for tonight.

The decision was reached after 27 precincts sent in their results.

RULE 45 ▶
 # figure
(L. 41)

Use figures for

❑ **Dates. (Use *st, d,* or *th* only if the day comes before the month.)**
   The tax report is due on April 15 (*not* April 15ᵗʰ)

   We will drive to the camp on the 23d (or *23rd* or *23ʳᵈ*) of May.

❑ **All numbers if two or more *related* numbers both above and below ten are used in the same sentence.**
   Mr. Carter sent in 7 receipts, and Ms. Cantrell sent in 22.

   But: The 13 accountants owned three computers each.

❑ **Measurements (time, money, distance, weight, and percent).**
   The $500 statue we delivered at 7 a.m. weighed 6 pounds.

❑ **Mixed numbers.**
   Our sales are up 9½ (or *9 1/2*) percent over last year.

RULE 46 ▶
 # word
(L. 57)

Spell out

❑ **A number used as the first word of a sentence.**
   Seventy-five people attended the conference in San Diego.

❑ **The shorter of two adjacent numbers.**
   We have ordered 3 two-pound cakes and one 5-pound cake for the reception.

❑ **The words *million* and *billion* in even amounts (do not use decimals with even amounts).**
   Not: A $5.00 ticket can win $28,000,000 in this month's lottery.

   But: A $5 ticket can win $28 million in this month's lottery.

❑ **Fractions.**
   Almost one-half of the audience responded to the question.

Note: When fractions and the numbers twenty-one through ninety-nine are spelled out, they should be hyphenated.

ABBREVIATIONS

RULE 47 ▶
abbreviate none
(L. 67)

In general business writing, do not abbreviate common words (such as *dept.* or *pkg.*), compass points, units of measure, or the names of months, days of the week, cities, or states (except in addresses).
   Almost one-half of the audience indicated they were at least 5 feet 8 inches tall.

Note: Do not insert a comma between the parts of a single measurement.

RULE 48 ▶
abbreviate measure
(L. 87)

In technical writing, on forms, and in tables, abbreviate units of measure when they occur frequently. Do not use periods.
   14 oz   5 ft 10 in   50 mph   2 yrs 10 mo

RULE 49 ▶
abbreviate lowercase
(L. 87)

In most lowercase abbreviations made up of single initials, use a period after each initial but no internal spaces.
   a.m.   p.m.   i.e.   e.g.   e.o.m.

   Exceptions: mph   mpg   wpm

RULE 50 ▶
abbreviate ≡
(L. 87)

In most all-capital abbreviations made up of single initials, do not use periods or internal spaces.
   OSHA   PBS   NBEA   WWW   VCR   MBA

   Exceptions: U.S.A.   A.A.   B.S.   Ph.D.   P.O.   B.C.   A.D.

Part 4
Advanced Formatting

Keyboarding in Health Services

Within the health services job cluster, there is an enormous range of job opportunities in the medical and health care industry. Hundreds of different occupations exist in health care practice, including business-oriented positions. In fact, career opportunities within this cluster are among the fastest growing in the national marketplace. The current job outlook is quite positive because the growth in managed care has significantly increased opportunities for doctors and other health professionals, particularly in the area of preventive care. In addition, the aging population requires more highly skilled medical workers.

Opportunities in Health Careers

Consider health care jobs, medical careers, health care management, and medical management. Various job possibilities exist in these areas, and work as a medical transcriber, clinical technician, nurse, medical analyst, surgical technician or surgeon, physical therapist, orderly, pharmacist, or medical researcher can most likely be easily found. Interestingly, keyboarding skill is important for all of these positions.

Objectives

KEYBOARDING

- Type at least 43 words per minute on a 5-minute timed writing with no more than 5 errors.

LANGUAGE ARTS

- Refine proofreading skills and correctly use proofreaders' marks.
- Use capitals, punctuation, and grammar correctly.
- Improve composing and spelling skills.
- Recognize subject/verb agreement.

WORD PROCESSING

- Use the word processing commands necessary to complete the document processing activities.

DOCUMENT PROCESSING

- Format reports, multipage letters, multipage memos, and tables.

TECHNICAL

- Answer at least 90 percent of the questions correctly on an objective test.

Unit 13

Skill Refinement

LESSON 61
Skillbuilding and Report Review

LESSON 62
Skillbuilding and Letter Review

LESSON 63
Skillbuilding, Memo, and E-Mail Review

LESSON 64
Skillbuilding and Table Review

LESSON 65
Skillbuilding and Employment Document Review

2

SKILLS THAT A LEADER NEEDS

A good leader must have the prerequisite skills if he or she is to be effective in business. Many textbook and business journal writers have used various terms to describe these skills. Zander lists such skills as being critical to success as a leader and identifies them as the ability to delegate responsibilities, to be fair with subordinates, and to be consistent.[2] However, Zander also discusses communications, human relations, and a sense of humor as special skills that a leader *should* possess. These skills are often acquired on the job with the assistance of mentors within the firm.

PROBLEM SOLVING

Dealing with problems is a delicate business. On the one hand, leaders do not want to anger anyone, especially union personnel, by being too harsh. On the other hand, they must confront problems head-on. Leaders should first make a special effort to identify clearly the real problem. Second, they should pinpoint the individual factors that may be causing the problem. Finally, they should take definite steps to correct the problem.

LEADERSHIP SKILLS NEEDED IN BUSINESS

Sally Rodriguez

Leadership skills are needed now more than ever in business and industry if our nation is to maintain a leading role in the business world of tomorrow. With the advent of a common European community without boundaries, the Asian influence throughout the world, and the development of a common North American business community, we must have leaders with vision and the appropriate skills for meeting the challenges of the new, very technical century.

Each of the new skills that a successful leader needs is discussed in the following pages.

LEADERSHIP

Leadership has been defined in a variety of of an individual when he or she is directing the activ goal.î[1]

A successful leader is one who is committed and services, for improving the firmís market positi her employees. A leader possesses a value system th Leaders who make decisions affecting the firm, emp beliefs that influence decision making.

[1] Judith R. Gordon, *A Diagnostic Approach to Organizational* 2002, p. 393.

y, 3rd ed., McGraw-Hill/Irwin, New York, 2002, pp. 274-

MEMO TO: Frank Janowicz, Ticket Manager

FROM: Sam Steele, Executive Director

DATE: March 1, 20--

SUBJECT: Ticket Sales Campaign

We tentatively have scheduled 114 concerts for Orchestra Hall for the calendar year beginning September 1, 20--. The attached list shows the new season ticket prices for the main floor, mezzanine, balcony, and gallery.

These prices are grouped in 11 different concert categories, which reflect the varied classical tastes of our patrons. These groupings also consider preferences for day of the week, time of day, and season of the year.

Please see me at 3 p.m. on March 10 so that we can review our ticket sales campaign. Last year's season ticket holders have had ample time to renew their subscriptions; we must now concentrate on attracting new season subscribers. I shall look forward to reviewing your plans on the tenth.

lpu
Attachment

Skillbuilding and Report Review

Goals

- Improve speed and accuracy
- Refine language arts skills in the use of commas
- Format reports

A. Type 2 times.

A. WARMUP

```
1      A queen quickly adjusted 12 blinds as the bright sun      11
2  blazed down from the sky; she then paced through the 19      22
3  rooms (all very large) next to the castle for 38 minutes.    33
   |  1  |  2  |  3  |  4  |  5  |  6  |  7  |  8  |  9  |  10  |  11  |  12
```

SKILLBUILDING

B. Take three 12-second timed writings on each line. The scale below the last line shows your wpm speed for a 12-second timed writing.

B. 12-SECOND SPEED SPRINTS

```
4  Most of those autos on the road had only one or two people.
5  Those boys and girls did the right thing by doing the work.
6  Some of the men ran to the gym to work out with their kids.
7  All of the new male workers were given a tour of the plant.
   I I I I 5 I I I I 10 I I I 15 I I I 20 I I I 25 I I I 30 I I I 35 I I I 40 I I I 45 I I I 50 I I I 55 I I I 60
```

C. DIAGNOSTIC PRACTICE: SYMBOLS AND PUNCTUATION

If you are not using the GDP software, turn to page SB-2 and follow the directions for this activity.

LANGUAGE ARTS

D. Study the rules at the right.

D. COMMAS

Note: The callout signals in the left margin indicate which language arts rule from this lesson has been applied.

RULE ▶

,series

The underlines call attention to a point in the sentence where a comma might mistakenly be inserted.

Use a comma between each item in a series of three or more.
> We need to order paper, toner, and font cartridges_for the printer.
> They saved their work, exited their program, and turned off their computers_when they finished.

Note: Do not use a comma after the last item in a series.

RULE ▶

,transitional expression

Use a comma before and after a transitional expression or independent comment.
> It is critical, therefore, that we finish the project on time.
> Our present projections, you must admit, are inadequate.
> *But:* You must admit_our present projections are inadequate.

Note: Examples of transitional expressions and independent comments are *in addition to, therefore, however, on the other hand, as a matter of fact*, and *unfortunately*.

Edit the sentences to correct any errors in the use of the comma.

8 The lawyer the bank and the courthouse received copies.
9 The closing was delayed therefore for more than an hour.
10 The abstract deed and contract were all three in order.
11 Ms. Sperry's flight was delayed however for two hours.
12 Happily the drinks snacks and napkins arrived on time.
13 This offer I think will be unacceptable to the board.

DOCUMENT PROCESSING

Report 61-35 ▶

Business Report

,transitional expression

The ¶ symbol indicates the start of a new paragraph. In a business report, paragraphs are blocked (not indented).

Word Processing Manual Review:

L. 21–24: *All*
L. 23: Bold
L. 26: Alignment and Font Size

Reference Manual

Review: R-8A: Business Report.

,series

UTI EMPLOYEE TRAINING PROGRAMS
Asako Kudo, Training Coordinator

¶ Various training techniques are used in business and industry to ~~update~~ *help* employees ^ *acquire new* skills ~~and to assist them in acquiring new skills. It should be no surprise, therefore, that conscientious employees are eager to participate in training programs.~~ Some ~~of the various~~ *effective* techniques that United Transportation Inc. *(UTI)* uses in its training programs are ~~described below.~~ *discussed in this report.*

ON-THE-JOB TRAINING AND LECTURES

¶ Two of the most frequently used and *highly effective* training methods are on-th*e*-job training and lectures.

¶ **On-the-Job Training.** *On* the job training saves time and money by *enabling* ~~permitting~~ individuals *to* train at the workplace. ~~This method lets~~ the trainer use*s* the workstation in place of a classroom. ~~While there are many benefits from this type of experience,~~ on-the-job training does require careful coordination to *e*insure that learning objectives are achieved.

¶ **Lectures.** Lectures are often used because they are a low-cost method of *instruction* ~~training~~. Lectures, which require little action on the part of the trainer, may not be effective when introducing employees to new techniques and work program*s*.

CONFERENCES

¶ In ~~the~~ *a* conference ~~method of instruction,~~ small groups of employees are taught by a ~~conference~~ director, manager, or outside consultant. ~~This method of instruction results in~~ *Conferences provide* considerable give-and-take ~~between the director and the employees.~~ For learning to occur, the ~~director~~ *trainer* must be *skilled* in the use of interactive tech*n*iques.

(Continued on next page)

DISTANCE EDUCATION

¶ A growing segment of UTI's training is now delivered on-line via the internet. Some of these courses, called distance education (DE), are designed and managed by UTI, but an increasing number are designed and managed by form independent vendors, such as educational institutions and management-consulting firms. These on-line courses are not only cost-effective, but also permit the trainee to complete the course at a time that is convenient for *him or her* them.

¶ The UTI Training Department estimates that within five years, 80% or more of its training modules will be delivered on-line, at a projected annual cost savings of at least $575,000 dollars.

Report 61-36 ▶

Academic Report

The ¶ symbol indicates the start of a new paragraph. In an academic report, paragraphs are indented.

Word Processing Manual Review:

L. 27: Page Numbering and Page Break
L. 29: Line Spacing
L. 35: Italics
L. 41: Footnotes

Reference Manual

Review: R-8C and R-8D: Academic Report

,series

,transitional expression

LEADERSHIP SKILLS NEEDED IN BUSINESS
Sally Rodriguez

¶ Leadership skills are needed now more than ever in business and industry if our nation is to maintain a leading role in the business world of tomorrow. With the advent of a common European community without boundaries, the Asian influence throughout the world, and the development of a common North American business community, we must have leaders with vision and the appropriate skills for meeting the challenges of the new, very technical century.

¶ Each of the new skills that a successful leader needs is discussed in the following pages.

LEADERSHIP

¶ Leadership has been defined in a variety of ways. One definition is "the behavior of an individual when he or she is directing the activities of a group toward a shared goal."[1]

¶ A successful leader is one who is committed to ideas—ideas for future products and services, for improving the firm's market position, and for the well-being of his or her employees. A leader possesses a value system that is ethically and morally sound. Leaders who make decisions affecting the firm, employees, and society have a set of beliefs that influence decision making.

SKILLS THAT A LEADER NEEDS

¶ A good leader must have the prerequisite skills if he or she is to be effective in business. Many textbook and business journal writers have used various terms to describe these skills. Zander lists such skills as being critical to success as a leader and identifies them as the ability to delegate responsibilities, to be fair with subordinates, and to be consistent.[2] However, Zander

(Continued on next page)

also discusses communications, human relations, and a sense of humor as special skills that a leader *should* possess. These skills are often acquired on the job with the assistance of mentors within the firm.

PROBLEM SOLVING

¶ Dealing with problems is a delicate business. On the one hand, leaders do not want to anger anyone, especially union personnel, by being too harsh. On the other hand, they must confront problems head-on. Leaders should first make a special effort to identify clearly the *real* problem. Second, they should pinpoint the individual factors that may be causing the problem. Finally, they should take definite steps to correct the problem.

[1] Judith R. Gordon, *A Diagnostic Approach to Organizational Behavior*, 2nd ed., Allyn and Bacon, Boston, 2002, p. 393.
[2] Raymond T. Zander, *Office Management Today*, 3rd ed., McGraw-Hill/Irwin, New York, 2002, pp. 274–275.

Report 61-37

Business Report

Open the file for Report 61-36 and make the following changes.

1. Change the report from academic style to business style.
2. Assume that Aaron Wojak wrote the report, and change the byline accordingly.
3. Delete the third paragraph. Note that this results in the elimination of the first footnote.
4. Add a fourth side heading, THE LEADER AS TEACHER. Then add the following paragraph:

   Those who are in leadership positions often assume that workers learn how to perform a job simply by doing it without guidance. The real leader plans well-structured orientation sessions for new workers and does the same for all workers whenever there is new technology to be learned or when there is a change in policy or procedure.

   (**Note:** If necessary, force a page break to prevent the new side heading from appearing at the bottom of the first page.)
5. Finally, add a footnote at the end of the paragraph you inserted in step 4:

   Ahmed Bazarak, "The Leader as Teacher," *The Manager's Newsletter*, July 18, 2004, pp. 14-17.

Skillbuilding and Letter Review

Goals

- Type at least 40wpm/5'/5e
- Format business letters and personal-business letters

A. Type 2 times.

A. WARMUP

```
1     Quist & Zenk's sales were exactly $247,650; but the      10
2  cost of goods sold was $174,280 (70.37%). The profit made   22
3  was small after other, extensive expenses were subtracted   34
   | 1 | 2 | 3 | 4 | 5 | 6 | 7 | 8 | 9 | 10 | 11 | 12
```

SKILLBUILDING

B. MAP

Follow the GDP software directions for this exercise in improving keystroking accuracy.

Strategies for Career Success

Corrective Feedback

Sometime in your career, you will give someone corrective feedback. You can use positive communication to do this and not appear to criticize the person.

Here are some things you should not do. Do not correct the person in front of others. Avoid giving feedback when you are angry. Stay away from personal comments (for example, "That idea will get us nowhere!"). Do not diminish a person's enthusiasm (for example, "We've never done that before, and we're not starting now.").

Here are some things you should do. Listen to the person's side of the situation. Express yourself in a positive way (for example, "You're getting much closer."). Be specific about what the person can do to correct the situation. Follow up within a short time and identify all progress.

YOUR TURN Think about the last time you received corrective feedback. Did the person giving you feedback use techniques to create a positive outcome?

C. Take two 5-minute timed writings. Review your speed and errors.

Goal: At least 40wpm/5'/5e

C. 5-MINUTE TIMED WRITING

```
 4        Digital photography has revolutionized the way we take   11
 5   pictures. A digital camera puts our photos in a format that    23
 6   makes them easy to print and share with others. Using a        34
 7   digital camera also has the advantage that we can quickly      46
 8   print out our photos and see the results of our efforts. We    58
 9   can also insert our photos into word processing documents,     70
10   send them by e-mail to our friends, or post them on the Web    82
11   where they can be viewed by all. We can even connect our       93
12   camera to a television set and have our images displayed in   105
13   a slide show presentation.                                    111
14        Another advantage of digital photography is that the     121
15   expense of developing your own photos is much less because    133
16   you do not have to buy many rolls of film, nor do you have    145
17   to have your photos developed by others. Also, your photos    157
18   can be edited if you do not like what you see. You can crop   169
19   the photo, adjust its color or contrast, take out red-eye     180
20   imperfections, and even add or delete elements from the       192
21   photo or from other photos you have taken.                    200
     | 1 | 2 | 3 | 4 | 5 | 6 | 7 | 8 | 9 | 10 | 11 | 12
```

DOCUMENT PROCESSING

Correspondence 62-55

Personal-Business Letter in Modified-Block Style

The ¶ symbol indicates the start of a new paragraph. In a personal-business letter, paragraphs are blocked (not indented).

 Refer to **Reference Manual**

Review: R-3D: Personal-Business Letter

October 1, 20-- | Dr. Anthony L. Robbins | 2345 South Main Street | Bowling Green, OH 43402 | Dear Anthony:

¶ Thank you for your letter of September 25, in which you inquired about my trip to New York City. Your letter brought back a lot of memories of those days when I was one of your students.

¶ I plan to leave on October 15 for a two-week business and vacation trip to the city. While at Columbia University, I will be conducting a workshop on the utilization of voice-activated equipment.

¶ My work at Columbia will be completed on October 22, after which I plan to attend a number of plays, visit the Metropolitan Museum of Art, and take one of the sightseeing tours of the city.

¶ If you and your wife would care to join me on October 22, please let me know. I would be most happy to make reservations at the hotel for you and to purchase theater tickets. Why don't you consider joining me in the "Big Apple."

Sincerely, | Bryan Goldberg | 320 South Summit Street | Toledo, OH 43604

Correspondence
62-56

Business Letter in
Modified-Block Style

**Word
Processing
Manual
Review:**

L. 50: Ruler Tabs and Tab Sets

**Reference
Manual**

Review: **R-3B:** Business
Letter in Modified-Block
Style

June 3, 20--

Director of Product Development

Hampton Associates, Inc.

830 Market St.

San Francisco, Ca 94103-1925

Dear Director of Product Development:

¶ I recently read an article in Business Week concerning how computer buyers can make standards happen. It was a very interesting article. It indicates that if customers demand products standard when they purchase computers, participate in standard-setting groups, and band together with other customers, they will do better in the long run. Have you had customer groups help you or provide you with information on the adoption of more standards, such as in the areas of industry wide interfaces, a mix and match of computer gear and programs, and building the best system for each application utilized?

These standards include

¶ I would appreciate any data that you might furnish for me with regard relationship to customers and your firm working together to set past or future standards.

Sincerely yours,

Alice Karns

Vice President

urs

Correspondence
62-57

Business Letter
in Block Style

**Word
Processing
Manual
Review:**

L. 33: Envelopes

**Reference
Manual**

Review pages **R-3A** and
R-6A of the Reference
Manual.

Revise Correspondence 62-56, making the following changes:

1. Change the letter to block style.
2. Change the date to June 5, 20--.
3. Send the letter to Ms. Heidi M. Fischer at Gramstad Brothers, Inc., located at 5417 Harbord Drive in Oakland, CA 94618.
4. Change the salutation.
5. Combine the second and third paragraphs into one paragraph.

6. Add the following text as a new third paragraph:

   Some of my colleagues and I would like to get involved with others in an effort to make desired changes. I am confident that there are others around the Bay area who feel the same way.

7. Prepare an envelope for the letter.

Skillbuilding, Memo, and E-Mail Review

Goals

- Improve speed and accuracy
- Refine language arts skills in composing paragraphs
- Format memos and an e-mail message

A. Type 2 times.

A. WARMUP

```
1        "When is the quarterly jury report due?" asked Glenn.    11
2   He had faxed forms* to 64 of the 135 prospective jurors.      22
3   Only about one dozen of 596 citizens could not be located.    34
    | 1 | 2 | 3 | 4 | 5 | 6 | 7 | 8 | 9 | 10 | 11 | 12
```

SKILLBUILDING

PPP   PRETEST → PRACTICE → POSTTEST

PRETEST
Take a 1-minute timed writing. Review your speed and errors.

B. PRETEST: Discrimination Practice

```
4        The entire trip on a large train was better than we       11
5   had hoped. Polite police looked out for both the young and    23
6   old. One unit was outnumbered by herds of frolicking deer.    35
    | 1 | 2 | 3 | 4 | 5 | 6 | 7 | 8 | 9 | 10 | 11 | 12
```

PRACTICE
Speed Emphasis:
If you made no more than 1 error on the Pretest, type each *individual* line 2 times.
Accuracy Emphasis:
If you made 2 or more errors, type each *group* of lines (as though it were a paragraph) 2 times.

C. PRACTICE: Left Hand

```
7   rtr trip trot sport train alert courts assert tragic truest
8   asa mass salt usage cased cease astute dashed masked castle
9   rer rear rest overt rerun older before entire surest better
```

D. PRACTICE: Right Hand

```
10  mnm menu numb hymns unmet manly mental namely manner number
11  pop post coop opera pools opens polite proper police oppose
12  iui unit quit fruit suits built medium guided helium podium
```

POSTTEST
Repeat the Pretest timed writing and compare performance.

E. POSTTEST: Discrimination Practice

F. PACED PRACTICE

If you are not using the GDP software, turn to page SB-14 and follow the directions for this activity.

G. COMPOSING: PARAGRAPH

Read through the paragraphs in the 5-minute timed writing in Lesson 62. Compose a paragraph to include the type of operating system, application software, and utility programs loaded on the computers used in your keyboarding class.

DOCUMENT PROCESSING

Correspondence 63-58

Memo

Review: R-4D: Memo

(!) The ¶ symbol indicates the start of a new paragraph. In a memo, paragraphs are blocked (not indented).

(!) Remember to type your reference initials.

MEMO TO: Frank Janowicz, Ticket Manager | **FROM**: Sam Steele, Executive Director | **DATE**: March 1, 20-- | **SUBJECT**: Ticket Sales Campaign

¶We tentatively have scheduled 114 concerts for Orchestra Hall for the calendar year beginning September 1, 20--. The attached list shows the new season ticket prices for the main floor, mezzanine, balcony, and gallery.

¶These prices are grouped in 11 different concert categories, which reflect the varied classical tastes of our patrons. These groupings also consider preferences for day of the week, time of day, and season of the year.

¶Please see me at 3 p.m. on March 10 so that we can review our ticket sales campaign. Last year's season ticket holders have had ample time to renew their subscriptions; we must now concentrate on attracting new season subscribers. I shall look forward to reviewing your plans on the tenth.

urs | Attachment

Correspondence 63-59

E-Mail Message

Review: R-5C: E-mail Message in Internet Explorer, or **R-5D:** E-mail Message in Yahoo!

Type the e-mail greeting, body, closing, and signature below in correct format.

Greeting: Mr. Phillips:

Body: ¶ Please send information and prices on the security software you recently advertised in *PC Magazine*.

¶ We are interested in implementing a new security program for the personal computers in our main office and would like to study the specifications and features your system provides.

¶ Thank you for your assistance.

Closing: Charles

Signature: C. H. Cox
E-mail address: chcox@mailserver.net
Phone: 770-555-2843

MEMO TO: Edo Dorati, Cabaret pops Conductor
FROM: Sam Steele, Executive Director
DATE: March 2, 20--
Subject: Erving Berlin Concert
Our Patron Advisory Program Committtee recomments inits their
attached letter that the Erving Berlin concert begin with some pre-
World War I hits, followed by music from the '20s and '30s. Favorites
from this era are hit songs from Music Box Review, Puttin' on The
Ritz, and Follow the the Fleet. After the intermission the committee
suggest songs from the '40s and '50s, hits from Annie get Your Gun,
Call me Madam, Easter parade. A planning meeting has been
scheduled for you, Dolly Carpenter (the Rehearsals Coordinator), and
me on Mar. 9 at 10 A.M. at Orchestra Hall. I shall look foreward to
seeing you then.

urs

Attachment

c: Dolly Carpenter

MEMO TO: Dolly Carpenter, Rehearsals Coordinator
FROM: Sam Steele, Executive Director
DATE: March 3, 20--
SUBJECT: Summer Cabaret Pops Concerts
We are pleased that you will be our rehearsals coordinator for this summer's Cabaret Pops concerts. The five biweekly concerts will run from June 13 through August 8.
As the concert schedule is much lighter during the summer months, I am quite confident that you will be able to use the Orchestra Hall stage for all rehearsals. This is the preference of Edo Dorati, who will be the conductor for this year's Cabaret Pops concerts.
I look forward to seeing you on June 1.

Skillbuilding and Table Review

Goals

- Type at least 40wpm/5'/5e
- Format tables

A. Type 2 times.

A. WARMUP

```
1        There were two big questions: (1) Would both have to      11
2   be present to pick up the license? and (2) Is a blood test     23
3   required? Jeff and Faye were quite dizzy with excitement.      34
    |  1  |  2  |  3  |  4  |  5  |  6  |  7  |  8  |  9  |  10  |  11  |  12
```

SKILLBUILDING

B. Take a 1-minute timed writing on the first paragraph to establish your base speed. Then take four 1-minute timed writings on the remaining paragraphs. As soon as you equal or exceed your base speed on one paragraph, advance to the next, more difficult paragraph.

B. SUSTAINED PRACTICE: ALTERNATE-HAND WORDS

```
4        The town council decided to shape its destiny when a      11
5   rich landowner lent a hand by proposing to chair the audit     23
6   committee. He will be a good chairman, and eight civic         34
7   club members will work to amend some troublesome policies.     46

8        One problem relates to the change in profit for many      11
9   of the firms in the city. As giant property taxes do not       22
10  relate to income, they wish to make those taxes go down.       33
11  The result means increases in their sales or income taxes.     45

12       All eight members of the town council now agree that      11
13  it is time to join with other cities throughout the state      23
14  in lobbying with the state legislature to bring about the      35
15  needed change. The right balance in taxes is the goal.         46

16       The mayor pointed out that it is not only business        10
17  property owners who would be affected. Homeowners should       22
18  see a decrease in property taxes, and renters might see        33
19  lower rents, as taxes on rental property would be lowered.     45
    |  1  |  2  |  3  |  4  |  5  |  6  |  7  |  8  |  9  |  10  |  11  |  12
```

C. Take two 5-minute timed writings. Review your speed and errors.

Goal: At least 40wpm/5′/5e

C. 5-MINUTE TIMED WRITING

20	The computer has changed the way you do things in the	11
21	office today. Jobs that used to take many hours to complete	23
22	now can be done in less time. A quick review of ways in	34
23	which your computer can help you streamline your work may	46
24	be in order.	49
25	Most software programs include helpful wizards that	59
26	can guide you through any project. You can use a stored	70
27	template, or you can create your own style. You do not need	82
28	to write your thoughts in longhand on paper before you type	94
29	them. Composing and revising documents as you type them	105
30	will save you lots of time.	111
31	Your computer is valuable for more than just writing	122
32	letters. Using different software applications, you can	133
33	create dazzling presentations for all to see. You can also	145
34	build databases for sorting and storing all types of data,	156
35	format spreadsheets, create your own calendar and colorful	168
36	charts, and perform calculations. You can even publish your	180
37	own newsletter and make business cards. It is exciting to	192
38	consider the ways you can use a computer.	200

| 1 | 2 | 3 | 4 | 5 | 6 | 7 | 8 | 9 | 10 | 11 | 12 |

DOCUMENT PROCESSING

**Table►
64-23**

Boxed Table

Word Processing Manual Review:

L. 36: Table—Create; AutoFit to Contents
L.37: Table—Merge Cells
L.38: Center a Table Horizontally and Center Page
L.39: Table—Align Text in a Column

Reference Manual

Review: R-13A: Boxed Table

$700 COMPOUNDED ANNUALLY FOR 7 YEARS AT 7 PERCENT		
Beginning of Year	**Interest**	**Value**
First	$00.00	$ 700.00
Second	49.00	749.00
Third	52.43	801.43
Fourth	56.10	857.53
Fifth	60.03	917.56
Sixth	64.23	981.79
Seventh	68.72	1,050.51
Eighth	78.68	1,129.19

Table
64-24

Open Table

Word Processing Manual Review:

L. 37: Tables—Borders

Reference Manual

Review: R-13B: Open Table

1. Insert a table with 3 columns and 9 rows.
2. Merge the cells in Row 1, and center the title in all-caps, bold, and 14-point font. Press ENTER 1 time.
3. Center the subtitle in upper- and lower-case, bold, and 12-point font. Press ENTER 1 time.
4. Center and bold the column headings.
5. Type the information in the body of the table.
6. Automatically adjust the column widths.
7. Center the table horizontally and vertically.
8. Spell-check, preview, and proofread your table for spelling and formatting errors before printing it.

SALES CONFERENCES
All Sessions at Regional Offices

Date	City	Leader
October 7	Boston	D. G. Gorham
October 17	Baltimore	James B. Brunner
October 24	Miami	Becky Taylor
November 3	Dallas	Rodney R. Nordstein
November 10	Minneapolis	Joanne Miles-Tyrell
November 17	Denver	Becky Taylor
November 26	Los Angeles	Rodney R. Nordstein

Table
64-25

Ruled Table

Reference Manual

Review: R-13C: Ruled Table

SECOND HALF-YEAR SALES
Ending December 31, 20--

Month	Sales Quotas ($)	Actual Sales ($)
July	335,400	350,620
August	370,750	296,230
September	374,510	425,110
October	390,270	390,110
November	375,890	368,290
December	360,470	378,690
TOTAL	2,207,290	2,209,050

Skillbuilding and Employment Document Review

Goals

- Improve speed and accuracy
- Refine language arts skills in proofreading
- Format employment documents

A. Type 2 times.

A. WARMUP

```
1      Only 6 of the 18 competitors weighed more than 149#.      11
2   All Big Five matches were scheduled in Gym #3. Amazingly,    23
3   about 1/3 of the #1 Jaguars were picked to acquire titles.   35
    |  1  |  2  |  3  |  4  |  5  |  6  |  7  |  8  |  9  |  10  |  11  |  12
```

SKILLBUILDING

B. PROGRESSIVE PRACTICE: NUMBERS

If you are not using the GDP software, turn to page SB-11 and follow the directions for this activity.

C. TECHNIQUE PRACTICE: BACKSPACE KEY

Type each word as shown until you reach the backspace sign (←). Then backspace 1 time and replace the previously typed character with the one shown.

First Letter
Middle Letter
Last Letter

```
4   h←fall s←dash h←lead k←heel p←cage b←rare d←bark l←date t←sold
5   has←lf far←te mak←de roo←am do←ive fas←ce war←ve wee←ak yok←lk
6   sale←t they←m helm←d wall←k pals←e milk←d told←l quip←t main←l
```

D. PROGRESSIVE PRACTICE: ALPHABET

If you are not using the GDP software, turn to page SB-7 and follow the directions for this activity.

LANGUAGE ARTS

E. Compare this paragraph with the fourth paragraph of Report 61-36 on page 217. Edit the paragraph to correct any errors.

E. PROOFREADING

```
7       A successful leader is one who is commited to ideas-
8   ideas for future product and services for improving the
9   firms market position, and for the wellbeing of his or her
10  employes. A leeder possesses a value system that is
11  ethicly and morally sound. leaders who make decisions
12  effecting the firm, employees, and society, have set of
13  beliefs that influence decision making.
```

Report 65-38

Traditional Resume

Go To Word Processing Manual Review:

L. 51: Fonts

Refer to Reference Manual

Review: R-12A: Resume

1. Press ENTER 6 times.
2. Insert an open table with 2 columns and 5 rows.
3. Merge the cells in Row 1.
4. Change to center alignment.
5. Type the individual's name in Arial Bold, all-caps, and 14-point font. Press ENTER 2 times.
6. Change to 12-point Arial Bold, and type the street address, city, state, and ZIP Code. Press ENTER 1 time.
7. Type the phone number and e-mail address. Press ENTER 1 time.
8. Apply a bottom border to Row 1.
9. Move to Row 2, Column A. Press ENTER 1 time; then type the section heading in 12-point Times New Roman Bold, all-caps.
10. Move to Column B, press ENTER 1 time, and type the information pertaining to the section. Press ENTER 1 time after the final line in Row 2, Column B.
11. Move to Row 3, Column A, and type the second section heading. Then move to Column B, and type the corresponding information for this section. Press ENTER 1 time after the final line in Row 3, Column B.
12. Move to Row 4, and repeat steps 9 and 10 until all remaining sections have been completed. (Do not insert a hard return at the end of the references section information.)
13. Manually adjust the column widths as needed.

Note: The table is shown with "Show Gridlines" active.

TIMOTHY J. ROBINSON	
5816 Foxfire Road, Lawton, OK 73501 **Phone: 405-555-3039; e-mail: trobinso@lcc.edu**	
EDUCATION	Lawton Community College, Lawton, Oklahoma Associate in Business degree, Office Systems, June 2003 Specialization in computer applications software (Microsoft Word, Excel, Access), business communication, and office systems management Frederick High School, Frederick, Oklahoma Graduated: May 2001

EXPERIENCE	*Computer Systems Technician*, September 2001-Present Selkirk & Associates, Lawton, Oklahoma
	   Duties include installing and updating computer software programs throughout the firm.
	
	Secretary II, July 1999–August 2001 (part-time) Kittredge Insurance Agency, Frederick, Oklahoma
	   Duties included typing and word processing while reporting to the administrative assistant to the owner.

ACTIVITIES	College Choir, 2001–2003 Business Students Club, 2001–2003 (Secretary, 2002–2003) Varsity Basketball, 2001–2003 Intramural Soccer, 2001–2003
REFERENCES	Available upon request.

March 10, 20-- | Mrs. Denise F. Klenzman | Director of Human Resources | Cole Enterprises | 3714 Crestmont Avenue | Norman, OK 73069 | Dear Mrs. Klenzman:

¶ Please consider me an applicant for the position of Computer Systems Coordinator with your firm. I became aware of the new position through a friend who is an employee at Cole Enterprises. I have been employed at Selkirk & Associates since graduating from high school in 2001. During this time I have also earned an assoc. in business degree at Lawton Community College. The resume enclosed shows that I have had several courses in computer application soft ware and office systems. I am confident that my educational background experience and my computer systems experience make me highly qualified for the position with your firm. You may call me for an interview at 405-555-3039.

Sincerely yours, | Timothy J. Robinson | 5816 Foxfire Road | Lawton, OK 73501 | Enclosure

Progress and Proofreading Check

Documents designated as Proofreading Checks serve as a check of your proofreading skill. Your goal is to have zero typographical errors when the GDP software first scores the document.

March 19, 20-- | Mrs. Denise F. Klenzman | Director of Human Resources | Cole Enterprises | 3714 Crestmont Avenue | Norman, OK 73069

Dear Mrs. Klenzman:

¶ Thank you for the opportunity to meet with you yesterday and to learn of the exciting career opportunities at Cole Enterprises. It was inspiring for me to learn about future plans for your forward-looking company.

¶ I am confident that my education and my experience qualify me in a special way for your position of computer systems coordinator. I am familiar with all of your present equipment and software.

¶ I would very much like to join the professional staff at Cole Enterprises. Please let me know when you have made your decision.

Sincerely yours, | Timothy J. Robinson | 5816 Foxfire Road | Lawton, OK 73501

Unit 14

Reports

LESSON 66
Itineraries

LESSON 67
Agendas and Minutes of Meetings

LESSON 68
Procedures Manual

LESSON 69
Reports Formatted in Columns

LESSON 70
Report Review

Presentation Software Guide   Cartwright Services, Page 2

FORMATTING SLIDES

Once you have written your presentation, you can place your key points on slides using presentation software. Follow these steps to prepare your presentation slides.

• Select a template or background that is appropriate for every slide.
• Select a layout such as text copy or bulleted or numbered lists.
• Use the edit, copy, and paste commands to add text to your presentation slides.

FORMATTING THE PRESENTATION

After you finish preparing the slides for your presentation, you may want to change the method by which each slide appears on the screen or the way individual points are displayed on the screen. In presentation software, moving from one slide to another is known as transition. Transition is accomplished by following these steps:

• Select the slides you want to control by the transition method.
• Select a transition method such as Cover Right or Wipe Left.
• Run through the slide show to determine whether or not you are satisfied with the transition.

Slide presentations can also be formatted so that each point you make on an individual slide appears individually on the screen. To structure your slides this way, follow these steps:

... y a build effect.
... Fly From Left.
... ermine whether or not you are satisfied with

... f a slide, and it can be added easily to selected
... resentation. Several clip art images are included in
... e of them can be used in slides that you prepare. If
... lip are images from other packages. To insert a clip
... age, follow these steps:

... t the clip art to appear.
... image.
... e clip art library.
... rect location on the slide.
... e if it is to appear on all slides.

CALIFORNIA PLANNING MEETING

Itinerary for Nancy Perkins

July 8-10, 20--

MONDAY, JULY 8

2:45 p.m.-4:05 p.m.   Flight from Houston to Los Angeles; United Flight 834; seat 10C; nonstop

TUESDAY, JULY 9

10 a.m.-11:15 a.m.   Flight from Los Angel... seat 4A; nonstop

WEDNESDAY, JULY 10

7 p.m.-11:15 p.m.   Flight from Sacramen... 7B; nonstop; dinner

NOTES

1. Adam Broderick, chief engineer for Natural Gas... Los Angeles.
2. At 7 p.m. on July 8, you will have dinner with C... the Hollywood & Vine Restaurant.
3. You will have a 9 a.m. tour of the wastewater tre... Wednesday, July 10.
4. At 12 noon on Wednesday, July 10, you will have... at J. C. Crawford's. Topic: Senate Bill 4501-68.

PERFORMING SUCCESSFULLY

Ginger Nichols

We have been involved in giving performances since our very early years, when we played a part in a class play or participated in competitive sports events at our school. The most terrifying part of each performance was probably the fear that we would "freeze" when it came our turn to perform. Whenever we find ourselves in this predicament, the best thing to do is to accept that fear and to learn to let it work for us, not against us. We need to recognize that nervousness or fear may set in during our performance. Then, when it does happen (if it does), we will be ready to cope with it and overcome it.

If you forget some of your lines in a recitation, try to remember other lines and recite them. Doing so may help those forgotten lines to "pop back" into your memory so that you put them in at a later time, if possible.

You always want to leave your audience with the idea that you have given them something worthwhile that they can use or apply to their own lives. For maximum impact on your audience and to make sure that they remember what you say, use audiovisual aids to reinforce your message. Remember, however, that audiovisual aids are nothing more than aids. The real message should come in the words you choose when giving your presentation.

Study your speech well; even rehearse it if necessary. However, do not practice it to the extent that it appears that you are merely reading what is written down on the paper in front of you. Much of your personality should be exhibited while you are giving your speech. If you are an enthusiastic, friendly person who converses well with people face-to-face, then that same persona should be evident during your speech. A good piece of advice is to just go out there and be yourself—you will be much more comfortable by doing so, and your audience will relate to you better than if you try to exhibit a different personality when at the podium.

No matter how rapidly you speak in general, slow down when you are in front of a group. The fact that you are nervous can cause your speech rate to increase. The best way to slow down your speaking is to breathe deeply. Doing so also causes your nervous system to relax, allowing you to proceed with your speech calmly.

Finally, possibly the best advice for giving a successful speech is to be prepared. You will be more confident if you are thoroughly prepared. Do your research, rehearse your speech, and make notes about where you want to give emphasis or use an audiovisual aid.

Itineraries

Goals

- Type at least 41wpm/5'/5e
- Format itineraries

A. Type 2 times.

A. WARMUP

```
1        Had Phil been given a quiz on a subject that had been    11
2   reviewed by Max and Kay? Frank scored 89 on that quiz; Sue    23
3   scored 93 (*math only). Both tests were taken on 10/25/04.    35
    |  1  |  2  |  3  |  4  |  5  |  6  |  7  |  8  |  9  |  10  |  11  |  12
```

SKILLBUILDING

B. Take three 12-second timed writings on each line. The scale below the last line shows your wpm speed for a 12-second timed writing.

B. 12-SECOND SPEED SPRINTS

```
4   This is not the person who is my first choice for this job.
5   The day was bright as the sun shone on the clear blue lake.
6   All of you should take a long walk when the sun sets today.
7   This line has many easy words in it to type your very best.
    |    5    |    10    |    15    |    20    |    25    |    30    |    35    |    40    |    45    |    50    |    55    |    60
```

Keyboarding Connection

Observing Netiquette

Netiquette is proper conduct for e-mail users. It shows courtesy and professionalism and conveys a good impression of you and your company. Since e-mail is close to speech, it is the most informal of business documents.

Check your e-mail daily. Try to answer it the same day it arrives. Don't let it accumulate in your mailbox; you risk offending the sender. Use regular capitalization. All-caps indicate SHOUTING; all-lowercase letters convey immaturity. Most readers tolerate an infrequent typo, but if your message is filled with errors, you appear unprofessional. Use your spell-checker, and don't overwhelm people with unnecessary e-mails. Use discretion. Make sure the information is relevant to each e-mail recipient.

Be considerate. Be professional. Anything you write can wind up in your personnel file. E-mail that criticizes another person can be forwarded to him or her without your knowledge.

YOUR TURN   Review your next e-mail message for the use of netiquette.

C. PROGRESSIVE PRACTICE: ALPHABET

If you are not using the GDP software, turn to page SB-7 and follow the directions for this activity.

D. Take two 5-minute timed writings. Review your speed and errors.

Goal: At least 41wpm/5'/5e

D. 5-MINUTE TIMED WRITING

8	Making a successful presentation to an audience is a	11
9	skill that is absolutely essential in your career. The art	23
10	of speaking before a group requires planning and hard work.	35
11	Although different speakers prepare in much different ways,	47
12	a speaker should try to adhere to certain rules.	56
13	As the speaker, you are quite visible to people in the	68
14	audience. Therefore, you should always try to make a good	79
15	first impression. When you walk to the podium to speak, you	91
16	give the audience a chance to notice your neat appearance,	103
17	good posture, and confident manner. You will improve the	114
18	quality of your voice if you stand up straight and hold	126
19	your shoulders back and stomach in.	133
20	As you talk, use your eyes, face, and hands to help	143
21	you connect with your listeners. Maintain eye contact by	155
22	just moving your eyes over the group without focusing on	166
23	any one person. Use hand movements and facial expressions	177
24	to convey meanings to your audience. By utilizing these	189
25	techniques, you will improve your speaking skills, and your	201
26	effort will be noted.	205

| 1 | 2 | 3 | 4 | 5 | 6 | 7 | 8 | 9 | 10 | 11 | 12

FORMATTING

E. ITINERARIES

An itinerary is a proposed outline of a trip that provides a traveler with information such as flight times and numbers, meeting times, travel dates, and room reservations. An itinerary may also include notes of special interest to the traveler.

Report 66-39

Itinerary

Refer to Reference Manual

Review R-11C: Itinerary

1. Press ENTER 6 times to leave an approximately 2-inch top margin.
2. Insert an open table with 2 columns and 10 rows.
3. Merge the cells in Row 1, and center the title in all-caps, bold, and 14-point font. Press ENTER 2 times.
4. Center the subtitle in upper- and lower-case, bold, and 12-point font. Press ENTER 2 times.
5. Center and bold the date. Press ENTER 1 time.
6. Move to Row 2, Column A, and type the date in all-caps; then press ENTER 1 time.

7. Move to Row 3, Column A, and type the time. Then move to Column B and type the corresponding information for this time. Press ENTER 1 time after the final line in Column B.
8. Move to Row 4 and repeat steps 5 and 6 until all dates, times, and entries have been completed. (Do not insert a hard return at the end of the final itinerary entry.)
9. Manually adjust the column widths as needed.

Note: The table is shown with "Show Gridlines" active.

↓6X

14 pt **PORTLAND SALES MEETING** ↓2X	
12 pt **Itinerary for Arlene Gilsdorf** ↓2X	
March 12-18, 20-- ↓1X	
THURSDAY, MARCH 12 ↓1X	
5:10 p.m.-5:55 p.m.	Flight from Detroit to Minneapolis; Northwest 83 (Phone: 800-555-1222); e-ticket; Seat 8D; nonstop ↓1X
6:30 p.m.-8:06 p.m.	Flight from Minneapolis to Portland; Northwest 2363; e-ticket; Seat 15C; nonstop; dinner ↓1X
SUNDAY, MARCH 15	
10:35 a.m.-12:22 p.m.	Flight from Portland to Los Angeles; United Airlines 360; e-ticket; Seat 15F; nonstop; breakfast
TUESDAY, MARCH 17	
8 a.m.-9:22 a.m.	Flight from San Francisco to Los Angeles; United Airlines 748; e-ticket; Seat 10D; nonstop; snack
WEDNESDAY, MARCH 18	
3:40 p.m.-5:50 p.m.	Flight from Los Angeles to Detroit; Southwest 327; e-ticket; Seat 17D; nonstop; snack

INTERCO SEMINAR
Itinerary for Mrs. Helen Kyslowsky
September 25-29, 20--

WEDNESDAY, SEPTEMBER 25

6:50 p.m. - 9:10 p.m.   *Flight from Columbus to Boston;*
America West 2053;
Seat 13 F; nonstop

FRIDAY, SEPTEMBER 27

9 a.m. - 10:17 a.m.   *Flight from Boston to New York City;*
US Airways 454; Seat 10 D; nonstop

SUNDAY, SEPTEMBER 29

2:07 p.m. - 4:18 p.m.   *Flight from New York City to Columbus;*
US Airways 324; Seat 9A; nonstop

CALIFORNIA PLANNING MEETING | **Itinerary for Nancy Perkins** | **July 8-10, 20--** | **MONDAY, JULY 8** | Leave at 2:45 p.m. and arrive at 4:05 p.m. Houston to Los Angeles; United Flight 834; Seat 10C; nonstop | Marriott (310-555-1014) King-sized bed; nonsmoking room; late arrival guaranteed (Reservation No. 45STX78) | **TUESDAY, JULY 9** | Leave at 10 a.m. and arrive at 11:15 a.m. Los Angeles to Sacramento; American Flight 206; Seat 4A; nonstop | **WEDNESDAY, JULY 10** | Leave at 7 p.m. and arrive at 11:15 p.m. Sacramento to Houston; United Flight 307; Seat 7B; nonstop; dinner

Agendas and Minutes of Meetings

Goals

- Improve speed and accuracy
- Refine language arts skills in the use of hyphens, abbreviations, and agreement
- Format agendas and minutes of meetings

A. Type 2 times.

A. WARMUP

```
1        Rex Yantz was calm before quitting his job at the zoo    11
2   on 7/10/03. On 8/23/03 he applied for a job at Vance &        22
3   Walton, "specialists" in corporate law and bankruptcies.      33
    |  1  |  2  |  3  |  4  |  5  |  6  |  7  |  8  |  9  |  10  |  11  |  12
```

SKILLBUILDING

B. DIAGNOSTIC PRACTICE: SYMBOLS AND PUNCTUATION

If you are not using the GDP software, turn to page SB-2 and follow the directions for this activity.

C. DIAGNOSTIC PRACTICE: NUMBERS

If you are not using the GDP software, turn to page SB-5 and follow the directions for this activity.

D. Type 2 times!

D. TECHNIQUE PRACTICE: SHIFT/CAPS LOCK

```
4        RHONDA KORDICH was promoted on APRIL 1 to SENIOR
5   SECRETARY. The SOLD sign replaced the FOR SALE sign at
6   1904 ELM DRIVE. The trip to DULUTH was on INTERSTATE 35.
```

LANGUAGE ARTS

E. Study the rules at the right.

E. HYPHENS

Note: The callout signals in the left margin indicate which language arts rule from this lesson has been applied.

RULE ▶

-compound adjective

The underline calls attention to a point in the sentence where a hyphen might mistakenly be inserted.

Hyphenate compound adjectives that come before a noun (unless the first word is an adverb ending in -ly).

We reviewed an up-to-date report on Wednesday.

But: The report was up_to_date.

But: We reviewed the highly_rated report.

Note: A compound adjective is two or more words that function as a unit to describe a noun.

F. AGREEMENT

RULE ▶

agreement singular
agreement plural

Use singular verbs and pronouns with singular subjects; use plural verbs and pronouns with plural subjects.

I was happy with my performance.

Janet and Phoenix were happy with their performance.

Among the items discussed were our raises and benefits.

G. ABBREVIATIONS

RULE ▶

abbreviate none

In general business writing, do not abbreviate common words (such as *dept.* or *pkg.*), compass points, units of measure, or the names of months, days of the week, cities, or states (except in addresses).

Almost one-half of the audience indicated they were at least 5 feet 8 inches tall.

Note: Do not insert a comma between the parts of a single measurement.

Edit the sentences to correct any errors in grammar and mechanics.

```
 7  The Queens visited Hickory to look at four bedroom homes.
 8  Cindy Wallace has a part time job after school.
 9  The accountants was extremely busy from March through April.
10  Lydia and Margaret were invited to present their report.
11  The portfolio include several technology stocks.
12  The planning committee will meet on Tue., Sept. 26.
13  Please credit the acct. for the amt. of $55.48.
14  The mgr. said the org. will move its headquarters to NC.
```

FORMATTING

H. AGENDAS

An agenda is a list of topics to be discussed at a meeting. It may also include a formal program of a meeting and consist of times, rooms, speakers, and other related information. Follow these steps to format an agenda:

1. Press ENTER 6 times to leave an approximately 2-inch top margin.

2. Center and type the name of the company or committee in all-caps, bold, and 14-point font.

3. Press ENTER 2 times, and then center and type Meeting Agenda in upper- and lowercase, bold, and 12-point font.

4. Press ENTER 2 times, and then center and type the date in upper- and lowercase, bold, and 12-point font.

5. Press ENTER 2 times, change the line spacing to double, and turn off bold.

6. Type all the items in the agenda, and then highlight the items and apply a number format to them.

Remember to position the numbers at the left margin.

```
                          ↓6X
        14 pt  ALLIANCE CORPORATION STAFF MEETING  ↓2X

              12 pt↓  Meeting Agenda
                                        ↓2X
                   November 17, 20--
                                        ↓2X
       1.  Approval of minutes of October 15 meeting
                                        ↓2X
       2.  Progress reports of new district offices

       3.  Discussion of attendance at the National Hardware Association's meeting

       4.  Multimedia installation update: B. Harris

       5.  Annual fund drive: T. Henderson
```

I. MINUTES OF MEETINGS

Minutes of a meeting are a record of items discussed during a meeting. To format meeting minutes, follow these steps:

1. Press ENTER 6 times to leave an approximately 2-inch top margin.
2. Insert an open table with 2 columns and 6 rows.
3. Merge the cells in Row 1, and center the title in all-caps, bold, and 14-point font. Press ENTER 2 times.
4. Center Minutes of the Meeting in upper- and lowercase, bold, and 12-point font. Press ENTER 2 times.
5. Center the date; then press ENTER 1 time.
6. Move to Row 2, Column A; then type the first section heading, ATTENDANCE, in bold, all-caps.
7. Move to Column B, and type the information pertaining to the section. Press ENTER 1 time after the final line in all Column B entries.
8. Move to Row 3, Column A, and type the second section heading. Then move to Column B and type the corresponding information for this section. Press ENTER 1 time after the final line in Row 3, Column B.
9. Move to Row 4 and repeat steps 6 and 7 until all remaining sections have been completed.
10. Type the closing and signature lines in Column B of the final row. Remember to press ENTER 4 times to allow room for the signature. Do not press ENTER after typing the signature line.
11. Manually adjust the column widths as needed.

Note: The table is shown with "Show Gridlines" active.

14 pt ↓6X **PLANNING COMMITTEE** ↓2X **12 pt** **Minutes of the Meeting** ↓2X **February 10, 20--** ↓1X	
ATTENDANCE	The Planning Committee meeting was called to order at 1 p.m. on February 10, 20—, by Michelle North, chairperson. Members present were Cal Anderson, L. T. Braddock, Lisa Samson, Sharon Owens, and J. R. Stern. ↓1X
OLD BUSINESS	The committee reviewed bids for the purchase of a new computer for the Cheyenne office. We will accept the lower of two bids that have been submitted.
NEW BUSINESS	The committee reviewed a proposal for a new complex in Helena. After much discussion, the committee agreed to contact the Helena county clerk's office to get information on zoning ordinances.
ADJOURNMENT	The meeting was adjourned at 2:45 p.m. The next meeting is scheduled for March 22 in Room 16. ↓1X
	Respectfully submitted, ↓4X L. T. Braddock L. T. Braddock, Secretary

**Go To** Word Processing Manual

J. WORD PROCESSING: HYPHENATION

Study Lesson 67 in your word processing manual. Complete all of the shaded steps while at your computer. Then format the jobs that follow.

Report 67-42

Agenda

Word Processing Manual Review:

Review: **L. 28:** Bullets and Numbering

Reference Manual

Review: **R-11A:** Meeting Agenda

Report 67-43

Agenda

↓6X

14 pt **ALLIANCE CORPORATION STAFF MEETING** ↓2X

12 pt↓ **Meeting Agenda** ↓2X

November 17, 20-- ↓2X

1. Approval of minutes of October 15 meeting ↓2X

2. Progress reports of new district offices

3. Discussion of attendance at the National Hardware Association's annual meeting

4. Multimedia installation update: B. Harris

5. Annual fund drive: T. Henderson

APEX MULTIMEDIA CORPORATION
Meeting Agenda
October 13, 20--

1. Call to order
2. Approval of minutes of September 10 meeting
3. Progress reports on Sherman contract
    (Julia Adams)
4. Upgrading of 8.0 presentation media
5. CD-ROM development program (Ray Sanchez)
6. Internet configuration (JoAnn Hubbard)
7. Adjournment

Note: The table is shown with "Show Gridlines" active.

↓6X
14 pt **PLANNING COMMITTEE** ↓2X

12 pt↓ **Minutes of the Meeting** ↓2X

February 10, 20-- ↓1X

ATTENDANCE	The Planning Committee meeting was called to order at 1 p.m. on February 10, 20--, by Michelle North, chairperson. Members present were Cal Anderson, L. T. Braddock, Lisa Samson, Sharon Owens, and J. R. Stern. ↓1X
OLD BUSINESS	The committee reviewed bids for the purchase of a new computer for the Cheyenne office. We will accept the lower of two bids that have been submitted.
NEW BUSINESS	The committee reviewed a proposal for a new complex in Helena. After much discussion, the committee agreed to contact the Helena county clerk's office to get information on zoning ordinances.
ADJOURNMENT	The meeting was adjourned at 2:45 p.m. The next meeting is scheduled for March 22 in Room 16. ↓1X
	Respectfully submitted, ↓4X L. T. Braddock, Secretary

PERSONEL COMMITTEE
N ∧

Minutes of the Meeting

May 14, 20--

ATTENDENCE
A∧

A meeting of the Personnel Committee was held in
special   on May 14, 20--,
the office of Mr. Cameron. Members present were
All

(Continued on next page)

except Richard Dixon, who was repre-sented by Monica Zick man. The meeting was called to order at 2 p. m.

Old Business A copy of the survey is attached. Eighty-eight employees participated in a survey that had been completed by Andrea Fields. The minutes of the last monthly meeting were read.

NEW BUSINESS Ms. ~~Samuels~~ Daniels discussed the need for planning a campaign for ∧ job applicants letting ∧ about vacancies know ∧ occur that within the company. Frank Lundquist will draft a fli̶er to be sent to the Park view sentinel *ital*. Programs for the N P A convention to be held in Des Moines were distributed to all members. Each committee member ~~were~~ was ∧ asked to distribute copies to ∧ all employees in his or her department.

ADJOURN ^MENT The meeting was adjourned at 3:25 p̶a.m. The next meeting has been scheduled for July 10 in the conference center.

Respectfully submitted,

Brandon Stinson, Secretary

Procedures Manual

Goals

- Type at least 41wpm/5′/5e
- Format a procedures manual

A. Type 2 times.

A. WARMUP

```
1       Zach sharpened the ax for Quinn just to help him win    10
2   the $100 tree-cutting event to be held in Kildeer on May 8  23
3   (if it doesn't rain). The prize will be $250--fantastic!    34
    | 1 | 2 | 3 | 4 | 5 | 6 | 7 | 8 | 9 | 10 | 11 | 12
```

SKILLBUILDING

B. MAP

Follow the GDP software directions for this exercise in improving keystroking accuracy.

C. Take two 5-minute timed writings. Review your speed and errors.

Goal: At least 41wpm/5′/5e

C. 5-MINUTE TIMED WRITING

```
4       Taking photos with a digital camera is a process that   11
5   is quite unique and very different from taking photos with  23
6   film. Most digital cameras store images on a device such as 35
7   a memory card or a memory stick. The number of photos you   46
8   can store on a card or stick depends on how many megabytes  58
9   it can hold. Once you reach the limit of the memory device, 70
10  you can store no new images until you either transfer or    82
11  delete the old ones to make room for new ones.              91
12      The advantages of using a memory device are many. For   102
13  example, the card or stick can be used over and over; or,   114
14  when the device is full, just simply remove it and put in a 126
15  new device. You can also move the images to the computer,   137
16  where they can reside on your hard drive for as long as you 149
17  want. If the memory card or stick you have does not have    161
18  enough memory, you can upgrade the megabyte size. Finally,  172
19  you can see instantly any images you have taken with the    184
20  camera. If you decide not to keep an image in the camera,   195
21  you can delete it to make room for other images.            205
    | 1 | 2 | 3 | 4 | 5 | 6 | 7 | 8 | 9 | 10 | 11 | 12
```

D. PROCEDURES MANUAL

Organizations often prepare procedures manuals to assist employees in identifying the steps or methods they must follow to accomplish particular tasks. To format a procedures manual:

1. Type the manual as a single-spaced report.
2. Place a header on every page except the first page. The header may include such items as the title of the manual (at the left margin) and the company name and page number (at the right margin).
3. Place a footer on every page including the first page. The footer should be in italics and may include the same information as the header, or it may identify the content of that page (for example, "Training Program").

Employees' Manual   Chandler Industries, Page 7

The purpose of this procedures manual is to assist managers who are responsible for developing training programs for new employees who have been hired in any of the seven regional branches of Chandler Industries. The basic content of this training program is outlined in the following paragraphs. ↓2X

INTRODUCTION ↓2X

This section identifies specific ways the manual should be used at Chandler Industries as well as the content of the manual. Answers are provided to the following questions: ↓2X

1. Where does the training manual fit within the training program?
2. For whom is the manual designed, and what does it contain?
3. How should the manual be used?
4. Can the manual be used in a classroom setting?
5. Can the manual be used as self-paced instructional material?
6. Can study guides accompany the manual? ↓2X

PROGRAM PHILOSOPHY AND GOALS ↓2X

This section reveals the nature of the training program. The statements below provide the context for all courses within Chandler Industries. The focus of the section is as follows: ↓2X

• Why does this program exist, and who benefits from it?
• What company needs are satisfied by this program?
• What goals, tasks, and competencies are satisfied by this program?
• What specific skills does this training program develop?

Training Program

DOCUMENT PROCESSING

Report 68-46

Procedures Manual

Word Processing Manual Review:

L. 27: Page Numbering
L. 42: Headers and Footers

1. Turn on hyphenation.
2. In page numbering, change the page number to start at page 7, and then create a header as follows: Type `Employees' Manual` at the left margin. Type `Chandler Industries, Page 7` aligned at the right margin.
3. Create a footer by typing *Training Program* in italic and aligned at the left margin.
4. Type the following portion of a procedures manual.

Employees' Manual   Chandler Industries, Page 7

¶ The purpose of this procedures manual is to assist managers who are responsible for developing training programs for new employees who have been hired in any of the seven regional branches of Chandler Industries. The basic content of this training program is outlined in the following paragraphs.

(Continued on next page)

INTRODUCTION

¶ This section identifies specific ways the manual should be used at Chandler Industries as well as the content of the manual. Answers are provided to the following questions:

1. Where does the training manual fit within the training program?
2. For whom is the manual designed, and what does it contain?
3. How should the manual be used?
4. Can the manual be used in a classroom setting?
5. Can the manual be used as self-paced instructional material?
6. Can study guides accompany the manual?

PROGRAM PHILOSOPHY AND GOALS

¶ This section describes the nature of the training program. The statements below provide the context for all courses within Chandler Industries. The focus of the section is as follows:

• Why does this program exist, and who benefits from it?
• What company needs are satisfied by this program?
• What goals, tasks, and competencies are satisfied by this program?
• What specific skills does this training program develop?

Training Program

Report 68-47 ▶

Procedures Manual

1. In page numbering, change the page number to start at page 2.
2. Create a header as follows:
   Type `Presentation Software Guide` at the left margin. Type `Cartwright Services, Page 2` aligned at the right margin.
3. Type *Formatting* as a footer at the left margin and in italic.

Presentation Software Guide   Cartwright Services, Page 2

FORMATTING SLIDES

¶ Once you have written your presentation, you can place your key points on slides using presentation software. Follow these steps to prepare your presentation slides.

• Select a template or background that is appropriate for every slide.
• Select a layout such as text copy or bulleted or numbered lists.
• Use the edit, copy, and paste commands to add text to your presentation slides.

FORMATTING THE PRESENTATION

¶ After you finish preparing the slides for your presentation, you may want to change the method by which each slide appears on the screen or the way individual points are displayed on the screen. In presentation software, moving from one slide to another is known as transition. Transition is accomplished by following these steps:

• Select the slides you want to control by the transition method.
• Select a transition method such as Cover Right or Wipe Left.
• Run through the slide show to determine whether or not you are satisfied with the transition.

(Continued on next page)

Remember to single-space the entire list if all items in the list are 1 line long.

Remember to insert a blank line between items in a multiline list in a single-spaced document.

¶ Slide presentations can also be formatted so that each point you make on an individual slide appears individually on the screen. To structure your slides this way, follow these steps:

- Select the slides to be controlled by a build effect.
- Select a build effect style such as Fly From Left.
- Run through the slide show again to determine whether or not you are satisfied with the build effect.

Formatting

Report 68-48
Procedures Manual

1. Open the file for Report 68-47.
2. Remove the third bulleted item under the FORMATTING SLIDES heading.
3. Add the following sections to the end of the report.

ADDING CLIP ART

¶ Clip art # enhances *can* the appearance of a slide, and it can be easily added to selected slides or to every other slide in your presentation. Several clip art images are included in this presentation package, and any one of them can be used in slides that you prepare. If you choose, however, you can insert clip art images from other packages. To insert a clip art *image* from your presentation package, follow these steps:

- Select the slide on which you want the clip art to appear.
- Click the icon for adding a clip art image. This icon is found on the menu bar.
- Select the image from the software clip art library. *and size and move it to its new location* The slide can come from the presentation package or you can retrieve it from another clip art package.
- Size and move the image to its correct location on the presentation slide.
- Copy the image to the master slide if it is to appear on all slides.

¶ You can also change the appearance of the clip art image by (1) changing the colors used in the image; (2) flipping the image so that its horizontal or vertical position is reversed (mirror image); (3) changing the contrast or brightness of the image; and (4) cropping the image so that unwanted sections are eliminated from view.

Reports Formatted in Columns

Goals

- Improve speed and accuracy
- Refine language arts skills in spelling
- Format magazine articles

A. Type 2 times.

A. WARMUP

```
1      On 12/30/02 Jim gave Alex and Pam a quiz--it was quite  11
2   difficult! Neither scored higher than 82%; their average    22
3   was 79. They should retake the quiz by the 4th or 5th.      32
    |  1  |  2  |  3  |  4  |  5  |  6  |  7  |  8  |  9  |  10  |  11  |  12
```

SKILLBUILDING

B. PACED PRACTICE

If you are not using the GDP software, turn to page SB-14 and follow the directions for this activity.

PPP PRETEST → PRACTICE → POSTTEST

PRETEST
Take a 1-minute timed writing. Review your speed and errors.

C. PRETEST: Horizontal Reaches

```
4      Four famous adults gazed at a wren on our farm gate.   11
5   A group of gawking writers wrote facts about an additional  23
6   upward gain in wildlife numbers on their supply of pads.    34
    |  1  |  2  |  3  |  4  |  5  |  6  |  7  |  8  |  9  |  10  |  11  |  12
```

PRACTICE
Speed Emphasis:
If you made no more than 1 error on the Pretest, type each *individual* line 2 times.
Accuracy Emphasis:
If you made 2 or more errors, type each *group* of lines (as though it were a paragraph) 2 times.

D. PRACTICE: In Reaches

```
7   wr wrap wren wreak wrist wrote writer unwrap writhe wreaths
8   ou pout ours ounce cough fouls output detour ousted coupons
9   ad adds dead adult ready blade advice fading admits adheres
```

E. PRACTICE: Out Reaches

```
10  fa fact farm faith sofas fakes faulty unfair famous defames
11  up upon soup upset group upper upturn supply uplift upsurge
12  ga gate gave cigar gains legal gazing legacy gawked garbage
```

POSTTEST
Repeat the Pretest timed writing and compare performance.

F. POSTTEST: Horizontal Reaches

G. Type this list of frequently misspelled words, paying special attention to any spelling problems in each word.

G. SPELLING

13 personnel information its procedures their committee system
14 receive employees which education services opportunity area
15 financial appropriate interest received production contract
16 important through necessary customer employee further there
17 property account approximately general control division our

Edit the sentences to correct any misspellings.

18 The revised systom was adopted by the finantial division.
19 Four employes want to serve on the new property commitee.
20 Approximatly ten proceedures were included in the contract.
21 Further informasion will be recieved from the customers.
22 Their was much interest shown by the production personal.
23 The services in that aria are necesary for needed control.

FORMATTING

H. MAGAZINE ARTICLES

Magazine articles can be formatted as two-column reports. Follow these steps:

1. Press ENTER 6 times to leave an approximately 2-inch top margin on page 1.
2. Center and type the article title in all-caps, bold, and 14-point.
3. Press ENTER 2 times; then center and type the byline in upper- and lower-case, bold, and 12-point.
4. Press ENTER 2 times and change to left alignment.
5. Turn on hyphenation, if needed.
6. Format the document for a 2-column layout; then change to justified alignment. (Remember to select "This point forward" from the "Apply to" section of the Columns dialog box.)
7. Type the article single-spaced; insert 1 blank line before and after all side headings.
8. Create a header to print on all pages except page 1 to identify the author's name and the page number at the top right of every page. Use only the author's last name and the page number in the header (for example, Davis 2).

Sample Document (shown at top)

↓6X
14 pt **MEMBER BUYING SERVICES** ↓2X
12 pt **Brenda T. Mysweski** ↓2X

Policyholders of AICA (and their dependents) are eligible for a wide range of discount services. These services provide you with a variety of items you can purchase, from automobiles to computers to jewelry. Here are some examples of the merchandise and services that are available to all AICA members. ↓2X

AUTO PRICING ↓2X

You can order the most sophisticated auto information guide on the market. The guide will give you information on retail prices, vehicle specifications, safety equipment, and factory-option packages. ↓2X

When you are ready to place your order for an automobile, a team of company experts will work with you and with the prospective dealer to ensure that you are getting the best possible price through a network of nationwide dealers. You are guaranteed to get the best price for the automobile you have chosen.

Once you have purchased your automobile, AICA will provide all your insurance needs. Discounts on policy rates are provided for completion of a driver-training program, for installed antitheft devices, and for installed passive restraint systems such as air bags.

Finally, we can make your purchase decision and easy one by always providing a low-rate finance plan for you. You can be certain that you are getting the most competitive interest rate for the purchase of your automobile when you finance with AICA.

CAR RENTAL DISCOUNTS

When you need to rent an automobile while traveling, special rates are available to you from five of the largest car rental agencies.

ROAD AND TRAVEL SERVICES

You can enjoy the security of emergency road service through the AICA Road and Travel Plan. This plan also includes discounts on hotels and motels.

As an AICA traveler, you can take advantage of our exclusive discounts and bonuses on cruises and tours. Our travel plan provides daily and weekend trips to over 100 destinations. Take advantage of this wonderful opportunity to let AICA serve all your travel needs.

MERCHANDISE BUYING

Each quarter a buying services catalog will be sent to you. This catalog includes a variety of items that can be purchased through AICA—and you'll never find better prices! Through the catalog you can purchase jewelry, furniture, sports equipment, electronics, appliances, and computers. To place an order, all you have to do is call AICA toll-free at 1-800-555-3838. Your order will arrive within 10 to 15 days.

Go To **Word Processing Manual**

I. WORD PROCESSING: COLUMNS

Study Lesson 69 in your word processing manual. Complete all of the shaded steps while at your computer. Then format the jobs that follow.

DOCUMENT PROCESSING

Report 69-49

Magazine Article in Two Columns

MEMBER BUYING SERVICES | Brenda T. Mysweski

¶ Policyholders of AICA (and their dependents) are eligible for a wide range of discount services. These services provide you with a variety of items you can purchase, from automobiles to computers to jewelry. Here are some examples of the merchandise and services that are available to all AICA members.

AUTO PRICING

¶ You can order the most sophisticated auto information guide on the market. The guide will give you information on retail prices, vehicle specifications, safety equipment, and factory-option packages.

¶ When you are ready to place your order for an automobile, a team of company experts will work with you and with the prospective dealer to ensure that you are getting the best possible price through a network of nationwide dealers. You are guaranteed to get the best price for the automobile you have chosen.

(Continued on next page)

¶ Once you have purchased your automobile, AICA will provide all your insurance needs. Discounts on policy rates are provided for completion of a driver-training program, for installed antitheft devices, and for installed passive restraint systems such as air bags.

¶ Finally, we can make your purchase decision an easy one by always providing a low-rate finance plan for you. You can be certain that you are getting the most competitive interest rate for the purchase of your automobile when you finance with AICA.

CAR RENTAL DISCOUNTS

¶ When you need to rent an automobile while traveling, special rates are available to you from five of the largest car rental agencies.

ROAD AND TRAVEL SERVICES

¶ You can enjoy the security of emergency road service through the AICA Road and Travel Plan. This plan also includes discounts on hotels and motels.

¶ As an AICA traveler, you can take advantage of our exclusive discounts and bonuses on cruises and tours. Our travel plan provides daily and weekend trips to over 100 destinations. Take advantage of this wonderful opportunity to let AICA serve all your travel needs.

MERCHANDISE BUYING

¶ Each quarter a buying services catalog will be sent to you. This catalog includes a variety of items that can be purchased through AICA—and you'll never find better prices! Through the catalog you can purchase jewelry, furniture, sports equipment, electronics, appliances, and computers. To place an order, all you have to do is call AICA toll-free at 1-800-555-3838. Your order will arrive within 10 to 15 days.

Report 69-50

Magazine Article in Two Columns

INTERVIEW TECHNIQUES | By Paul Sanford

The interview process enables a company to gather information about you that was not provided on your resume or application form. This information may includes such items as your career goals, appearance, personality, poise, attitudes, and ability to express yourself verbally.

APPEARANCE

There are several things you should keep in mind when going to an interview. You should plan your wardrobe carefully because first impressions are lasting ones when you walk into the interviewer's office. If you are not quite certain about what you should wear, dress conservatively. Whatever you choose, be sure that your clothing is clean, neat, and comfortable. You should

(Continued on next page)

also pay attention to ~~important~~ details such as clean hair, shined shoes, well-groomed nails, and appropriate jewelry and other accessories.

MEETING THE INTERVIEWER

Be sure to arrive at the interview site a few minutes early. Stand when you meet the interviewer ~~for the first time~~. If ~~a handshake is~~ the interviewer offered s to shake hands, shake hands in a confident, firm manner. It is also a good idea not to smoke or chew gum during the interview.

THE INTERVIEW PROCESS

Maintain ~~good~~ direct eye contact with the interviewer when you respond to his or her questions. Listen intently to everything that is said. Be aware of ~~the~~ any movements you make with your eyes, your hands, and other parts of your body during the interview. Too much movement may be a signal to the interviewer that you are nervous, that you lack confidence, or that you are not certain of your answers.

During the interview ~~process~~, the interviewer will judge not only what you say but also how you say it. As you ~~speak~~ answer questions, you will be judged on grammar, articulation, vocabulary, and tone of voice. The nonverbal skills that the interviewer may ~~be~~ judged are your attitude, enthusiasm, listening abilities, and promptness in responding to questions.

ENDING THE INTERVIEW

Let the interviewer determine when it is time to close the interview. When this time arrives, ask the interviewer when he or she expects to make a decision on hiring for this position and when you ~~can~~ may expect to hear about the job. Thank the interviewer for taking the time to meet with you, and express a ~~positive~~ desire to work for the company.

After the interview, send a follow-up letter to remind the interviewer of your name and your ~~continued~~ interest in the company. Let that person know how to contact you by providing a telephone number where you can be reached, either at home or at your current work location.

Report 69-51 ▶

Magazine Article in Two Columns

Go To

Word Processing Manual Review:

L. 30:
Cut/Copy/Paste

Open the file for Report 69-49 and make the following changes:

1. Make Maria Sanchez the author of the article.
2. Make the MERCHANDISE BUYING section the second paragraph in the article.
3. Add the following section to the end of the article:

MISCELLANEOUS SERVICES | In addition to the above services, AICA provides permanent life insurance, pension plan funding, cash management, and credit card programs. At your request, detailed catalogs will be sent to you that explain each of these services.

Report Review

Goals

- Type at least 41wpm/5'/5e
- Improve speed and accuracy
- Review report formats

A. Type 2 times.

A. WARMUP

```
1        Felix Quayle sat in Seat #14 when he won the jackpot;   11
2  Van Gill sat in Seat #23 but did not win a prize. Do you      22
3  think Row 19 (Seats #1560 and #1782) will be lucky for me?     34
   |  1  |  2  |  3  |  4  |  5  |  6  |  7  |  8  |  9  |  10  |  11  |  12
```

SKILLBUILDING

B. Take a 1-minute timed writing on the first paragraph to establish your base speed. Then take four 1-minute timed writings on the remaining paragraphs. As soon as you equal or exceed your base speed on one paragraph, advance to the next, more difficult paragraph.

B. SUSTAINED PRACTICE: ROUGH DRAFT

```
4        The possibility of aging and not being able to live as   11

5  independently as we want to is a prospect that no one wants    23

6  to recognize. One resource designed to counter some of the     35

7  negative realities of aging is called the Handyman Project.    47

                          program
8        This type of project helps support elders and disabled   12

9  residents in their efforts to maintain their homes. As the     24

10 name implies, "handy" volunteers perform minor home repairs    36

11 such as tightening leaky faucets and fixing broken windows.    48

12 Other types of work include: painting, plumbing, yard          11

13 work, and carpentry. The volunteers are all as diversified     23

14 as the word itself. You may find a retiree working next too    35
                                   assisting
15 an executive or a student helping a licensed electrician.      47
```

(Continued on next page)

16   Their back grounds may vary, but that they share is the   11

17   ~~hope~~ *desire* to put their ~~capabilities~~ to good use. Volunters ~~take~~ *find*   23

18   a high level of personal satisfaction after ~~doing~~ *finishing* a job   35

19   ~~but~~ *and* spending time with *an elder who really needs the* help.   47

| 1 | 2 | 3 | 4 | 5 | 6 | 7 | 8 | 9 | 10 | 11 | 12

C. Take two 5-minute timed writings. Review your speed and errors.

Goal: 41wpm/5′/5e

C. 5-MINUTE TIMED WRITING

23   In most offices, many products that are used each day   11

24   are made of materials that can now be recycled. Amazingly,   23

25   items made of glass, steel, aluminum, plastics, and paper   34

26   can be recycled to make many products that we need. Also,   46

27   the recycling process can help the environment.   56

28   Some unique examples of the process of recycling the   66

29   items we often throw away are listed here. Those old coffee   78

30   filters can be used to make soles for new shoes. Pieces of   90

31   paper that are thrown away each day can be used to make   101

32   tissue paper and paper towels. Most plastics that are used   113

33   in soda bottles can be recycled for insulation for jackets   125

34   and car interiors. Used lightbulbs and some glass products   137

35   can also be used to replace the surface on our streets.   148

36   Look around the room in which you are working. If you   159

37   are not already taking part in a recycling program, you may   171

38   want to recycle some items that you no longer need. Items   183

39   such as used paper, file folders, and aluminum cans can be   194

40   collected very quickly. What other items can you add?   205

| 1 | 2 | 3 | 4 | 5 | 6 | 7 | 8 | 9 | 10 | 11 | 12

Report 70-52

Agenda

Crandall First National Bank | Meeting Agenda | May 15, 20--

1. Call to Order
2. Approval of minutes of April 16 meeting
3. Mortgage loans (J. William Hokes)
4. Installment loans (Lorraine Hagen)
5. Series EE bonds (Joni Ellickson)
6. Club memberships (Louise Abbey)
7. Certificates of deposit (Louise Abbey) Robert Hunt
8. Closing remarks
9. Adjournment

Report 70-53

Minutes of a Meeting

LITTLETON WATERCOLOUR SOCIETY
Minutes of the Meeting
October 23, 20--

CALL TO ORDER The meeting was called to order by Sandra Garvy at 8 p.m. in the Littleton library conference room.

OLD BUSINESS Susan Firtz furnished each member with a list of artists and the names of the watercolor paintings each artist is entering in the Fall Arts Fair.

NEW BUSINESS John Cahmpion informed members that a new supply of canvas and oil paint arrived. Members can check out any items their to begin winter projects. He reminded everyone that Winter Fair will be held December 14 at the Expo.

ADJOURNMENT The meeting was adjourned at 9:45 p.m. The next meeting will be held November 12.

Respectfully submitted,

Catherine Argetes

Type the article in two
columns and balance
the columns.

**Progress and
Proofreading
Check**

Documents designated
as Proofreading Checks
serve as a check of
your proofreading skill.
Your goal is to have
zero typographical
errors when the GDP
software first scores
the document.

PERFORMING SUCCESSFULLY
Ginger Nichols

¶ We have been involved in giving performances since our very early years, when we played a part in a class play or participated in competitive sports events at our school. The most terrifying part of each performance was probably the fear that we would "freeze" when it came our turn to perform. Whenever we find ourselves in this predicament, the best thing to do is to accept that fear and to learn to let it work for us, not against us. We need to recognize that nervousness or fear may set in during our performance. Then, when it does happen (if it does), we will be ready to cope with it and overcome it.

¶ If you forget some of your lines in a recitation, try to remember other lines and recite them. Doing so may help those forgotten lines to "pop back" into your memory so that you put them in at a later time, if possible.

¶ You always want to leave your audience with the idea that you have given them something worthwhile that they can use or apply to their own lives. For maximum impact on your audience and to make sure that they remember what you say, use audiovisual aids to reinforce your message. Remember, however, that audiovisual aids are nothing more than aids. The real message should come in the words you choose when giving your presentation.

¶ Study your speech well; even rehearse it if necessary. However, do not practice it to the extent that it appears that you are merely reading what is written down on the paper in front of you. Much of your personality should be exhibited while you are giving your speech. If you are an enthusiastic, friendly person who converses well with people face-to-face, then that same persona should be evident during your speech. A good piece of advice is to just go out there and be yourself—you will be much more comfortable by doing so, and your audience will relate to you better than if you try to exhibit a different personality when at the podium.

¶ No matter how rapidly you speak in general, slow down when you are in front of a group. The fact that you are nervous can cause your speech rate to increase. The best way to slow down your speaking is to breathe deeply. Doing so also causes your nervous system to relax, allowing you to proceed with your speech calmly.

¶ Finally, possibly the best advice for giving a successful speech is to be prepared. You will be more confident if you are thoroughly prepared. Do your research, rehearse your speech, and make notes about where you want to give emphasis or use an audiovisual aid.

Unit 15

Correspondence

March 1, 20--

Mr. Rodney Graae
Thompson Corporation
42 Harris Court
Trenton, NJ 08648

We are indeed interested in designing a new corporate logo and the corresponding stationery for your fine corporation. As I indicated in our recent telephone conversation, we have a design staff that has won many national awards for letterhead form design, and we consider it an honor to be contacted by you.

Within a month, we will submit several basic designs to you and your board of directors. At that time, please feel free to make any comments and suggestions that will help us finalize a design. Here is a modified price list for the printed stationery:

	Cost
00 sheets)	$ 80.00
s (1,000 cards)	39.50
ures (1,000 sheets)	219.30
	92.00

...can be of further service.

November 8, 20--

CONFIDENTIAL

Mrs. Katie Hollister
11426 Prairie View Road
Kearney, NE 68847

Dear Mrs. Hollister:

Subject: Site for New Elementary School

As you are aware, your 160-acre farm, located in th...
Tyro township, is a part of Independent School Dis...
schools occupies 2 acres and is adjoined by an 8-ac...
planning stages for a fourth elementary school. As...
District 17 Board has directed me to initiate discuss...
acres of land.

Please call me at your convenience to arrange a me...
and me. I look forward to our discussions.

Yours truly,

Irvin J. Hagg
Superintendent

lcv
c: District 17 Board

MEMO TO: All Employees

FROM: Adrienne Barzanov

DATE: March 2, 20--

SUBJECT: New Building Site

We have consulted with several architects and have finalized plans to build a new administrative center at 6400 Easton Plaza. This memo provides general information about plans for the center's exterior and interior development.

EXTERIOR PLANS

Exterior plans will maintain the historical integrity and beauty of the surrounding area and reflect the architecture of other buildings in the office park. Landscaping plans include a parklike area, a picnic area, and a small pond.

INTERIOR PLANS FOR STAFF

Staff will be located within the new facility as follows:

1. Accounting will be located on the first floor in the west wing.

2. Sales and marketing will be located on the first floor in the east wing. All staff will be grouped according to product line.

3. All other staff will be located on the second floor. Exact locations will be determined at a later date.

INTERIOR PLANS FOR SPECIAL FACILITIES

Conference rooms will be located in the center of the building on the first floor to provide easy access for everyone. All rooms will be equipped with state-of-the-art technology.

Our new center will also include a full-service cafeteria, a copy center, a library, an athletic center, and an on-site day care center.

Construction of the new center will begin when we obtain the necessary permits.

mwr

Multipage Letters

Goals

- Improve speed and accuracy
- Refine language arts skills in the use of commas
- Format multipage letters

A. Type 2 times.

A. WARMUP

```
1       We were quite dazzled when the plumber drove up in a      11
2   C-150 pickup truck! She was joined by 26 young people (all    23
3   students) who gazed intently as she welded six of the rods.   35
    |  1  |  2  |  3  |  4  |  5  |  6  |  7  |  8  |  9  |  10  |  11  |  12
```

SKILLBUILDING

B. Take three 12-second timed writings on each line. The scale below the last line shows your wpm speed for a 12-second timed writing.

B. 12-SECOND SPEED SPRINTS

```
4   Pam knew that five girls in the other car were on the team.
5   The women drove eight blue autos when they made some trips.
6   All the girls in four other autos may go on the same trips.
7   Spring is the time of the year when they have a lot of pep.
      5     10     15     20     25     30     35     40     45     50     55     60
```

C. DIAGNOSTIC PRACTICE: SYMBOLS AND PUNCTUATION

If you are not using the GDP software, turn to page SB-2 and follow the directions for this activity.

LANGUAGE ARTS

D. Study the rules at the right.

D. COMMAS

Note: The callout signals in the left margin indicate which language arts rule from this lesson has been applied.

RULE ▶

,nonessential expression

The underline calls attention to a point in the sentence where a comma might mistakenly be inserted.

Use a comma before and after a nonessential expression.

Andre, who was there, can verify the statement.

But: Anyone_ who was there_ can verify the statement.

Van's first book, *Crisis of Management*, was not discussed.

Van's book_ *Crisis of Management*_ was not discussed.

Note: A nonessential expression is a group of words that may be omitted without changing the basic meaning of the sentence. Always examine the noun or pronoun that comes before the expression to determine whether the noun needs the expression to complete its meaning. If it does, the expression is *essential* and does *not* take a comma.

Use a comma between two adjacent adjectives that modify the same noun.

We need an intelligent, enthusiastic individual for this job.

But: Please order a new bulletin board for our main conference room.

Note: Do not use a comma after the second adjective. Also, do not use a comma if the first adjective modifies the combined idea of the second adjective and the noun (for example, *bulletin board* and *conference room* in the second example).

Edit the sentences by inserting any needed punctuation.

8 The school president Mr. Roberts will address the students.
9 The fall planning meeting which is held in Charlotte has been canceled.
10 Students planning to take the certification test must register for the orientation class.
11 The sleek luxury car is scheduled for delivery next week.
12 Margaret brought her fast reliable laptop to the meeting.
13 A stamped addressed envelope should be included with the survey.

FORMATTING

E. MULTIPAGE LETTERS

To format a multipage letter:

1. Type the first page on letterhead stationery, and type continuation pages on plain paper that matches the letterhead.
2. Insert a page number at the top right of the second and succeeding pages.

> 2
>
> A copy of the formal complaint is enclosed for your review. I shall call you in about a week to arrange a time and place for our meeting.
>
> I have never been involved with anything like this before. Any help that you give me will be appreciated.
>
> Sincerely,
>
> Ms. Jeanne M. Hoover
> Attorney-at-Law
>
> rmv
> Enclosure

DOCUMENT PROCESSING

Correspondence 71-64 ▶

Business Letter in Modified-Block Style

Refer to   Reference Manual

Review: R-5A and R-5B: Multipage Business Letter

October 16, 20-- | Miss Florence B. Glashan | Attorney-at-Law | 2406 Shadows Glade | Dayton, OH 45426-0348 | Dear Miss Glashan: |
¶ It was good to meet you at the convention for trial attorneys in Detroit last week. In addition to the interesting program highlights of the regular sessions, I find that the informal discussions with people like you are an added plus at these meetings. Your contribution to the program was very beneficial to me.
¶ You may recall that I told you I had just been appointed by the court to defend a woman here in Dayton who has been charged with embezzling large sums of money from her previous employer. The defendant had been employed at a large department store for more than 25 years. Because of her valuable years of experience in accounting with the store, she was in charge of accounts receivable at the store. Her previous employer, the plaintiff in the case, claims that she embezzled $18,634 in 2000, $39,072 in 2001, and $27,045 in 2002.

(Continued on next page)

¶ I feel that it is my responsibility to represent my client and to provide the best defense possible. I recall that you mentioned that you had represented defendants in similar cases in previous years. As I prepare for this defense, perhaps you might help me in the following ways:

1. Please send me the appropriate citations for all similar trials in which you participated.
2. Also, please provide me with any other case citations that you think might be helpful to me in this case.
3. Arrange to meet with me soon so that I can benefit from your experience as I prepare for the trial.

¶ A copy of the formal complaint is enclosed for your review. I shall call you in about a week to arrange a time and place for our meeting. Please let me know if there is additional information that would be helpful in preparing for this case.

¶ I have never been involved with anything like this before. Any help that you give me will be appreciated. I shall look forward to working with you.

Sincerely, | Ms. Jeanne M. Hoover | Attorney-at-Law | urs | Enclosure

Correspondence 71-65

Business Letter in Block Style

April 3, 20-- | Mr. Michael McGinty | District Manager | Starr & Morgan Company | One DuPont circle | Washington, DC 20036-2133 |

Dear Mike:

¶ It was good to see you at our sales conference in Reston, Virginia, last week. Your winning the "golden apple" award for the most sales for the year was well deserved. When you first became part of our sales team, you showed great enthusiasm for your job immediately. There is no doubt in my mind that Starr & Morgan Company is very well represented in the Washington area. We particularly want to commend you for obtaining the Westminster Account. Acquiring this account has been a major objective for a number of years. None of our other company's sales representatives have been able to accomplish this feat. Just the idea of a new account of over $500,000 is quite mind-boggling. How did you do it? Did you:

1. spend considerable time with the President, Mr. Arch Davis, or the Director of Purchasing, Ms. Betsy Matin?
2. Conduct a series of hands-on workshops for the employees and managers?
3. Develop a special marketing campaign for Westminster and customize it for Westminster?
4. Combine various strategies in your efforts to obtain this important account?

(Continued on next page)

¶ ~~Can you~~ Please let me know what approaches ~~were~~ you used to make this sale?

Successes of this nature do not happen without a lot of hard work. You are

to be commended for putting forth your best efforts to sign the account.

¶ If ~~it~~ we can ~~be arranged,~~ a ~~presentation by you~~ like to have you make a presentation to our ~~next~~ time sales ~~conference~~ annual meeting, we

would ~~seem very appropriate. The other~~ They sales representatives would benefit

~~much~~ greatly having you share from your success story. Our ~~next~~ annual meeting will be held in late September in

Richmond, Virginia. Again, co**n**gratulations on ~~your receipt of~~ receiving this prestigious award.

All of us here in the home office are | pleased / greatly | with the performance

of our entire sales team. Indications are that this will be a year when our sales records

~~are~~ will be broken and we will again be in the media spotlight.

Sincerely yours, | Robert D. Miley (Pres) | urs | c: R. Olson, Director of

Sales

Correspondence 71-66

Business Letter in Modified-Block Style

Open the file for Correspondence 71-64 and make the following changes:

1. Change the addressee to Ms. Cynthia Barnes, Attorney-at-Law.
2. Change the office address to:
   4066 Quarry Estates
   Dayton, OH 45429-1362.
3. Change the salutation and header as needed.
4. Add this sentence at the end of the second paragraph:
   The defendant is also being accused of embezzling $35,680 in 2003.

Special Letter Features

Goals
- Type at least 42wpm/5'/5e
- Format special letter features

A. Type 2 times.

A. WARMUP

```
1        Six citizens from 14th Avenue East joined 83 other      10
2   residents to discuss the #794 proposal* for a new swimming   22
3   pool. Barry Kelm quoted numbers about current pool usage.     34
    | 1 | 2 | 3 | 4 | 5 | 6 | 7 | 8 | 9 | 10 | 11 | 12
```

SKILLBUILDING

B. MAP

Follow the GDP software directions for this exercise in improving keystroking accuracy.

Strategies for Career Success

Audience Analysis

Knowing your audience is fundamental to the success of any message. Ask the following questions to help identify your audience.

What is your relationship to your audience? Are they familiar—people with whom you work or people unknown to you? The latter will prompt you to conduct some research to better communicate your purpose. What is the attitude of your audience? Are they hostile or receptive to your message? How will your message benefit them? What is your anticipated response? Asking these questions first can help prevent message mishap later.

When writing to a diverse audience, direct your message to the primary audience. These key decision makers will make a decision or act on the basis of your message. Determine the level of detail, organization, formality, and use of technical terms and theory.

YOUR TURN Compose a thank-you e-mail to a friend. How would it differ from an interview thank-you letter?

C. Take two 5-minute timed writings. Review your speed and errors.

Goal: At least 42wpm/5'/5e

C. 5-MINUTE TIMED WRITING

```
 4      Whether you are searching for your first job or are      11
 5  looking to change jobs, your networking skills may play a    22
 6  crucial role in how successful you are in that endeavor.     34
 7  Networking can be defined in some respects as a group of     45
 8  people who are linked closely together for the purpose of    56
 9  achieving some sort of end result. In this case, the end     68
10  result will be to establish new contacts who might be able   80
11  to assist you in your job search.                            86
12      Your network is made up of dozens of people you have     97
13  met. You can never be sure who has the potential of helping 109
14  you the most in your job search. Therefore, it is important 121
15  that you consider all acquaintances. You should certainly   133
16  network with business associates, and especially those you  145
17  have met at various meetings and conferences. And don't     156
18  forget former teachers in whose classes you were enrolled.  168
19  Former classmates provide an excellent base on which to     179
20  build your network, and friends and family should also be   190
21  included. Finally, use the Internet to nurture any online   202
22  contacts you have made over the years.                      210
    | 1  | 2  | 3  | 4  | 5  | 6  | 7  | 8  | 9  | 10 | 11 | 12
```

D. MULTIPLE ADDRESSES

Often a letter may be sent to two or more people at the same address or to different addresses:

1. If a letter is addressed to two people at the same address, type each name on a separate line above the same inside address.
2. If a letter is addressed to two people at different addresses, type each name and address, one under the other. Press ENTER 2 times between the addresses.
3. If a letter is addressed to three or more people, type the names and addresses side by side, with one at the left margin and another beginning at the center-point. Insert 1 blank line before typing the third name and address at the left margin.

November 19, 20-- ↓4X

Dr. Albert Russell, Professor
Department of English
Appalachian State University
Boone, NC 28608 ↓2X

Dr. Kay Smith, Professor
Director of Business
Grove City College
Grove City, PA 16127 ↓2X

Dear Dr. Russell and Dr. Smith:

E. ON-ARRIVAL NOTATIONS

On-arrival notations (such as *CONFIDENTIAL*) should be typed on the second line below the date, at the left margin. Type the notation in all-caps. Press ENTER 2 times to begin the inside address.

November 19, 20-- ↓2X

CONFIDENTIAL ↓2X

Mr. and Mrs. Earl Walters
3408 Washington Boulevard
New Tripoli, PA 18066 ↓2X

Dear Mr. and Mrs. Walters:

F. SUBJECT LINES

A *subject line* indicates what a letter is about. Type the subject line below the salutation at the left margin, preceded and followed by 1 blank line. (The term *Re* or *In re* may be used in place of *Subject*.)

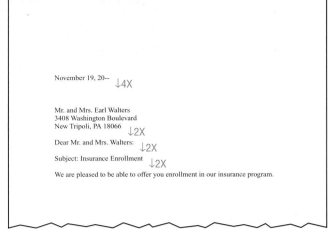

November 19, 20-- ↓4X

Mr. and Mrs. Earl Walters
3408 Washington Boulevard
New Tripoli, PA 18066 ↓2X

Dear Mr. and Mrs. Walters: ↓2X

Subject: Insurance Enrollment ↓2X

We are pleased to be able to offer you enrollment in our insurance program.

Word Processing Manual

G. WORD PROCESSING: SORT

Study Lesson 72 in your word processing manual. Complete all of the shaded steps while at your computer. Then format the jobs that follow.

DOCUMENT PROCESSING

Correspondence 72-67

Business Letter in Block Style

November 8, 20--

CONFIDENTIAL

Mrs. Katie Hollister

11426 Prairie View Rd.

Kearney, NE 68847

Dear Mrs. Hollister:

Subject: Site For New Elementary School

¶ As you are aware, your 160 acre farm, located in the northeast quarter northeast of Section 26 in Tyro township, is a part of independent School District 17. Each of our three elementary schools occupies two 2 acres and is adjoined by an 8-acre park. We are now in the early planning stages for a third fourth elementary school. As your large farm is centrally located, the District 17 Board has directed me to initiate discussions with you for the purchase of 8 10 acres of land.

(Continued on next page)

¶ I look forward to our discussions. Please call me at your convenience to arrange a meeting with you and/or your attorney and me.

Yours truly,

Irvin J. Hagg

Superintendent

urs

c: District 17 Board

Correspondence 72-68

Business Letter in Block Style

Sort each bulleted list in the letter in ascending order.

October 4, 20-- | Ms. Deborah Campbell Wallace | 7835 Virginia Avenue Northwest | Washington, DC 20037 | Mr. Thomas E. Campbell | 3725 Stevens Road Southeast | Washington, DC 20020 | Dear Ms. Wallace and Mr. Campbell:

¶ We received your letter requesting instructions for transferring stock. The most common stock transfer situations are provided below. Determine which type of transfer you require and select the instructions that apply to your stock transfer.

- Name change
- Transferring shares to another individual(s)
- Transfers involving a deceased shareholder (individual ownership)
- Transfers involving a deceased shareholder (multiple owners)
- Transfers involving a minor
- Transfers involving a power of attorney
- Transfers involving a trust

¶ Every transfer requires a letter of instruction specifying how you want your shares transferred. The following items are required for all types of transfers:

- Name and address of new owner(s)
- Social security number or tax payer identification number
- Preferred form of ownership (that is, joint tenants or tenants in common)
- Indicate total shares that are being transferred
- Sign and date the form

¶ Please be sure to submit all required documentation and note that all documents submitted become part of the permanent record of transfer and will not be returned.

(Continued on next page)

¶ All transfers must have your signature(s) guaranteed by a financial institution participating in the Medallion Signature Guarantee Program.

¶ If you need additional information, you may visit our Web site for step-by-step instructions or you may call one of our customer service representatives at our toll-free number.

Sincerely, | William J. Shawley | Shareholder Services | urs

Correspondence ▶
72-69

Personal-Business
Letter in Block Style

(!) Format book titles
in italic instead of
underlining.

November 17, 20--

Dr. Arif Gureshi
8726 East Ridge Drive
Morehead, KY 40351-7268
Dear Dr. Gureshi:
Subject: The Middle East in the Year 2005
Discussion
¶ Your new book, The Middle East in the Year 2005, has gotten excellent reviews. The citizens of Morehead are pleased that a respected member of one of our local colleges is receiving national attention.
¶ Our book discussion group in Morehead, composed of members of the AAUW (American Association of University Women), has selected your book for discussion at our May meeting. We would very much like you to be a participant; your attendance at the meeting would be a real highlight.
¶ I shall call you next week. Our members are hoping that you will be able to attend and that an acceptable date can be arranged.
Sincerely,

Theresa A. Gorski
2901 Garfield Court
Morehead, KY 40351-2687

More Special Letter Features

Goals

- Improve speed and accuracy
- Refine language arts skills in composing paragraphs
- Format letters with special features

A. Type 2 times.

A. WARMUP

```
1      The 83 Lions Club members raised $6,690 (95% of the    11
2  requested sum) to resurface the tennis courts. Gayle was   22
3  amazed when sixteen jolly members picked up over 10% more. 34
   |  1  |  2  |  3  |  4  |  5  |  6  |  7  |  8  |  9  |  10  |  11  |  12
```

SKILLBUILDING

B. PACED PRACTICE

If you are not using the GDP software, turn to page SB-14 and follow the directions for this activity.

PPP PRETEST → PRACTICE → POSTTEST

PRETEST
Take a 1-minute timed writing. Review your speed and errors.

C. PRETEST: Vertical Reaches

```
4      The scents in the trunk scared the rest of the drama   11
5  class. One judge drank juice and ate pecans as the cranky  23
6  coach scolded the best junior and bought the pink dresses. 35
   |  1  |  2  |  3  |  4  |  5  |  6  |  7  |  8  |  9  |  10  |  11  |  12
```

PRACTICE
Speed Emphasis:
If you made no more than 1 error on the Pretest, type each *individual* line 2 times.
Accuracy Emphasis:
If you made 2 or more errors, type each *group* of lines (as though it were a paragraph) 2 times.

D. PRACTICE: Up Reaches

```
7  dr draft drank dryer drain drama dread dream drag drew drug
8  ju judge juice jumpy junks juror julep jumbo judo jump just
9  es essay nests tests less dress acres makes uses best rest
```

E. PRACTICE: Down Reaches

```
10  ca cable caddy cargo scare decay yucca pecan cage calm case
11  nk ankle blank crank blink think trunk brink bank junk sink
12  sc scale scalp scene scent scold scoop scope scan scar disc
```

POSTTEST
Repeat the Pretest timed writing and compare performance.

F. POSTTEST: Vertical Reaches

G. COMPOSING: PARAGRAPH

Compose a paragraph expressing your opinion on whether or not it is safe to make purchases online. Include precautions and potential dangers.

FORMATTING

H. TABLES WITHIN DOCUMENTS

To format a table that is part of a letter, memo, or report:

1. In a single-spaced document, press ENTER 2 times before and 1 time after the table. Be sure you are outside the table structure before pressing ENTER 1 time.
2. In a double-spaced document, press ENTER 1 time before and after the table.
3. Single-space the body of the table.
4. Adjust the column widths, and center the table within the margins of the document.
5. Never split a table between two pages if it will fit on one page. If a table will not fit at the bottom of the page on which it is first mentioned, place it at the top of the next page.

MEMO TO: Leo Guthrie

FROM: Paul Forester

DATE: January 10, 20--

SUBJECT: Sales Comparison

Listed below are the sales totals for the last two quarters. Please review the information before our staff meeting on Friday. ↓2X

SALES SUMMARY December 31, 20-- ↓1X		
↓1X Region	Third Quarter	Fourth Quarter
Northeast	456,321	512,980
Southeast	335,765	375,112
Northwest	425,666	457,034
Southwest	388,546	410,478

↓1X

Come to the meeting prepared to discuss plans for the upcoming sales promotions that will take place in our district.

I. COMPANY NAME IN CLOSING LINES

Some business firms show the company name in the closing lines of a letter. Type the company name in all-caps on the second line below the complimentary closing. Then press ENTER 4 times and type the writer's name.

Thank you for inviting me to participate in the discussion concerning this issue. ↓2X

Sincerely yours, ↓2X

HENDERSON AND SONS, INC. ↓4X

Mark Henderson, President ↓2X

mjd

J. BLIND COPY NOTATION

A *blind copy (bc:) notation* is used when the addressee is not intended to know that one or more other persons are being sent a copy of the letter. Type the *bc* notation on the file copy at the left margin on the second line after the last item in the letter.

When preparing a letter with a blind copy, print one copy of the letter; then add the blind copy notation and print another.

Thank you for inviting me to participate in the discussion concerning this issue.

Sincerely yours, ↓4X

Mark Henderson
President ↓2X

man ↓2X
bc: Mary Stevenson

K. DELIVERY NOTATION

Type a delivery notation (such as *By fax*) on the line below the enclosure notation (if used) or on the line below the reference initials. A delivery notation comes before a copy notation.

Sincerely yours, ↓4X

Mark Henderson
President ↓2X

opc
Enclosure
By fax
c: Mary Stevenson

L. POSTSCRIPT

If a postscript *(PS)* is added to a letter, it is typed as the last item in the letter, preceded by 1 blank line. If a blind copy notation and postscript are used, the bc: notation follows the postscript.

lte
Enclosure ↓2X

PS: You will be reimbursed for all expenses. Complete an expense report and submit it to your supervisor. ↓2X

bc: Mary Stevenson

Word
Processing
Manual

M. WORD PROCESSING: SHADING

Study Lesson 73 in your word processing manual. Complete all of the shaded steps while at your computer. Then format the jobs that follow.

Correspondence 73-70 ▶

Business Letter in Block Style

March 1, 20-- | Ms. Maureen Testa | Austin Communications | 37 Pittsburgh Road | Franklin, PA 16323 | Dear Ms. Testa:

¶ We are indeed interested in designing a new corporate logo and the corresponding stationery for your fine company. As I indicated in our recent telephone conversation, we have a design staff that has won many national awards for letterhead form design, and we consider it an honor to be contacted by you.

¶ Within a couple of weeks, we will submit to you and your committee several basic designs. Based on your evaluation and suggestions, we can go from there. Here is a modified price list for the printed stationery:

Automatically adjust the column widths and center the table horizontally.

Stationery	Cost
Letterhead (500 sheets)	$ 80.00
Business cards (1,000 cards)	39.50
Coated brochures (1,000 sheets)	219.30
Envelopes	92.00

¶ In the meantime, please call me if we can be of further service. Sincerely yours, | Samantha A. Steele | General Manager | urs | By fax | bc: Design Department

Correspondence 73-71 ▶

Business Letter in Block Style

Open the file for Correspondence 73-70 from Ms. Steele and make the following changes:

1. Send the letter to Mr. Rodney Graae | Thompson Corporation | 42 Harris Court | Trenton, NJ 08648
2. Change the word "company" in the first paragraph to corporation.
3. Revise the first two sentences of the second paragraph to say:

Within a month, we will submit several basic designs to you and your board of directors. At that time, please feel free to make any comments and suggestions that will help us finalize a design.

4. Change the table to a boxed table.
5. Apply 15 percent shading to the first row of the table.

Correspondence 73-72 ▶

Business Letter in Modified-Block Style

November 5, 20-- | Master Gyms, Inc. | 4201 Castine Court | Raleigh, NC 27613-5981 | Ladies and Gentlemen:

¶We have 494 apartments at Fountain Ridge. As the recreation coordinator, I have concerns not only about the leisure-time activities of our residents but also about the health and physical fitness of the more than 1,100 people who call Fountain Ridge home.

(Continued on next page)

¶ Our recreation facilities are excellent. In addition to our two outdoor tennis courts and swimming pool, we have the following indoor facilities: two racquetball courts, swimming pool, whirlpool bath, sauna, steam room, and two billiard tables. However, we have no workout equipment.

¶ During the next few months we will be equipping a new gymnasium. The dimensions of the gym are shown on the enclosed sketch. There will be exercise bicycles, treadmills, and rowing machines. In addition, we would like to install a muscle-toning machine that includes features such as the following: leg press, chest press, shoulder press, arm pull, leg pull, arm lift, leg lift, and sit-up board.

¶ The needs and interests of our residents are varied. Some residents will take full advantage of the equipment we have suggested for the gymnasium. However, many of our residents have expressed interests in an indoor track for walking; others would like to add a track for running. We hope to accommodate as many of the suggestions as we feel are feasible.

¶ The population of the residents in the Fountain Ridge complex consists of a mixture of young and middle-age adult couples as well as single residents. Some of the couples have children who would be old enough to enjoy the facilities. Therefore, safety and durability of the equipment are very important considerations. In addition, we would like to continue to develop our complex in a way that would invite family participation in our recreational activities.

¶ Do you have a sales representative serving this area who could meet with me within a week or ten days? As an alternative, perhaps you have some brochures, including prices, that could be sent to me.

Sincerely yours, | FOUNTAIN RIDGE | Rosa Bailey-Judd | Recreation Coordinator | urs | Enclosure | By fax | PS: Please send a current catalog and price list immediately so that we can prepare for our meeting with the sales representative.

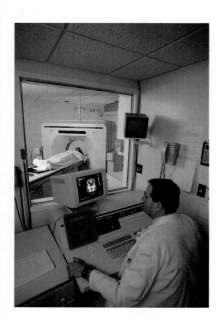

Multipage Memos With Tables

Goals

- Type at least 42wpm/5'/5e
- Format multipage memos with tables

A. Type 2 times.

A. WARMUP

```
1        Over 270 cars were backed up near the Baxter & Meintz   11
2   building after an 18-wheeler jackknifed at an icy junction.  23
3   About 1/3 to 1/2 of the cars were required to use a detour.  35
    |  1  |  2  |  3  |  4  |  5  |  6  |  7  |  8  |  9  |  10  |  11  |  12
```

SKILLBUILDING

B. PROGRESSIVE PRACTICE: ALPHABET

If you are not using the GDP software, turn to page SB-7 and follow the directions for this activity.

C. PROGRESSIVE PRACTICE: NUMBERS

If you are not using the GDP software, turn to page SB-11 and follow the directions for this activity.

Keyboarding Connection

Virus and Spam Prevention

Use caution when opening e-mail attachments or downloading files from the Internet. Download files only from reliable Web sites. Do not open files attached to an e-mail from an unknown source. Also question files attached to a known source. Some viruses replicate themselves and are sent through e-mail without users' knowledge.

Delete any e-mail with an odd subject, a chain e-mail, or electronic junk mail, commonly known as spam. If you're given the opportunity to unsubscribe from a spammer's list, think twice. Your reply will stop the messages on a reputable mailing list but may incite disreputable list marketers.

To protect against lost data, back up your files on a regular basis. Then you will be prepared if a virus infects your computer. New viruses are discovered daily, so update your antivirus software regularly.

YOUR TURN How do you handle junk mail via post? Do you notice similarities when dealing with spam?

D. Take two 5-minute timed writings. Review your speed and errors.

Goal: At least 42wpm/5'/5e

D. 5-MINUTE TIMED WRITING

4	Have you ever given any thought to starting your own	11
5	business? Obviously, there is some risk in starting out in	23
6	a venture such as this. However, if you realize there are	34
7	some issues to starting up a business, it may not seem to	46
8	be such a daunting undertaking. Let's quickly look at just	58
9	some of the issues that are involved in this task.	64
10	First of all, you need to think about whether you want	75
11	to do so badly enough to work long hours without knowing if	87
12	you will make any money at the end of the month. It would	99
13	be advantageous if you had worked previously for another	110
14	company as a manager or have managerial experience.	121
15	You have to have some sense for just how much money	131
16	you will need to start your business. It will take some	143
17	working capital to get you started. If you have put money	154
18	aside to invest in the company, there is a good possibility	166
19	you will succeed. If you don't have enough put aside, can	178
20	you get credit from a lending institution to assist you	189
21	through the first few months of operation? And, of course,	201
22	you'll also need to get credit from suppliers.	210

| 1 | 2 | 3 | 4 | 5 | 6 | 7 | 8 | 9 | 10 | 11 | 12

FORMATTING

Word Processing Manual

E. WORD PROCESSING: FIND AND REPLACE

Study Lesson 74 in your word processing manual. Complete all of the shaded steps while at your computer. Then format the jobs that follow.

DOCUMENT PROCESSING

Correspondence 74-73

Memo

MEMO TO: L. B. Chinn, Station Manager | **FROM**: Mitzi Grenell, News Director | **DATE**: May 5, 20-- | **SUBJECT**: FCC European Trip

¶ As you requested, this memo is being sent to you as one in a series to keep you informed about my upcoming trip to Europe. I have been invited by the Federal Communications Commission to participate in a study of television news in European countries. The invitation came from Jill Andrews, FCC vice-chair; and I am, of course, delighted to take part in this challenging project.

(Continued on next page)

¶ One function of this study will be to compare the news in countries that have a long history of free-access broadcasting with the programming in newly democratic countries. I have been assigned to lead a study group to six European countries to gather firsthand information on this topic. We will be visiting England, France, Germany, Poland, Romania, and Latvia from August 24 through September 3. In addition to me, our group will consist of the following members:

Arkady Gromov	Executive Editor *Miami Herald*	Miami, Florida
Manuel Cruz	News Director National Public Radio	Boise, Idaho
Katherine Grant	Station Manager WLBZ-TV	Bangor, Maine
Richard Logan	Operations Manager Cable News System	Provo, Utah

¶ Our initial plans are to spend at least one full day in each of the countries, meeting with the news staff of one or two of the major networks, touring their facilities, viewing recent broadcasts, and becoming familiar with their general operations.

¶ If you need to contact me during my absence, Barbara Brooks, our liaison at the Federal Communications Commission (1919 M Street, NW, Washington, DC 20554; phone: 202-555-3894), will be able to provide a location and phone number.

¶ Arrangements will be made with several different staff members in the News Department to handle my responsibilities here at Channel 5 while I am gone. Dave Gislason will be the contact person for the department. As you can imagine, this is an exciting time for me. Thank you for supporting the project.

| urs | PS: Thanks also for suggesting that this trip be combined with a vacation. My husband and I have discussed the possibility of his joining me for a two-week tour of the Scandinavian countries after the FCC trip has been completed. I shall let you know what our plans are by the end of May.

Correspondence 74-74 ▶

Memo

Open the file for Correspondence 74-73 and make the following changes:

1. Jill Andrews has just been promoted to FCC chair.
2. Finland has been added as a seventh country.
3. The trip has been extended through September 5.
4. Each occurrence of the word "news" (lowercase) has to be changed to news programming. (Do not replace News.)
5. Reggie Jordan, Staff Assistant, FCC, Washington, DC, will replace Manuel Cruz on the trip.
6. Gil Friesen will replace Dave Gislason as contact person.

MEMO TO: Terri Hackworth, Manager

FROM: Rosa Bailey Judd, Recreation Coordinator

DATE: April 14, 20--

SUBJECT: Fitness room

The new Fitness Room will be ready for use in about 1 month. Your leadership in bringing this about is sincerely appreciated. After ~~much~~ extensive investigation (much reading and several interviews), I likely will be requesting approval soon to purchase the following equipment:

No.	Type
4	exercise bicycles
2 1	treadmills
1	muscle-toning machine

Three other types of equipment were considered seriously, but those listed above enable users to reach objectives with out excessive cost. I am not quite ready to recommend the specific brands or the suppliers for these machines. As we expect that there will be very heavy usage, we are concerned with durability, warranties, and the availability of dependable service personnel. Thanks again for your full support and cooperation with this project.

urs

Memo Reports

Goals

- Improve speed and accuracy
- Format memo reports

A. Type 2 times.

A. WARMUP

```
1        The sizable judge asked three questions: "What's the      11
2   best time of the day for you to be in court? Can you leave     23
3   your job at exactly 4 p.m.? If not, 5 p.m. or 7 p.m.?"         34
    |  1  |  2  |  3  |  4  |  5  |  6  |  7  |  8  |  9  |  10  |  11  |  12
```

SKILLBUILDING

B. Take a 1-minute timed writing on the first paragraph to establish your base speed. Then take four 1-minute timed writings on the remaining paragraphs. As soon as you equal or exceed your base speed on one paragraph, advance to the next, more difficult paragraph.

B. SUSTAINED PRACTICE: SYLLABIC INTENSITY

```
4        Each of us has several bills to be paid on a monthly      11
5   basis. For most of us, a checkbook is the tool that we use     23
6   to take care of this chore. However, in this electronic        34
7   age, other ways of doing this have received rave reviews.      45

8        You will likely be surprised to learn that the most       11
9   basic way and the cheapest way to pay bills electronically     23
10  involves the use of a Touch-Tone phone. The time required      35
11  is approximately a third of that used when writing checks.     47

12       Several banking institutions offer or plan to offer       11
13  screen phones as a method for paying bills. It is possible     22
14  to buy securities, make transfers, and determine account       34
15  balances. You will save time by using a Touch-Tone phone.      45

16       A third type of electronic bill processing involves       10
17  using a microcomputer and a modem. Software programs have      21
18  on-screen checkbooks linked to bill-paying applications.       34
19  Other microcomputers use online services through a modem.      46
    |  1  |  2  |  3  |  4  |  5  |  6  |  7  |  8  |  9  |  10  |  11  |  12
```

C. TECHNIQUE PRACTICE: SPACE BAR

```
20       We will all go to the race if I win my event today.
21  Do you think that I will be able to finish the race at the
22  front of the pack, or do you think there are lots of very
23  fast runners out there who surely can finish ahead of me?
```

D. Edit this paragraph to correct any typing or formatting errors.

D. PROOFREADING: EDITING

```
24      Many home computer user like the challenge of haveing
25   the latest in both hardware and software technology. Their
26   are those however, who's needs likely can be satisfied at
27   a very low costs. A used 486-chip personnel computer with
28   color monitor and keyboard might be your's for under $ 300.
29   Check out th Yellow Page, or visit a used-computer store.
```

FORMATTING

E. REPORT HEADINGS IN MEMOS

There are times when a memo report is used rather than a cover memo to accompany a report. The memo and the report are combined into one, and headings are formatted as they are in a report.

DOCUMENT PROCESSING

Report 75-55

Memo Report

Refer to | **Reference Manual**

Review:
R-9C: Memo Report

MEMO TO: All Employees | **FROM:** Franklin Coates, Director | **DATE:** February 24, 20-- | **SUBJECT:** Security System

¶ Beginning March 1, we will install a new security access system. Complete installation should occur by the end of March. The system will include new magnetic card readers at all entrances. It will also provide a more secure working environment, especially in the evenings and on weekends. Entrances will lock and unlock automatically each day during working hours. Please carefully read and follow the detailed instructions for using the new system.

RECEIVING A NEW ACCESS CARD

¶ Once the new system is installed, you will need a new access identification card to enter the building during nonworking hours. Human Resources will begin taking pictures for new cards during the week of March 20. When you are called, report immediately. The cards will be issued as soon as they are ready. To receive your new card, you must turn in your old one.

(Continued on next page)

ENTERING THE BUILDING

¶ Entrances will automatically unlock each working day at 8 a.m and lock at 5 p.m. To enter the building during nonworking hours, slide your access identification card (with the magnetic strip facing left) through the card reader at the right of the entrance door. When the green light comes on, open the door. Do not hold the door open longer than 30 seconds.

¶ Once you enter the building during nonworking hours, please proceed immediately to the front desk and sign in. Record in the logbook your name, department, extension number, and arrival time.

LEAVING THE BUILDING

¶ Before leaving the building, you must sign out. Please record your departure time beside your name. Do not use the special latch handle to open the door, or the alarm will sound. Instead, use the push bar. Once you have opened the door, do not let it remain open longer than 30 seconds, or the alarm will sound. If you accidentally set off the alarm, return to the front desk and call the security company (the telephone number is at the top of the logbook). Be prepared to provide the security personnel with your name, extension number, and access card number.

¶ At times you may need to have the door held open for extended periods of time during nonbusiness hours. In these situations, please make arrangements with Building Maintenance by calling extension 4444.

¶ If you have questions about our new security access system and procedures, please contact me.

urs

Report 75-56

Memo Report

Mr. Coates has asked you to revise Report 75-55 as follows:

1. Use February 25 as the date.
2. Change "nonworking" to nonbusiness throughout the report.

3. Add the following sentence at the end of the second paragraph:
   New employees will be asked for a special form, to be provided by their supervisors.
4. Change "Building Maintenance" to Building Security in the next-to-last paragraph.

MEMO TO: All Employees
FROM: Adrienne Barzan
DATE: March 2, 20--
SUBJECT: New Building Site

¶ We have consulted with several architects and have finalized plans to build a new administrative center at 6400 Easton Plaza. This memo provides general information about plans for the center's exterior and interior development.

EXTERIOR PLANS

¶ Exterior plans will maintain the historical integrity and beauty of the surrounding area and reflect the architecture of other buildings in the office park. Landscaping plans include a parklike area, a picnic area, and a small pond.

INTERIOR PLANS FOR STAFF

¶ Staff will be located within the new facility as follows:

1. Accounting will be located on the first floor in the west wing.
2. Sales and marketing will be located on the first floor in the east wing. All staff will be grouped according to product line.
3. All other staff will be located on the second floor. Exact locations will be determined at a later date.

INTERIOR PLANS FOR SPECIAL FACILITIES

¶ Conference rooms will be located in the center of the building on the first floor to provide easy access for everyone. All rooms will be equipped with state-of-the-art technology.

¶ Our new center will also include a full-service cafeteria, a copy center, a library, an athletic center, and an on-site day care center.

¶ Construction of the new center will begin when we obtain the necessary permits.

Unit 16

Tables

LESSON 76
Tables With Footnotes or Source Notes

LESSON 77
Tables With Braced Column Headings

LESSON 78
Tables Formatted Sideways

LESSON 79
Multipage Tables

LESSON 80
Using Predesigned Table Formats

CITY BANK
Interest Rates Schedule
Effective Date: November 11, 2003

	Rate	APY*
Value Checking	0.00%	0.00%
City Checking	1.25%	1.27%
Prestige Checking	1.25%	1.27%
Golden Checking	1.50%	1.55%
Regular Savings	1.75%	1.90%
Young Savers	1.75%	1.90%
Christmas Club	1.75%	1.90%
Money Market—Tier I	2.25%	2.30%
Money Market—Tier II	2.50%	2.60%
Money Market—Tier III	2.75%	2.80%
Money Market—Tier IV	3.00%	3.10%
CD—6 month	2.25%	2.50%
CD—1 year	2.35%	2.65%
CD—2 year	2.45%	2.70%
CD—3 year	2.50%	2.75%

*APY=Annual Percentage Yield.

CITY BANK
Interest Rates Schedule
Effective Date: November 11, 2003

	Rate	APY
Value Checking	0.00%	0.00%
City Checking	1.25%	1.27%
Prestige Checking	1.25%	1.27%
Golden Checking	1.50%	1.55%
Regular Savings	1.75%	1.90%
Young Savers		
Christmas Club		
Money Market		
Money Market		
Money Market		
Money Market		
CD—6 month		
CD—1 year		
CD—2 year		
year		

CUSTOMER DATABASE INFORMATION
(Ohio District)
August 31, 2003

Customer	Address	City	ZIP	Telephone No.	Item	Stock No.
Westphal, Darlene	3309 Aaron Place Street	Kenton	44426	419-555-2384	Pentium Computer	4-138-CW
Roanne, Dennis	20604 Lucille Road South	Columbus	43230	614-555-2074	Laser Printer	3-895-LP
Byrnes, Carl	322 West Lyons Road	Mansfield	44902	216-555-2002	Laser Printer	3-895-LP
Dawson, Cynthia	5914 Bay Oaks Place	Chillicothe	45601	614-555-1399	Color Ink-Jet Printer	2-555-CIJ
Graupmann, Meg	10386 Power Drive	Steubenville	43952	614-555-7821	Pentium Computer	4-238-CW
Neusome, Jo	Box 365	Youngstown	44502	216-555-3885	Pentium Computer	4-238-CW
Shapiro, Tony	6823 Creekwood Drive	Columbus	43085	614-555-2934	Pentium Computer	4-238-CW
Garand, Lisa	26044 Manzano Court	Youngstown	44505	216-555-1777	Flatbed Color Scanner	6-882-CSC
Parker, Tom	936 Eastwind Drive	Cleveland	44121	216-555-2839	Laser Printer	3-895-LP

Tables With Footnotes or Source Notes

Goals

- Type at least 43wpm/5'/5e
- Change text direction
- Insert or delete rows or columns

A. Type 2 times.

A. WARMUP

```
1        Order #Z391 must be processed "quickly" and exactly      11
2   as specified! In January several orders were sent out by      22
3   mistake; regrettably, one order worth $5,680 was canceled.    34
    |  1  |  2  |  3  |  4  |  5  |  6  |  7  |  8  |  9  |  10  |  11  |  12
```

SKILLBUILDING

B. Take three 12-second timed writings on each line. The scale below the last line shows your wpm speed for a 12-second timed writing.

B. 12-SECOND SPEED SPRINTS

```
4   You paid for the ruby that she owned when he was just five.
5   Toby wishes to thank all eight of the girls for their time.
6   Yale is a very fine place to learn about the world of work.
7   She has a theory that the icy roads will cause a bad wreck.
    I I I I 5 I I I I 10 I I I I 15 I I I 20 I I I 25 I I I 30 I I I 35 I I I 40 I I I I 45 I I I I 50 I I I 55 I I I I 60
```

C. DIAGNOSTIC PRACTICE: SYMBOLS AND PUNCTUATION

If you are not using the GDP software, turn to page SB-2 and follow the directions for this activity.

Strategies for Career Success

Cell Phone Manners Matter

Mind your cell phone manners! Although the cell phone allows you to keep in touch with your boss, coworkers, and clients, it also requires you to consider your communication etiquette. One of the worst violations of etiquette and safety is driving and talking at the same time; and in some states such as New Jersey, cell phone use while driving is restricted to hands free devices. It is much safer to pull off the road to make a call.

Consider others when you use a cell phone in a public place (for example, a restaurant). If you use the phone in public, talk quietly and watch what you say. Cell phones in meetings can distract others; some companies prohibit them in business meetings.

When you call a cell phone user, keep your message brief.

YOUR TURN Observe cell phone users in a public place. Are they mindful of others when they use their phones?

D. Take two 5-minute timed writings. Review your speed and errors.

Goal: At least 43wpm/5'/5e

D. 5-MINUTE TIMED WRITING

```
 8        Starting up your own business may mean that you are    11
 9   thinking about acquiring an existing business. If so, is    22
10   that business doing well in the community? If you are going  34
11   to buy out an established business, you need to know the     45
12   reason the current owner wishes to sell the company. If      57
13   there are other businesses in the area, you should first     68
14   find out what reputation that business has built up in the   80
15   community. Do other businesses think highly of the company?  92
16        You must also consider what type of advertising you    103
17   plan to use to get your business off to a good start. You    114
18   might use ads in newspapers, on television, in magazines,    126
19   or on the Internet. When you start your ad campaign, you     137
20   should consider hiring an ad agency to put out the best      149
21   message for your company and its products. You should also   160
22   consider the types of ads being used by your competitors to  172
23   determine what has worked well for them.                     181
24        Yes, there are major issues that need to be addressed  192
25   when starting up your own business; and all of the issues    203
26   should be dealt with before you decide to take such a step.  215
     |  1  |  2  |  3  |  4  |  5  |  6  |  7  |  8  |  9  |  10  |  11  |  12
```

FORMATTING

E. TABLES WITH FOOTNOTES OR SOURCE NOTES

To format tables with footnotes or source notes:

1. When you insert a table, include an additional row at the bottom of the table for the footnote or source note.
2. Merge the cells in the bottom row.
3. In the bottom row, type the word Note: or Source: if there is a note or source for the table. Then type the information for the note or source.
4. If there is a footnote, type an asterisk (or another symbol) at the appropriate point within the table. Then type the information for the footnote.

F. WORD PROCESSING: TABLE—TEXT DIRECTION, AND TABLE—INSERT OR DELETE ROWS OR COLUMNS

Study Lesson 76 in your word processing manual. Complete all of the shaded steps while at your computer. Then format the jobs that follow.

DOCUMENT PROCESSING

Table 76-26 ▶

Boxed Table

Your completed table will look different from the one shown.

1. Insert a boxed table with 7 columns and 6 rows.
2. Select Row 1, and change the text direction to display vertically top to bottom.
3. Drag down on the bottom border of Row 1 until the column headings display in one continuous line without wrapping.
4. Type the information in the body of the table.

(Continued on next page)

5. Right-align the text in the number columns. **Note:** Do not change the left alignment of the column headings.
6. Merge the cells in the bottom row, and then type the table note.

7. Automatically adjust the column widths.
8. Center the table horizontally and vertically.

Always automatically adjust column widths and center tables horizontally and vertically.

Account Number	Blue Sierra Letterhead	Italian Renaissance Letterhead	Sonoma Desert Letterhead	Watercolor Wash Letterhead	Sandstone Marble Letterhead	Greek Acropolis Letterhead
GV-11	3,500	500	750	1,000	250	1,250
GV-29	2,500	250	250	500	500	250
GV-37	750	1,000	500	2,500	250	2,500
GV-10	250	500	1,000	250	1,500	250
Note: This information is subject to change.						

Table 76-27

Boxed Table

Open the file for Table 76-26 and make the following changes:

1. Delete the table note row.
2. Delete Column G.
3. Insert a column to the left of Column B.
4. Insert a row above Row 3. Type: GV-72 | 1,250 | 500 | 1,000 | 250 | 750 | 2,000
5. Type: French Patina Letterhead | 750 | 1,250 | 250 | 1,000 | 500
6. Right-align the text in the numbers columns as needed.
7. Apply 10 percent shading to Row 1.

Table 76-28

Boxed Table

Your completed table will look different from the one shown.

1. Insert a boxed table with 5 columns and 6 rows.
2. Select Row 1, and change the text direction to display vertically top to bottom.
3. Drag down on the bottom border of Row 1 until the column headings display in one continuous line without wrapping.
4. Type the information in the body of the table.
5. Right-align the text in the number columns. **Note:** Do not change the left alignment of the column headings.
6. Merge the cells in the bottom row, and then type the source note.
7. Automatically adjust the column widths.
8. Center the table horizontally and vertically.

Office Supply Account	LED Laser Printer	Internal Fax Modem	Cash Management System	Plain-Paper Laser Fax
OE-9	$405	$181	$199	$249
DD-7	395	150	205	234
US-2	410	125	183	252
OB-1	420	167	179	245
Source: March invoices				

Tables With Braced Column Headings

Goals

- Improve speed and accuracy
- Refine language arts skills in capitalization
- Format braced headings in tables

A. Type 2 times.

A. WARMUP

```
1        Six citizens from 14th Avenue East joined 83 other       10
2   residents to discuss the #794 proposal* for a new swimming    22
3   pool. Barry Kelm quoted numbers about current pool usage.      33
    |  1  |  2  |  3  |  4  |  5  |  6  |  7  |  8  |  9  |  10  |  11  |  12
```

SKILLBUILDING

B. DIAGNOSTIC PRACTICE: NUMBERS

If you are not using the GDP software, turn to page SB-5 and follow the directions for this activity.

C. MAP

Follow the GDP software directions for this exercise in improving keystroking accuracy.

LANGUAGE ARTS

D. Study the rules at the right.

D. CAPITALIZATION

RULE ▶

≡ noun #

Capitalize nouns followed by a number or letter (except for the nouns *line*, *note*, *page*, *paragraph*, and *size*).

Please read Chapter 5, which begins on page 94.

RULE ▶

≡ compass point

Capitalize compass points (such as *north*, *south*, or *northeast*) only when they designate definite regions.

From Montana we drove south to reach the Southwest.

Edit the sentences to correct any errors in capitalization.

```
4   The marketing manager had a reservation on flight 505 to Atlanta.
5   Please order two model 6M printers.
6   The desktop publishing seminar will be held in Room 101.
7   Study pages 120-230 for the unit test.
8   Please contact all representatives in the northern states.
9   Have you visited the city of Pittsburgh?
10  The population of the south continues to increase.
```

FORMATTING

E. BRACED COLUMN HEADINGS

A braced column heading is a heading that applies to more than one column (for example, *Retirement Account* in the table shown below):

1. To create a braced column heading, position the insertion point where you want the braced heading to appear.

2. Merge the cells over which the braced heading will appear.
3. Center the braced column heading over the appropriate columns.

DOCUMENT PROCESSING

Table 77-29

Boxed Table

1. Insert a boxed table with 6 columns and 6 rows.
2. Center and type the braced column headings in upper- and lowercase and bold.
3. Type the regular column headings in bold; right-align the number columns.
4. Follow the standard table format.
5. Merge cells as necessary.
6. Center the table horizontally and vertically.

INSURED ACCOUNT DEPOSITS For Melanie and Frank Bush					
First World Savings		**Individual Account**		**Retirement Account**	
Month	**Branch**	**M. Bush**	**F. Bush**	**M. Bush**	**F. Bush**
January	Reseda	$5,500	$2,350	$2,000	$10,000
February	Valencia	7,950	5,700	5,500	4,300
March	Van Nuys	2,400	7,300	9,300	2,550

Table 77-30

Boxed Table

1. Insert a boxed table with 4 columns and 6 rows.
2. Center and type the braced column headings in upper- and lowercase and bold.
3. Type the regular column headings in bold; right-align the number columns.
4. Follow the standard table format.
5. Merge cells as necessary.
6. Center the table horizontally and vertically.

CINEPLEX VIDEOS Sales Trends			
Western Region		**Total Sales**	
State	**Manager**	**Last Year**	**This Year**
California	George Lucas	$1,956,250	$2,135,433
Nevada	Marjorie Matheson	859,435	1,231,332
Washington	Valerie Harper	737,498	831,352

Open the file for Table 77-30 and make the following changes.

1. Change the column heading "Western Region" to Eastern Region.
2. Change the state names to New York | New Jersey | Delaware.
3. Change the managers' names to Robert DeLuca | Doris Lynch | Megan Bennett.

4. Change last year's amounts to $2,052,659 | 534,958 | 894,211.
5. Change this year's amounts to $3,345,312 | 2,311,478 | 925,138.

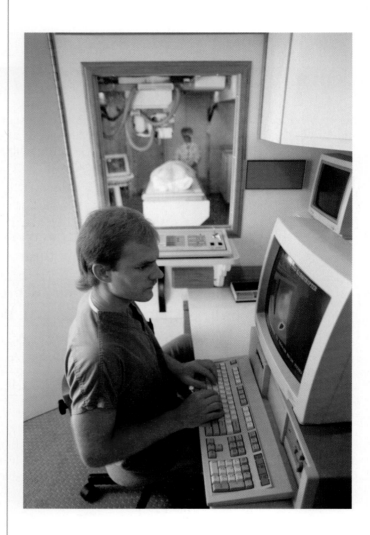

Tables Formatted Sideways

Goals

- Type at least 43wpm/5′/5e
- Format tables in landscape orientation

A. Type 2 times.

A. WARMUP

```
1        This week order a monitor with a resolution of 1280 x     11
2   1024 that supports an optimal refresh rate from V & Q Inc.     23
3   It will cost $573* (*a 9% savings) if ordered before July!     35
    | 1  | 2  | 3  | 4  | 5  | 6  | 7  | 8  | 9  | 10  | 11  | 12
```

SKILLBUILDING

B. PACED PRACTICE

If you are not using the GDP software, turn to page SB-14 and follow the directions for this activity.

Keyboarding Connection

Finding People on the Internet

Remember that long-lost friend from high school? Well, he or she may not be lost for long if you use the Internet's assistance. It is easy to search for a person on the Net by following a few simple steps.

Access a search engine. Click hyperlinks pertaining to finding people such as People Finder or People Search. Enter the information requested about the person, and press the Search button.

Conduct a search for Web sites where you can also find e-mail addresses. Enter the information about the person you are seeking. Click the Search button. Your search should list any names and e-mail addresses that match the name you entered.

YOUR TURN Access a search engine and try to locate the address of a high school friend.

C. Take two 5-minute timed writings. Review your speed and errors.

Goal: At least 43wpm/5'/5e

C. 5-MINUTE TIMED WRITING

4	This is the third in a series of timed writings on	10
5	starting up a new business. In this presentation, you will	22
6	consider some expense and merchandise issues as well as	33
7	some thoughts on the building you will move into or build.	45
8	There are several expenses that you will have to look	57
9	at for your new business. For example, do you realize how	69
10	much construction costs will be, or, if you are going to	80
11	rent a building, how much that expense will amount to? You	92
12	must also project expenses for insurance on the building	103
13	and its contents, utilities costs for running the business,	115
14	interest expense on any loans you secure to purchase or	126
15	renovate the building, and any advertising expenses.	137
16	You must also consider the amount of merchandise you	148
17	will have on hand when you first open your store. If you	159
18	have several lines of merchandise, you need to determine	171
19	how many products and how much of each product you will	182
20	keep on the shelves and how much you will keep in inventory	194
21	in your warehouse. To acquire this merchandise, you must	205
22	locate suppliers who will sell you what you need.	215

| 1 | 2 | 3 | 4 | 5 | 6 | 7 | 8 | 9 | 10 | 11 | 12

FORMATTING

Word Processing Manual

D. WORD PROCESSING: PAGE ORIENTATION

Study Lesson 78 in your word processing manual. Complete all of the shaded steps while at your computer. Then format the jobs that follow.

DOCUMENT PROCESSING

Table 78-32

Boxed Table

1. Format the table in landscape orientation.
2. Set 0.5-inch side margins for the page.
3. Insert a boxed table with 7 columns and 11 rows.
4. Type the following column headings in bold:

Customer | Address | City | ZIP | Telephone No. | Item | Stock No.

5. In Column A, type the customer's last name followed by a comma; then type the first name.

(Continued on next page)

CUSTOMER DATABASE INFORMATION

(Ohio District)

August 31, 20---

~~Maria~~ *Darlene* Westphal | 3309 aaron Place ~~Avenue~~ *Street* | Kenton | 44426 | 419-555-2384 | Pentium computer | 4-238-cw

Dennis Roanne | 20604 Lucile Rd. South | Columbus | 43230 | 614-555-2074 | laser printer | 3-895-LP

Carl Byrnes | 322 W. Lyons Road | Mansfield | 44902 | 216-555-2002 | ~~Color~~ Laser Printer | 3-895-LP

Cynthia Dawson | 5914 Bay Oaks Place | Chilicothe | 45610 | 614-555-1399 | Color Ink-Jet Printer | 2-550-cij

Meg Graupmann | 10386 power Dr. | Steubenville | 43952 | 614-555-7821 | Pentium Computer | 4-238-CW

Jo Neusome | Box 365 | Youngstown | 44502 | 216-555-3885 | Pentium computer | 4-238-CW

Tony Shapiro | 6823 Creekwood ~~Lane~~ *Drive* | Columbus | 43085 | 614-555-2934 | Pentium Computer | ~~5-987-PC~~ *4-238-CW*

Lisa Garand | 26044 Manzano Court | Youngstown | 44505 | 216-555-1777 | FlatBed Color Scanner | 6-8820-CSC

Tom Parker | 936 East wind Drive | Cleveland | 44121 | 216-555-2839 | Lasser Printer | 3-895-LP

Table 78-33

Boxed Table

Open the file for Table 78-32, and make the following changes:
1. Change the date to August 19, 20--.
2. Sort the table alphabetically by the customers' last names.

3. Change the font for the column headings to Arial Narrow, and shade the headings with a 10 percent fill.

Table
78-34
Boxed Table

1. Change the page orientation to landscape.
2. Insert a boxed table with 7 columns and 6 rows.
3. Use standard table format to type the headings and body of the table.
4. Bold and center-align the column headings.
5. Merge the cells in the bottom row; then type the table footnote.

REGIONAL SALES OFFICES
General Information*

Region	Street Address	City	State	ZIP	Telephone	Fax
East	8787 Orion Place	Columbus	OH	43240	614-555-4951	614-555-4999
Mid-Continent	1415 Elbridge Payne Road	Chesterfield	MO	63017	636-555-9940	636-555-9034
Southeast	3100 Breckinridge Boulevard	Duluth	GA	30096	770-555-7007	770-555-7422
West	21600 Oxnard Street	Woodland Hills	CA	91367	818-555-2675	818-555-2697
*Information on all regional offices is updated each year on July 1.						

Multipage Tables

Goals

- Improve speed and accuracy
- Refine language arts skills in spelling
- Format multipage tables

A. Type 2 times.

A. WARMUP

```
1       Please request this key item by June: an XYZ 2000      10
2  motherboard with 512-MB RAM. I don't expect delivery until  22
3  7/5; I realize this is a "great" investment for the money!   34
   | 1 | 2 | 3 | 4 | 5 | 6 | 7 | 8 | 9 | 10 | 11 | 12
```

SKILLBUILDING

PPP PRETEST → PRACTICE → POSTTEST

PRETEST
Take a 1-minute timed writing. Review your speed and errors.

B. PRETEST: Alternate- and One-Hand Words

```
4       They both blame the fight on the visitor. The girl    10
5  had no right to imply that the proxy was brave enough to    21
6  draw you into the unholy case. The union will reward you.   32
   | 1 | 2 | 3 | 4 | 5 | 6 | 7 | 8 | 9 | 10 | 11 | 12
```

PRACTICE
Speed Emphasis:
If you made no more than 1 error on the Pretest, type each *individual* line 2 times.
Accuracy Emphasis:
If you made 2 or more errors, type each *group* of lines (as though it were a paragraph) 2 times.

C. PRACTICE: Alternate-Hand Words

```
7  also angle field bushel ancient emblem panel sight fish big
8  both blame fight formal element handle proxy signs girl and
9  city chair giant island visitor profit right their laid cut
```

D. PRACTICE: One-Hand Words

```
10  acts hilly award uphill average poplin refer jolly adds him
11  area jumpy based homily baggage you'll serve union beat ink
12  case brave extra limply greater unholy wages imply draw you
```

POSTTEST
Repeat the Pretest timed writing and compare performance.

E. POSTTEST: Alternate- and One-Hand Words

F. PROGRESSIVE PRACTICE: ALPHABET

If you are not using the GDP software, turn to page SB-7 and follow the directions for this activity.

G. TECHNIQUE PRACTICE: ENTER KEY

13   Start a business. See the banker. Rent a building.
14 Check state codes. Check city codes. Get needed licenses.
15 Contact suppliers. Call utility companies. Buy furniture.
16 Hire the employees. Open the doors. Hope for customers.

LANGUAGE ARTS

H. SPELLING

17 assistance compliance initial limited corporation technical
18 operating sufficient operation incorporated writing current
19 advice together prepared recommend appreciated cannot based
20 benefit completing analysis probably projects before annual
21 issue attention location association participation proposed

22 The complience by the corporation was sufficient to pass.
23 I cannot reccomend the project based on the expert advise.
24 The location of the proposed annual meeting was an issue.
25 Your assistance in completeing the project is appreciated.
26 Together we prepared an analysis of their current operation.
27 The writing was incorporated in the initial asociation bid.

FORMATTING

I. MULTIPAGE TABLES

Tables should generally be formatted to fit on one page. However, if a table extends to another page, follow these formatting rules:

1. Repeat the column headings at the top of each new page.
2. Number all pages in the upper right-hand corner.

1

50 LONGEST RIVERS OF THE WORLD (Miles Rounded To Nearest Ten)		
River	**Outflow**	**Miles**
Nile	Mediterranean	4,160
Amazon	Atlantic Ocean	4,000
Chang	East China Sea	3,960
Huang	Yellow Sea	3,400
Ob-Irtysh	Gulf of Ob	3,360
Amur	Tatar Strait	2,740
Lena	Laptev Sea	2,730
Congo	Atlantic Ocean	2,720
Mekong	South China Sea	2,600
Niger	Gulf of Guinea	2,590
Yenisey	Kara Sea	2,540
Parana	Rio de la Plata	2,490
Mississippi	Gulf of Mexico	2,340
Missouri	Mississippi River	2,320
Murray-Darling	Indian Ocean	2,310
Volga	Caspian Sea	2,290
Purus	Amazon River	2,100
Medeira	Amazon River	2,010
Sao Francisco	Atlantic Ocean	1,990
Yukon	Bering Sea	1,980
Rio Grande	Gulf of Mexico	1,900
Brahmaputra	Bay of Bengal	1,800
Indus	Arabian Sea	1,800
Danube	Black Sea	1,780
Japura	Amazon River	1,750
Euphrates	Shatt al-Arab	1,700
Zambezi	Indian Ocean	1,700
Tocantins	Para River	1,680
Orinoco	Atlantic Ocean	1,600
Amu	Aral Sea	1,580
Paraguay	Parana River	1,580

2

50 LONGEST RIVERS OF THE WORLD (Miles Rounded To Nearest Ten)		
River	**Outflow**	**Miles**
Ural	Caspian Sea	1,580
Ganges	Bay of Bengal	1,560
Salween	Andaman Sea	1,500
Arkansas	Mississippi River	1,460
Colorado	Gulf of California	1,450
Dnieper	Black Sea	1,420
Negro	Amazon	1,400
Syr	Aral Sea	1,370
Irrawaddy	Bay of Bengal	1,340
Orange	Atlantic Ocean	1,300
Red	Atchafalaya River	1,290
Columbia	Pacific Ocean	1,240
Don	Sea of Azov	1,220
Peace	Slave River	1,210
Xi	South China Sea	1,200
Tigris	Shatt al-Arab	1,180
Angara	Yenisey River	1,150
Songhua	Amur River	1,150
Snake	Columbia River	1,040

Word Processing Manual

J. **WORD PROCESSING: REPEATING TABLE HEADING ROWS**

Study Lesson 79 in your word processing manual. Complete all of the shaded steps while at your computer. Then format the jobs that follow.

DOCUMENT PROCESSING

Table 79-35

Boxed Table

Follow these steps to create a multipage table:

1. Insert a boxed table with 3 columns and 52 rows.
2. Type the table as shown.
3. Apply 10 percent shading to the column headings row.
4. Repeat the table heading rows on page 2.
5. Number the pages in the upper right-hand corner.

50 LONGEST RIVERS OF THE WORLD (Miles rounded to nearest 10)		
River	**Outflow**	**Miles**
Nile	Mediterranean	4,160
Amazon	Atlantic Ocean	4,000
Chang	East China Sea	3,960
Huang	Yellow Sea	3,400
Ob-Irtysh	Gulf of Ob	3,360
Amur	Tatar Strait	2,740
Lena	Laptev Sea	2,730
Congo	Atlantic Ocean	2,720
Mekong	South China Sea	2,600
Niger	Gulf of Guinea	2,590
Yenisey	Kara Sea	2,540
Parana	Rio de la Plata	2,490
Mississippi	Gulf of Mexico	2,340
Missouri	Mississippi River	2,320
Murray-Darling	Indian Ocean	2,310
Volga	Caspian Sea	2,290
Purus	Amazon River	2,100
Medeira	Amazon River	2,010
Sao Francisco	Atlantic Ocean	1,990
Yukon	Bering Sea	1,980
Rio Grande	Gulf of Mexico	1,900
Brahmaputra	Bay of Bengal	1,800
Indus	Arabian Sea	1,800
Danube	Black Sea	1,780
Japura	Amazon River	1,750
Euphrates	Shatt al Arab	1,700
Zambezi	Indian Ocean	1,700
Tocantins	Para River	1,680
Orinoco	Atlantic Ocean	1,600
Amu	Aral Sea	1,580
Paraguay	Parana River	1,580

50 LONGEST RIVERS OF THE WORLD (Miles rounded to nearest 10)		
River	**Outflow**	**Miles**
Ural	Caspian Sea	1,580
Ganges	Bay of Bengal	1,560
Salween	Andaman Sea	1,500
Arkansas	Mississippi River	1,460
Colorado	Gulf of California	1,450
Dnieper	Black Sea	1,420
Negro	Amazon	1,400
Syr	Aral Sea	1,370
Irrawaddy	Bay of Bengal	1,340
Orange	Atlantic Ocean	1,300
Red	Atchafalaya River	1,290
Columbia	Pacific Ocean	1,240
Don	Sea of Azov	1,220
Peace	Slave River	1,210
Xi	South China Sea	1,200
Tigris	Shatt al Arab	1,180
Angara	Yenisey River	1,150
Songhua	Amur River	1,150
Snake	Columbia River	1,040

Table
79-36

Boxed Table

Open the file for Table 79-35, and make the following changes:

1. Sort the table alphabetically by river in ascending order.

2. Apply a double border at the bottom of Row 2.

Table
79-37

Boxed Table

Follow these steps to create a boxed table.

1. Change the page orientation to landscape.
2. Insert a boxed table with 5 columns and 7 rows.
3. Type the table as shown.
4. Apply 100 percent shading (black) to the title row.
5. Apply 10 percent shading to the column heading row.
6. Merge the cells in the bottom row; then type the table footnote.

INVESTMENT SUMMARY				
Limited Partnership	Date of Issue	Initial Cost	Dividend*	Owner
HS Properties	January 2001	$ 50,000	$ 6,066	Alpha Association
Northern Lumber	May 2001	50,000	4,750	CXT Corporation
ST1	February 2001	50,000	7,500	Smith & Sons, Incorporated
ST2	December 2001	100,000	12,250	Q and S Company
* Annual dividends based on current market analysis.				

Using Predesigned Table Formats

Goals

- Type at least 43wpm/5′/5e
- Format tables using TableAutoFormat

A. Type 2 times.

A. WARMUP

```
 1      "Just when can we expect to realize a profit of 5% or    11
 2   more?" This kind of question will be important to 2/3 of     22
 3   the shareholders; they own over 89% of the prime holdings.   34
        |  1  |  2  |  3  |  4  |  5  |  6  |  7  |  8  |  9  |  10  |  11  |  12
```

SKILLBUILDING

B. Take a 1-minute timed writing on the first paragraph to establish your base speed. Then take four 1-minute timed writings on the remaining paragraphs. As soon as you equal or exceed your base speed on one paragraph, advance to the next, more difficult paragraph.

B. SUSTAINED PRACTICE: NUMBERS AND SYMBOLS

```
 4      There is a need at this time to communicate our new      11
 5   pricing guidelines to our franchise outlets. In addition,    23
 6   they must be made aware of inventory implications. They      34
 7   will then be in a position to have a successful operation.   46

 8      Franchise operators could be requested to use either     11
 9   a 20% or a 30% markup. A $50 item would be marked to sell    23
10   for either $60 or $65. Depending on future prospects for     34
11   sales, half of the articles would be priced at each level.   46

12      Ms. Aagard's suggestion is to assign items in Groups     11
13   #1470, #2830, and #4560 to the 20% category. The Series 77   23
14   items* would be in the 30% markup category except for the    35
15   items with a base rate under $100. What is your reaction?    46

16      Mr. Chavez's recommendation is to assign a 30% markup    11
17   to Groups #3890, #5290, #6480, and #7180. About 1/4 of the   22
18   remainder (except for soft goods) would also be in the 30%   34
19   category. Groups #8340 and #9560 would have a 20% markup.    46
        |  1  |  2  |  3  |  4  |  5  |  6  |  7  |  8  |  9  |  10  |  11  |  12
```

C. Take two 5-minute timed writings. Review your speed and errors.

Goal: At least 43wpm/5′/5e

C. 5-MINUTE TIMED WRITING

```
20        Finding a job is a challenge in today's job market,    11
21   but there are some steps you can take to remain competitive  23
22   in the job market. First of all, be sure you know something  35
23   about the company. Do they have offices in a location to     46
24   which you would move, and is the position in that company    58
25   one in which you would like to spend the next five to ten    69
26   years?                                                       71
27        To be successful during your interview, you need to     81
28   know yourself. What are your strengths, and what are your    93
29   weaknesses, if any? Be sure to emphasize your unique skills 105
30   both in your resume and during the interview. Let others    116
31   know what makes you the best candidate for the job. Some    128
32   excellent traits to emphasize would be enthusiasm, a high   139
33   motivation level, and an excellent work ethic.              149
34        When you go for your interview, take into account how  160
35   you dress. Choose your wardrobe as you would for your first 172
36   day on the job. If you are uncertain as to the particular   183
37   dress code, always err on the side of conservatism. Also,   195
38   be watchful of your personal grooming. Make certain your    206
39   hair is trimmed and your shoes are polished.                215
   |  1  |  2  |  3  |  4  |  5  |  6  |  7  |  8  |  9  | 10  | 11  | 12
```

FORMATTING

Word Processing Manual

D. WORD PROCESSING: TABLE—AUTOFORMAT

Study Lesson 80 in your word processing manual. Complete all the shaded steps while at your computer. Then format the jobs that follow.

Table 80-38

Predesigned Table

1. Use a landscape page orientation.
2. Insert a table with 3 columns and 17 rows.
3. Type the table contents, and then AutoFit to contents.
4. Apply the 3D effects 2 Table AutoFormat.
5. Center the table horizontally and vertically.

CITY BANK Interest Rates Schedule Effective Date: November 11, 2003		
	Rate	**APY**
Value Checking	0.00%	0.00%
City Checking	1.25%	1.27%
Prestige Checking	1.25%	1.27%
Golden Checking	1.50%	1.55%
Regular Savings	1.75%	1.90%
Young Savers	1.75%	1.90%
Christmas Club	1.75%	1.90%
Money Market—Tier I	2.25%	2.30%
Money Market—Tier II	2.50%	2.60%
Money Market—Tier III	2.75%	2.80%
Money Market—Tier IV	3.00%	3.10%
CD—6 month	2.25%	2.50%
CD—1 year	2.35%	2.65%
CD—2 year	2.45%	2.70%
year	2.50%	2.75%

Table 80-39

Predesigned Table

Open the file for Table 80-38 and make the following changes:

1. Use a portrait page orientation.
2. Add 1 blank row between Christmas Club and Money Market—Tier 1.
3. Add 1 blank row between Money Market—Tier IV and CD—6 month.
4. Merge the cells in the inserted rows.
5. Type an asterisk (*) after "APY" in Column C.
6. Insert 1 blank row at the bottom of the table and type *APY=Annual Percentage Yield.
7. Apply a Table AutoFormat Table Professional.
8. Center the table horizontally and vertically.

Table
80-40

Predesigned Table

Follow these steps to insert a table using Table AutoFormat.

1. Insert the following table in default format.

2. Apply the Contemporary Table AutoFormat option.

3. Center the table horizontally and vertically.

BUILDING DIRECTORY Paulding Meeting Facility			
No.	Room Name	Seating	Square Feet
102	Alabama	35	400
104	Colorado	150	1,600
106	Delaware	25	350
108	Georgia	50	600
202	Montana	35	400
204	Nevada	50	600
206	New Jersey	300	3,200
208	Pennsylvania	350	3,600

Skills Assessment on Part 4

```
 1       Many business firms create their own special documents  11
 2  today by using software packages that are designed to do     23
 3  the job. These packages help people with limited design       34
 4  skills create pages with very little effort. The challenge,   46
 5  though, is for the person to design the pages effectively     57
 6  so that the reader will read them. After all, the reason      69
 7  for putting in all that time and money is to get people to    81
 8  read the articles.                                            84
 9       Designing pages that are easy to read is not quite as   95
10  easy as it seems. For example, a reader may be confused if   107
11  a page has too many headlines. Instead, a reader may want    119
12  to read fewer headlines that are printed in larger type.     130
13       Desktop publishers require just a few good tools to    141
14  interest the reader. A good plan to use is to be sure to     152
15  put the most important articles at the top of the first page 164
16  and the less important articles on the inside pages. The     176
17  use of bullets and side headings are also helpful guides to  188
18  help a reader zip through pages. A final suggestion is to    199
19  use pictures and graphics that can make the text much more   211
20  interesting to read.                                         215
 |  1  |  2  |  3  |  4  |  5  |  6  |  7  |  8  |  9  |  10  |  11  |  12
```

Correspondence Test 4-76

Memo Report

MEMO

TO: All employees

FROM: Paula Sullivan

Date: January 15, 20--

SUBJECT: Capital Communication Co.

Capital Communication Co. (CCC) operates the fourth-largest network in the U.S. In addition, CCC owns 8 television stations, 3 radio stations, and 4 newspapers.

HISTORY

CCC was started in 1962 by a subsidiary of Heartland Publications as a public service network. It began with three radio stations and added both radio and television stations until it went public in 1956. In 1987, it merged with Pacific

(Continued on next page)

Media Company and added 4 newspapers. CCCs largest news paper, *The San Antonio Times*, won a pulitzer Prize for feature writing last year.

EARNINGS With sales of $4.9 billion dollars for the most recent 12-month period and a net income of $486 million, it CCC continues to lead the "buy" list of most stock brokers. The following table shows a break down of its CCC's earnings.

CAPITAL COMMUNICATION COMPANY			
Company	Last Year	This Year	Next Year*
Radio	$ #1.3	$1.4	$1.4
Television	$1.8	$2.10	$2.2
Newspapers	$1.4	$1.5	$2.0
*Projected			

Sales (in Billio

urs

Correspondence
Test 4-77

Business Letter
in Block Style

January 10, 20-- | Mr. Owen F. Austin | 1734 Perry Street | Flint, MI 48504 | Dear Mr. Austin:

¶ I am sorry that time constraints shortened our telephone conversation yesterday. Given the circumstances as you presented them, you would be wise to consider drafting a general durable power of attorney as described in Section 495 of the new act.

¶ A power of attorney, under the old law, is effective only up to the time that a person is disabled or incompetent. Now the general durable power of attorney, under the new statute, will remain in effect until a person either revokes it or passes away.

¶ The new law will be very helpful to many elderly and infirm people. Sincerely yours, | C. F. Storden | Attorney-at-Law | urs | PS: You may want to discuss this matter with your children before calling my office for an appointment. | bc: Peggy Austin, Walter Austin

Boxed Table

Add 20 percent shading to the title row and 10 percent shading to column headings and total row.

AMERICAN TRADE (As a Percentage of Total)			
Exports		**Imports**	
Canada	22	Japan	20
Japan	12	Canada	19
Mexico	7	Mexico	6
United Kingdom	6	Germany	5
Germany	5	Taiwan	5
South Korea	4	South Korea	4
Other countries	44	Other countries	41
TOTAL	**100**	**TOTAL**	**100**

Unit 17

Formal Report Project

LESSON 81
Formal Report Project

LESSON 82
Formal Report Project

LESSON 83
Formal Report Project

LESSON 84
Formal Report Project

LESSON 85
Formal Report Project

INTERCULTURAL SEMINARS

Jordan D. Sylvester, Director

Human Resources Department

February 12, 20--

The Marketing Department has been conducting surveys of our worldwide offices, foreign customers, and prospective foreign customers over the last several months. Information received through the use of mailed questionnaires has made us aware of an urgent need to improve our communication skills at the international level.

PROBLEM

Some incidents have been reported to us in which we h
with foreign customers and prospective foreign custome
breakdowns in communication. Some of these setbacks
conscious negative acts on the part of our employees. H
to be lack of awareness of cultural differences and lack
that reflect these cultural differences. Indeed, there are
misunderstandings, insults, miscues, and avenues for pe
miscommunicate.

INTERCULTURAL SEMINARS

Three-day seminars designed to improve intercultural co
at regional sites in the United States and in foreign cities

- Beijing
- Hamburg
- Madrid
- Melbourne
- Oslo
- Rio de Janeiro
- Tokyo
- Warsaw

It will be our intent that all employees who have direct co
countries will participate in these seminars over a four-m

INTERCULTURAL SEMINARS

Submitted to

Jordan D. Sylvester, Director
Human Resources Department

red by

Reyes
Manager
Healthcare

12, 20--

CONTENTS

Formal Report Project

Goals

- Improve speed and accuracy
- Refine language arts skills in grammar
- Format a formal report

A. Type 2 times.

A. WARMUP

```
1       The jalopy quivered as it crossed over the 1/5-mile-    11
2   long bridge on Route 267 about 14 miles south @ Granite     22
3   Falls. The axle on Richard's truck broke as he whizzed by.  34
    |  1  |  2  |  3  |  4  |  5  |  6  |  7  |  8  |  9  |  10  |  11  |  12
```

SKILLBUILDING

B. MAP

Follow the GDP software directions for this exercise in improving keystroking accuracy.

C. Take a 1-minute timed writing on the first paragraph to establish your base speed. Then take four 1-minute timed writings on the remaining paragraphs. As soon as you equal or exceed your base speed on one paragraph, advance to the next, more difficult paragraph.

C. SUSTAINED PRACTICE: CAPITALIZATION

```
4       A visit to Europe is a vacation that many people dream  11
5   of doing. There are many countries to visit and hundreds of 23
6   sites to see if you can spend at least four weeks on the     34
7   continent. A trip to Europe is one you will never forget.   46

8       If you decide to visit Europe, the months of June and   11
9   July would probably be the prettiest, but they would also   23
10  be the busiest. England, France, and Germany are popular    34
11  countries to visit; Spain is popular for Americans as well. 46

12      In England you will want to visit St. Paul's Cathedral   11
13  and Big Ben. And, of course, when you are in England, you   23
14  do not want to pass up the opportunity to see Buckingham    34
15  Palace. Plan on staying a few days to see all the sites.    45

16      France certainly is a highlight of any European visit.  11
17  Paris offers many sites such as the Arc de Triomphe, the    22
18  Louvre, the Eiffel Tower, and the Gothic Cathedral of Notre 34
19  Dame. Other cities to visit are Nice, Lyon, and Versailles. 46
    |  1  |  2  |  3  |  4  |  5  |  6  |  7  |  8  |  9  |  10  |  11  |  12
```

D. Study the rules at the right.

D. AGREEMENT

RULE ▶

agreement pronouns

Some pronouns *(anybody, each, either, everybody, everyone, much, neither, no one, nobody,* and *one)* **are always singular and take a singular verb. Other pronouns** *(all, any, more, most, none,* and *some)* **may be singular or plural, depending on the noun to which they refer.**

> <u>Each</u> of the employees <u>has</u> finished <u>his or her</u> task.
> <u>Much</u> <u>remains</u> to be done.
> <u>Most</u> of the pie <u>was</u> eaten, but <u>most</u> of the cookies <u>were</u> left.

RULE ▶

agreement intervening words

Disregard any intervening words that come between the subject and verb when establishing agreement.

> The <u>box</u> containing the books and pencils <u>has</u> not been found.
> <u>Alex</u>, accompanied by Tricia, <u>is</u> attending the conference and taking <u>his</u> computer.

Edit the sentences to correct any errors in grammar.

20 Everybody who signed up for the trip are to be at Building 16.
21 All the tourists are sending cards to us from their hotels.
22 Everyone on the trip, including spouses, have been having fun.
23 Some of the postcards from their vacations are not arriving.
24 Two of the sales reps from Region 4 were given cash bonuses.
25 The fastest runner from all five teams are receiving a trophy.

FORMATTING

Word Processing Manual

E. WORD PROCESSING: STYLES

Study Lesson 81 in your word processing manual. Complete all of the shaded steps while at your computer. Then format the job that follows.

DOCUMENT PROCESSING

Report 81-58 ▶

Business Report

Reference Manual

Refer to Reference Manual pages R-8A and R-8B to review the correct format for business reports. Refer to Reference Manual page R-12C for a review of list formatting.

Report 81-58 begins in this lesson and is continued through Lesson 85. You will be applying styles throughout this report that automatically effect formatting changes to fonts, paragraph spacing, bold, and so on. You will therefore notice some differences from standard business report format. Such changes will be called out in directions and illustrations. Use the following guidelines to format the report.

1. First, change to 11-point Arial font; then press ENTER 6 times.
2. Type the title in all-caps, and press ENTER 1 time. **Note**: Do not apply any styles until you have typed the entire report for a given lesson.
3. Type the byline information and the date in upper- and lowercase, and press ENTER 1 time between each line.

4. Press ENTER 2 times after the date and continue typing the remainder of the report in the same way. Press ENTER only 1 time before and after all side headings.
5. Create a header that will display on all pages except the first page. Type the header in 10-point Arial italic. Type Human Resources Department at the left margin. Press TAB until you reach the right margin, type Page followed by 1 space, and insert an automatic page number. Add a bottom border and close the header.

After you have finished typing the entire document for a particular lesson, go back and make these changes:

1. Apply the Title style to the report title.
2. Apply the Subtitle style to the subtitle, byline, and date.
3. Apply the Heading 2 style to the side headings. **Note:** The Heading 2 style includes italic.
4. Apply the Heading 3 style to the paragraph headings, including the period at the end.

5. Type the table titles in 13-point Arial Bold. Type the table column headings in 11-point Arial Bold. Type the table body in 11-point Arial.
6. Apply 11-point Arial font to the body of the report as needed.
7. Use the default formatting for the footnotes at the bottom of the page.

Change to 11-point Arial first.

↓6X
INTERCULTURAL SEMINARS ↓1X   Apply the Title style.

Jordan D. Sylvester, Director ↓1X   Apply the Subtitle style.

Human Resources Department ↓1X

February 12, 20-- ↓2X

Arial 11 pt.

agreement intervening words

¶ The marketing department has been ~~doing~~ *conducting* surveys of our world wide offices, foreign customers, and prospective foreign customers over the last several months. Information received through the use of *mailed* questionnaires has made us aware of an urgent need to improve our communication skills at the international level. ↓1X

Apply the Heading 2 style.

agreement pronouns

PROBLEM ↓1X

¶ Some incidents have been reported to us in which we have failed to negotiate contract*s* with foreign customers and prospective foreign customers because of serious break downs in com*m*unication. ~~Very few~~ *Some* of these setbacks have been the result of conscious negative acts on the part of our employees. *However,* The main culprit seems to be lack of awareness of cultural differences and a lack of appreciation for the nuances that reflect these cultural differences. Indeed, there almost are unlimited possibilities for misunderstandings, insults, miscues, and avenues for people of good intent to miscommunicate. ↓1X

(Continued on next page)

Apply the Heading 2 style.

agreement intervening
words

Refer to   Reference
Manual

Refer to page R-12C of
the Reference Manual for
a review of list formatting.

agreement intervening
words

agreement pronouns

agreement pronouns

Save this unfinished
report. You will resume
work on it in Lesson 82.

INTERCULTURAL SEMINARS

↓1X

¶ Three day seminars designed to improve intercultural communication skills will be held at regional sites in the U. S. and in foreign cities where we have offices: ↓1X

- Beijing
- Hamburg
- Madrid
- Melbourne
- Oslo
- Rio de Janeiro
- Tokyo
- Warsaw ↓2X

¶ It will be our intent that all employees who have direct contact with people from other countries will participate in these seminars over a four-month period.

¶ It would be unreasonable to assume that a small team of people from our company would have the breadth of knowledge needed to conduct these seminars in 8 foreign countries. However, Angela Demirchyan, William Hamilton, and Chang Ho Han have agreed to work together as the coordinating team for this effort.

¶ Each of these individuals has worked over the past 2 months with the managers of our international offices as well as natives in specific countries to formulate a preliminary plan for these in-service programs. There Their plan will utilize the expertise of our employees who have had negotiating experience in each country and who have knowledge of local customs as demonstrated by natives. We are confident that through this team approach everyone will gain an understanding of problems only not from the position of our company but also from the perspective of those with whom they conduct business.

Formal Report Project

Goals

- Type at least 44wpm/5′/5e
- Format a formal report

A. Type 2 times.

A. WARMUP

```
1        The path will be covered by approximately 30 pieces    11
2   of slate from Quarry #19. Schreiner & Zimmer (the general    23
3   contractor) took the joint bid of $638, including delivery.  35
    |  1  |  2  |  3  |  4  |  5  |  6  |  7  |  8  |  9  |  10  |  11  |  12
```

SKILLBUILDING

B. Take three 12-second timed writings on each line. The scale below the last line shows your wpm speed for a 12-second timed writing.

B. 12-SECOND SPEED SPRINTS

```
4   There are many things to think about if you buy a used car.
5   Two of the main things are its age and the number of miles.
6   Take the car for a test drive in town and on the open road.
7   Pay a fee to an auto expert who will check it over for you.
    | | | | |5| | | |10| | | |15| | | |20| | | |25| | | |30| | | |35| | | |40| | | |45| | | |50| | | |55| | | |60
```

C. PROGRESSIVE PRACTICE: ALPHABET

If you are not using the GDP software, turn to page SB-7 and follow the directions for this activity.

Strategies for Career Success

Letter of Complaint

Is poor product or bad service getting you down? By writing a concise, rational letter of complaint, you have the possibility of the reader honoring your request.

In the first paragraph, give a precise description of the product or service (for example, model, serial number). Include a general statement of the problem (for example, "It is not working properly."). In the middle section, provide the details of what went wrong (for example, when it happened, what failed). Refer to copies of invoices, checks, and so on. Describe how you were inconvenienced, with details about time and money lost. State what you want (for example, refund, repair, replace). In the closing paragraph, ask for a timely response to the complaint (for example, "Please resolve this problem within the next two weeks.").

YOUR TURN Think about the last time that you experienced poor product or service. Did you write a letter of complaint?

D. Take two 5-minute timed writings. Review your speed and errors.

Goal: At least 44wpm/5'/5e

D.   5-MINUTE TIMED WRITING

8   Critical thinking is a skill that can be learned and   11
9   applied to more than a few situations. There are many ways   23
10 to describe critical thinking skill. The common theme that   34
11 runs through each of these descriptions is related to the   46
12 use of cognitive skill. With this skill, the person thinks   58
13 with a purpose in mind and likely directs some of the focus   70
14 toward goals. The person looks at a situation and decides   81
15 rationally what to believe or not to believe. In critical   93
16 thinking, the goal is to achieve understanding, judge more   105
17 than one viewpoint, and then solve problems. After a person   117
18 thinks through all the elements of the problem, a decision   129
19 is made based on all of the facts and exact findings. Bias,   141
20 prejudice, and feelings should not sway the final outcome.   152
21   Critical thinking is useful in reading, listening,   163
22 speaking, and writing. A critical thinker will ask great   174
23 questions. He or she listens carefully to others and gives   186
24 feedback. A critical thinker seeks the truth with zeal and   198
25 then willingly accepts change when new facts are presented.   210
26 Critical thinking is important for problem solving.   220

| 1 | 2 | 3 | 4 | 5 | 6 | 7 | 8 | 9 | 10 | 11 | 12

DOCUMENT PROCESSING

Report 81-58

(Continued)

Continue working on Multipage Business Report 81-58.

Refer to Reference Manual

Refer to page R-12C of the Reference Manual for a review of list formatting.

INSTRUCTIONAL APPROACH

¶ Alvarez and Hwang suggest a framework of instruction with the following: _three components_ ∧

1. The cognitive component includes information about communicating with people. _of other cultures_ ∧

2. The _a_ effective component is the area in which attention is given to attitudes, emotions, and resulting behaviors as they are _a_ effected by human interaction in a multi-cultural environment.

(Continued on next page)

3. The experiential component is the "hands-on" element ~~which~~ _that_ suggests different possibilities. Others have found that the use of simulations is a natural for this type of experience. The writing of letters, memos, and reports to persons in other cultures also provides beneficial learning experiences. In addition, the use of tutors can be very helpful to workers unfamiliar with a particular culture.[1]

SEMINAR CONTENT

¶ The cognitive, affective, and experiential ~~frames~~ _components_ would be applied as appropriate for each of the topics included. The coordinating team members have utilized the resources available to them at our ③ local universities.

¶ Most colleges and universities now provide instruction in international communication. While the content at times is integrated into several business administration courses, there has been a trend in recent years to provide a course ~~or courses~~ specifically designed for business interaction in an intercultural setting. The very nature of this type of study makes it very difficult to segment the broad topical areas, as all elements are so closely intertwined. However, the tentative seminar plan is to cover the content as described in Table 1.

¶ The seminars must reflect the broad involvement of our international operations. There is a need for many workers in our domestic offices to develop an appreciation of the intercultural challenge. This is true not only for those in the marketing and sales areas. Those in our Finance Department and our Legal Department are _increasingly_ involved not only with foreign companies but also with huge multinational corporations that, at times, are as large as or larger than the biggest companies in the ~~entire~~ United States.

¶ Demirchyan, Hamilton, and Han suggest the following list of tentative instructional topics:[2]

---

[1] Ana Maria Alvarez and Allen Hwang, "Communication Across Cultures," _International Business World,_ April 2006, pp. 39-42.

[2] Angela Demirchyan, William Hamilton, and Chang Ho Han, _The Dynamics of Intercultural Seminars_, Gateway Publishing, Boston, 2005.

(Continued on next page)

Refer to **Reference Manual**

Review the format for placing a table in a report on page R-8B of the Reference Manual.

↓2X

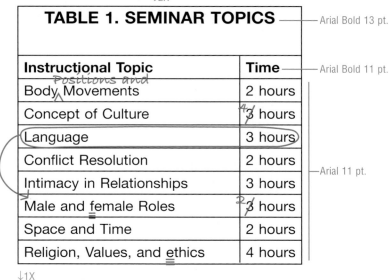

Instructional Topic	Time
Body Positions and Movements	2 hours
Concept of Culture	3 hours
Language	3 hours
Conflict Resolution	2 hours
Intimacy in Relationships	3 hours
Male and female Roles	3 hours
Space and Time	2 hours
Religion, Values, and ethics	4 hours

Arial Bold 13 pt.
Arial Bold 11 pt.
Arial 11 pt.

↓1X

Apply the Heading 3 style.

¶ **Body Positions and Movements.** Body language, that is, facial expressions, gestures, and body movements, conveys messages about attitude and may be interpreted differently by people in different cultures. For example, firm handshakes are the norm in the U.S.; loose handshakes are the custom in some other countries. The way we stand, sit, and hold our arms may convey different messages in different cultural settings.

Apply the Heading 3 style.

¶ **Concept of culture.** This session will be an over view of the various cultures in which we conduct business, including e-commerce. Clooney identifies the need for varied marketing strategies within the different economic, political, and cultural environments:

> International Web use and access are growing exponentially, and many businesses are wanting to capitalize on this trend and grab their fair share of this global market. English-speaking audiences are not expected to continue to dominate this market. Certainly, more than a literal translation will be required to reach this culturally diverse audience.[3]

Refer to **Reference Manual**

Refer to page R-8B for a review of long quotations.

Case studies will be reviewed that are considered classics in the field of international communication. In addition, Summaries of some of our own successes and failures will be reported.

Save this unfinished report. You will resume work on it in Lesson 83.

---

[3] Arlene D. Clooney, "Cultural Comparisons in E-Commerce," December 19, 2005, <http://www.ecommerce.com/news.htm>, accessed on January 18, 2006.

Formal Report Project

Goals

- Improve speed and accuracy
- Refine language arts skills in composing
- Format a formal report

A. Type 2 times.

A. WARMUP

```
1      The 16 young farmers (only 50% over 30 years of age)    11
2  gathered in Room 209 to begin discussing the earthquake     22
3  threat; an extra door prize was given as a "joke present."  34
   |  1  |  2  |  3  |  4  |  5  |  6  |  7  |  8  |  9  |  10  |  11  |  12
```

SKILLBUILDING

PPP PRETEST → PRACTICE → POSTTEST

PRETEST
Take a 1-minute timed writing. Review your speed and errors.

B. PRETEST: Common Letter Combinations

```
4      The insurance agent read the report before giving it   11
5  to your deputy director. This weekly action showed that     22
6  the agent really knew the actual input on a daily basis.    33
   |  1  |  2  |  3  |  4  |  5  |  6  |  7  |  8  |  9  |  10  |  11  |  12
```

PRACTICE
Speed Emphasis:
If you made no more than 1 error on the Pretest, type each *individual* line 2 times.
Accuracy Emphasis:
If you made 2 or more errors, type each *group* of lines (as though it were a paragraph) 2 times.

C. PRACTICE: Word Beginnings

```
7  re- repel renew remit relax refer ready react really reveal
8  in- inept inert inset input infer index incur inches insert
9  be- bears beams beach below being began befit beauty beside
```

D. PRACTICE: Word Endings

```
10  -ly truly madly lowly early daily apply hilly simply weekly
11  -ed sized hired dated cited based acted added opened showed
12  -nt plant meant giant front event count agent amount fluent
```

POSTTEST
Repeat the Pretest timed writing and compare performance.

E. POSTTEST: Common Letter Combinations

F. PROGRESSIVE PRACTICE: NUMBERS

If you are not using the GDP software, turn to page SB-11 and follow the directions for this activity.

G. COMPOSING A DOCUMENT

Compose a 1-page document in which you describe how you can use the Styles feature in a resume you are preparing for a job search. You might include features such as fonts, font sizes, indentations, and spacing to control the appearance of your resume. Use default margins, double spacing, and two paragraphs in your document. Provide a title, and type your name at the top of the document.

In paragraph 1, you could include information on using styles for those items you want to highlight in your resume such as (1) your name and address at the top of the resume, (2) the section headings that often run down the left side of the resume, and (3) any bullets you want to include for items that contain multiple entries.

In paragraph 2, you could include a brief discussion on (1) the margins to use for your resume, (2) line spacing to use for individual entries, and (3) line spacing to use between entries.

Include a brief summary statement to emphasize the importance of proofreading your document and the need for accuracy in a resume.

FORMATTING

Word Processing Manual

H. WORD PROCESSING: INSERT CLIP ART AND FILES

Study Lesson 83 in your word processing manual. Complete all of the shaded steps while at your computer. Then format the job that follows.

DOCUMENT PROCESSING

Report 81-58

(Continued)

Continue working on Report 81-58.

Insert clip art that is related to communication and similar to this example.

Set the clip art at a size of 1-inch square, and place it at the right margin even with the first line of the Language paragraph.

¶ **Conflict Resolution**. Whether people are involved in negotiating a contract, working together to remedy product quality issues, or resolving contract interpretations, the need for tact and skill is particularly important in the foreign setting. Many of the seminar topics have implications in the area of conflict resolution. While every effort should be made to prevent conflict, there is a need for guidance in resolving disagreements in foreign cultures.

¶ **Intimacy in Relationships**. The degree of physical contact that is acceptable varies considerably. Hugs and kisses are the standard, even in the business office, in some countries. By contrast, the act of touching a person is considered an extreme invasion of privacy in other places. The use of first names may or may not be acceptable. To ask a personal question is extremely offensive in some cultures. While socializing with business clients is to be expected in some countries, it would be highly inappropriate in others. These are only a few of the relationship concerns that will be explored.

¶ **Language**. It is obvious that language differences play a major part in business miscommunication. Whenever there is an interpreter or a written translation involved, the chances for error are increased. There are over 3,000 languages used on the earth. Just as with English, there are not only

(Continued on next page)

grammar rules but also varied meanings as words are both spoken and written. Even with the English language, there are differences in usage between the English used in the United States and that used in England.

¶ Although English is the language usually used in international communication, the topics identified in Table 1 illustrate the complexity of communicating accurately; and the problem continues to grow. For example, literal translations of American advertising and labeling have sometimes resulted in negative feelings toward products. As world trade increases, so does the need for American businesses to understand the complexities of cultural differences. Gregorian offers this example:

> A businessperson must change his or her expectations and assumptions away from what is customary and acceptable in the United States in terms of personal and social conduct to what is customary and acceptable within the culture of the country where they are conducting business. Any other assumption can have serious consequences and undesirable results. In the other person's mind, you are the foreigner and therefore you will be the one who might look out of place or act in a way that is considered socially unacceptable.[4]

¶ A good sense of humor is an asset not only in our personal lives but also in the business environment. However, it probably should be avoided in multicultural settings because the possibilities for misinterpretation are compounded. Do not use humor that makes fun of a particular individual, group, or culture. Remember that what may appear to be humorous to you may have a negative connotation in another culture.

¶ **Male and Female Roles.** There are major contrasts in the ways male and female roles are perceived in different cultures. The right to vote is still withheld from women in countries all over the world. Opportunities for female employment in the business environment vary considerably. Pay differentials for men and women continue to exist even when they are performing the same tasks. Opportunities for advancement for men and women often are not the same.

¶ **Space and Time.** The distance one stands from someone when engaged in conversation is very important. If a person stands farther away than usual, this may signal a feeling of indifference or even a negative feeling. Standing too close is a sign of inappropriate familiarity. However, it should be recognized that different cultures require a variety of space for business exchanges to take place. In the United States, that space is typically from three to five feet, but in the Middle East and in Latin American countries, this distance is considered too far.

¶ There is also the element of time--a meeting that is scheduled for 9 a.m. likely will start on time in the United States, but in some other cultures the meeting may not start until 9:30 or even 10 o'clock. Punctuality and time concepts vary with the customs and practices of each country. Patience really can be a virtue.

---

[4] Gerald Gregorian, *Comparing Cultural Differences*, Dana Publishing Company, Los Angeles, 2003, p. 49.

Insert clip art that is related to time and similar to this example. The style should be similar to the first clip art you inserted.

Set the clip art at a size of 1-inch square, and place it at the right margin even with the first line in the second paragraph of the Space and Time paragraph.

Save this unfinished report. You will resume work on it in Lesson 84.

Formal Report Project

Goals

- Type at least 44wpm/5′/5e
- Format a formal report

A. Type 2 times.

A. WARMUP

```
1        The new schedule* has the Lynx at their home park on    11
2   July 27 with the zany Waverley Blackhawks. The Lynx scored   23
3   five fourth-quarter goals in their last game to win 8 to 4!  34
    | 1 | 2 | 3 | 4 | 5 | 6 | 7 | 8 | 9 | 10 | 11 | 12
```

SKILLBUILDING

B. DIAGNOSTIC PRACTICE: SYMBOLS AND PUNCTUATION

If you are not using the GDP software, turn to page SB-2 and follow the directions for this activity.

C. Take two 5-minute timed writings. Review your speed and errors.

Goal: At least 44wpm/5'/5e.

C. 5-MINUTE TIMED WRITING

4	Proofreading skill is developed with practice. You may	11
5	want to master several techniques that will help develop	23
6	and improve your proofreading skills.	30
7	In order to be a successful proofreader, you will want	41
8	to schedule time to read through the completed job several	53
9	times. At the first reading, check your work to see if the	65
10	margins are correct and the page numbers are in the right	77
11	places. Determine if the spacing and the font styles are	80
12	correct. With each reading, zoom in on a specific type of	100
13	error. If possible, read your work out loud and read only	111
14	one word at a time. You may find that placing a ruler under	123
15	each line as you read it will give your eyes a manageable	135
16	amount of text to read.	140
17	At the next reading, be sure that the content of the	150
18	document follows a logical order. If any cited works are	162
19	included, be sure the citations are in the proper format	173
20	with complete and accurate data. Check to be sure that all	185
21	the basic rules of grammar, spelling, and punctuation have	197
22	been followed. Proofread your document when you are fresh	208
23	and alert. Remember, proofreading takes time and patience.	220

| 1 | 2 | 3 | 4 | 5 | 6 | 7 | 8 | 9 | 10 | 11 | 12 |

Keyboarding Connection

Sending E-Mail Attachments

Your e-mail program will tell you if an attachment has been sent, but the attachment may arrive in unusable or partially usable form. Often the sender and recipient need to use the same or compatible software to open and use each other's documents, especially if the files contain visuals, records, or spreadsheets.

Send a test e-mail by attaching a test document and ask your receiver to send you one in return. If the test fails with a word processing document, open your word processor, and save the document again as a text file. You may lose some formatting (indents, bold, bullets), but any e-mail program, as well as any word processor, can usually read the file.

YOUR TURN Open a word processing file. Save it as a text file. Open the text file in your word processor. What formatting has changed? Send both files to yourself as e-mail attachments. Open them and note any changes.

Table 84-42 ▶

Boxed Table

TABLE 2. FOREIGN-CITY SEMINARS		
City	**First Seminar**	**Second Seminar**
Melbourne	May 2-4	July 5-7
Rio de Janeiro	May 9-11	July 11-13
Beijing	May 16-18	July 18-20
Hamburg	May 23-25	July 25-27
Tokyo	June 6-8	August 1-3
Warsaw	June 13-15	August 8-10
Oslo	June 20-22	August 15-17
Madrid	June 27-29	August 22-24

— Arial Bold 13 pt.
— Arial Bold 11 pt.
— Arial 11 pt.

Report 81-58 ▶

(Continued)

Continue working on Report 81-58.

¶ **Religion, Values, and Ethics**. While we can recognize the difficult challenge presented by language differences, this category (religion, values, and ethics) is in some ways the area that can bring about the most serious breakdowns in relations with those from other cultures.

• The very nature of religious beliefs suggests that this is a delicate area for those involved in business transactions in foreign countries. Also, religious beliefs affect the consumption of certain products throughout the world. Examples are tobacco, liquor, pork, and coffee.

• Values are a reflection of religious beliefs for most people. We often hear references to right and wrong as applied to the ideals and customs of a society. Values relate to a range of topics, and they may pertain to areas such as cleanliness, education, health care, and criminal justice. Such values are often very personal and as such can have a variety of interpretations. The more interpretations there are, the more likely it is that miscommunication will occur.

• Ethics can be considered as standards of conduct that reflect moral beliefs as applied to both one's personal life and one's business life.

¶ Huntington suggests that now more than ever, a code of ethics is essential within the business environment. When this code of ethics is missing or if it is not enforced, chaos and financial ruin for everyone associated is often the result.

A code of ethics is increasingly being recognized as an intrinsic and critical component in any business environment. Newspapers are filled with reports of scandalous, unconscionable, nonethical behavior that has led to the downfall of otherwise successful businesses. The lack of ethics in business conduct has led to disastrous effects for both the businesses in question and the consumers and their investments in these companies.[5]

---

[5] Marilyn C. Huntington, *Business Ethics and Workplace Compliance*, Horizon Publishing Company, New York, 2005, p. 53.

TENTATIVE SEMINAR SCHEDULE

Insert clip art that is related to world travel and similar to this example. The style should be similar to that of the earlier clip art you inserted.

Set the clip art at a size of 1-inch square, and place it at the right margin even with the first line of the first paragraph.

¶ As indicated earlier, it is our intent that all employees who have direct contact with people in other cultures will participate in these seminars. For that reason there will be two identical three-day seminars scheduled at each foreign site. Only selected employees in our regional sites in the United States will participate. These people have been tentatively identified on the basis of the extent of their involvement with persons from other countries.

¶ As all employees in our foreign offices will participate, a decision has been made to schedule these seminars through the summer. A tentative schedule for these seminars is shown in Table 2.

↓2X
(Insert Table 84–42 here)
↓1X

The Marketing Department is to be commended for calling our attention to the seriousness of our international communication problem. Angela Demirchyan, William Hamilton, and Chang Ho Han also deserve our sincere thanks for their planning efforts for our intercultural communication seminars. As can be seen, special attention is being given to the seminar topics for these in-service programs. Efforts are also being made to identify instructors and resource persons who will develop instructional strategies that will be effective, interesting, and well received by the participants. These seminars will help significantly in increasing our market share in the international market.

Save this unfinished report. You will resume work on it in Lesson 85.

Formal Report Project

Goals

- Improve speed and accuracy
- Refine language arts skills in proofreading
- Format a formal report

A. Type 2 times.

A. WARMUP

```
1        Bev ordered the following: 24 #794 napkin boxes, 48      11
2    #265B quarts of ketchup, and 72 reams of 20-1b white print   22
3    paper. Did you receive the prize jalapeno peppers we sent?   34
     |  1  |  2  |  3  |  4  |  5  |  6  |  7  |  8  |  9  |  10  |  11  |  12
```

SKILLBUILDING

B. Type the columns 2 times. Press TAB to move from column to column.

B. TECHNIQUE PRACTICE: TAB

```
4    M. A. Barnes     Julie Herden    Lynn Masica     Don Trueblood
5    Nathan Favor     Brett Irvin     Lisa O'Keefe    Matthew Utbert
6    Lee Chinn        Rick Kenwood    J. E. Perry     Jill Voss-Walin
7    Xavier Saxon     Lance King      Chad Quinn      Robin Yager
```

C. PACED PRACTICE

If you are not using the GDP software, turn to page SB-14 and follow the directions for this activity.

LANGUAGE ARTS

D. Compare this paragraph with lines 4-7 on page 305.

D. PROOFREADING

```
8         A visitt to Europe is a vacation that many people dreem
9    of doing. There are many countrys to visit and hundreds
10   of sights to see if you can spend at least for weeks on the
11   continnent. A trip too Europe is one you will never forget.
```

Report
85-59

Title Page

Refer to
Reference
Manual

Refer to page R-7B of
the Reference Manual
to format the title page.

Create a title page for Report 81-58 as a separate document using standard format and making these changes:

1. Change to 11-point Arial before typing any part of the title page.
2. Type INTERCULTURAL SEMINARS as the title.
3. The report is to be submitted to Jordan D. Sylvester, Director, Human Resources Department. Type Jordan D. Sylvester, Director on one line followed by the department name on the next line.
4. The report is being prepared by Lydia Reyes, Marketing Manager, Gold Coast Healthcare.
5. The date is February 12, 20--.
6. When you are finished typing the title page, apply the Title style to the title.

Report
85-60

Table of Contents

Refer to
Reference
Manual

Refer to page R-7D of
the Reference Manual
to format the table of
contents.

Create a table of contents for Report 81-58 as a separate document using standard format. The table of contents shown is incomplete. Refer to your report to compose and complete the table of contents. Make these changes:

1. Change to 11-point Arial before typing any part of the table of contents page.
2. Refer to the finished report to compose and type the table of contents. The entries should include all side headings and paragraph headings from the report. Refer to the finished report for the page numbers.
3. Type the side headings in all-caps at the left margin.
4. Type the paragraph headings in upper- and lowercase indented 0.5 inch from the left margin.
5. Do not include the report header.

(Continued on next page)

↓6X

Title style **CONTENTS** ↓X2

Arial 11 pt.

Report 85-61

Bibliography

Refer to | **Reference Manual**

Refer to page R-9B of the Reference Manual to format the bibliography page. Arial 11 pt.

Spell-check your report for errors. Proofread it for omitted or repeated words, errors that form a new word, and formatting errors.

Type the bibliography for Report 81-58, shown here as a separate document using standard format. Follow these steps:

1. Change to 11-point Arial.
2. Type the bibliography in standard format.

3. When you are finished with all entries, apply the Title style to "BIBLIOGRAPHY."
4. Do not include the report header.

Title style **BIBLIOGRAPHY**

Alvarez, Ana Maria, and Allen Hwang, "Communication Across Cultures," *International Business World*, April 2006, pp. 39-42.

Clooney, Arlene D., "Cultural Comparisons in E-Commerce," December 19, 2005, <http://www.ecommerce.com/news.htm> accessed on January 18, 2006.

Demirchyan, Angela, William Hamilton, and Chang Ho Han, *The Dynamics of Intercultural Seminars*, Gateway Publishing, Boston, 2005.

Gregorian, Gerald, *Comparing Cultural Differences*, Dana Publishing Company, Los Angeles, 2003.

Huntington, Marilyn C., *Business Ethics and Workplace Compliance*, Horizon Publishing Company, New York, 2005.

Report 81-58

(Continued)

Progress and Proofreading Check ✓

Documents designated as Proofreading Checks serve as a check of your proofreading skill. Your goal is to have zero typographical errors when the GDP software first scores the document.

Finalize the report project:

- Proofread all the pages for format and typing errors.
- Assemble the pages in this order: title page, table of contents, body, bibliography, and a blank page for a back cover sheet.
- Staple the report pages together.

Unit 18

International Formatting

LESSON 86
International Formatting (Canada)

LESSON 89
International Formatting (Germany)

LESSON 87
International Formatting (Mexico)

LESSON 90
International Formatting (Japan)

LESSON 88
International Formatting (France)

16 April 20--

Mr. Henry R. Defforey
Human Resources Director
Gemey Techtronics
Avenue Raymond Poincore
75116 Paris
FRANCE

Dear Mr. Defforey:

...d in an employee exchange this coming year. As ...s of our 26 production employees will benefit both

...hrough the various units of our production ...rials division and continuing right on through our ...a projected rotation plan for you to review. ...oyee rotations we discussed at our last meeting. ...e if there are any changes you wish to make. You ...tech.com>, or, if you wish to speak to me directly,

...this coming year. As soon as we have agreed on ...s for all affected employees. I know that ...ticipating this collaborative effort.

MEXICO TRAVEL DESTIN...

Most Popular Attracti...

April 15, 20--

INTRODUCTION

Since the mid-1990s, national parks in Mexico have b... visitors from the Americas, Europe, and Asia. As a re... requests have been made for travel brochures and ma... Therefore, in the next few weeks, we will be publishi... maps to accommodate these requests.

BROCHURES

The brochures will include a detailed description of t... beginning and ending visitation schedules, highlights... photography locations. Brochures will be prepared on... in the table below. The fourth column indicates how... ranked among the top ten most popular sites in Mexic...

Area	Site
Northern	Cumbres de Majalca
Northern	Cumbres de Monterrey
Northern	Sierra del Pinacate
Central	El Tepozteco
Central	Iztaccihuatl y Popocatepetl
Central	Malinche
Southern	Bonampak/Yaxchilan Monuments
Southern	Chichén Itzá
Southern	Dzibilchaltun
Southern	Sian Káan Biosphere Reserve

MAPS

Maps will be supplied for the locations listed above, w... visitors from the nearest cities to the tourist attraction... stations will be highlighted, and approximate walking... maps. Individual maps will be prepared for each area... southern), and a comprehensive map for all three visi... Please send any advertising pieces you wish to promo... Relations Director.

---

18 April 20--

Ms. Sharla D. Enterline
Project Coordinator
Carroll Technology
8723 Hill Avenue
Bowling Green, KY 42823

Dear Ms. Enterline:

The following information is being sent to assist you with Japanese mailing rules. As a service to your employees, I am providing the following summary of these rules.

A Japanese mailing address consists of the name, street address, town, city, prefecture, postal code, and country. The illustration below shows how an address should appear on an envelope going to Japan.

Address Items	Address Example
Name	Mr. Yoshifumi Uda
Street Address, Town (first address)	1-17, Akai-cho
City, Prefecture (second address), Postal Code	Minato-ku, Tokyo 108-8005
JAPAN	JAPAN

Please e-mail me if you have questions about mailing rules in Japan. You can reach me at <shiroshi@tadashi.jp.com>.

Very sincerely,

S. Hiroshi
Shipping Department

hk
c: K. Tachikawa

International Formatting (Canada)

Goals

- Type at least 45wpm/5'/5e
- Format international documents

A. Type 2 times.

A. WARMUP

```
1        The lynx at the zoo fought wildly and had to be moved    11
2   quickly to a new cage (#248-I or #357-II). These adjoining    23
3   cages place the lynx (all of them) into individual areas.     34
    |  1  |  2  |  3  |  4  |  5  |  6  |  7  |  8  |  9  |  10  |  11  |  12
```

SKILLBUILDING

B. DIAGNOSTIC PRACTICE: NUMBERS

If you are not using the GDP software, turn to page SB-5 and follow the directions for this activity.

C. Take three 12-second timed writings on each line. The scale below the last line shows your wpm speed for a 12-second timed writing.

C. 12-SECOND SPEED SPRINTS

```
4   The car will now have to turn off on the lane to the lake.
5   Mark must type these lines fast and press for a high speed.
6   We had a lunch at the lake and went for a walk in the park.
7   Take this disk to have it fixed by the end of your workday.
    | | | | 5 | | | | 10 | | | | 15 | | | | 20 | | | | 25 | | | | 30 | | | | 35 | | | | 40 | | | | 45 | | | | 50 | | | | 55 | | | | 60
```

D. Take two 5-minute timed writings. Review your speed and errors.

Goal: At least 45wpm/5'/5e

D. 5-MINUTE TIMED WRITING

8	During good economic times, businesses have trouble	11
9	finding and keeping their skilled workers. As a result,	22
10	some places may offer great benefits to their workers. This	34
11	could include such things as sick leave, life insurance,	45
12	profit sharing, paid time off each year, and flextime.	56
13	The concept of flextime was introduced to the work	67
14	force quite a few years ago. Companies adopted the concept	78
15	for a lot of reasons. Among the top reasons for flexible	90
16	work schedules at that time were to reduce the number of	101
17	cars on the road, to help workers to meet their families'	113
18	needs and demands, and also to attract more women back to	124
19	the work force.	128
20	Businesses can manage such a schedule in a few ways.	138
21	Employees may have a chance to choose when to arrive and	150
22	leave for the day. This policy allows people who like to	161
23	work early in the day to start early and end early and vice	173
24	versa. Other companies may allow their employees to work	185
25	extended hours for four days and then enjoy three days off.	197
26	This type of benefit has helped both workers and companies.	209
27	Companies recognize that their workers are more productive	220
28	and absences are lower.	225

| 1 | 2 | 3 | 4 | 5 | 6 | 7 | 8 | 9 | 10 | 11 | 12 |

Keyboarding Connection

Effective Teleconferencing for Meetings

Teleconferencing is a useful way to conduct meetings with businesspersons across the globe. To make the best use of teleconference meetings, follow these guidelines.

Since sound quality varies greatly, use the best equipment available. Allow individual participants enough time to use their technology. Participants should select a conference leader and alternate that leadership. Distribute agendas to everyone in advance, possibly via e-mail.

Be sensitive to time zone differences. Since it is possible someone will experience an inconvenient time, consider rotating the times of the meetings. Assign someone to prepare and e-mail to the participants a brief summary covering the main discussion topics and action items of the teleconference.

YOUR TURN List what you think are the advantages and disadvantages of conducting meetings via teleconference.

E. METRIC PAPER SIZE

Paper size for correspondence in the United States is typically 8.5 × 11 inches. However, correspondence in many foreign countries is often formatted on metric-sized paper. The most popular of these is called A4 paper, and it measures 210 × 297 millimeters—approximately 8.25 × 11.75 inches.

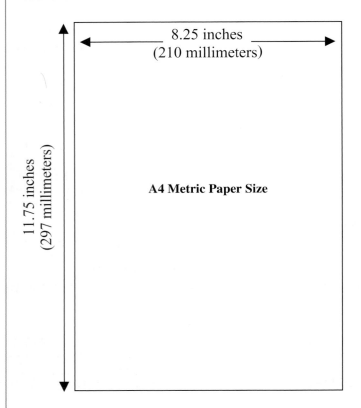

8.25 inches
(210 millimeters)

11.75 inches
(297 millimeters)

A4 Metric Paper Size

F. METRIC ENVELOPE SIZE

A standard large envelope (No. 10) measures 9.5 × 4.125 inches. A large envelope for metric size paper is called DL, and it measures 110 × 220 millimeters—approximately 4.33 × 8.67 inches. The No. 10 envelope is not as deep as the metric envelope, but it is slightly wider.

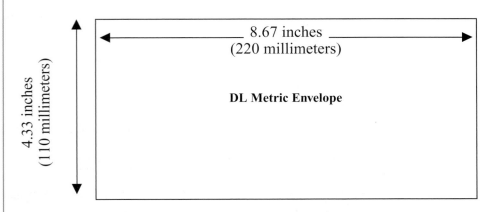

8.67 inches
(220 millimeters)

4.33 inches
(110 millimeters)

DL Metric Envelope

G. INTERNATIONAL ADDRESSES IN LETTERS

International addressing is becoming more common with the increased popularity of the Internet and frequently requires changes to the address lines, such as the addition of special codes, abbreviations, and capitalization. Individual organizational preferences for international address formatting will vary. Therefore, the most technologically efficient formats for international addresses will be used, including the use of all caps and the name of the country spelled out as the last entry of the address, as shown in the examples below.

Canada Address Example:

8437 Dixie Road ◄——————— Street Address [street number followed by street name]

Brampton, ON L6T 5P6 ◄——— City/Province/Postal Code [2 spaces after the province; 1 space between first 3 and last 3 characters]

CANADA ◄——————— Country Name [typed in all-capitals]

Mexico Address Example:

Av. Chapultepec 28 ◄——————— Street Address [street name followed by street number]

06724 Mexico D.F. ◄——————— Postal Code/City [postal code and city name; "Mexico D.F." denotes Mexico City]

MEXICO ◄——————— Country Name [typed in all-capitals]

France Address Example:

14, Rue Royale ◄——————— Street Address [street number followed by a comma and then street name]

75008 Paris ◄——————— Postal Code/City

FRANCE ◄——————— Country Name [typed in all-capitals]

Germany Address Example:

Mannesmannufer 2 ◄——————— Street Address [street name followed by street number]

D-40213 Duesseldorf ◄——————— Postal Code/City [international sorting code followed by postal code and city name]

GERMANY ◄——————— Country Name [typed in all-capitals]

Japan Address Example:

10-1, Toranomon 2-chome ◄——— Division of the City [lot and building number, followed by neighborhood name, followed by area number]

Minato-ku Tokyo 105-8436 ◄— City, District/City Name/Postal Code

JAPAN ◄——————— Country Name [typed in all-capitals]

H. DAY/MONTH/YEAR FORMAT

In international correspondence, the date line is often formatted in this sequence: day, month, year. Thus, the first line of a letter to a foreign recipient may appear as shown in the illustration.

12 April 20--

Mr. James E. Burillon
Sales Director
Avian Industries
14, Rue Royale
75008 Paris
FRANCE

Dear Mr. Burillon:

Word Processing Manual

I. WORD PROCESSING: PAPER SIZE

Study Lesson 86 in your word processing manual. Complete all of the shaded steps while at your computer. Then format the jobs that follow.

DOCUMENT PROCESSING

Situation: You work for World-Tech Industries, an international computer manufacturer located in Vancouver, Canada. World-Tech Industries has a client base in both the United States and Canada. For the purposes of this simulation, your name will be Hiroki Kayano. Your e-mail address is hkayano@worldtech.com and your phone number is +1.702.555.1839.

For the next five days, you will prepare documents for several World-Tech executives. Your firm follows formatting guidelines for metric paper and envelope size and international addresses, dates, phone numbers, and measurements. You will use A4 metric paper and DL metric envelopes for all documents.

Today is April 14, and you will spend your first day preparing documents, which appear in your in-basket. Proofread your work carefully and check for spelling, punctuation, grammar, and formatting errors so that your documents are mailable.

Correspondence 86-78

Business Letter in Modified-Block Style

14 April 20-- | Mr. Alec R. Cousins | Manager, Computer Services | Columbia Enterprises, Ltd. | 338 Dunsmuir Street | Vancouver, BC V4B 5R9 | CANADA | Dear Mr. Cousins:

¶ Thank you for your recent computer order. As you requested, we have added the DVD drives to the 50 computers. There will be no extra charge for exchanging the DVD drives for the ZIP drives that come standard with the C-420 model you ordered.

¶ Your order will be shipped ten business days from the date of your order. Our order processing and shipping departments are online, and you can check the progress of your order by going to <www.worldtech.com> and clicking on Customer Orders.

¶ We look forward to the opportunity to serve your computer needs for many years to come.

Sincerely, | Sharon T. Yates | Sales Manager | hk | c: Terry Mourieux, Pamela Phillips | PS: The special software you ordered with your computers will be installed at our factory, ready for your use when your computers arrive.

(!) Type *hk* as the reference initials for this simulation.

Table 86-43

Boxed Table

Prepare Table 86-43 on A4 paper, in landscape orientation. **Note:** Entries are arranged in ascending order by kilometers from Vancouver, British Columbia.

CUSTOMER SHIPPING ADDRESSES AND DISTANCE				
Name	**Address**	**City/Province**	**Postal Code**	**Kilometers**
Francis Stevens	17820 Attwood Road	Prince George, BC	V2N 653	520
Helene Abrams	269 Acadia Drive, SE	Calgary, AB	T2J 0A6	673
Connie Visocki	39 Blackburn Drive, SW	Edmonton, AB	T6W 1C5	817
Clarence Brewer	157 Caribou Street, E.	Moose Jaw, SK	S6H 0R4	1,266
Christine Osborn	P.O. Box 613	The Pas, MB	R9A 1K7	1,597
Andrew Svenson	14 Island Drive	Flin Flon, MB	R8A 058	1,850
Gary Fitzpatrick	635 Agnes Street	Winnipeg, MB	R3E 1X8	1,869
Lazo Aida	P.O. Box 1016	Churchill, MB	R0B 0E0	2,152
Note: Distance is measured in kilometers from Vancouver.				

**Table
86-44**

Boxed Table

Open the file for Table 86-43 and make the following changes:

1. Rearrange the entries in Column A so that the last name is given first, followed by a comma, followed by the first name.

2. Rearrange the entries in the table by placing the last names of the customers in alphabetic order.

International Formatting (Mexico)

Goals

- Improve speed and accuracy
- Refine language arts skills in the use of abbreviations
- Format international documents

A. Type 2 times.

A. WARMUP

```
1      On 4/25/05 Jamie exercised by "power walking" on the    11
2  athletic tracks. She also zipped along the city's favorite  23
3  route (Polk Street & Bell Avenue). It was a quick walk!     34
   |  1  |  2  |  3  |  4  |  5  |  6  |  7  |  8  |  9  |  10  |  11  |  12
```

SKILLBUILDING

B. PROGRESSIVE PRACTICE: ALPHABET

If you are not using the GDP software, turn to page SB-7 and follow the directions for this activity.

C. Type the paragraph 2 times, concentrating on each letter typed.

C. TECHNIQUE PRACTICE: CONCENTRATION

```
4      El uso de la bicicleta es muy popular en Barranquilla.
5  Cuando el tiempo es bueno a toda la gente joven le gusta ir
6  a pasear en bicicletas. Me gusta ir a montar en bicicleta,
7  especialmente cuando hace sol y el tiempo es agradable.
```

LANGUAGE ARTS

D. Study the rules at the right.

D. ABBREVIATIONS

RULE ▶
abbreviate measure

In technical writing, on forms, and in tables, abbreviate units of measure when they occur frequently. Do not use periods.
14 oz   5 ft 10 in   50 mph   2 yrs 10 mo

RULE ▶
abbreviate lowercase

In most lowercase abbreviations made up of single initials, use a period after each initial but no internal spaces.

a.m.	p.m.	i.e.	e.g.	e.o.m.
Exceptions:	mph	mpg	wpm	

RULE ▶
abbreviate ≡

In most all-capital abbreviations made up of single initials, do not use periods or internal spaces.

OSHA	PBS	NBEA	WWW	VCR	MBA
Exceptions:	U.S.A.	A.A.	B.S.	Ph.D.	P.O.
	B.C.	A.D.			

Edit the sentences to correct any errors in the use of abbreviations.

8 A mixture of 25 lb of cement and 100 lb of gravel was used.
9 The desk height must be reduced from 2 ft. 6 in. to 2 ft 4 in.
10 The 11 a. m. meeting was changed to 1 p. m. because of a
11 conflict.
12 The eom statement was published over the Internet on the W.W.W.
13 She enlisted in the U.S.M.C. after she received her MBA degree.
14 His Ph. D. dissertation deals with the early history of NATO.

FORMATTING

E. INTERNATIONAL URLs

Uniform resource locators (URLs) identify a site on the World Wide Web where specific information can be found. In international URLs, an abbreviation for a country is often included in the URL, as shown in red below.

Country	Uniform Resource Locator (URL)
Canada	http://www.pearlson.animate.chap2.ca
France	http://www.education.grad.up.fr
Germany	http://www.mercedes.de
Japan	http://www.sushi.co.jp
Mexico	http://www.reloj.baja.mx

F. WORD PROCESSING: INSERT SYMBOL

Accents and other marks are used in many languages to indicate how words should be pronounced. Some examples of accents used in Mexico, where Spanish is spoken, are shown below.

Symbol	Spanish Word	English Translation
ñ	Señor, Señorita	Mr., Mrs.
í	el río	river
ó	adiós	good-bye

DOCUMENT PROCESSING

Correspondence 87-79

E-Mail Message

Refer to **Reference Manual**

Refer to page R-5C and R-5D: E-Mail Message.

Today is April 15, your second day, and you will prepare an e-mail message and a business report with a table. Begin with the e-mail. Type the e-mail greeting, `Hi, Mr. Noriega:`, and the body shown below in correct format. Type `Hiroki` as the closing, and type this signature: `Hiroki Kayano | E-Mail: hkayano@ worldtech.com | Phone: +1.702. 555.1839.` Save the e-mail message, but do not send it.

¶ As you know, sales in our international divisions have been accelerating since the advent of our new Jefe automobile. As a result, several new manufacturing plants will open in the next eight years. The first five of these plants will open in France and Germany.

¶ To market our new manufacturing plants and promote the Jefe, our Marketing Division is planning to open new Web sites on the Jefe home page. The following links will be added to advertise our plant expansion:

abbreviate lowercase

- Bordeaux, France: http://www.bordeaux.fr.jefe.new.html
- Toulouse, France: http://www.toulouse.fr.jefe.new.html
- Grenoble, France: http://www.grenoble.fr.jefe.new.html
- Hamburg, Germany: http://www.hamburg.de.jefe.new.html
- Stuttgart, Germany: http://www.stuttgart.de.jefe.new.html

Refer to **Reference Manual**

Refer to page R-12C of the Reference Manual for a review of list formatting.

¶ You will be notified when the Web sites go online. Until then, plan to work with your Marketing Division personnel to implement the marketing plan we discussed at our meeting last month (the Henderson Proposal). When the sites go online, we hope to maximize our exposure on the WWW. If they are as successful as we believe they will be, our promotional campaign may also be implemented at our plants in Piedras Negras, Morelia, and Cancún.

abbreviate ≡

Type the report on A4-size paper.

MEXICO TRAVEL DESTINATIONS
Most Popular Attractions
April 15, 20--

¶ Since the mid-1990s, national parks in Mexico have become popular tourist sites for visitors from the Americas, Europe, and Asia. As a result, an increasing number of requests have been made for travel brochures and maps from our Visitors' Bureau. Therefore, in the next few weeks, we will be publishing several new brochures and maps to accommodate these requests.

BROCHURES

¶ The brochures will include a detailed description of the site, providing information on beginning and ending visitation schedules, highlights of the site, and popular photography locations. Brochures will be prepared on the sites and locations shown in the table below. The fourth column indicates how many years each site has been ranked among the top ten most popular sites in Mexico.

Type the copy at the right in boxed table format, inserting the table into the report.

abbreviate measure

Accent used in Sian Káan

Area	Site	State	Top 10
Northern	Cumbres de Majalca	Chihuahua	2 yrs
Northern	Cumbres de Monterrey	Nuevo Leon	2 yrs
Northern	Sierra del Pinacate	Mexicali	4 yrs
Central	El Tepozteco	Morelos	10 yrs
Central	Iztaccihuatl y Popocatepetl	Morelos	10 yrs
Central	Malinche	Puebla	3 yrs
Southern	Bonampak/Yaxchilan Monuments	Chiapas	7 yrs
Southern	Chichén Itzá	Merida	15 yrs
Southern	Dzibilchaltun	Yucatán	5 yrs
Southern	Sian Káan Biosphere Reserve	Quintana Roo	4 yrs

(Continued on next page)

MAPS

¶ Maps will be supplied for the locations listed above, with detailed insets to guide visitors from the nearest cities to the tourist attractions. Walking trails and resting stations will be highlighted, and approximate walking times will be noted on the maps. Individual maps will be prepared for each area (northern, central, and southern), and a comprehensive map for all three visitor areas will also be available. Please send any advertising pieces you wish to promote to Señor Garcia, Public Relations Director.

ñ used in Señor

International Formatting (France)

Goals

- Type at least 45wpm/5′/5e
- Format international documents

A. Type 2 times.

A. WARMUP

```
1      On May 4, 2004, Kaye gave a dazzling talk on graphics;   11
2  it was quite fantastic! She is also writing an excellent    23
3  book about graphics with text. It might sell for $23.85.    34
   |  1  |  2  |  3  |  4  |  5  |  6  |  7  |  8  |  9  |  10  |  11  |  12
```

SKILLBUILDING

B. DIAGNOSTIC PRACTICE: SYMBOLS AND PUNCTUATION

If you are not using the GDP software, turn to page SB-2 and follow the directions for this activity.

C. PACED PRACTICE

If you are not using the GDP software, turn to page SB-14 and follow the directions for this activity.

Keyboarding Connection

Protecting Your Files With Antivirus Programs

A virus is a computer program intentionally written to contaminate your computer system. Viruses can enter your system from files downloaded from the Internet or can be acquired from infected files sent to you via e-mail, diskette, or other storage media.

You can protect your computer by purchasing an antivirus program. These programs periodically scan your computer system for viruses. They also scan files that you bring into the system. Some antivirus manufacturers allow you to download a trial copy of their software from their Web site. You can try the software for a few days before you decide if you want to buy it.

YOUR TURN If you want to visit antivirus sites to find out what they have to offer, search for *antivirus software* on your search engine.

D. Take two 5-minute timed writings. Review your speed and errors.

Goal: At least 45wpm/5'/5e

D. 5-MINUTE TIMED WRITING

4	Technology surrounds us. It is everywhere you look.	11
5	People use cellular phones to speak to one another just	22
6	about anywhere. They carry their pagers so that they can be	34
7	reached at any time. Everyone, from the busy executive to	45
8	the college student, is now quite used to being available	57
9	at all hours of the day or night.	64
10	In recent years, busy travelers have become used to	74
11	using their laptops everywhere. They use computer ports in	86
12	airports, hotel rooms and lobbies, and even taxis. This	97
13	technology allows the busy traveler to have access to the	109
14	Internet while on the go. Using the laptop, the user can	120
15	access the latest weather report, sports scores, and news,	132
16	almost as soon as they happen.	138
17	Using the latest technology, you can keep up with your	150
18	work and maintain contact with your office. You can even	161
19	access your bank accounts and pay bills while waiting in	172
20	traffic. Also, if you are in a new place, you can find a	184
21	restaurant or call for directions as needed. The technology	196
22	options that have become available to almost everyone are	207
23	quite amazing. We are living in a small world that seems to	219
24	be getting smaller each day.	225

| 1 | 2 | 3 | 4 | 5 | 6 | 7 | 8 | 9 | 10 | 11 | 12 |

FORMATTING

E. DOT-STYLE TELEPHONE NUMBERS

In the United States, hyphens are used in telephone numbers. A hyphen is used after the 3-digit area code and after the first 3 digits of the telephone number; for example, 701-555-1234. Another format, used in many countries, is to replace the hyphens with periods; for example, 701.555.4832 or 818.555.3424.

F. INTERNATIONAL TELEPHONE ACCESS CODES

Special access codes are needed to make a phone call from one country to another. To make an international call, dial the IDD (International Direct Dialing) code first. Then dial the country code for the country you are calling, next the area code (if any), and finally the phone number. The IDD code in many countries changes periodically.

The United States and Canada have the same IDD (011) and country code (1). When you provide a United States (or Canadian) telephone number in a document being sent to an international address, use a plus sign (+) in front of the area code, instead of the IDD code, followed by 1 (the country code for the United States). For example, if you are writing a letter to an international address and you are giving your own phone number in Los Angeles, you would express your number as +1.323.555.8923. Some of the more common access codes are listed below.

| Country | From U.S. to Foreign Country | | From Foreign Country to U.S. | |
	IDD Code	Country Code	IDD Code	Country Code
Canada	011	1	011	1
France	011	33	00	1
Germany	011	49	00	1
Italy	011	39	00	1
Japan	011	81	001	1
Mexico	011	52	98	1
Taiwan	011	886	002	1
United Kingdom	011	44	00	1
Note: The United States and Canada have the same IDD (011) and country code (1).				

DOCUMENT PROCESSING

Today is April 16, your third day, and you will prepare a letter, a table, and an e-mail message. Begin with the letter.

Correspondence 88-80

Business Letter in Block Style

Type the letter on A4-size paper.

16 April 20-- | Mr. Henry R. Defforey | Human Resources Director | Gemey Techtronics | Avenue Raymond Poincore | 75116 Paris | FRANCE | Dear Mr. Defforey:

¶ I am pleased that we will be involved in an employee exchange this coming year. As we discussed earlier, the exchange of our 26 production employees will benefit both companies.

¶ We plan to rotate all 26 employees through the various units of our production process, starting from the raw materials division and continuing right on through our shipping operations. I have enclosed a projected rotation plan for you to review. Included in the plan are all the employee rotations we discussed at our last meeting. Please review the plan and e-mail me if there are any changes you wish to make. You can e-mail me at ssouthern@worldtech.com, or, if you wish to speak to me directly, you can call +1.214.555.9090.

(Continued on next page)

¶ I look forward to working with you this coming year. As soon as we have agreed on the rotation plan, we can make copies for all affected employees. I know that everyone from our end is eagerly anticipating this collaborative effort.

Sincerely, | Sheila T. Southern | Human Resources Manager | hk | Enclosure | c: Ted Lambeer, Shirley Gouet

Table 88-45 ▶

Boxed Table

Type the table on A4-size paper.

Apply 20 percent shading to the column headings.

ROTATION PLAN Tech-Group Inc. and Gemey Techtronics		
Department	**Rotation Start Date**	**Rotation End Date**
Raw Materials	3 July 20--	August 11 20--
Board assembly	14 August 20--	22 September 20--
Drive and Assembly	25 Sept. 20--	3 November 20--
Power Unit	6 November 20--	15 December 20--
Testing & Evaluation	18 December 20--	2 Feburary 20--

Correspondence 88-81 ▶

E-Mail Message

Type the e-mail greeting, Hi, Mr. Deforey:, and the body shown below in correct format. Type Hiroki as the closing, and type this signature: Hiroki Kayano |

E-Mail: hkayano@worldtech.com | Phone: +1.702.555.1839. Save the e-mail message, but do not send it.

¶ I am sending you this e-mail to alert you to a change we must make in the rotation plan I sent you last week. We will have to refit several of our board assembly production unit relay systems during the week of 14 August through 18 August. To avoid significantly altering the remaining rotation plan, I would like to suggest that we use one-half of the drive assembly rotation period to complete the board assembly rotation. ¶ Please respond to my e-mail as soon as possible so that we can make whatever changes are necessary.

International Formatting (Germany)

Goals

- Improve speed and accuracy
- Refine language arts skills in spelling
- Format international documents

A. Type 2 times.

A. WARMUP

```
 1      Did Jacqueline get 62% of the vote in the election on    11
 2   9/04/00? I think Buzz* (*Kelly) voted for her at 7:35 p.m.   23
 3   that evening, and she was really excited when Jackie won.    34
     | 1 | 2 | 3 | 4 | 5 | 6 | 7 | 8 | 9 | 10 | 11 | 12
```

SKILLBUILDING

B. MAP

Follow the GDP software directions for this exercise in improving keystroking accuracy.

C. Take a 1-minute timed writing on the first paragraph to establish your base speed. Then take four 1-minute timed writings on the remaining paragraphs. As soon as you equal or exceed your base speed on one paragraph, advance to the next, more difficult paragraph.

C. SUSTAINED PRACTICE: PUNCTUATION

```
 4      One of the strengths you must have if you are going to   11
 5   be a success in business is good writing skills. You must    23
 6   practice your writing skills every day if you want them to   35
 7   improve. Perfection of writing skills takes much practice.   46

 8      You must always strive to write clearly, concisely,      11
 9   and accurately. Remember always that your writing can be     22
10   examined by more people than just the one to whom you have   34
11   written. It's often looked at by other readers as well.      45

12      You want to be sure that your letters always convey a    11
13   positive, helpful attitude. Don't forget, you represent      22
14   more than yourself when you write--you also represent your   34
15   company! This is an important, useful rule to remember.      45

16      Try to stay away from negative words like "can't" or     11
17   "won't." Readers also do not like phrases such as "because   23
18   of company policies" or "due to unforeseen circumstances."   34
19   Using these words and phrases never helps resolve problems.  46
     | 1 | 2 | 3 | 4 | 5 | 6 | 7 | 8 | 9 | 10 | 11 | 12
```

D. Type this list of frequently misspelled words, paying special attention to any spelling problems in each word.

D. SPELLING

20 means valve entry patient officer similar expenses industry
21 quality judgment academic provisions previously cooperation
22 foreign closing indicated secretary especially construction
23 monitoring assessment continuing registration manufacturing
24 products policies capacity presently accordance implemented

Edit the sentences to correct any misspellings.

25 Every company offiser will have simaler expenses next week.
26 In my judgement, we must insist on co-operation from all.
27 My secretery said that she traveled to a foriegn country.
28 We must continue monitering the progress for assesment.
29 The new policeis must be implimented for all products.

FORMATTING

E. METRIC UNITS OF MEASUREMENT

The metric system of measurement was devised in 1670. It is based on units of 10 and is used by almost every nation in the world. The five common measurements in the metric system are length, area, volume, capacity, and weight and mass. The table below gives the basic units of measure used in the metric and U.S. systems.

Quantity	Metric Units of Measure	U.S. Units of Measure
Length	millimeter, centimeter, meter, kilometer	inch, foot, yard, mile
Area	square centimeter, square meter, hectare	square inch, square foot, square yard
Volume	cubic centimeter, cubic decimeter, cubic meter, liter, hectoliter	cubic inch, cubic foot, fluid ounce, pint, gallon
Weight	milligram, gram, kilogram, tonne	ounce, pound, ton

DOCUMENT PROCESSING

Correspondence 89-82

E-Mail Message

Highlighted words are spelling words from the language arts activities.

Today is April 17, your fourth day, and you will prepare an e-mail message, a business letter, and a multipage business report with tables. Begin with the e-mail. Type the e-mail greeting, Hi, Mr. Neuberger:, and the body shown below in correct for-mat. Type Hiroki as the closing, and type this signature: Hiroki Kayano | E-Mail: hkayano@worldtech.com | Phone: +1.702.555.1839. Save the e-mail message, but do not send it.

¶ The total conversion of our manufacturing plant in Wiesbaden to a metric system, which was discussed previously, is six months away. Ms. Schneider has asked for your continuing support and cooperation as you prepare employees who are presently transferring to the Wiesbaden plant in accordance with the provisions of our policies. Please send me the summary report used when you were monitoring the conversion last year.

¶ The metric system will be quite foreign to many employees, especially the younger ones, who were not involved in the planning stages. The summary report will give them a head start on metrication as indicated in the assessment.

¶ Call Ms. Schneider Thursday morning (+1.702.555.2354) to discuss the Frankfurt plant closing. Plant operations will be transferred to Wiesbaden in July. She has asked that you use your judgment to monitor the quality of the operation closely until the transfer has been fully implemented.

Correspondence 89-83

Business Letter in Block Style

Type the letter on A4-size paper.

17 April 20-- | Ms. Geraldine Sommer | Marketing Department | Deutsch Lebensmittel, Inc. | Mannesmannufer 2 | D-40213 Dusseldorf | GERMANY | Dear Ms. Sommer:

¶ Amalia Rios has asked that I send a copy of the summary report on metrics that we completed last year. As you recall, I sent you that report previously to share with the new employees at our Stuttgart plant.

¶ If you wish, you can e-mail me the copy that accompanied the report, and my secretary will distribute it as needed.

Sincerely, | Klaus Neuberger | Human Resources Manager | hk

Type the report on
A4-size paper.

Insert clip art that is
related to measurements
and similar to this example.
Set the clip art at a size
of about 1-inch square,
and place it at the right
margin even with the first
line of the Language
paragraph.

(!) Insert 1 blank line
between the two
tables.

METRIC SUMMARY REPORT
April 17, 20--

¶ The metric system was devised by Gabriel Mouton, a French man, in 1607. It is a system based on units of 10 and is considered by ~~some~~ many to be more accurate and easier to use than the imperial system of measure used in the United States. When it was first defined, a meter was considered to be 1/10,000,000 of the distance from the Pole to the Equator.

¶ The most common metric measurements are for length, area, volume, capacity, and weight and mass. For our wiesbaden plant, the most crucial measurements for new employees from the U.S. will be volume and weight. Comparisons between these two measures appear in Table 1 (comparing volume measures) and Table 2 (comparing weight measures).

Table 1. METRIC/U.S. COMPARISONS FOR VOLUME		
Metric Unit	**Metric Example**	**U.S. Equivalent**
Cubic centimeter	1 cubic centimeter	0.061 cubic inch
Cubic decimeter	1,000 cubic centimeters	0.053 cubic ft
Cubic meter	1,000 cubic decimeters	1.31 cubic yards
Liter	1 cubic decimeter	1.76 pints
Hectoliter	100 Liters	21.99 ~~gal~~ gallons

Table 2. METRIC/U.S. COMPARISONS FOR WEIGHT		
Metric Unit	**Metric Example**	**U.S. Equivalent**
Miligram	1 milligram	0.015 grain
gram	1,000 milligrams	0.035 ounce
Kilogram	1,000 grams	2.205 ~~lbs~~ pounds
Tonne	1,000 kilograms	0.984 ton

(Continued on next page)

Reference Manual

Refer to page R-12C of the Reference Manual for a review of list formatting.

The tilde (~) is usually found next to the 1 on the top row of the keyboard.

¶ Employees will quickly adapt to the metric system when they use it daily. *on a basis* Although we encourage all employees to make calculations in the metric system, it may be helpful for the first few days if they are aware of the conversion factors involved in comparing the 2 measurement systems. The following conversions may therefore be helpful to them:

- Multiply inches by 2.45 to get centimeters
- Multiply feet by 0.305 to get meters
- Multiply miles by 1.6 to get kilometers
- Divide lbs. by 2.2 to get kilograms
- Multiply ounces by 28 to get grams
- Multiply fluid ounces by 30 to get milliliters
- Multiply gallons by 3.8 to get liters

¶ More detailed conversions and metric information can be obtained by visiting the web site for the U.S. metric association at http://lamar.colostate.edu/~hillger/.

International Formatting (Japan)

Goals
- Type at least 45wpm/5′/5e
- Format international documents

A. Type 2 times.

A. WARMUP

```
1        James used a dozen of Harold's power trucks to quickly   11
2   move over 17 large boxes on 11/30/00. I think these trucks    23
3   (just the diesels) may need maintenance work on 3/24/01.      34
    |  1  |  2  |  3  |  4  |  5  |  6  |  7  |  8  |  9  |  10  |  11  |  12
```

SKILLBUILDING

PPP PRETEST → PRACTICE → POSTTEST

PRETEST
Take a 1-minute timed writing. Review your speed and errors.

B. PRETEST: Close Reaches

```
4        Uncle Bert chased a fast, weary fox into the weeds of   11
5   the swamp. He hoped to grab the old gray fox under the        22
6   bridge with a rope as he darted swiftly from his cold lair.   34
    |  1  |  2  |  3  |  4  |  5  |  6  |  7  |  8  |  9  |  10  |  11  |  12
```

PRACTICE
Speed Emphasis:
If you made no more than 1 error on the Pretest, type each *individual* line 2 times.
Accuracy Emphasis:
If you made 2 or more errors, type each *group* of lines (as though it were a paragraph) 2 times.

C. PRACTICE: Adjacent Keys

```
7   as asked asset based basis class least visas ease fast mass
8   op opera roped topaz adopt scope troop shops open hope drop
9   we weary wedge weigh towed jewel fewer dwell wear weed week
```

D. PRACTICE: Consecutive Fingers

```
10  sw swamp swift swoop sweet swear swank swirl swap sway swim
11  un uncle under undue unfit bunch begun funny unit aunt junk
12  gr grade grace angry agree group gross gripe grow gram grab
```

POSTTEST
Repeat the Pretest timed writing and compare performance.

E. POSTTEST: Close Reaches

F. Take two 5-minute timed writings. Review your speed and errors.

Goal: At least 45wpm/5'/5e

F.   5-MINUTE TIMED WRITING

```
13      Anyone with a supervisory position will occasionally    11
14  have to deal with a problem employee. If you learn to deal  23
15  with this type of worker in a good way, it will benefit     34
16  everyone within the organization. As a manager, you should  46
17  address the problem as soon as you are made aware of it.     57
18  However, if you are extremely upset, it may be best to wait  69
19  until you calm down and have time to plan what you will      80
20  say. Avoid using an approach based on reaction, which can    86
21  often be ineffective and too emotional. Speaking up too      92
22  quickly might bring you unwanted results.                    103
23      When you talk to an employee, be sure you get to the     111
24  real issue. Present the facts and tell the employee exactly  122
25  what he or she is doing wrong on the job. Do not express     134
26  your own personal opinion. You need to present a positive    146
27  and mutually fair solution to the employee in question to    157
28  solve a problem. At the end of the meeting, ask the person   169
29  to explain his or her problem to you and the changes that    181
30  are necessary. By following this procedure, you know that    192
31  everyone understands what is happening. Set up a time to     204
32  meet in a few days to follow up with this person.            215
                                                                 225
```

| 1 | 2 | 3 | 4 | 5 | 6 | 7 | 8 | 9 | 10 | 11 | 12 |

DOCUMENT PROCESSING

Correspondence ▶ 90-84

Business Letter in Block Style

Type the letter on A4-size paper.

Today is April 18, your fifth day, and you will prepare several letters, an e-mail message, and a table. Begin with the letter.

18 April 20-- | Mr. Kouji Tachikawa | Chief Technology Officer | Tadashi Corporation | 7-1, Shiba 5-chome | Minato-ku, Tokyo 108-8001 | JAPAN | Dear Mr. Tachikawa:

¶ It is a distinct pleasure to learn that we will be working together to develop the training manual to be used in our joint venture. Your company has long been known for its excellence in developing instructional materials, and Carroll Technology is pleased to play a collaborative part with you in this venture.

¶ Our development teams have been working with their counterparts in Tadashi over the past several weeks. Your suggestion that we pool our personnel resources was indeed an excellent one that will give us a head start in the development stage.

(Continued on next page)

¶ If I may make one suggestion, I believe it would be helpful for the personnel in our mailing and shipping department to have a better understanding of the labeling procedures used in Japan for distributing the training manuals. Could you please send me some information that might be helpful in this regard? I will do the same for you by sending you the labeling procedures used at Carroll Technology.

Sincerely | Sharla D. Enterline | Project Coordinator | hk | c: Roberta Akiyama, Samuel Hiroshi, Charlene Brandenburger

Correspondence 90-85

E-Mail Message

Type the e-mail greeting, Hi, Ms. Enterline:, and the body shown below in correct format. Type Hiroki as the closing, and type this signature: Hiroki Kayano |

E-mail: hkayano@worldtech.com | Phone: +1.702.555.1839. Save the e-mail message, but do not send it.

¶ It is my pleasure to inform you that Samuel Hiroshi will be forwarding to your office a summary of the package labeling procedures used at Tadashi Inc. Employees from many different foreign countries have used these procedures to help them understand mailing requirements in Japan.

¶ After receiving the procedures, feel free to e-mail Mr. Hiroshi with any questions you may have. You can reach him at shiroshi@tadashi.jp.com. If you prefer, you can call Mr. Hiroshi at +81.3.34543113.

Correspondence 90-86

Business Letter in Block Style

Type the letter on A4-size paper.

18 April 20-- | Ms. Sharla D. Enterline | Project Coordinator | Carroll Technology | 8723 Hill Avenue | Bowling Green, KY 42823 | Dear Ms. Enterline:

¶ The following information is being sent to assist you with Japanese mailing rules. As a service to your employees, I am providing the following summary of these rules.

¶ A Japanese mailing address consists ~~mainly~~ of the name, street address, town, city, prefecture, postal code, and country. The illustration below shows how an address should appear on an envelope going to Japan.

(Continued on next page)

346 UNIT 18 | Lesson 90

Address Items	Address Example
Name ~~St.~~ *Street* Address, Town (①st address) City, Prefecture (②d address), ⌃*Postal* Code JAPAN	Mr. Yoshifumi Uda 1-17, Akai-cho Minato-ku, Tokyo 108-8005 JAPAN

¶ Please ~~E~~-mail me if you have questions about mailing rules in ~~japan~~. You can reach me at <shiroshi@tadashi.jp.com>.

Very sincerely, | S. Hiroshi | Shipping (Dept.) | hk | c: K. Tachikawa

Table
90-46
Boxed Table

Your line endings will be different from those shown here.

JAPANESE POSTAL CODE REGULATIONS Prepared by Hiroki Kayano	
Postal Code Rule	**Example**
The first line of a Japanese address is used for the addressee's name.	Mr. Takashi Imaizumi Mr. Kazuki Terada
The second line provides a street name or building number.	Kifune 3-402 (this represents building 402 on the 3rd street within the Kifune neighborhood)
The third line gives the city, prefecture (a district within the city), and postal code.	Meito-ku, Nagoya 112-3844 Minato-ku, Tokyo 105-8436
The fourth line gives the name of the country to which the document or package is being mailed.	JAPAN

Correspondence
90-87
Business Letter
in Block Style

Type the letter on A4-size paper.

Progress and Proofreading Check ✔

Documents designated as Proofreading Checks serve as a check of your proofreading skill. Your goal is to have zero typographical errors when the GDP software first scores the document.

18 April 20-- | Mr. Fujio Okuda | Sales Manager | Naruto Publishing Company | 7-35, Kitashinagawa 6-chome | Shinagawa-ku, Tokyo 141-0001 | JAPAN | Dear Mr. Okuda:

¶ We are pleased to have this opportunity for two of our computer textbooks to be translated into Japanese and for you to do the same for two of your textbooks in the computer area. As we agreed at our meeting in Takasaki last week, sales for both of our book companies should improve substantially with these translations.

¶ I am enclosing with this letter the first three units of *Computer Essentials* so that your editors can begin the translation process. We will do the same here at Globe Publishing when your first three units from *Global Computers* arrive in Chicago.

¶ Should your editorial staff have any questions during the translation, they can e-mail me at shaddock@worldtech.com or call me at +1.402.555.3848.

Sincerely, | Shannon Haddock | Editorial Director | hk | Enclosure

Unit 19

Medical Office Documents

LESSON 91
Medical Office Documents

LESSON 94
Medical Office Documents

LESSON 92
Medical Office Documents

LESSON 95
Medical Office Documents

LESSON 93
Medical Office Documents

RECOVERING FROM KNEE SURGERY

Dr. Alec Pera, M.D.

November 5, 20--

Specific procedures should be followed by patients who are recovering from knee surgery. Depending on the particular surgery that ... patients with knee replacements vary greatly. Hea... only a few therapy sessions to recover from their ... with no family or friends to help them at home ma... to aid their mobility. Some patients may benefit f... facility. To enhance the rate of recovery, patients ... needs that may require attention before their oper...

To promote full recovery, Lakewood Hospital has ... physical and occupational therapy for patients' use... Service (PRTS) and Lakewood Hospital have coll... sequence of procedures to follow.

Prior to your surgery, we recommend that you:

1. Determine any special equipment that will be ...

2. Learn correct techniques for performing day-to... out of bed, driving your automobile, taking sho... up and down stairs.

3. Learn what exercises will help facilitate your r...

After surgery, patients must participate in physica...

- Extend their knee straight or bend it past 90 de...

- Place weight on their knee to ensure that they ... their weight.

- Use the knee without discomfort (this may tak...

MEMO TO: Dr. Alec Pera

FROM: Dr. Charlene T. Gutierrez, Director of Plastic Surgery

DATE: November 5, 20--

SUBJECT: Mr. Owensby's Surgery

On Friday I visited with Mr. Bryan Owensby to discuss his options relative to the muscle transfer we plan to complete following radiation treatment. Mr. Owensby is a 53-year-old male who recently had multiple lesions excised.

Mr. Owensby is aware that our goal is to provide healthy tissue that could tolerate the radiation treatment he would need to destroy the malignant cells on his upper thigh. At this time, we plan to complete a skin graft from the contralateral thigh to provide the healthy tissue for radiation treatment. I believe this will give Mr. Owensby the best ...

... ed, and this may be an option if the contralateral ... ... derstands the risks and complications of either ... ... through our offices. Thank you for this opportunity ...

... ethna, Dr. Monica Stevens

**DESCRIPTIONS AND TREATMENTS
OF ADULT BRAIN TUMORS**
November 4, 20--

Type of Tumor	Description/Treatment
Astrocytomas	Tumors that start in brain cells. Treatment includes surgery, chemotherapy, and radiation.
Brain Stem Gliomas	Tumors located in the bottom part of the brain, that connects to the spinal cord. Treatment includes radiation and biological therapy.
Cerebellar Astrocytomas	Tumors that occur in the area of the brain called the cerebellum. Treatment is similar to that for Astrocytomas.
Craniopharyngiomas	Tumors that occur near the pituitary gland. Treatment includes surgery and radiation.
Gliomas	The general name for tumors that come from the supportive tissue of the brain; for example, astrocytoma or oligodendroglioma. They may be benign or malignant.
Oligodendroglial	Tumors that begin in brain cells that provide support and nourishment for the cells that transmit nerve impulses. Treatment includes surgery, chemotherapy, and radiation.

Medical Office Documents

Goals

- Improve speed and accuracy
- Refine language arts skills in punctuation
- Format medical office documents

A. Type 2 times.

A. WARMUP

```
1       The taxes* were quickly adjusted upward by 20 percent    11
2   because of the improvements to her house (built in 1901).    23
3   A proposed law might not penalize good homeowners like her.  34
    |  1  |  2  |  3  |  4  |  5  |  6  |  7  |  8  |  9  |  10  |  11  |  12
```

SKILLBUILDING

B. MAP

Follow the GDP software directions for this exercise in improving keystroking accuracy.

C. Take a 1-minute timed writing on the first paragraph to establish your base speed. Then take four 1-minute timed writings on the remaining paragraphs. As soon as you equal or exceed your base speed on one paragraph, advance to the next, more difficult paragraph.

C. SUSTAINED PRACTICE: ALTERNATE-HAND WORDS

```
4        A downturn in world fuel prices signals a lower profit   11
5   for giant oil firms. In fact, most downtown firms might       22
6   see the usual sign of tight credit and other problems. The    34
7   city must get down to business and make plans in the fall.    46

8        The hungry turkeys ate eight bushels of corn that were   11
9   given to them by our next-door neighbors. They also drank     22
10  the eight bowls of water that were left in the yard. All in   34
11  all, the birds caused quite a bit of chaos early that day.    46

12       A debate on what to do about that extra acreage in the   11
13  desert dragged on for four hours. One problem is what the     23
14  effect may be of moving the ancient ruins to a much safer     34
15  place. City officials must always protect our environment.    46

16       Molly was dressed in a plain pink dress at the annual    11
17  meeting that was taking place at the hotel in Tempe later     23
18  that last week in September. The agenda included four very    34
19  controversial topics that have often generated much debate.  46
    |  1  |  2  |  3  |  4  |  5  |  6  |  7  |  8  |  9  |  10  |  11  |  12
```

D. Study the rules at the right.

D. PUNCTUATION

RULE ▶

: explanatory material

Use a colon to introduce explanatory material that follows an independent clause.

The computer satisfies three criteria: speed, cost, and power.
But: The computer satisfies the three criteria of speed, cost, and power.
Remember this: only one coupon is allowed per customer.

Note: An independent clause can stand alone as a complete sentence. Do not capitalize the word following the colon.

RULE ▶

. polite request

Use a period to end a sentence that is a polite request.

Will you please call me if I can be of further assistance.

Note: Consider a sentence a polite request if you expect the reader to respond by doing as you ask rather than by giving a yes-or-no answer.

Edit the sentences to correct any errors in punctuation.

20 We need the following items, pens, pencils, and paper.
21 May I suggest that you send the report by Tuesday?
22 These are some of your colleagues: Bill, Mary, and Ann.
23 Would you please pay my bills when I am on vacation?
24 Our flag is these three colors; red, white, and blue.
25 Would you please start my car to warm it up for me.

DOCUMENT PROCESSING

Situation: You work for Lakewood Hospital in Springfield, Oregon. For the purposes of this simulation, your name will be Lucille R. Medford. Your e-mail address is lmedford@lakewood.com.

For the next five days, you will prepare documents for several units within the hospital—Admissions, Billing, Dermatology, Oncology, and Surgery. You will also format various documents including correspondence and medical reports for these units.

Today is November 1. You will spend your first day working in the Admissions Office preparing the documents that appear in your in-basket for today. Proofread your work carefully and check for spelling, punctuation, grammar, and formatting errors so that your documents are mailable.

**Correspondence ▶
91-88**

Business Letter in Block Style

: explanatory material

November 1, 20-- | Ms. Nancy J. Dodson | 3727 Harris Street | Eugene, OR 97405-4246 | Dear Ms. Dodson:

¶ Thank you for contacting us and considering us as your primary care provider. We are confident that you will be pleased with our services and our patient care, and we look forward to many years of serving your health needs.

¶ Now that you have made your final selection, we would like you to complete the enclosed Patient Information Form and send it back to us at your earliest convenience. As you can see, the form asks mostly for personal information so that we can contact you or your employer if necessary. In addition, the form requests the following information: the name, address, and telephone number of your insurance company and your insurance policy number.

(Continued on next page)

¶ Again, welcome to Lakewood Hospital! If there is any additional information we can provide about our services, do not hesitate to call us at 555-2300 or e-mail me at lmedford@lakewood.com.

Sincerely, | Lucille R. Medford | Office Manager | ap | Enclosure

Table 91-47

Table

Create a patient information form using the illustration below and these steps:

1. Insert a table with 1 column and 15 rows.
2. Split cells as shown to provide room for individual entries.
3. Type the information as shown.
4. Bold the information in Rows 1, 7, and 11.
5. Insert blank lines above and below the centered section headings, and type the headings in 12-point Arial.
6. Insert 5 spaces between the parentheses in Rows 4 and 9.
7. Insert 1 blank line above the information in Rows 2 to 6, 8 to 10, and 12 to 15.
8. Apply 10 percent shading to Rows 1, 7, 11, and 15.

Arial 12 pt. ↓1X **PATIENT INFORMATION** ↓1X

↓1X Date:

Name: (last, first)	Birth Date:

Street Address:	Phone: ( )

City:	State:	ZIP:

E-Mail

EMPLOYER INFORMATION

Employer:

Street Address:	Phone: ( )

City:	State:	ZIP:

INSURANCE INFORMATION

Name of Company:

Address:

Phone:	Policy Number:

Signature:	Date:

:explanatory material

.polite request

MEMO TO: Dr. Abraham Kramer
FROM: Paula Campbell
DATE: November 1, 20--
SUBJECT: Radiology Lab Closing

¶ Next week the Radiology Lab in Building D will be closed for repairs. I realize that this is the week you were going to take a group of interns to see our new equipment.

¶ I have arranged to have the Radiology Lab in Building C open for you to use so that you do not have to postpone the meeting with the interns. I am sending over a passkey for the lab. The passkey will open three doors: main entry, hall entry, lab door.

¶ Would you please give me a call on Ext. 75 if this lab substitution is not satisfactory with you.

ap

c: Dr. Arnold, Dr. Kazinofski

Medical Office Documents

Goals

- Type at least 46wpm/5'/5e
- Format medical office documents

A. Type 2 times.

A. WARMUP

```
1      Missy examined these items: the #4261 oil painting, a     11
2   Bowes & Elkjer porcelain vase, and the 86-piece collection   23
3   of glazed antique pitchers. There were 337 people present.   34
    | 1 | 2 | 3 | 4 | 5 | 6 | 7 | 8 | 9 | 10 | 11 | 12
```

SKILLBUILDING

B. Take three 12-second timed writings on each line. The scale below the last line shows your wpm speed for a 12-second timed writing.

B. 12-SECOND SPEED SPRINTS

```
4   Their home is on a lake that is right south of the prairie.
5   They have a boat and motor and spend a lot of time fishing.
6   Kay caught so many fish that she gave some to the old lady.
7   She was so pleased that a young girl would do this for her.
    | | | | 5 | | | 10 | | | 15 | | | 20 | | | 25 | | | 30 | | | 35 | | | 40 | | | 45 | | | 50 | | | 55 | | | 60
```

C. PROGRESSIVE PRACTICE: ALPHABET

If you are not using the GDP software, turn to page SB-7 and follow the directions for this activity.

Strategies for Career Success

Business Communication

There are five components to the communication process, whether written or oral.

The sender is the person who initiates the communication process. The message is the information that needs to be communicated (for example, "There will be a meeting at . . ."). The channel is the method for transmitting the message (for example, e-mail, letter, memo, orally). The audience is the person(s) who receives the message. Feedback is the response given to the sender by the audience that enables the sender to determine if the message was received as intended.

The most effective communication within companies must flow not only downward but also upward.

YOUR TURN Suppose you send a memo to 20 people in your department announcing a meeting to discuss your company's new policy on flextime. Who is the sender? What is the message? What is the channel you use to transmit the message? Who is the audience? What is the ultimate feedback?

D. Take two 5-minute timed writings. Review your speed and errors.

Goal: At least 46wpm/5'/5e

D. 5-MINUTE TIMED WRITING

8	The first impression you make on a job interview will	11
9	be a lasting one, and you will want it to be favorable. A	23
10	safe choice is to dress conservatively. If you have time,	34
11	find out what people who are currently employed at this	45
12	company wear to work. You can acquire this information by	57
13	simply calling the human resources office. Or, you could	68
14	observe what the current employees are wearing when you	80
15	pick up a job application from a company.	88
16	As you plan the details of your appearance before your	99
17	job interview, be cognizant of all the details. You will	111
18	want to present a neat and clean appearance. Your clothing	122
19	should be clean and very neatly pressed. Your hair and your	134
20	nails should be neatly groomed, and your shoes should be	146
21	clean and polished. You should use only a small amount of	157
22	perfume or cologne and wear only basic jewelry. Plan to	169
23	arrive for the appointment in time to make a final check of	181
24	your appearance before the interview.	188
25	Your appearance may not be the sole factor that will	199
26	secure the job, but it will help you make a positive first	211
27	impression. Remember to dress for the position you would	222
28	like rather than the position you have.	230

| 1 | 2 | 3 | 4 | 5 | 6 | 7 | 8 | 9 | 10 | 11 | 12

DOCUMENT PROCESSING

This is November 2, the second day of your assignment at Lakewood Hospital. Today you are assigned to the Billing Office, where you will complete documents related to the activities in that office. Your first assignment is to prepare a report describing the billing process at Lakewood Hospital.

LAKEWOOD BILLING PROCESS

November 2, 20--

¶ The billing process at Lakewood Hospital will be undergoing review soon. This report will explain how fees are determined, how transactions are recorded, how payments are made, and how overdue accounts are collected.

Determining Fees

¶ Fees that a physician charges for services should be fair both to the patients that are under his or her care and to the medical profession. A doctors' fees should be based on the following criteria:

(Continued on next page)

Refer to **Reference Manual**

Refer to page R-12C of the Reference Manual for a review of list formatting.

- the amount of time involved in providing ~~the~~ service
- the level of skill required in providing the service
- the degree of expertise required to interpret the results of the service provided

¶ Fees should be identified in a fee schedule that lists procedures performed and the charges assessed for those procedures. The fee schedule should be made available to patients if it's requested. If patients inquire ~~as to~~ about the amount of the fee, an estimate should be given to the patient. In all instances, this estimate should be made available to the patient before treatment begins.

RECORDING TRANSACTIONS

¶ A record of all patient visits must be maintained. A charge slip should be used to record all procedures. The charge slip includes information such as a checklist of all procedures; a checklist of all diagnoses; space for additional information; and an area for all previous charges, payments, and balances. As the doctor performs procedures, annotations and changes are made to the charge slip so that it is ~~always~~ kept current. The charge slip should be attached to the patient's chart. When all procedures have been completed, a copy of the charge slip is sent to the patient to indicate the charges incurred during the patient's visit.

MAKING PAYMENT ARRANGEMENTS

¶ A patient's bill can be paid by one of the following methods:

- A patient can pay the bill by cash or check at the conclusion of the visit.
- A patient can pay fixed amounts of the bill at ~~any~~ designated times, weekly or monthly.
- A bill (statement) can be sent to the patient at the conclusion of the visit.
- A bill can be sent to the Health Insurance Carrier.

COLLECTING OVERDUE ACCOUNTS

¶ There are a number of reasons why a patient might not pay a bill. Whatever the reason, however, steps must be taken to collect delinquent accounts. Depending on the number of days the account has been overdue, here are some suggestions for steps that can be taken to collect payment:

(Continued on next page)

1. Attach a reminder when the bill is sent if payment is over ~~thirty~~ 30 days overdue (this is the usual grace period given to accounts).

2. If payment is not received after the reminder is sent, it may be necessary to call the patient to request payment.

3. The next step would be to attach a personal note to a statement that is over due, possibly as long as 60 days.

4. Make one further attempt to telephone the patient for payment.

5. Send a collection letter for payment. The letter should be friendly, but firm. Remind the patient that the account is overdue. Offer to assist the patient in making payments on a fixed schedule by establishing a payment plan. Leave your telephone number so the patient can call you if there are any questions that need to be answered regarding the bill.

6. The final alternative in collecting an unpaid bill is to turn over the account to a collection agency or go to court for legal action. This is a costly step for both caregivers and patients, and it should be used only as a last resort.

Table 92-48

Boxed Table

Press the SPACE BAR 10 times between the phone number and the e-mail address.

STATEMENT

WENDY NEWMAN, M.D.
Lakewood Hospital
970 Kruse Way
Springfield, OR 97477

Phone: 541-555-2300   E-Mail: billing@lakewood.com

Patient: Marion W. Fleming
Address: 1654 Franklin Boulevard
City/State/ZIP: Eugene, OR 97403

Date	Description	Charge	Payment	Balance
3/18/06	EKG	185.00	50.00	135.00
3/18/06	Laboratory work	125.00	25.00	100.00
3/19/06	X-ray	85.00	0.00	85.00
3/21/06	Cholesterol check	75.00	25.00	50.00
3/21/06	Laboratory work	80.00	25.00	55.00
Total Due				**425.00**

Medical Office Documents

Goals

- Improve speed and accuracy
- Refine language arts skills in composing
- Format medical office documents

A. Type 2 times.

A. WARMUP

```
1        Did you hear the excellent quartet of junior cadets?     11
2   Everybody in that crowd (estimated at over 500) applauded     23
3   "with gusto." The sizable crowd filled the 3/4-acre park.     35
    | 1 | 2 | 3 | 4 | 5 | 6 | 7 | 8 | 9 | 10 | 11 | 12
```

SKILLBUILDING

PPP PRETEST → PRACTICE → POSTTEST

PRETEST
Take a 1-minute timed writing. Review your speed and errors.

B. PRETEST: Discrimination Practice

```
4        Did the new clerk join the golf team? James indicated    11
5   to me that Patricia invited her prior to last Wednesday. He   23
6   believes she must give you a verbal commitment at once.       34
    | 1 | 2 | 3 | 4 | 5 | 6 | 7 | 8 | 9 | 10 | 11 | 12
```

PRACTICE
Speed Emphasis:
If you made no more than 1 error on the Pretest, type each *individual* line 2 times.
Accuracy Emphasis:
If you made 2 or more errors, type each *group* of lines (as though it were a paragraph) 2 times.

C. PRACTICE: Left Hand

```
7   vbv bevy verb bevel vibes breve viable braves verbal beaver
8   wew went week weans weigh weave wedges thawed weaker beware
9   ded dent need deals moved ceded heeded debate edging define
```

D. PRACTICE: Right Hand

```
10  klk kale look kilts lakes knoll likely kettle kernel lacked
11  uyu buys your gummy dusty young unduly tryout uneasy jaunty
12  oio oils roil toils onion point oriole soiled ration joined
```

POSTTEST
Repeat the Pretest timed writing and compare performance.

E. POSTTEST: Discrimination Practice

F. PROGRESSIVE PRACTICE: NUMBERS

If you are not using the GDP software, turn to page SB-11 and follow the directions for this activity.

G. COMPOSING AN E-MAIL MESSAGE

Compose an e-mail message to your employer, Dr. Natalie Benson nbenson @lakewood.com, informing Dr. Benson of the appointments you have scheduled for Tuesday, April 17, 20--. The first appointment is with James Mitchell, who is coming for his annual physical—make this appointment at 9 a.m. The second appointment is with Karen McDaniels, who is going to have her blood pressure and cholesterol checked. She will see Dr. Benson at 10 a.m. The final appointment is with Mary Ann Bradley, who will see the doctor about flu symptoms. Be sure you use an appropriate greeting, closing, and signature. Save but do not send this e-mail message.

DOCUMENT PROCESSING

Correspondence 93-90

Business Letter in Modified-Block Style

This is November 3, the third day of your assignment. You will work in a specialty area—the Dermatology Unit. Dermatology is a branch of science dealing with the skin and its structure, functions, and diseases.

November 3, 20-- | Dr. Stanley G. Streisand | Professor of Medical Science | Hillside Medical College | 110 Sunset Drive | Eugene, OR 97403-2120 | Dear Dr. Streisand:

¶ Thank you for the invitation to address the students in your medical science class on the topic of dermatology. As you know, this is my specialty; I am particularly interested in the topic of skin rashes and their causes and treatments.

¶ I recognize that your students are beginning medical school students, so my presentation will focus on a very general talk about dermatology. I am enclosing a copy of a paper I presented at the AMA meeting in San Francisco last week that I think would be appropriate for your students. The audience at my AMA presentation was primarily first-year nursing students who were interested in a general background of the more common types of skin rashes.

¶ Please send me a copy of your program with directions on how to reach your classroom on the day of my presentation. I look forward to meeting with your students.

Sincerely yours, | Angela Miller, M.D. | ap | Enclosure | PS: Please let me know how many students you have in your class so I can prepare an adequate number of handouts for them.

(Continued on next page)

COMMON SKIN RASHES
Their Causes and Cures
Dr. Stanley G. Streisand

¶ Skin rashes are caused by many different things. They are often recognized by symptoms of reddening, itching, blistering, dryness, or scabbing of the skin. Some of the more common ailments that fall into the category of skin rashes are dermatitis, eczema, and psoriasis. This paper will discuss these three common types of skin rashes.

DERMATITIS

¶ Dermatitis is often referred to as *contact dermatitis*. Some of the more common substances that cause dermatitis are soaps, rubber, jewelry, plants, household and industrial chemicals, cosmetics, and perfumes. Contact dermatitis is further classified as either *allergic contact dermatitis* or *irritant contact dermatitis*.

¶ *Allergic Contact Dermatitis.* This skin rash occurs after contact is made with certain substances, called allergens. The rash occurs as a reaction of the body's immune system to expel the allergen from your skin. Some common allergens are metals in jewelry, cosmetics, and rubber boots.

¶ *Irritant Contact Dermatitis.* This skin rash does not require exposure to an allergen but can develop when you come in contact with certain substances—skin cleansers, detergents, solvents, and oils.

Instead of underlining a word, use italic.

(Continued on next page)

ECZEMA

¶ Eczema, also known as atopic dermatitis, causes the skin to appear red and blotchy all over. The disease occurs at any age but mainly from infancy to childhood. It affects about 3 percent of the United States population. There are two types of eczema—atopic eczema and hand eczema.

¶ Atopic Eczema. This form of eczema is caused by the house dust mite, by heat, by contact with woolen clothing, by detergents, and by stress.

¶ Hand Eczema. Hand eczema is caused by sensitive skin, too much exposure to wet work, detergents, oils, and greases.

PSORIASIS

¶ Psoriasis is a chronic skin disease characterized by inflammation and skin scaling. This disease affects about 5.5 million people in the United States. It occurs in all age groups and affects both men and women. When psoriasis develops, patches of skin redden and become covered with scales. The skin then cracks and may cause severe irritation in places like the elbows, knees, face, scalp, and lower back.

¶ It is believed that psoriasis is a disorder of the immune system in which there are not enough white blood cells to help protect the body against infection and diseases of this type.

Medical Office Documents

Goals

- Type at least 46wpm/5′/5e
- Format a formal report

A. Type 2 times.

A. WARMUP

```
1      Mr. Baxter will move to 1749 Larkin Street; his old      11
2  home is in Gray's Woods, just east of the corner of Parson   22
3  and 167th Avenue. The house sizes are quite different!       33
   |  1  |  2  |  3  |  4  |  5  |  6  |  7  |  8  |  9  |  10  |  11  |  12
```

SKILLBUILDING

B. DIAGNOSTIC PRACTICE: SYMBOLS AND PUNCTUATION

If you are not using the GDP software, turn to page SB-2 and follow the directions for this activity.

C. Take two 5-minute timed writings. Review your speed and errors.

Goal: At least 46wpm/5'/5e

C. 5-MINUTE TIMED WRITING

```
 4        Innovative technology may bring new problems for our      11
 5   homes and businesses. A rising shift to use a cell phone is    23
 6   causing many people to look at the etiquette of cell phone     35
 7   usage. Are there times and places where a cell phone should    47
 8   not be used?                                                   49
 9        People want to be able to stay in touch, no matter        60
10   where they are or what they are doing. However, in some        71
11   places cell phone usage is inappropriate or not allowed.       82
12   For example, you would not want a ringing cell phone to        93
13   disrupt an entire production if you are enjoying a concert    105
14   or play. As a consideration to everyone in the audience,      117
15   the management may make an announcement asking audience       128
16   members to turn off their cell phones or pagers before the    140
17   production begins. Making this request gives everyone the     151
18   chance to enjoy the show.                                     156
19        Often you see someone driving a car while talking on a   168
20   cell phone. Talking on the phone while you are driving is     179
21   not a good idea. When you are talking on the phone and not    191
22   concentrating on driving, you may cause an accident. If you   203
23   are driving a vehicle in traffic, your full focus should be   215
24   on the road. Be cognizant of this. Do not use your cell       226
25   phone when driving.                                           230
     |  1  |  2  |  3  |  4  |  5  |  6  |  7  |  8  |  9  |  10  |  11  |  12
```

DOCUMENT PROCESSING

Table 94-49

Boxed Table

This is November 4, the fourth day of your assignment. Today you are working in the Oncology Unit. Oncology is a branch of science dealing with the study of tumors.

You will begin by typing this boxed table. Insert 1 blank line after the information in each row.

DESCRIPTIONS AND TREATMENTS OF ADULT BRAIN TUMORS	
Types of Tumors	**Description and Treatment**
Astrocytomas	Tumors that start in brain cells. Treatment includes surgery, chemotherapy, and radiation.
Brain stem gliomas	Tumors located in the bottom part of the brain, which connects to the spinal cord. Treatment includes radiation and biological therapy.

(Continued on next page)

Cerebellar astrocytomas	Tumors that occur in the area of the brain called the cerebellum. Treatment is similar to that for astrocytomas.
Craniopharyngiomas	Tumors that occur near the pituitary gland. Treatment includes surgery and radiation.
Oligodendrogliomas	Tumors that begin in brain cells that provide support and nourishment for the cells that transmit nerve impulses. Treatment includes surgery, chemotherapy, and radiation.

Correspondence 94-91

Business Letter in Block Style

November 4, 20-- | Dr. Samuel Abbott | Sacred Heart Medical Center | 267 Ferry Street | Eugene, OR 97401-2409 | Dear Sam: | Subject: Paul R. Williams.

¶ On September 3 I examined Mr. Williams and discovered a Stage 1A, Cleaved B cell follicular lymphoma in the left inguinal region. I conducted a surgical excision and recommended radiation therapy. Mr. Williams completed his radiation therapy four weeks ago and feels well at this time. He has no complaints, his appetite and energy are normal, and he looks good. His weight is down five pounds upon my recommendation four weeks ago that he lose some excess weight.

¶ There are no abdominal or inguinal lymph nodes to his scrotal sac exam. There are, however, three- to four-millimeter nodes in the right inquinal region that appear totally unchanged from his original exam on September 3. His lungs are clear, his heartbeat is regular, the liver and spleen are not enlarged, and there are no palpable masses.

¶ It appears to me that Mr. Williams has recovered satisfactorily from his radiation therapy. He has requested a second opinion, and I am therefore recommending that he make an appointment with you at his earliest convenience. We will prepare a referral for Mr. Williams and forward it to your office in a day or two.

Sincerely, | Donna Stensland, M.D. | ap

Table 94-50

Boxed Table

Open the file for Table 94-49 and make the following changes:

1. Press ENTER 1 time after the title, change to 12-point Times New Roman, and type the subtitle November 4, 20-- in bold.
2. Add this entry to the table so that it will appear in alphabetical order:

   Gliomas

   The general name for tumors that come from the supportive tissue of the brain; for example, astrocytomas or oligodendrogliomas. They may be benign or malignant.

3. Apply a Table AutoFormat of your choice. Select one with distinctive borders and shading that will make the table easier to read.

RECOVERING FROM KNEE SURGERY

Dr. Alec Pera, M.D.

November 5, 20--

¶ Specific procedures should be followed by patients who are recovering from knee surgery. Depending on the particular surgery that was performed, postoperative needs of patients with knee replacements vary greatly. Healthy, young individuals may require only a few therapy sessions to recover from their surgery completely. Older individuals with no family or friends to help them at home may need special assistance or equipment to aid their mobility. Some patients may benefit from a short stay in a rehabilitation facility. To enhance the rate of recovery, patients should identify and address any special needs that may require attention before their operation.

Refer to Reference Manual

Refer to page R-12C of the Reference Manual for a review of list formatting.

¶ To promote full recovery, Lakewood Hospital has developed a coordinated pathway of physical and occupational therapy for patients' use. Patient Rehabilitation and Therapy Service (PRTS) and Lakewood Hospital have collaborated on recommending a specific sequence of procedures to follow.
¶ Prior to your surgery, we recommend that you:
1. Determine any special equipment that will be required to promote your recovery.
2. Learn correct techniques for performing day-to-day activities such as getting in and out of bed, driving your automobile, taking showers, getting up from a seat, and going up and down stairs.
3. Learn what exercises will help facilitate your recovery.
¶ After surgery, patients must participate in physical therapy to ensure that they can:
- Extend their knee straight or bend it past 90 degrees.
- Place weight on their knee to ensure that they have the strength and stability to hold their weight.
- Use the knee without discomfort (this may take several months).

Prepare this e-mail message. Type the e-mail greeting, Hi, Dr. Lockhart:, and the body shown below in correct format. Type Anna as the closing, and type this signature: Anna Padilla | E-Mail: apadilla@lakewood.com | Phone: 541-555-2303. Save the e-mail message, but do not send it.

Mr. Walden came in today with a crusted lesion in his back. Lesion was removed using 1% Xylocaine with epinephrine loc. Wound was closed with 4.0 nylon sutures. Stitches should be removed in approximately 10 days. Sutures should be kept dry for 3 days. Mr. Walden is to call if he has questions or if problems arise.

Dr. Charlene T. Gutierrez, Director of Plastic Surgery, was asked to assist Dr. Alec Pera with surgery on Bryan Owensby. After an office visit with Mr. Owensby, Dr. Gutierrez dictated the following memo to Dr. Pera. Use November 5, 20--, as the date and type the subject Mr. Owensby's Surgery. Type Dr. Gutierrez's title on the same line as her name, and use a comma and space between them.

Progress and Proofreading Check

Documents designated as Proofreading Checks serve as a check of your proofreading skill. Your goal is to have zero typographical errors when the GDP software first scores the document.

On Friday I visited with Mr. Bryan Owensby to discuss his options relative to the muscle transfer we plan to complete following radiation treatment. Mr. Owensby is a 53-year-old male who recently had multiple lesions excised.
¶ Mr. Owensby is aware that our goal is to provide healthy tissue that could tolerate the radiation treatment he would need to destroy the malignant cells on his upper thigh. At this time, we plan to complete a skin graft from the contralateral thigh to provide the healthy tissue for radiation treatment. I believe this will give Mr. Owensby the best opportunity for early healing.
¶ A free tissue transfer was also discussed, and this may be an option if the contralateral graft is unsuccessful. Mr. Owensby understands the risks and complications of either method. Scheduling is pending jointly through our offices. Thank you for this opportunity to participate in Mr. Owensby's care.
ap | c: Dr. Taiwo Owakoniro, Dr. Lewis Sethna, Dr. Monica Stevens

Unit 20

Legal Office Documents

LESSON 96
Legal Office Documents

LESSON 97
Legal Office Documents

LESSON 98
Legal Office Documents

LESSON 99
Legal Office Documents

LESSON 100
Legal Office Documents

[Document 1 — Summons]

```
1   STATE OF KANSAS                    →6" right tab  IN DISTRICT COURT
2                                                                    ↓2X
3   COUNTY OF DOUGLAS                  NORTHEAST JUDICIAL DISTRICT
                                                                     ↓2X
                                       6" right tab
5   PEOPLE'S BANK          →3" tab  )  NO. ____ 20 underscores
6   607 New Hampshire Street        )
7   Lawrence, KS 66044-2243         )
8                          →3" tab  )
9   →1" tab    Plaintiff,  →3" tab  )
10                                  )
11  →1" tab    vs.        →3" tab   )            →6" right tab  SUMMONS
12                                  )
13  JOHN COUZINS and GLORIA COUZINS,)
14                                  )
15         Defendants.             )  ↓2X
16
17  THE STATE OF KANSAS TO THE ABOVE-NAMED DEFENDANTS:  ↓2X
18
19  →1" tab    You are hereby summoned and required to appear and defend against the
20  Complaint in this action, which is hereby ser...
21  undersigned an Answer or other proper response w...
22  of the Summons and Complaint upon you, exclusiv...
23
24         If you fail to do so, judgment by de...
25  relief demanded in the Complaint.
26
27         SIGNED this ____ day of Decemb...
28        5 underscores
29                       →3" tab ____...
30                                Ann B...
31                                806 K...
32                                Lawren...
33                                Teleph...
34                                Attorn...
35
```

[Document 2 — Last Will and Testament, page 1]

LAST WILL AND TESTAMENT
OF
IRMA J. GOMEZ ↓2X

→1" tab I, IRMA J. GOMEZ, residing in Corvallis, Oregon, do hereby make and declare this to be my Last Will and Testament, hereby revoking any and all former Wills and Codicils by me at any time heretofore made. ↓2X

ARTICLE I ↓2X

This will is made in Oregon and shall be governed, construed, and administered according to Oregon law, even though subject to probate or administered elsewhere. The Oregon laws applied shall not include any principles or laws relating to conflicts or choice of laws.

ARTICLE II

Whenever used herein, words importing the singular shall include the plural and words importing the masculine shall include the feminine and neuter, and vice versa, unless the context otherwise requires.

ARTICLE III

I am married and my husband's name is Ricardo E. Gomez. All references hereinafter made to "husband" or "spouse" shall refer to him and no other; and if he is not my legal husband at the time of my death, then he shall be deemed for the purpose of this, my last Will and Testament, to have predeceased me. I was formerly married to Henry Woo, who is now deceased. There were three (3) children born of my marriage to Henry Woo. The names of those children are as follows: Judy Parsons, Henry Wayne, and Randy Woo.

ARTICLE IV

If My Spouse Survives. Except as may otherwise be provided hereunder in this Article IV, if my spouse survives me, I devise to my spouse all my interest in household furniture and furnishings, books, apparel, art objects, collections, jewelry, and similar personal effects; sporting and recreational equipment; all other tangible property for personal use; all other like contents of my home and any vacation property that I may own or reside in on the date of my death; all animals; any motor vehicles that I may own on the date of my death; and any unexpired insurance on all such property.

ARTICLE V

If My Spouse Does Not Survive. Except as may be otherwise provided in this Article IV, if my spouse does not survive me, I devise the property described above in this Article (except motor vehicles) to my children who survive me, to be divided

1

[Document 3 — Last Will and Testament, page 2]

among them as they shall agree, or in the absence of such agreement, as my Personal Representative shall determine, which determination shall be conclusive.

ARTICLE VI

If any beneficiary named or described in this Will fails to survive me for 120 hours, all the provisions in this Will for the benefit of such deceased beneficiary shall lapse, and this Will shall be construed as though the fact were that he or she predeceased me.

ARTICLE VII

All estate, inheritance, transfer, succession, and any other taxes plus interest and penalties thereon (death taxes) that become payable by reason of my death upon property passing under this instrument shall be paid out of the residue of my estate without reimbursement from the recipient and without apportionment. All death taxes upon property not passing under this instrument shall be apportioned in the manner provided by law. ↓2X

IN WITNESS WHEREOF, I have hereunto affixed my hand and seal this ____ day of _____ 20-character underscore _____, 20--. ↓2X
   5-character underscore

→3" tab   underscores to the right margin
                    IRMA J. GOMEZ   →6" right tab   Testator

The foregoing instrument, consisting of TWO (2) pages (this page included), was on this ____ day of _____, 20--, subscribed on each ...omez, the above-named Testator and by her ... be her Last Will, in the presence of us, and each ...his presence, and in the presence of each other, ... attesting witnesses thereto. ↓2X

_____ ...esiding at _____

_____ ...esiding at _____

2

Legal Office Documents

Goals

- Type at least 47wpm/5′/5e
- Format legal office documents

A. Type 2 times.

A. WARMUP

```
1        Marshal bought five chances for the contest. He won     11
2   six prizes and was given a check for $2,350--these prizes    22
3   are equal to 1/4th of Jill's winnings for all of last year.  34
    | 1 | 2 | 3 | 4 | 5 | 6 | 7 | 8 | 9 | 10 | 11 | 12
```

SKILLBUILDING

B. DIAGNOSTIC PRACTICE: NUMBERS

If you are not using the GDP software, turn to page SB-5 and follow the directions for this activity.

C. Take three 12-second timed writings on each line. The scale below the last line shows your wpm speed for a 12-second timed writing.

C. 12-SECOND SPEED SPRINTS

```
4   They saw the sun shine through after days and days of rain.
5   She hopes to get a much higher math score on the next test.
6   Jo did not study for the math exam she took late last week.
7   This time he spent at least ten days studying for the test.
    | | | | 5 | | | 10 | | | 15 | | | 20 | | | 25 | | | 30 | | | 35 | | | 40 | | | 45 | | | 50 | | | 55 | | | 60
```

Keyboarding Connection

Capturing an Image From the Internet

Would you like to copy an image or graphic from the Internet? It's easy!

Point to the image or graphic and press the right mouse button. When the shortcut menu appears, choose Save Picture As (or Save Image As). The Save Picture dialog box appears. Select the appropriate drive and name the file if necessary. Click Save. The image is usually saved with a .gif, .jpg, or .bmp file extension. To insert the image into a Word document, choose Picture from the Insert menu, and select From File. Locate the file, and click Insert. You could also right-click the image, choose Copy, and then click the Paste button in Word.

YOUR TURN Conduct a Web search and locate an image or graphic to save. Right-click the image, choose Save Picture As, name the file, and save the image. Insert the image into a word processing document.

D. Take two 5-minute timed writings. Review your speed and errors.

Goal: At least 47wpm/5'/5e

D. 5-MINUTE TIMED WRITING

```
 8        Many businesses across the country are adopting a new      11
 9   dress code called business casual. Depending on the type of     23
10   place for which you work, business casual can have various      35
11   meanings. Most places allow their workers to dress down a       46
12   notch from what was expected in the past. If people wore        58
13   suits and ties in the past, then the business casual code       69
14   would allow them to stop wearing ties and suit jackets. It      81
15   is quite necessary for a business to formulate dress code       93
16   guidelines for workers to follow when business casual goes     105
17   into effect.                                                   107
18        Surveys of various companies show mixed results when      118
19   employees were given a choice of dressing more casually.       129
20   Some companies feel business casual is a perk that works       141
21   for employees. However, other companies report that job       152
22   productivity rates zoom down when workers are allowed to       163
23   dress down. More research is needed.                           171
24        When you feel good about the way you look, you will       181
25   show this attitude in your performance. If your company has    193
26   adopted a business casual dress code, you must keep in mind    205
27   that business casual does not mean that you can dress in a     217
28   sloppy manner. A neat appearance and good grooming always      229
29   enhance a business casual look.                                235
```

`| 1 | 2 | 3 | 4 | 5 | 6 | 7 | 8 | 9 | 10 | 11 | 12`

FORMATTING

E. LEGAL DOCUMENTS

Court rules (federal, state, appellate, and so on) and law office preferences determine the format of legal documents including margins, line numbering, line spacing, line lengths, page numbering, indents, alignment, and bolding. Therefore, the legal documents and guidelines in this unit have been designed to serve as simplified examples of acceptable legal formats.

Legal documents are typed on either 8.5- × 14-inch legal paper or 8.5- × 11-inch paper. Court documents often include numbered lines for easy reference in a court of law. *Legal cap* is the name given to the vertical rules that appear at the left and right margins. In legal documents, the *venue* states the name and location of the court and county. The *caption* states the court, the names of the parties, the docket (case) number, the title of the document, and sometimes the name of the judge.

Follow these general formatting guidelines for legal documents in this unit. Refer to the summons shown in the illustration.

- Use default margins all around, single spacing, left alignment, and no bold.
- Set a 1-inch tab, and indent paragraphs 1 inch; press ENTER 2 times between paragraphs.
- Set a 6-inch right tab, and type 20 underscores for the case number.
- Single-space court documents (such as an affidavit of possession, a summons, a complaint, and a judgment), and number all lines. Restart line numbers on each page.

(Continued on next page)

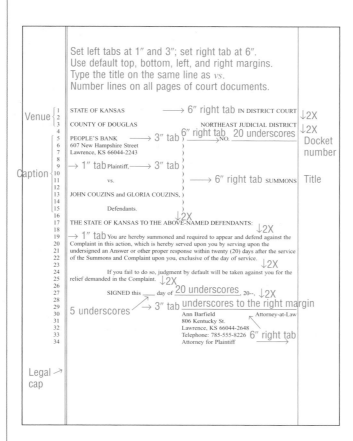

- Single-space noncourt documents (such as a warranty deed and last will and testament), and do not number lines.
- For multipage documents, insert a centered page number at the bottom of each page.
- Set a 3-inch tab, and type the closing parentheses at 3 inches; for signature lines, type continuous underscores from this 3-inch tab setting to the right margin.
- Type 20 underscores for months and case numbers and 5 underscores for dates; insert spaces before and after underscores when the underscores appear in the middle of a sentence.

Word Processing Manual

F. WORD PROCESSING: LINE NUMBERING

Study Lesson 96 in your word processing manual. Complete all of the shaded steps while at your computer. Then format the jobs that follow.

DOCUMENT PROCESSING

An affidavit is a sworn written statement made under oath.

Report 96-67

Affidavit of Possession

Add line numbering for all lines in this document. When this document is actually typed, the line numbers will vary from those shown here.

1   AFFIDAVIT OF POSSESSION ↓2X

2

3 STATE OF VERMONT ↓2X

4

5 COUNTY OF WINDSOR ↓2X

6

7 → 1″ tab   Eric Wesley, being first duly sworn, deposes and says: ↓2X

8

9   That he is an adult person and is a resident of Windsor County,

10 Vermont, and that his mailing address is P.O. Box 801, Ludlow, VT 05149. ↓2X

11

(Continued on next page)

₁₂ That he knows the history, ownership, and occupancy of the
₁₃ following-described property situated in Windsor County, Vermont, to wit:

₁₄

₁₅ All that part of the Southeast Quarter of the Northeast Quarter of
₁₆ Section Nine (9), Township Seventy-two (72), further described as follows:
₁₇ Beginning at the Northeast corner of said Southeast Quarter of the Northeast
₁₈ Quarter; thence South along the East line of said quarter 1000.00 feet;
₁₉ thence west 575.00 feet; thence North 200.00 feet; thence West 204.00 feet;
₂₀ thence North 800.00 feet; thence East 979.00 feet.

₂₁

₂₂ That the record title holder in fee simple of the above property is
₂₃ Eric Wesley, a single person; that he is presently in possession of the above-
₂₄ described premises;

₂₅

₂₆ That ownership of the aforesaid property is based upon an
₂₇ unbroken chain of title through immediate and remote grantors by deed of
₂₈ conveyance which has been recorded for a period of more than twenty-one
₂₉ (21) years, to wit: Since August 21, 1943, at 2 a.m.;

₃₀

₃₁ That the purpose of this Affidavit of Possession is to show proof of
₃₂ ownership by providing and recording evidence of possession for
₃₃ marketable title as required by the Marketable Record Title Act of the State
₃₄ of Vermont.   ↓2X

₃₅   5 underscores
₃₆ DATED this _____ day of May 2006, at Ludlow, Vermont. ↓2X

₃₇
₃₈   underscores to the right margin
        _____
₃₉   ⟶ 3" tab Blake Crawford 6" right tab ⟶ Attorney-at-Law
₄₀   ↓2X
₄₁ Subscribed and sworn to before me this ____ day of May 2006.

₄₂
₄₃   _____
₄₄   Shirley Blakely   Notary Public
₄₅   Windsor County, Vermont
₄₆   My Commission Expires July 17, 2012

Underscore is 5 characters wide.

Underscore starts at 3-inch left tab and ends at the right margin.

Signature title ends at 6-inch right tab.

Underscore starts at 3-inch left tab and ends at the right margin.

Correspondence ▶ 96-94

Business Letter in Block Style

August 30, 20-- | Mr. Eric Wesley | P.O. Box 801 | Ludlow, VT 05149 | Dear Mr. Wesley:

¶ Enclosed is your copy of the Affidavit of Possession that was filed on your behalf with the Windsor County Courthouse.

¶ As you can see, only the Southeast Quarter of your property was included in the affidavit. We will have to file an additional affidavit if you want to add the Northwest Quarter as well as your Franklin County properties. All affidavits must be completed prior to your property being advertised in the *Windsor News*.

¶ I will be out of the office all of next week. If you have questions, please call my associate, Betty Yu.

Sincerely, | Blake Crawford | urs | Enclosure | c: Marvin Steele, Beverley Perez

Legal Office Documents

Goals

- Improve speed and accuracy
- Refine language arts skills in the use of punctuation
- Format legal office documents

A. Type 2 times.

A. WARMUP

```
1      Jacqueline kept prize #2490 instead of #3761 because   11
2  it was worth 58.5% more value. That was a great prize! Last  23
3  year the law firm of Adams & Day donated all grand prizes.   34
   |  1  |  2  |  3  |  4  |  5  |  6  |  7  |  8  |  9  |  10  |  11  |  12
```

SKILLBUILDING

B. PROGRESSIVE PRACTICE: ALPHABET

If you are not using the GDP software, turn to page SB-7 and follow the directions for this activity.

C. PACED PRACTICE

If you are not using the GDP software, turn to page SB-14 and follow the directions for this activity.

LANGUAGE ARTS

D. Study the rules at the right.

D. SEMICOLONS

RULE ▶
; no conjunction

Use a semicolon to separate two closely related independent clauses that are not connected by a conjunction (such as *and, but*, or *nor*).

Management favored the vote; stockholders did not.

But: Management favored the vote, but stockholders did not.

RULE ▶
; series

Use a semicolon to separate three or more items in a series if any of the items already contain commas.

Staff meetings were held on Thursday, May 7; Monday, June 7; and Friday, June 12.

Note: Be sure to insert the semicolon between (not within) the items in a series.

Edit the sentences to correct any errors in the use of semicolons.

```
4  Paul will travel to Madrid, Spain; Lisbon, Portugal, and
5  Nice, France.
6  Mary's gift arrived yesterday, Margie's did not.
7  Bring your textbook to class; I'll return it tomorrow.
8  The best days for the visit are Monday, May 10, Tuesday,
9  May 18, and Wednesday, May 26.
10 Jan is the president; Peter is the vice president.
```

A seller who provides a warranty deed warrants (or guarantees) that he or she has full ownership of a property and has the right to sell it. The seller also guarantees all rights of the property to the buyer.

WARRANTY DEED ↓2X

→ 1″ tab   THIS INDENTURE, made this ⁵ ᵘⁿᵈᵉʳˢᶜᵒʳᵉˢ _____ day of October, 2006, between Maria J. Lopez, Grantor, whether one or more, and Barbara Denman, Grantee, whether one or more, whose post office address is 315 Clark Avenue, Ames, IA 50010-3314. ↓2X

     WITNESSETH, for and in consideration of the sum of SEVENTY-FIVE THOUSAND and 00/100 DOLLARS ($75,000), Grantor does hereby GRANT to Grantee, all of the following real property lying and being in the County of Story, State of Iowa, and described as follows, to-wit:

Lots Seventeen (17) and Eighteen (18), Block Seventy-three (73), Original Townsite of Ames, Iowa, SUBJECT TO easements, special or improvement taxes and assessments, mineral conveyances, rights-of-way and reservations of record.

(THIS DEED IS IN FULFILLMENT OF THAT CERTAIN CONTRACT FOR DEED ENTERED INTO BY AND BETWEEN THE SAME PARTIES ON THE DATE HEREOF.)

     And the said Grantor for herself, her heirs, executors and administrators, does covenant with the Grantee that she is well seized in fee of the land and premises aforesaid and has good right to sell and convey the same in manner and form aforesaid: that the same are free from all encumbrances, except installments of special assessments or assessments for special improvements which have not been certified to the County Treasurer for collection, and the above granted lands and premises in the possession of said Grantee, against all persons lawfully claiming or to claim the whole or any part thereof, the said Grantor will warrant and defend.

     WITNESS, the hand of the Grantor.

→ 3″ tab _____ underscores to the right margin _____

        Maria J. Lopez

(Continued on next page)

STATE OF IOWA

County of Story

On this _____ day of October, 2006, before me, a notary public within and for said County and State, personally appeared Maria J. Lopez, to me known to be the person described in and who executed the within and foregoing instrument and acknowledged to me that she executed the same as her free act and deed.

_____

Boyd H. Fraser   *6" right tab* →   Notary Public
Story County, Iowa
My Commission Expires June 15, 2012

Table 97-52 ▶

Boxed Table

(!) Your finished table will have different line endings for column B when you resize the column widths to fit the contents.

WARRANTY DEED TERMINOLOGY State of Iowa	
Term	*Definition*
Appurtenance	Something attached to the land
Consideration	The value of the property
Escrow	A system of document transfer in which the document is given to a third party to hold until the conditions of the agreement have been met
Grantee	The person who is buying the property
Grantor	The person who owns the property
Mortgage	The pledge of property as security for a loan
Tenement	Something that can be possessed, such as land or a building
Warranty deed	A deed in which the seller forever guarantees clear title to the land

Type the e-mail greeting, body, closing, and signature as indicated below in correct format:

1. Type `Hi, David:` as the greeting, type the body shown below, and type `Yen` as the closing.

2. Type this signature: `Yen Nguyen | E-Mail: ynguyen@webmail.net | Phone: 712-555-3435`

3. Save the e-mail message in GDP, but do not send it.

¶ You might recall last week that I indicated there might be some fore closure property available and that it would be auctioned at the Story *County* Courthouse. On September 9 3 properties in southern Story <u>c</u>ounty will be auctioned as foreclosures. These properties are located adjacent to the lots you purchased last year. I know that you would be interested in expanding your lot size with this purchase. Specifically, they are located in Spring Township, Lot 23; Aiken Township, Lot 17; and Andrews Township, Lot 9.

¶ I expect these properties will sell for around $36,000 each; their excellent location may force the bidding into the $40,000 *or $50,000* range. If you cannot be present for the auction but would like to place a bid on the properties, please let me know so that I can act on your behalf as your agent. If you *elect* ~~want~~ to do this, send me the bidding range you wish to present for each of the Properties or for all 3 as one combined property. I need confirmation from you no later than September 7 so that I can register *as* your agent to present your bid.

; no conjunction

; series

; no conjunction

Legal Office Documents

Goals

- Type at least 47wpm/5′/5e
- Format legal office documents

A. Type 2 times.

A. WARMUP

```
1      Janet bought dozens of disks (5 or 6) to store her        10
2   article, "The Internet Sanctions." She quickly sent it to    23
3   her editor, Max Pavlow, on the 18th or 19th of September.    34
    |  1  |  2  |  3  |  4  |  5  |  6  |  7  |  8  |  9  |  10  |  11  |  12
```

SKILLBUILDING

B. DIAGNOSTIC PRACTICE: SYMBOLS AND PUNCTUATION

If you are not using the GDP software, turn to page SB-2 and follow the directions for this activity.

C. Type the paragraph 2 times, concentrating on each letter typed.

C. TECHNIQUE PRACTICE: SHIFT/CAPS LOCK

```
4      Raymond and Karen must travel through TENNESSEE and
5   KENTUCKY on TUESDAY and WEDNESDAY. Raymond will speak in
6   NASHVILLE on the topic of COMPUTER AWARENESS; Karen will
7   speak in LOUISVILLE, and her talk is on INTERNET ACCESS.
```

Strategies for Career Success

Enhance Your Presentation With Visual Aids

Visual aids capture people's attention while increasing their retention. Use visual aids to present an outline of your presentation, explain detailed technical or numerical information, and summarize your key points.

Be selective. Don't bombard your audience with visuals. Your visual aids should support and clarify your verbal presentation. Consider the size of your audience and the size of the room before selecting your visuals. Audiences have little patience for visuals that are too small to read. Types of visual aids are overhead transparencies, slides, photographs, flip charts, maps, flowcharts, posters, handouts, and computer graphics including tables, graphs, and charts.

Limit the amount of information on a visual. Use simple graphics. Continue displaying the current visual until you are ready to discuss the next one. Always keep the projector or overhead on.

YOUR TURN In what ways would your visual aids differ if your audience had 10 people or 110?

D. Take two 5-minute timed writings. Review your speed and errors.

Goal: At least 47wpm/5′/5e

D. 5-MINUTE TIMED WRITING

8	From the time you start attending school, you begin to	11
9	develop new skills in making friends and getting along with	23
10	people. These skills are used throughout your life journey.	35
11	If you want to be successful in any business or career, you	47
12	can't be a loner. You must learn skills for working with	59
13	people from all cultures.	64
14	In a corporation, people use their unique skills to	74
15	work as a team in order to accomplish their goals. Like a	86
16	finely tuned orchestra or a football team, all members must	98
17	work together to achieve a desired objective. If a person	110
18	does not work efficiently within the group, then other team	122
19	members may have to work harder to compensate so that the	133
20	effort of the team will not fall short.	141
21	Working with others allows you the chance to learn	152
22	from other people. You may also learn some things about	163
23	yourself. To get along with your coworkers, you may have to	175
24	overlook the personal faults of others. Everyone has some	186
25	faults, and your faults may be just as disconcerting to	198
26	other people as their faults are to you. Your ability to	209
27	work with people will also enhance your quest for career	220
28	advancement. You can expect amazing results when you work	232
29	with your team.	235

| 1 | 2 | 3 | 4 | 5 | 6 | 7 | 8 | 9 | 10 | 11 | 12 |

Report 98-69 ►

Summons

Add line numbers for all lines in this court document. When this document is actually typed, the line numbers will vary from those shown here.

A summons is a document that notifies a defendant that a lawsuit has been filed and an appearance must be made before the court, at a specified time, to answer the charges.

1 STATE OF KANSAS　　　　　　⟶ 6″ right tab　IN DISTRICT COURT
　　　　　　　　　　　　　　　　　　　　　　　↓2X
2
3 COUNTY OF DOUGLAS　　　　　　NORTHEAST JUDICIAL DISTRICT
　　　　　　　　　　　　　　　　　　　　　　　↓2X
4
5 PEOPLE'S BANK　　⟶ 3″ tab　)—6″ right tab→ NO. _____ 20 underscores _____
6 607 New Hampshire Street　　)
7 Lawrence, KS 66044-2243　　)
8　　　　　　　　　　⟶ 3″ tab　)
9 ⟶ 1″ tab　Plaintiff,　　⟶ 3″ tab　)
10　　　　　　　　　　　　　　　)
11 ⟶ 1″ tab　vs.　　⟶ 3″ tab　)　　　　⟶ 6″ right tab　SUMMONS
12　　　　　　　　　　　　　　　)
13 JOHN COUZINS and GLORIA　　)
14 COUZINS,　　　　　　　　　　)
15　　　　　　Defendants.　　)　↓2X
16
17 THE STATE OF KANSAS TO THE ABOVE-NAMED DEFENDANTS: ↓2X
18
19 ⟶ 1″ tab　You are hereby summoned and required to appear and defend
20 against the Complaint in this action, which is hereby served upon you by
21 serving upon the undersigned an Answer or other proper response within
22 twenty (20) days after the service of the Summons and Complaint upon
23 you, exclusive of the day of service. ↓2X
24
25　　　　　　If you fail to do so, judgment by default will be taken against you
26 for the relief demanded in the Complaint.
27
28　　　　　SIGNED this _____ day of December 20--.
29　　　　　5 underscores
30　　　　　　　　　⟶ 3″ tab _____ underscores to the right margin _____
31　　　　　　　　　　Ann Barfield　6″ right tab→　Attorney-at-Law
32　　　　　　　　　　806 Kentucky Street
33　　　　　　　　　　Lawrence, KS 66044-2648
34　　　　　　　　　　Telephone: 785-555-8226
35　　　　　　　　　　Attorney for Plaintiff

Type the title on the same line as *vs.*

MEMO TO: Raymond Ruiz

FROM: Charlotte Libretto

DATE: December 28, 20--

SUBJECT: Client listing

¶ As you requested, I am now enclosing an up-to-date new client list for our Atlanta area clients. This list is current as of this last week, and it includes clients in the counties of Carroll, Cobb, Douglas, Fulton, and paulding. Please note that the total billing hours are also shown in this list.

¶ Douglas and Fulton counties represent the greatest number of clients over all, although this list doesn't not reveal the total number of clients per county. Just in the past quarter, these two counties represented nearly eighty 80 % of our client base. Cobb County clients do not represent a sizable percentage of our client base, but the opening of three two new law offices in that county will most certainly generate considerable new business in the coming months.

¶ We will send you an updated list biweekly. The next list will most certainly show substantial gains in Cobb County, and we expect business in Douglas and Fulton counties to continue growing because of the tremendous growth in the area West of Atlanta. If you have any questions about any of our new clients, please call our main office at 770-555-1843.

urs | Enclosure | c: Blair Kiplan

Table
98-53
Boxed Table

Press ENTER to create the 2-line column heading as displayed before automatically adjusting column widths.

CLIENT LIST December 28, 20--			
Name	**Address**	**County**	**Billing Hours**
Jose Azteca	128 Holly St.	Douglas	25
Carroll Bryan	323 Newnan St.	Carroll	28
Margie Coulon	301 Bradley St.	Paulding	15
Thomas Henry	2900 Shady Grove	Cobb	22
Debra Johnson	215 Griffin Dr.	Cobb	34
Maria Mateo	156 Cypress Circle	Fulton	10
Luther Nicholson	6703 Burns Rd.	Paulding	12
Pearl Nix	106 Alice Lane	Douglas	18
James Presley	622 North Ave.	Carroll	23
Janie Ramey	1202 Park St.	Fulton	32
Heather Sanders	248 Lakeshore Dr.	Cobb	12
Thomas Tarpley	2950 Chapel Hill Rd.	Douglas	29
Vickie Thomas	4821 Hope Rd.	Carroll	9
Kim Wong	111 Pierce St.	Fulton	18
Ray Young	108 Waverly Way	Douglas	30
Tong Zhen	286 Laurel Terrace	Paulding	35

Keyboarding Connection

Coping With Spam

Have you received heaps of unsolicited e-mail, commonly known as spam? Everyone wants to get rid of those irritating online sales pitches. Contrary to popular advice, however, there is not much you can do about them. You can make use of various filters, but they aren't foolproof.

If you end up on a spammer's list and receive a courteous e-mail asking you to reply if you wish to be removed from the list, *do not reply*. The spammer may interpret your reply to mean that you read e-mail, and you may be put on the hot list. The best action is to try to avoid divulging your e-mail address to spammers. Most important, use an alternate account if posting to any kind of online forum.

YOUR TURN How do you deal with postal "junk mail" that you receive? Are there similarities in dealing with spam?

Legal Office Documents

Goals

- Improve speed and accuracy
- Refine language arts skills in spelling
- Format legal office documents

A. Type 2 times.

A. WARMUP

```
1     Zeke sharpened his ax so that he could quite easily     11
2  saw through 15 very large pine trees. Each load will sell  23
3  for $175 (to Blake & James Inc.) at next Friday's auction. 35
   |  1  |  2  |  3  |  4  |  5  |  6  |  7  |  8  |  9  |  10  |  11  |  12
```

SKILLBUILDING

B. MAP

Follow the GDP software directions for this exercise in improving keystroking accuracy.

C. Take a 1-minute timed writing on the first paragraph to establish your base speed. Then take four 1-minute timed writings on the remaining paragraphs. As soon as you equal or exceed your base speed on one paragraph, advance to the next, more difficult paragraph.

C. SUSTAINED PRACTICE: ROUGH DRAFT

```
4      The pattern of employment in our country is undergoing  11
5   some major changes. Companies are slowly decreasing their  23
6   permanent staff to just a core group of managers and other 35
7   high-powered people and are using temporaries for the rest. 47

8      This trend is creating an acͨcordion aftermath in many   11
9   firms: the ability to expand and contract as the time or̲ and  23
10  the balance sheets dictate. H̶a̶v̶e̶ Having this range of flexibility 35
11  w̶o̶u̶l̶d̶ will be a key ingredient in the competͥative fight to come. 47

12     All of these changes w̶o̶u̶l̶d̶ will make it tough for a̶l̶l̶ the unions 11
13  to stay a float. They do not have a satisfactͦory method of  23
14  organizing such employeͤs. Unions c̶a̶n̶ could try to change in̲ ̲to  35
15  social agencͤeis, providing aid to members outside of work.   47

16     Such services as elder or child care, counseling, debt   11
17  managͤment, and even health care may#be of great as̲s̲istance   23
18  as employers find it more and more dif̲ficult to offer these  35
19  benͤfits. unions may find their niche by filling this gap.    47
    |  1  |  2  |  3  |  4  |  5  |  6  |  7  |  8  |  9  |  10  |  11  |  12
```

LANGUAGE ARTS

D. Type this list of frequently misspelled words, paying special attention to any spelling problems in each word.

D. SPELLING

20 distribution executive extension requested specific carried
21 recommended alternative programs access budget issued seize
22 objectives indicated calendar family could these until your
23 administrative accommodate possibility students fiscal past
24 transportation employee's categories summary offered estate

Edit the sentences to correct any misspellings.

25 The execitive requested an extention on spicific programs.
26 I have recomended alternitive programs for early next week.
27 These objectives were indacated for the new calender year.
28 These passed administrative goals will accomodate the team.
29 These categories could be included in the employee summery.

DOCUMENT PROCESSING

Report 99-70

Last Will and Testament

Insert a centered page number at the bottom of each page.

A last will and testament is a legal document stating how a person wants his or her property distributed after death.

LAST WILL AND TESTAMENT
OF
IRMA J. GOMEZ ↓2X

→ 1″ tab   I, IRMA J. GOMEZ, residing in Corvallis, Oregon, do hereby make and declare this to be my Last Will and Testament, hereby revoking any and all former Wills and Codicils by me at any time heretofore made. ↓2X

ARTICLE I ↓2X

This will is made in Oregon and shall be governed, construed, and administered according to Oregon law, even though subject to probate or administered elsewhere. The Oregon laws applied shall not include any principles or laws relating to conflicts or choice of laws.

ARTICLE II

Whenever used herein, words importing the singular shall include the plural and words importing the masculine shall include the feminine and neuter, and vice versa, unless the context otherwise requires.

(Continued on next page)

ARTICLE III

I am married and my husband's name is Ricardo E. Gomez. All references hereinafter made to "husband" or "spouse" shall refer to him and no other; and if he is not my legal husband at the time of my death, then he shall be deemed for the purpose of this, my last Will and Testament, to have predeceased me. I was formerly married to Henry Woo, who is now deceased. There were three (3) children born of my marriage to Henry Woo. The names of those children are as follows: Judy Parsons, Henry Wayne, and Randy Woo.

ARTICLE IV

If My Spouse Survives. Except as may otherwise be provided hereunder in this Article IV, if my spouse survives me, I devise to my spouse all my interest in household furniture and furnishings, books, apparel, art objects, collections, jewelry, and similar personal effects; sporting and recreational equipment; all other tangible property for personal use; all other like contents of my home and any vacation property that I may own or reside in on the date of my death; all animals; any motor vehicles that I may own on the date of my death; and any unexpired insurance on all such property.

ARTICLE V

If My Spouse Does Not Survive. Except as may be otherwise provided in this Article IV, if my spouse does not survive me, I devise the property described above in this Article (except motor vehicles) to my children who survive me, to be divided among them as they shall agree, or in the absence of such agreement, as my Personal Representative shall determine, which determination shall be conclusive.

ARTICLE VI

If any beneficiary named or described in this Will fails to survive me for 120 hours, all the provisions in this Will for the benefit of such deceased beneficiary shall lapse, and this Will shall be construed as though the fact were that he or she predeceased me.

ARTICLE VII

All estate, inheritance, transfer, succession, and any other taxes plus interest and penalties thereon (death taxes) that become payable by reason of my death upon property passing under this instrument shall be paid out of the residue of my estate without reimbursement from the recipient and without apportionment. All death taxes upon property not passing under this instrument shall be apportioned in the manner provided by law. ↓2X

(Continued on next page)

IN WITNESS WHEREOF, I have hereunto affixed my hand and seal this _____ day of ____20-character underscore____, 20--. ↓2X

↖ 5-character underscore

⟶ 3″ tab _____underscores to the right margin_____

IRMA J. GOMEZ → 6″ right tab Testator
↓2X

The foregoing instrument, consisting of TWO (2) pages (this page included), was on this _____ day of _____, 20--, subscribed on each page and at the end thereof by Irma J. Gomez, the above-named Testator and by her signed, sealed, published and declared to be her Last Will, in the presence of us, and each of us, who thereupon, at his request, in his presence, and in the presence of each other, have hereunto subscribed our names as attesting witnesses thereto. ↓2X

Center the last 2 lines.

_____30-character underscore_____ residing at _____

_____ residing at _____

Correspondence
99-97

Business Letter
in Block Style

Refer to Reference Manual

Refer to page R-12C of the Reference Manual for an overview of formatting lists.

July 1, 20-- | Mrs. Irma J. Gomez | 768 Southwest Adams Avenue | Corvallis, OR 97333-4523 | Dear Mrs. Gomez: | Subject: Will Provisions ¶ Your last will and testament has been drafted and is enclosed for your review. Please review it carefully for any specific omissions or deletions. ¶ Although your will has been drafted as you indicated, there are still a couple of alternative inclusions that I would recommend.
• Do you wish to include a fiduciary powers summary in the will?
• What division of estate do you wish to include for your family? ¶ These inclusions could be rather comprehensive. Therefore, could we schedule a meeting for next Tuesday to accommodate these changes? Please call my administrative assistant so she can put you on my calendar. Sincerely, | Andrea L. Grainger | Attorney-at-Law | urs | Enclosure | c: T. Carter, S. Rohrer, A. Winchester

Legal Office Documents

Goals

- Type at least 47wpm/5'/5e
- Format legal office documents

A. Type 2 times.

A. WARMUP

```
1      Val Lopez and Jack Drew quickly bought six tickets for    11
2  Sam's $24,600 collector's auto (a 1957 Chevrolet). Over the   23
3  past month, its value increased by 1.5%. That is fantastic!   35
   | 1 | 2 | 3 | 4 | 5 | 6 | 7 | 8 | 9 | 10 | 11 | 12
```

SKILLBUILDING

PPP PRETEST → PRACTICE → POSTTEST

PRETEST
Take a 1-minute timed writing. Review your speed and errors.

B. PRETEST: Horizontal Reaches

```
4      Bart enjoyed his royal blue race car. He bragged about    11
5  how he learned to push for those speed spurts that helped     23
6  him win those races. The car had a lot of get-up-and-go.      34
   | 1 | 2 | 3 | 4 | 5 | 6 | 7 | 8 | 9 | 10 | 11 | 12
```

PRACTICE
Speed Emphasis:
If you made no more than 1 error on the Pretest, type each *individual* line 2 times.
Accuracy Emphasis:
If you made 2 or more errors, type each *group* of lines (as though it were a paragraph) 2 times.

C. PRACTICE: In Reaches

```
7  oy toy ahoy ploy loyal coyly royal enjoy decoy annoy deploy
8  ar fare arch mart march farms scars spear barns learn radar
9  pu pull push puts pulse spurt purge spuds pushy spurs pupil
```

D. PRACTICE: Out Reaches

```
10  ge gear gets ages getup raged geese lunge pages cagey forge
11  da dare date data dance adage dazed sedan daubs cedar daily
12  hi high hick hill hinge chief hires ethic hiked chili hitch
```

POSTTEST
Repeat the Pretest timed writing and compare performance.

E. POSTTEST: Horizontal Reaches

F. Take two 5-minute timed writings. Review your speed and errors.

Goal: At least 47 wpm/5'/5e

F. 5-MINUTE TIMED WRITINGS

13	Company loyalty may be a thing of the past. A worker	11
14	who stayed and worked in one place for thirty or more years	23
15	is rare these days. People are moving to different jobs at	35
16	a faster pace than in the past. Changing jobs many times	46
17	over a career no longer carries the stigma of the past.	57
18	People are looking for new challenges.	65
19	Those who change jobs are able to market their skills	76
20	and to get salary increases. Hopping from job to job can	87
21	pay amazing returns for some careers. Businesses are quite	99
22	willing to offer higher pay and more perks to attract the	111
23	best and most skilled people. People who change jobs a lot	123
24	have the experience and knowledge that other companies are	134
25	willing to retain.	138
26	The opportunity to change jobs is there not only for	149
27	younger workers but also for older workers who are well	160
28	into their careers. For example, computer technology has	172
29	been experiencing a boom. The Internet industry has a big	183
30	demand for computer programmers. People with knowledge in	195
31	this field can request higher salaries. A company may even	207
32	offer additional benefits in order to attract experienced	208
33	workers with great credentials. It is really up to each	229
34	person to decide what to do.	235

| 1 | 2 | 3 | 4 | 5 | 6 | 7 | 8 | 9 | 10 | 11 | 12 |

Strategies for Career Success

Letter of Resignation

When you plan to leave a job, you should write a resignation letter, memo, or e-mail to your supervisor and send a copy to Human Resources. Follow these guidelines to write an effective resignation.

Start a resignation letter positively, regardless of why you are leaving. Include how you benefited from working for the company, or compliment your coworkers.

In the middle section, state why you are leaving. Provide an objective, factual explanation and avoid accusations. Your resignation becomes part of your permanent company record. If it is hostile, it could backfire on you when you need references. Stipulate the date your resignation becomes effective (provide at least a two-week notice).

End the letter of resignation with a closing of goodwill (for example, "I wish all of you the best in the future.").

YOUR TURN List the benefits of *not* "burning your bridges" (showing anger or bitterness) in your letter of resignation.

Report
100-71

Complaint

A complaint uses the same format as a summons, as shown in Report 98-69.

Add line numbers for all lines in this court document, and restart line numbers on each page.

Type the title on the same line as *vs.*

Press ENTER 2 times before each Roman numeral.

All Roman numerals are centered between the margins.

A complaint is the initial document filed with a court by a plaintiff to begin an adversarial or action at law proceeding. A judgment is the decision of the court.

1 STATE OF NORTH DAKOTA   IN DISTRICT COURT

2

3 COUNTY OF WALSH   NORTHEAST JUDICIAL DISTRICT

4

5 WALSH COUNTY BANK   )   NO _____

6 170 Main Street   )

7 Adams, ND 58210   )

8   )

9   Plaintiff,   )

10   )

11   vs.   )   COMPLAINT

12   )

13 KENNEDY FARMERS, INC.   )

14 JAMES D. KENNEDY and   )

15 CAROL KENNEDY,   )

16   )

17   Defendants   )

18

19 PLAINTIFF FOR ITS CAUSE OF ACTION AND COMPLAINT

20 AGAINST THE DEFENDANTS, COMPLAINS, ALLEGES AND SHOWS

21 TO THE COURT:

22

23   I.

24   That defendants owe plaintiff $5,685.00, plus interest and charges,

25 under the terms of a promissory note executed April 10, 20--, a copy of

26 which is attached hereto and incorporated by reference as "Exhibit A."

27

28   II.

29   That defendants have not, upon due demand, satisfied their

30 obligation under the terms of the promissory note.

31

32   III.

33   That Kennedy Farmers, Inc., is a North Dakota for-profit

34 corporation duly organized under the corporate laws of the State of North

35 Dakota.

36

37   IV.

38 That the registered agent of Kennedy Farmers, Inc., is James D. Kennedy.

(Continued on next page)

1   V.

V.

2   That James D. Kennedy executed a Commercial Guaranty for the
3 note dated April 10, 20--, a copy of which is attached hereto and
4 incorporated herein by reference as "Exhibit B."
5

VI.

7   That Carol Kennedy executed a Commercial Guaranty on the
8 prior promissory note No. 7249, and the Commercial Guaranty provides
9 that the guaranty extends to ". . . all renewals of, extensions of,
10 modifications of, refinancings of, consolidations of, and substitutions for
11 the promissory note or agreement." A copy of that Commercial Guaranty is
12 attached hereto and incorporated hereby by reference as "Exhibit D."
13

VII.

15   That the indebtedness was the renewal of a prior promissory note
16 executed by Kennedy Farmers, Inc., to Walsh County Bank on June 17, 20--,
17 which was in the original principal amount of $6,685.00, a copy of which is
18 attached hereto and incorporated by reference as "Exhibit C."
19

VIII.

21   That James D. Kennedy and Carol Kennedy are personally liable
22 for the amount of the debt, as is the corporation, Kennedy Farmers, Inc.
23

24   WHEREFORE, PLAINTIFF DEMANDS JUDGMENT AGAINST
25 THE DEFENDANTS, AND EACH OF THEM, AS FOLLOWS:
26

27 1. For the amount of $3,585.00, plus interest on that amount from
28   and after April 10, 20--, at the rate of 10.75% per annum; and
29   for its costs, late charges, and disbursements in this action;
30

31 2. For such other and further relief as the Court may deem
32   appropriate.
33

34 SIGNED this _____ day of December, 20--.
35
36 _____
37 Harold E. Jensen   Attorney-at-Law
38 405 1st Street
39 Adams, ND 58210
40 Telephone: 701-555-4832
41 Attorney for Plaintiff

Reference Manual

Refer to page R-12C of the Reference Manual for an overview of formatting lists.

A judgment uses the same format as a summons, as shown in Report 98-69.

Add line numbers in this court document.

1 STATE OF ARIZONA   IN DISTRICT COURT

2

3 COUNTY OF MARICOPA   CENTRAL JUDICIAL DISTRICT

4

5 Timothy Barnes d/b/a Barnes Computers)   CIVIL NO. 43-89-D-00145

6 1651 West Baseline Road   )

7 Tempe, AZ 85283   )

8   )

9   Plaintiff,   )

10   )

11   vs   )   JUDGMENT

12   )

13 Maricopa Hospital Association   )

14 d/b/a Maricopa Nursing Care   )

15   )

16   Defendant   )

17

18 ¶ The defendant, Maricopa Hospital Association,

19 d/b/a Maricopa Nursing Care, having been

20 regularly served with process, and having failed

21 to appear and answer the plaintiff's Complaint filed

22 herein, and the default of said defendant having

23 been duly entered, and it appearing that said

24 defendant is not an infant or an incompetent

25 person, and an affidavit of nonmilitary service

26 having been filed herein, and it appearing by the

27 affidavits of plaintiff that plaintiff is entitled to

28 judgment herein,

29 ¶ IT IS THEREFORE ORDERED AND ADJUDGED, that

30 the plaintiff have and recover from the

31 defendant, Maricopa Hospital Association d/b/a

32 Maricopa Nursing Care, the sum of $8,000.00

33 plus interest thereon from and after August 10,

34 20--, until paid, together with costs in the sum

35 of $252.75.

36 ¶ SIGNED this _____ day of _____, 20-- .

37

_____

Clerk of the District Court

Use the same format as in the affidavit shown in Report 96-67.

Add line numbers for all lines in this court document.

Progress and Proofreading Check

Documents designated as Proofreading Checks serve as a check of your proofreading skill. Your goal is to have zero typographical errors when the GDP software first scores the document.

1 AFFIDAVIT OF POSSESSION

2

3 STATE OF OREGON

4

5 COUNTY OF LINN

6

7   I, MARILYN T. HUGGINS, being first duly sworn, depose and say:

8

9   That I am the petitioner in the above-entitled suit.

10

11   That the respondent, RICHARD M. HUGGINS, and I are the

12 parents of BENJAMIN T. HUGGINS. That BENJAMIN T. HUGGINS is

13 currently residing exclusively with me. Respondent is currently residing

14 away from the home at 1529 South Oak Street, Albany, Oregon. That I am a

15 fit and proper person to have immediate and temporary custody of

16 BENJAMIN T. HUGGINS.

17

18   I believe that these pending dissolution proceedings will aggravate

19 this situation; therefore, I believe that it is necessary and appropriate for

20 the Court to issure an Order restraining and enjoining respondent from

21 physically or verbally abusing or harassing me or our child in any way.

22

23   _____

24

25   Subscribed and sworn to before me this _____ day of

26 _____, 20--.

27

28   _____

29   Notary Public for Oregon

30   My commission expires January 7, 2012

Skills Assessment
on Part 5

5-Minute Timed Writing

1   When you submit your resume to apply for a job, you   11
2 want your resume to be noticed. Here are some things you   22
3 might do to make certain your resume receives the time and   34
4 focus it deserves.   38
5   First, be neat. Review each page to make sure that it   49
6 is free of typos and spelling errors. Check each page for   60
7 correct grammar. Remember that this document will make the   72
8 first impression with a potential employer. You want the   83
9 document to represent you in the best way. Use white paper   95
10 of good quality to print your resume.   103
11   Second, try to be creative. Make your resume unique. A   114
12 future employer may be looking for specific things when he   126
13 or she scans the pages of your resume. Be sure to provide   137
14 facts that explain exactly what skills you have acquired in   149
15 positions you have held in the past. Avoid using the same   161
16 buzzwords that everyone else uses.   168
17   Finally, state a career objective on your resume. Some   179
18 experts suggest that by stating a career objective, you are   191
19 showing a career path. Others think that stating a career   203
20 objective may limit many job possibilities. If you state a   215
21 career objective, make sure the objective is in line with   226
22 the specific job for which you are applying.   235

| 1 | 2 | 3 | 4 | 5 | 6 | 7 | 8 | 9 | 10 | 11 | 12

13 July 20-- | Mr. Antoine Lauvergeon | Marketing Director | Alatel Inc. | 54, Rue la Boetie | 75382 Paris | France | Dear Mr. Lauvergeon:

¶ As we predicted, our jefe effort marketing was a tremendous success in the 5 new plants opened last Spring in France and Germany. In fact, sales at those two plants have surpassed our Switzerland and Italy sales over the same period. Much of this sucess is due to your timely marketing campaign that was conducted during the first quarter. Congratulations to you and your staff on this fine effort.

Because of this positive experience, we have decided to expand our promotional campaign at our plants in Negras Piedras, Morelia, and Puebla. Would you please put together a proposal for these plants and send it to me by the end of next week. We are excited about this oportunity and look forward to recieving your proposal.

¶ Again, nice work on the France and Germany effort.

Sincerely, | Harold Deforey | V.P. Marketing | c: Mari Lynn Somnolet, James Lafforgue

HEMATOLOGY REPORT

Patient Name:			Date:	
	WBC			Glucose
	Hemoglobin			Cholesterol
	PMN			BUN
	Bands			Calcium
	Lymphs			Phosphorous
	Mono			Bilirubin
	Eos			Uric acid
	Baso			Alkaline phosphate
	Platelets			Albumin
	Thyroid			Protein, total

1 STATE OF NEBRASKA   IN DISTRICT COURT
2
3 COUNTY OF WAYNE   NORTHEAST JUDICIAL DISTRICT
4
5 PAUL C. CREWS   )   NO. _____
6 601 Thorman Street   )
7 Wayne, NE 66787-2243)
8   )
9   Plaintiff,   )
10   )
11   vs.   )   SUMMONS
12   )
13 ANGELINA WASHINGTON)
14   )
15   Defendant.   )
16
17 THE STATE OF NEBRASKA TO THE ABOVE-NAMED DEFENDANTS:
18
19   You are hereby summoned and required to appear and defend
20 against the Complaint in this action, which is hereby served upon you by
21 serving upon the undersigned an Answer or other proper response within
22 twenty (20) days after the service of the Summons and Complaint upon
23 you, exclusive of the day of service.
24
25   If you fail to do so, judgment by default will be taken against you
26 for the relief demanded in the Complaint.
27
28   SIGNED this _____ day of May, 20--.
29
30   _____
31   Jeremy Richfield   Attorney-at-Law
32   Box 148
33   Wayne, NE 67878-2648
34   Telephone: 402-555-1205
35   Attorney for Plaintiff

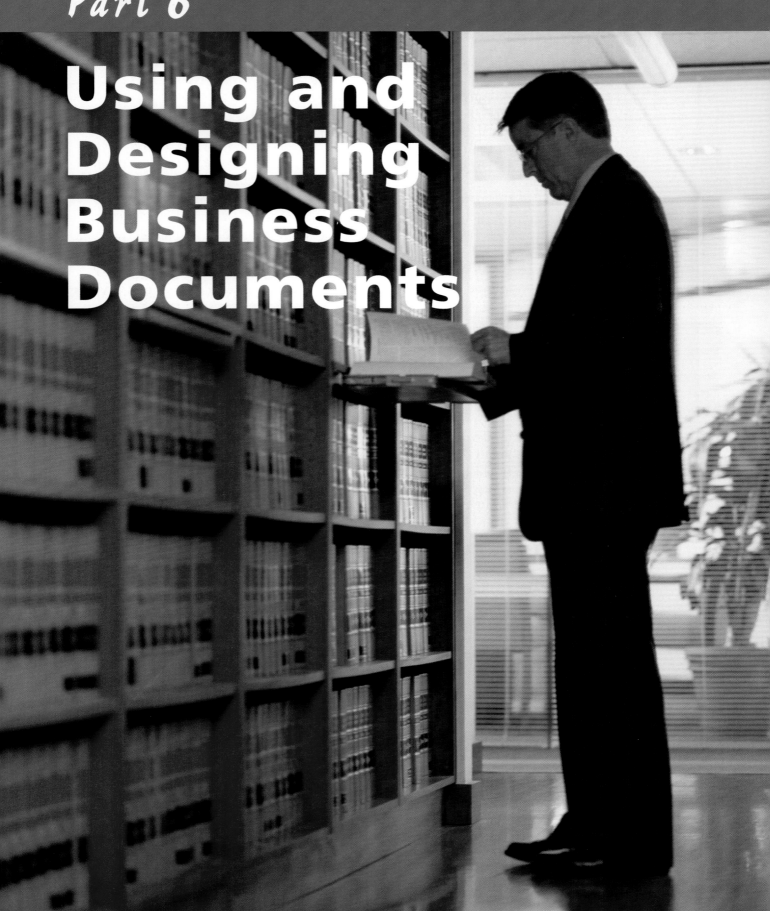

Part 6

Using and Designing Business Documents

Keyboarding in Legal Services Careers

A career in legal services can take many forms. Lawyers, of course, are responsible for legal work, but a number of other positions in the legal services field are available. Often, lawyers assign tasks to paralegals. Paralegals—also referred to as legal assistants—have taken on a larger percentage of responsibilities in recent years. Another profession in the law field, that of court reporter, requires excellent communication skills. Court reporters are responsible for taking exact notes in court, in meetings, and at any other event where an accurate account of the proceedings is needed. Keyboarding skills are important for many job functions in legal services careers, and they can prove to give a job candidate an advantage.

Paralegals can work in many different business settings, but they are found most commonly in law firms and government offices. Court reporters are responsible for providing an accurate and detailed legal record of any proceeding. For individuals working in the legal services field, strong communication skills, written and spoken, are very important, but being able to convey ideas in a typed report in a timely manner is even more important.

Objectives

KEYBOARDING

- Type at least 50 words per minute on a 5-minute timed writing with no more than 5 errors.

LANGUAGE ARTS

- Refine proofreading skills and correctly use proofreaders' marks.
- Use capitals, punctuation, and grammar correctly.
- Improve composing and spelling skills.
- Recognize subject/verb agreement.

WORD PROCESSING

- Use the word processing commands necessary to complete the document processing activities.

DOCUMENT PROCESSING

- Design office forms, office publications, and Web pages.

TECHNICAL

- Answer at least 90 percent of the questions correctly on an objective test.

Unit 21

Using and Designing Office Forms

LESSON 101
Using Correspondence Templates

LESSON 102
Using Report Templates

LESSON 103
Designing Letterheads

LESSON 104
Designing Notepads

LESSON 105
Designing Miscellaneous Office Forms

 From the Desk of Amber Bristol

 From the Desk of Amber Bristol

❑ *Urgent*
❑ *Do Today*
❑ *Follow-Up*

❑ *Urgent*
❑ *Do Today*
❑ *Follow-Up*

From the Desk of Amber Bristol

 From the Desk of Amber Bristol

❑ *Urgent*
❑ *Do Today*
❑ *Follow-Up*

❑ *Urgent*
❑ *Do Today*
❑ *Follow-Up*

Memorandum

To:	Naoe Okubo, Senior Graphics Artist
CC:	Roy Phillips, Marketing Manager
From:	Gloria Hernandez, Vice President
Date:	June 17, 20--
Re:	Web Site Redesign

Our Web site needs a complete reorganization and redesign. I know this assignment will be a major challenge, and I have full confidence in your experience and ability. Within the next week, please contact five Web design firms and make arrangements for a formal presentation to you and your staff. Invite Roy Phillips and his staff in marketing as well. When you have chosen the two best candidates, submit your findings to our key executives in a formal presentation. The better of the two will then be chosen.

Because our Web site is critical to our sales and marketing efforts, you must make this assignment a top priority. If you need temporary help to support you in your efforts, let me know.

Thank you for your continued good work, Naoe. I look forward to the presentation and your recommendations.

wn

WINTER SPORTS

2820 Cerillos Road • Santa Fe, NM 87505 • 505-555-3496 • www.wintersports.com

Using Correspondence Templates

Goals

- Improve speed and accuracy
- Refine language arts skills in grammar
- Format correspondence using a template

A. Type 2 times.

A. WARMUP

```
1        The secretary made a reservation on Flight #847; it      11
2    departs at exactly 3:05 on July 6. A sizable number of       22
3    key executives (about 1/2) requested seats in Rows G to M.   33
     |  1  |  2  |  3  |  4  |  5  |  6  |  7  |  8  |  9  |  10  |  11  |  12
```

SKILLBUILDING

B. Take three 12-second timed writings on each line. The scale below the last line shows your wpm speed for a 12-second timed writing.

B. 12-SECOND SPEED SPRINTS

```
4   Bob will lend all the keys to you if you will fix the leak.
5   Ruth wanted to thank you for all of the work you did today.
6   Both of the books will have to be sent to her by next week.
7   Dick paid her half of the money when she signed the papers.
    I I I I 5 I I I 10 I I I 15 I I I 20 I I I 25 I I I 30 I I I 35 I I I 40 I I I 45 I I I 50 I I I 55 I I I 60
```

C. PROGRESSIVE PRACTICE: ALPHABET

If you are not using the GDP software, turn to page SB-7 and follow the directions for this activity.

D. PROGRESSIVE PRACTICE: NUMBERS

If you are not using the GDP software, turn to page SB-11 and follow the directions for this activity.

LANGUAGE ARTS

E. Study the rules at the right.

RULE ▶
adjective/adverb

E. ADJECTIVES AND ADVERBS AND AGREEMENT

Use comparative adjectives and adverbs (-er, more, and less) when referring to two nouns or pronouns; use superlative adjectives and adverbs (-est, most, and least) when referring to more than two.

The <u>shorter</u> of the <u>two</u> training sessions is the <u>more</u> helpful one.

The <u>longest</u> of the <u>three</u> training sessions is the <u>least</u> helpful one.

RULE ▶

agreement nearer noun

If two subjects are joined by *or, either/or, neither/nor,* or *not only/but also,* make the verb agree with the subject nearer to the verb.

Neither the coach nor the <u>players</u> <u>are</u> at home.

Not only the coach but also the <u>referee</u> <u>is</u> at home.

But: <u>Both</u> the coach and the referee <u>are</u> at home.

Edit the sentences to correct any errors in grammar.

8 Of the three printers, the faster one was the most expensive.
9 Of the two phones purchased, the first one is the better model.
10 The quietest of the five printers is also the less expensive.
11 Not only the manager but also the employees wants to attend.
12 Neither the printer nor the monitors is in working order.
13 Either Mr. Cortez or his assistants have to sign the order.
14 Coffee or soft drinks is available for the afternoon session.
15 Not only the manual but also the software were mailed.

FORMATTING

F. FILLING IN FORMS

Many business forms can be created by using templates that are provided within word processing software. When a template is opened, a generic form is displayed on the screen. Specific information that is appropriate for that form may then be added.

Template forms contain data fields that correspond to blank sections on printed forms. For example, a memo template may include the guide words *To:, CC:, From:, Date:,* and *Re*: for the subject. Templates are usually designed so that you can replace data in fields easily by clicking in the field and typing or by selecting the information you want to replace and typing. Built-in styles are also readily available.

You can customize a generic template by filling in repetitive information (such as the company name and telephone number) and save it as a new template. Then each time you open that newly created template, the customized information appears automatically.

Word Processing Manual

G. WORD PROCESSING: CORRESPONDENCE TEMPLATES

Study Lesson 101 in your word processing manual. Complete all of the shaded steps while at your computer. Then format the jobs that follow.

DOCUMENT PROCESSING

Form 101-1 ▶

Memo Template

Note: You may want to read and print the information in the template before deleting it.

1. Select the first memo template listed in your word processing software.
2. Follow the directions on the template to type the information for this memo, using the built-in styles as needed.
3. Use the month/day/year format for the date.

4. Type the information for the memo from the copy shown on the next page.

Note 1: In the body of the memo, the cursor will automatically drop down 1 blank line below a paragraph when you press the ENTER key.

Note 2: Remove any extra text boxes that may appear on the page as part of the default memo template.

To: Naoe Okubo, Senior Graphics Artist

CC: Mr. Roy Phillips, Marketing Manager

From: Gloria Hernandez, Vice President

Date: June 17, 20--

Re: Website Redesign

¶ Our web site needs a complete redesign and reorganization. I know this assignment *will be* a major challenge, and I have full confidence in your skill *experience* and ability. Within the next week, ~~you should~~ *please* contact ⑤ web design firms and make arrangements for a formal presentation to you and your staff. ~~Please~~ invite Roy Phillips and his staff in Marketing as well. When you have chosen the two best candidates, submit your findings to *our* key executives in a *formal* presentation. The better of the two will then be chosen.

¶ Because our web site is ~~crucial~~ *critical* to our sales and marketing efforts, you must make this assignment a top priority. If you need temporary help to support you in your efforts, let me know. Thank you for your continued good work, Naoe. I look forward to *the* ~~your~~ presentation and your recommendations.

urs

adjective/adverb

adjective/adverb

Form 101-2

Letter Template

1. Select the first letter template listed in your word processing software.
2. Follow the template directions to type the information for this letter using the built-in styles as needed.
   Note: Delete the company slogan text box at the bottom of the template.
3. The company name is Global Web Resources.
4. Type each line of the return address on a separate line. (The setup of the return address should be similar to the arrangement you use for the inside address.)

The return address is as follows:
   575 Eighth Avenue, Suite 1104
   New York, NY 10018
   212-555-3495
   www.globalwebresources.com

5. Use the default spacing provided by the template between the date and the inside address.
6. Type the rest of the information into the template, as indicated in the copy below, using standard business letter format for a block-style letter.
   Note: Save this job as FORM 101-2.

June 23, 20-- | Naoe Okubo | Contempo Fashions | 22802 Soledad Canyon | Santa Clarita, CA 91355 | Dear Ms. Okubo:

¶ Thank you for your request for more information on Web page design, layout, and graphics. I have enclosed some brochures that address some of your questions.

¶ Ms. Ina Phillips is our senior account manager in your area. Either her staff members or Ms. Phillips is going to schedule an appointment with you and your staff for a formal presentation of our design portfolios this week. The best way to answer your questions and to help you reach a decision is to

agreement nearer noun

(Continued on next page)

have you see examples of some of the Web sites we have developed for other clients in the fashion industry. I know you will be impressed by the creativity and innovative concepts that Global Web Resources is known for in this business.

¶If you would like a preview now, please go to www.globalwebresources.com and click the link entitled Professional Images to see some of our best designs. Again, thank you for your interest in our services.

Sincerely, | Linda Vigil | Vice President | urs | Enclosures

adjective/adverb

Press SHIFT + ENTER 2 times after typing "Vice President" to position your reference initials correctly at the left margin.

Form ▶
101-3

Memo Template

agreement nearer noun

Select the first memo template listed in your word processing software.

To: Roy Phillips, Marketing Manager | **CC:** Gloria Hernandez, Vice President | **From:** Naoe Okubo, Senior Graphics Artist | **Date:** August 7, 20-- | **Re:** Web Site Redesign

¶I have contacted five Web design firms for formal presentations in our executive boardroom. A schedule of the meeting dates and times is attached. Because Ms. Hernandez has indicated that this assignment is to take top priority, not only current projects but also future work is to be put on hold. If you need any temporary help with any projects in progress, let me know.

¶The Web design firms that have been scheduled are very innovative and creative. The presentations should be exciting. Ask your staff to prepare for the meeting by visiting the Web sites and doing some research on each company. Please forward this memo to the members of your staff.

urs | Attachment

Keyboarding Connection

Transferring Text From a Web Page

Have you ever wished you could copy the text from a Web page? You can!

To select the desired text to copy, click in front of the text and drag to the end of it. (If the text won't highlight, try to click at the end of the desired text and drag backward.) To copy the Web text, from the Edit menu, select Copy. Open your word processing document. Position the cursor where you want to paste the text. From the Edit menu of the word processor, select Paste. The text will appear in the word processing document.

When you copy text information from the Web, you must cite the source in your word processing document by giving the URL (Web page address), Web page name, and author, if given.

YOUR TURN Open a Web page. Copy some text and paste it in a word processing document.

Using Report Templates

Goals

- Type at least 48wpm/5′/5e
- Format reports using a template

A. Type 2 times.

A. WARMUP

```
1        I am glad the office measures just 15 × 23* (*feet)    11
2   because the carpet is quite expensive! At $64/yard, we      22
3   can't afford any mistakes; contact v&zcarpets@mail.com.     33
    | 1 | 2 | 3 | 4 | 5 | 6 | 7 | 8 | 9 | 10 | 11 | 12
```

SKILLBUILDING

B. PACED PRACTICE

If you are not using the GDP software, turn to page SB-14 and follow the directions for this activity.

C. Take two 5-minute timed writings. Review your speed and errors.

Goal: At least 48wpm/5'/5e

C. 5-MINUTE TIMED WRITING

```
 4        Job stress is not that uncommon in today's workplace.   11
 5   There may be many causes of job stress; but the most likely  23
 6   reasons it occurs are overwork, possible layoffs, conflicts  35
 7   with people at work, or just simply working in a job that    47
 8   is no longer to your liking.                                 52
 9        Symptoms of job stress are common to many people, and   63
10   they include changes in sleeping patterns, short temper,     75
11   upset stomach, headache, and low morale. Although many of    86
12   us suffer from one or more of the above symptoms, we should  98
13   take them seriously if the symptoms continue or if we tend  110
14   to experience three or four of the symptoms at the same     121
15   time continuously.                                          125
16        Sometimes it is possible to reduce the stress in your  136
17   work by taking a commonsense approach to the situation. If  148
18   you think that you are being overworked, take a vacation or 160
19   avoid taking work home with you. If you are concerned about 172
20   layoffs, then be certain that you are prepared to make a    183
21   career change if it is required. If you have conflicts with 195
22   your boss or with others at the office, try to work them    207
23   out by discussing the issues with the people involved to be 219
24   certain they understand all aspects of the conflict. Then,  231
25   work together to minimize any future conflicts.             240
     | 1 | 2 | 3 | 4 | 5 | 6 | 7 | 8 | 9 | 10 | 11 | 12
```

FORMATTING

Word Processing Manual

D. WORD PROCESSING: REPORT TEMPLATES

Study Lesson 102 in your word processing manual. Complete all of the shaded steps while at your computer. Then format the jobs that follow.

DOCUMENT PROCESSING

Form 102-4 ▶

Report Template

Note: You may want to read and print the information in the template before deleting it.

1. Select the first report template listed in your word processing software.
2. Type the information for this report using the built-in template styles as needed.
3. On the title page, type the following address:

   575 Eighth Avenue, Suite 1104
   New York, NY 10018
   212-555-3495
   www.globalwebresources.com.

4. The company name is Global Web Resources.
5. The title is Web Design Proposal.
6. The subtitle is Strategies for the Online Presence of Contempo Fashions.
7. Use the same title and subtitle on the second page of the report.
8. Type the rest of the information into the template, as indicated in the copy below.

Introduction

¶ Two major issues need to be addressed in terms of the website design for Contempo Fashions. The site's most obvious weakness is its lack of unity. The content seems to be out of sync with the design. This division is definitely noticeable to the casual observer.

¶ Often those in charge of content don't have any background in html or coding of any kind, and feel locked into the current design because they simply don't know what their options are. Those in charge of the design can get caught up in trying to create an attractive page that doesn't really work effectively with the content. Global Web Resources is in the business of providing workable solutions that address both these needs.

Content Issues

¶ The content is by far the first and most important element in a web site. If the content is not effective, it doesn't matter how attractive the design is because no one will bother to read beyond the first page or even the first line. Spelling and grammar must be checked with meticulous care. The credibility of your company is at stake. The readability of the web site can be dramatically improved. Headings, subheadings, bullets, and numbers are critical in making your pages readable. Visitors to your site scan for major headings and want to move quickly and efficiently to any items of interest. Visual separation between paragraphs is also critical for readability. The use of

(Continued on next page)

whitespace created by inserting blank lines between paragraphs is generally more effective than indenting paragraphs. Short lines and short pages make readers want to look at your *site* pages ~~rather than avoid them~~.

Design Issues

¶ The design of the web site is ⟨done⟩ ⟨well⟩ overall. Appropriate fonts, colors, and art were used in a manner that complements the image of Contempo Fashions. The site's navigation is intuitive ~~and easy to use~~. However, the design is dated and needs a new look.

¶ The ②groups that are now managing the site must be given guidance in working together to produce a unified site that is both attractive and effective. The goals of the design group and those in charge of content must be brought into alignment in order to make the content work within the context of the current design. Global Web Resources has a web design solution that will bring the needs of *both* ~~these~~ groups into alignment. Your redesigned site will be visually appealing, informative, and intuitive to the visitor. *We* look forward to our *meeting* ~~detailed presentation~~ this week.

Form 102-5

Report Template

Open the file for Form 102-4 and make the following changes:

1. On the title page, change the address as follows:

   8502 North Ashley Street
   Tampa, FL 33604
   813-555-1205
   www.CTI.com.

2. The company name is CompuTek International.
3. Change the report title both on the title page and on the first page of the report to Web Site Proposal.
4. Change the report subtitle both on the title page and on the first page of the report to Content and Design Recommendations for Contempo Fashions.
5. Delete the second paragraph under the heading "Introduction."
6. Delete the second paragraph under the heading "Content Issues."
7. Delete the last paragraph of the report.

8. Move the insertion point to the end of the first paragraph under the heading "Design Issues," and press ENTER 1 time.
9. Use the Heading 1 style to add the heading Solutions.
10. Move to the end of the report, and add the following paragraphs.
   Paragraph 1:

   Your Web site should always have new and updated content so that your visitors will have good reason to return. If you continue with your current Web site plan, the maintenance of your site will become a major responsibility. Hundreds of files will need to be maintained whenever you want to make a fundamental change to your site.

(Continued on next page)

The best approach is to let your writers post new content themselves without having to worry about design issues. This is accomplished through a database-driven Web site.

Paragraph 2:
Building a database-driven Web site requires a great deal of technical expertise and tools such as scripting languages and relational database software. Your operating system must be compatible with these languages and databases. Server-side programming is also critical here. CompuTek International would build a database-driven site design and host the site to minimize technical troubleshooting issues. We look forward to our meeting this week.

Designing Letterheads

Goals

- Improve speed and accuracy
- Refine language arts skills in composing
- Design letterheads

A. Type 2 times.

A. WARMUP

```
1        Does Quentin know if 1/2 of the January order will be    11
2   ready? At 5:30 about 46% of the orders still hadn't been      22
3   mailed! Mr. Gray expects a very sizable loss this month.      34
    |  1  |  2  |  3  |  4  |  5  |  6  |  7  |  8  |  9  |  10 |  11 |  12
```

SKILLBUILDING

B. DIAGNOSTIC PRACTICE: SYMBOLS AND PUNCTUATION

If you are not using the GDP software, turn to page SB-2 and follow the directions for this activity.

C. These paragraphs are made up of very short words, requiring the frequent use of the SPACE BAR. Do not pause before or after pressing the SPACE BAR. Type the paragraph 2 times.

C. TECHNIQUE PRACTICE: SPACE BAR

```
4         He had the car in the shop and knew that the cost for
5   the work might be high. If the bill for the work was to be
6   more than he could pay, he knew that he would skip it. It
7   did not make any sense to put more money into the old car.
8         If you are near the old shop, come in to see if you can
9   pay the bill at that time. If you are not able to pay it at
10  that time, you can come back to see us when you are able.
```

LANGUAGE ARTS

D. COMPOSING A MEMO

Compose the body of a memo to explain basic design guidelines. Refer to page 411—Section E, Designing a Form—frequently. Use the following suggestions for composing each paragraph:

Paragraph 1. Explain that a simple, balanced design is essential and that typefaces (fonts), attributes, and sizes should be limited.

Paragraph 2. Explain that white space should be used to make text easier to read and graphics easier to see.

Paragraph 3. Explain that word processing software is a powerful tool that makes experimenting easy.

FORMATTING

E. DESIGNING A FORM

Use the following guidelines to design an attractive, effective form:

1. Keep all elements of your design simple and balanced.
2. Limit the number of typefaces, attributes (bold, italics, and so on), and sizes. Using two typefaces is a good rule of thumb.
3. Use white space liberally to separate and open up text and graphics.
4. Use different alignments (left, center, right, and full) to add interest and emphasis.
5. Experiment and change—word processing software makes both easy to do.

Word Processing Manual

F. WORD PROCESSING: SMALL CAPS AND TEXT BOXES

Study Lesson 103 in your word processing manual. Complete all of the shaded steps while at your computer. Then format the jobs that follow.

DOCUMENT PROCESSING

Form 103-6

Letterhead Form

Note: When creating, sizing, or positioning a text box, switch to a whole-page view. When typing text, switch to a page-width view or larger as desired. As you add information to the text box, adjust the size of the text box as needed.

1. Change the left and right margins to 0.25 inch, and press ENTER 2 times.
2. Apply a border to the bottom of the second blank line.
3. Insert a picture of an elementary school or kindergarten.
4. Drag and size the picture so that it looks like the one in the illustration at the left and on page 410.
5. Create a text box next to the school, about the size and in the same position as the one in the illustration, to hold the business name.
6. Remove the line around the text box, and change the fill to none.

7. Change to Arial 18-point small caps, and center and type Tutor Time.
8. Change the font color as desired to coordinate with the picture.
9. Create a text box, about the size and in the same position as the one in the illustration, to hold the address of the business.
10. Remove the line around the text box, and change the fill to none.
11. Change the font to Arial 10 point, and right-align and type the lines of the address:

```
4219 Richmond Avenue,
Suite 205
Houston, TX 77027
713-555-7337
www.tutortime.com
```

(Continued on next page)

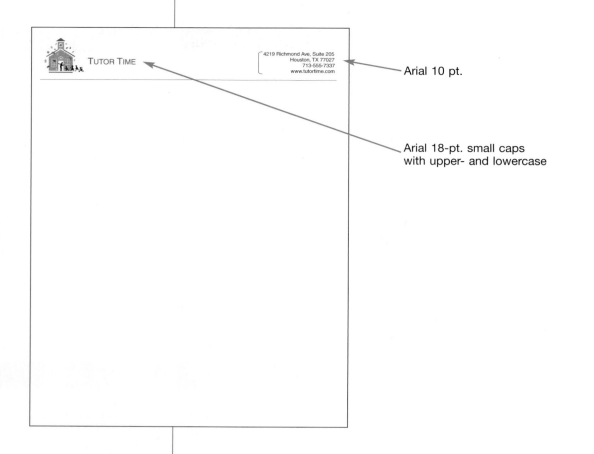

TUTOR TIME

4219 Richmond Ave, Suite 205
Houston, TX 77027
713-555-7337
www.tutortime.com

Arial 10 pt.

Arial 18-pt. small caps
with upper- and lowercase

Form 103-7

Letterhead Form

1. Press ENTER 2 times, and insert a picture of your favorite winter sport.
2. Drag and size the picture so that it looks like the one in the illustration on the left and on page 411.
3. Create a text box, about the size and in the same position as the one in the illustration, to hold the name of the business.
4. Remove the line around the text box, and change the fill to none.
5. Change to Times New Roman Italic 24-point small caps, and type Winter Sports with upper- and lowercase.
6. Change the font color of the business name to coordinate with one of the colors in the picture.
7. Create a text box, about the size and in the same position as the one in the

illustration, to hold the address of the business.
8. Change the font to Times New Roman 10 point and center and type the lines of the address, all on one continuous line.

   2820 Cerillos Road
   Santa Fe, NM 87505
   505-555-3496
   www.wintersports.com

9. Insert a diamond-shaped symbol between each item in the address block as shown in the illustration. Insert 1 space before and after the symbol.
10. Add a fill to the text box to coordinate with one of the colors in the picture.

(Continued on next page)

Times New Roman Italic 24-pt. small caps with upper- and lowercase

Times New Roman 10 pt.

WINTER SPORTS

2820 Cerillos Road ◆ Santa Fe, NM 87505 ◆ 505-555-3496 ◆ www.wintersports.com

Form 103-8

Letterhead Form

1. Create a letterhead design of your own—for you personally, for your school, or for a business.
2. Insert at least one picture that enhances the theme of the letterhead.
3. Remember to include complete information in the address block.
4. Try using fonts that you have not yet applied—experiment with point sizes and attributes.

Strategies for Career Success

Designing the Page for Readability

A well-designed document is appealing to the eye, is easy to read, and shows you are professional and competent. Follow these simple guidelines to increase the readability of your documents.

Use white space (that is, empty space) to make material easier to read by separating it from other text. Side margins should be equal. Create white space by varying paragraph length. The first and last paragraphs should be short—three to five typed lines.

Use bulleted or numbered lists to emphasize material. Lists are normally indented on the left. Make sure all the items in the list are grammatically parallel in structure. Use headings to introduce new material. Use full caps sparingly. Consider desktop publishing software to visually enhance your document. Remember to balance graphics, lists, and text.

YOUR TURN Review a document you have recently written. What page design and format techniques did you use to make the document more readable?

Designing Notepads

Goals

- Type at least 48wpm/5′/5e
- Design notepads

A. Type 2 times.

A. WARMUP

```
1        This series* (*2 films, 9 minutes) by J. Zeller goes    11
2   beyond the "basics" of computers. Viewers keep requesting    22
3   an extension on the dates; this includes 3/2, 5/5, and 8/9.  34
    |  1  |  2  |  3  |  4  |  5  |  6  |  7  |  8  |  9  |  10  |  11  |  12
```

SKILLBUILDING

B. MAP

Follow the GDP software directions for this exercise in improving keystroking accuracy.

C. Take two 5-minute timed writings. Review your speed and errors.

Goal: At least 48wpm/5'/5e

C. 5-MINUTE TIMED WRITING

4	Employers are always searching for people who have	10
5	salable skills. Having salable skills makes you unique and	22
6	desirable as an employee. Developing skills and qualities	34
7	such as a pleasing personality, a good sense of humor, a	45
8	positive attitude, an ability to get along with people, and	57
9	the ability to manage your time and prioritize your work	69
10	may help you find a job.	74
11	A tenacious person is persistent and maintains strong	85
12	work habits. He or she does not give up on a task easily	96
13	and always expects to finish the assigned task.	106
14	A good sense of humor and a positive attitude are two	117
15	traits that can help a person advance on the job. Although	128
16	there are times to be serious at work, sometimes you have	140
17	to look at things humorously. If you maintain a positive	151
18	attitude, other workers will like to work with you.	162
19	When you acquire the skills to manage your time and	172
20	prioritize your work, you will be successful in anything	184
21	you try to do. When you are given an assignment, ask for	195
22	guidelines so that you will know what needs to be done and	207
23	in what order. Then try to complete the assignment in a	218
24	timely fashion. The skills may be difficult to learn, but	230
25	you will be glad you can manage your time and work.	240

| 1 | 2 | 3 | 4 | 5 | 6 | 7 | 8 | 9 | 10 | 11 | 12

FORMATTING

Word Processing Manual

D. WORD PROCESSING: PRINT OPTIONS

Study Lesson 104 in your word processing manual. Complete all of the shaded steps while at your computer. Then format the jobs that follow.

Form 104-9 ▶

Notepad Form

Many ink-jet printers do not print beyond the bottom half inch on a sheet of paper. Keep this in mind when positioning objects at the bottom of a page.

1. Press ENTER 2 times, and insert a picture of an office desk or a picture related to an office notepad.
2. Drag and size the picture so that it looks similar to the one in the illustration on this page.
3. Create a text box, about the size and in the same position as the one in the illustration, to hold the words "From the Desk of Amber Bristol."
4. Remove the line around the text box, and change the fill to none.
5. Change to Arial Bold 18 point, and center and type From the Desk of Amber Bristol inside the text box.
6. Create a text box, about the size and in the same position as the one in the illustration, to hold the check box list at the bottom of the notepad.
7. Remove the line around the text box, and change the fill to none.
8. Insert a check box using Wingdings Italic 18 point. Space 1 time.
9. Change to Arial Italic 28 point, type Urgent inside the text box, and press ENTER 1 time.
10. Repeat steps 8 and 9 for the remaining lines in the check box list, adding the words Do Today and Follow-Up.
11. Change to a whole-page view, and select and copy the entire document.
12. Move to the end of the document and insert three hard page breaks to create three additional blank pages.
13. Paste the copied document into each of the three newly created pages.
14. Use the print option to print four pages per sheet on 8.5- × 11-inch paper.

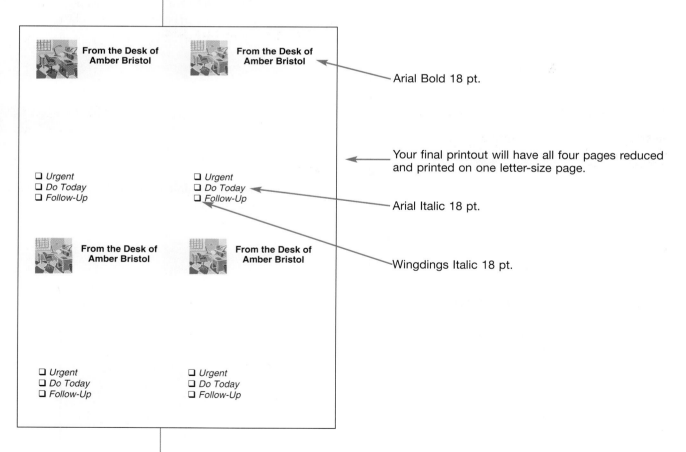

From the Desk of Amber Bristol — Arial Bold 18 pt.

Your final printout will have all four pages reduced and printed on one letter-size page.

❑ Urgent / ❑ Do Today / ❑ Follow-Up — Arial Italic 18 pt.

Wingdings Italic 18 pt.

1. Press ENTER 2 times, and insert a picture of an office desk or a picture related to a musical note or a personalized office note.
2. Drag and size the picture so that it looks similar to the one in the illustration on this page.
3. Create a text box, about the size and in the same position as the one in the illustration, to hold the words "Just a Note to Say . . ."
4. Remove the line around the text box, and change the fill to none.
5. Change to a script font of your choice in 20-point bold and italic.
6. Center and type Just a Note to Say followed by 1 space and 3 periods with 1 space after each period.

7. Create a text box, about the size and in the same position as the one in the illustration, to hold the words at the bottom of the notepad.
8. Change to the same script font used in the first text box, also in 20-point size, and center and type From the Desk of Darin Diaz inside the text box.
9. Change to a whole-page view, and select and copy the entire document.
10. Move to the end of the document, and insert three hard page breaks to create three additional blank pages.
11. Paste the copied document into each of the three newly created pages.
12. Use the print option to print four pages per sheet on 8.5- × 11-inch paper.

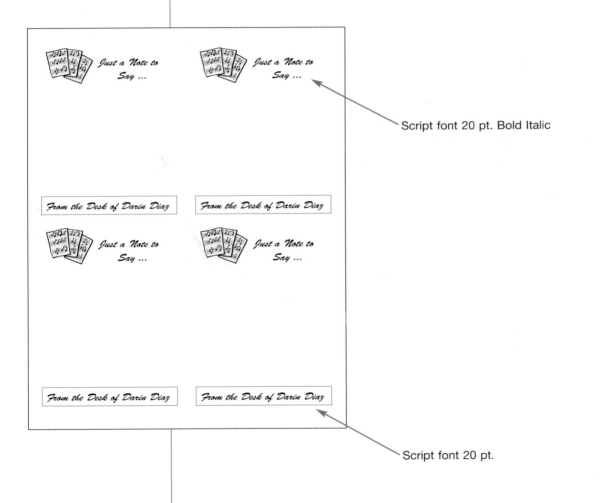

Script font 20 pt. Bold Italic

Script font 20 pt.

1. Create a notepad design of your own— for you personally, for your school, or for a business.
2. Insert at least one picture that enhances the theme of the notepad.

3. Insert at least one text box with a fill.
4. Try using fonts that you have not yet applied. Experiment with point sizes and attributes.

Designing Miscellaneous Office Forms

Goals

- Improve speed and accuracy
- Refine language arts skills in proofreading
- Design miscellaneous office forms

A. Type 2 times.

A. WARMUP

```
1        Item #876 won't be ordered until 9/10. Did you gather    11
2   all requests and input them exactly as they appeared? Zack    23
3   will never be satisfied until he contacts jack@orders.com.    34
    |  1  |  2  |  3  |  4  |  5  |  6  |  7  |  8  |  9  |  10  |  11  |  12
```

SKILLBUILDING

PPP   PRETEST → PRACTICE → POSTTEST

PRETEST
Take a 1-minute timed writing. Review your speed and errors.

B. PRETEST: Vertical Reaches

```
4        The man knelt on the lawn and used a knife with skill    11
5   to raise the valve away from the brace. His back ached in     23
6   vain as he crawled over the knoll to fix the flawed valve.    34
    |  1  |  2  |  3  |  4  |  5  |  6  |  7  |  8  |  9  |  10  |  11  |  12
```

PRACTICE
Speed Emphasis:
If you made no more than 1 error on the Pretest, type each *individual* line 2 times.
Accuracy Emphasis:
If you made 2 or more errors, type each *group* of lines (as though it were a paragraph) 2 times.

C. PRACTICE: Up Reaches

```
7  aw away award crawl straw drawn sawed drawl await flaw lawn
8  se self sense raise these prose abuse users serve send seem
9  ki kind kites skill skier skims skips skits kilts king skid
```

D. PRACTICE: Down Reaches

```
10  ac ache track paced brace races facts crack acute back aces
11  kn knob knife kneel knows knack knelt known knoll knot knew
12  va vain vague value valve evade naval rival avail vats vase
```

POSTTEST
Repeat the Pretest timed writing and compare performance.

E. POSTTEST: Discrimination Practice

F. SUSTAINED PRACTICE: SYLLABIC INTENSITY

```
13        People continue to rent autos for personal use or for    11
14   their work, and the car-rental business continues to grow.     23
15   When you rent a car, look carefully at the insurance cost.     35
16   You might also have to pay a mileage charge for the car.       46

17        It is likely that a good deal of insurance coverage is    11
18   part of the standard rental cost. But you might be urged       23
19   to procure extra medical, property, and collision coverage.    35
20   If you accept, be ready to see your rental charge increase.    46

21        Perhaps this is not necessary, as you may already have    11
22   the kind of protection you want in a policy that you have      23
23   at the present time. By reviewing your own auto insurance      34
24   policy, you may easily save a significant amount of money.     46

25        Paying mileage charges could result in a really large    11
26   bill. This is especially evident when the trips planned        22
27   involve destinations that are many miles apart. Complete a     34
28   total review of traveling plans before making a decision.      43
```

LANGUAGE ARTS

G. Compare these lines with lines 25-28 in the Sustained Practice drill above. Edit the lines to correct any errors.

G. PROOFREADING

```
29        Paying milage charges could result in a very large
30   bill. This is especially evident when the trips planned
31   involve destinations that are manymiles apart. complete a
32   total review of traveling plans before making a decsion.
```

DOCUMENT PROCESSING

Form
105-12

Directory Form

1. Change the page orientation to landscape.
2. Change the top margin to 2.3 inches, and the other margins to 0.75 inch.
3. Press ENTER 1 time.
4. Create a boxed table with 4 columns and 17 rows.
5. Select the entire table and change the font to Arial Bold 18 point.
6. Type these column headings in Row 1: Name | Department | Phone Number | E-Mail Address. Change the alignment in the row to center.
7. Move to the top of the document, and insert a picture, associated with a

directory, in the same position as the one in the illustration on the left and on page 419.
8. Insert a text box, about the size and in the same position as the one in the illustration, to hold the heading.
9. Change to Arial 48 point, and center and type Directory at a Glance inside the text box.
10. Remove the line around the text box, and change the fill to none.
11. Add shading to the cells in Row 1 of the boxed table, using a color that complements the picture.

(Continued on next page)

Directory at a Glance

— Arial 48 pt.

Name	Department	Phone Number	E-Mail Address

— Arial Bold 18 pt.

Form 105-13

Sign-In Form

1. Change the top margin to 2 inches and the other margins to 0.75 inch.
2. Create a boxed table with 4 columns and 30 rows.
3. Select Row 1 and change the font to Arial Bold 18 point.
4. Type these column headings in Row 1: Name | Time In | Doctor's Name | Purpose. Change the alignment in the row to center.
5. Adjust the column widths manually so they appear similar to the column widths in the illustration on the left and on page 420.
6. Select Rows 2-29 and change the font to Arial Bold 12 point.
7. Insert a picture of an office desk or clip art related to an office notepad.
8. Move the insertion point outside the table, then insert a text box, about the size and in the same position as the one in the illustration, to hold the name of the medical group.
9. Change to Times New Roman 48 point, and center and type Facey Medical Group.
10. Remove the line around the text box, and change the fill to none.
11. Create a text box, about the size and in the same position as the one in the illustration, to hold the date line.
12. Change to Arial Bold 12 point, and type Date: followed by a series of underlines to form a date line similar to the one in the illustration.
13. Remove the fill and the lines around the text box.
14. Create a text box, about the size and in the same position as the one in the illustration, to hold the names of the doctors.
15. Change to Times New Roman Italic 12 point, and type the following doctors' names in a bulleted list:

    Dr. Mary Chavez
    Dr. Irving K. Levine
    Dr. Evelyn Jones
16. Remove the line around the text box, and change the fill to none.
17. Change the font color of the words on the form as desired to coordinate with the picture.

(Continued on next page)

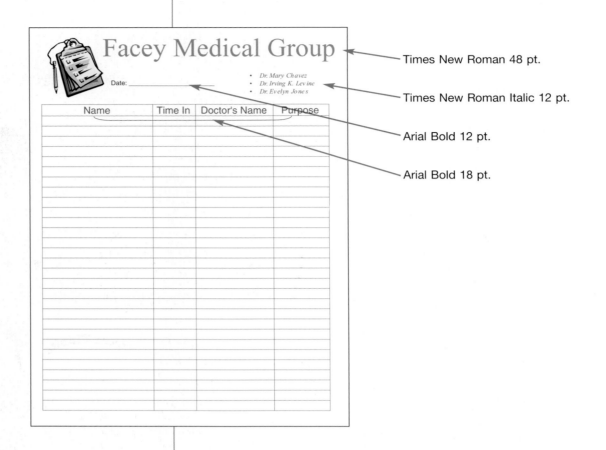

Facey Medical Group ← Times New Roman 48 pt.

Date: _____

- *Dr. Mary Chavez*
- *Dr. Irving K. Levine*
- *Dr. Evelyn Jones*

← Times New Roman Italic 12 pt.

Name	Time In	Doctor's Name	Purpose

← Arial Bold 12 pt.

← Arial Bold 18 pt.

Form 105-14 ▶

Memo Template

Select the first memo template listed in your word processing software.

Progress and Proofreading Check

Documents designated as Proofreading Checks serve as a check of your proofreading skill. Your goal is to have zero typographical errors when the GDP software first scores the document.

To: Gloria Hernandez, Vice President | **CC:** Roy Phillips, Marketing Manager | **From:** Naoe Okubo, Senior Graphics Artist | **Date:** September 3, 20-- | **Re:** Web Site Redesign

¶ I have finished evaluating the five Web design firms that made formal presentations to our Web site team last week. The two finalists are Global Web Resources and CompuTek International. Their portfolios and presentations were very impressive. I believe either firm would be an excellent choice. Mr. Phillips agrees with this assessment.

¶ I have arranged for a formal presentation to our key executives for Wednesday afternoon of next week in our corporate dining room. We will have a luncheon first followed by the presentations. I have attached key information from the portfolios of both firms as well as details of Wednesday's meeting. Please let me know if you need any further information.

urs | Attachment

Unit 22

Designing Office Publications

The Traveler's Connection

A Newsletter From E-Travel.com

Volume 9, Issue No. 5   Spring 20--

In This Issue:
A Few Tips for the Smart Traveler, Page 1
Planning Your Travel Online, Page 1
Focus on Dallas-Fort Worth, Page 2
Texas Tidbits, Page 2
Thistle Hill, Page 2

A Few Tips for the Smart Traveler

We all have visions of the perfect vacation. They usually include a beautiful hotel, a comfortable room, great food, and wonderful entertainment. Unfortunately, sometimes our vision doesn't exactly align itself with reality, and our dream has suddenly turned into a nightmare. You can avoid this situation if you will do some smart advance planning.

Here are some smart travel tips that can turn your dream vacation into a reality:

- Do your homework. Your best bet is to find out all you can about your destination before you do anything else. Find a good travel agent, do your own research on the Internet, and buy some good travel books on your destination in your favorite bookstore.

- Carry medications and other essentials with you. To avoid a disaster, carry everything you can't function without in the event that your luggage is lost. This would include medications, money, tickets, toiletries, visas, passports, eyeglasses, and anything else you can think of that is irreplaceable in the course of a day or two.

- Buy travel insurance. If you are taking an expensive vacation and are not completely sure you can make it, buying travel insurance is a wise expenditure. Many people today have children and aging parents whose needs are unpredictable.

- Confirm all reservations. Be sure that all your reservations including hotels, cars, and entertainment are confirmed and that you have the different confirmation numbers and phone numbers written down. Nothing can ruin a trip faster than finding out that you don't have a place to sleep or suitable transportation. You will find that if you take these tips to heart, your vacation will be just as wonderful as you imagined!

Planning Your Travel Online

The Internet has opened up a wealth of information that used to be the domain of individual travel agencies. If you have a computer and Internet access, you can make reservations, buy tickets, book entertainment packages, and do any number of other things.

Page 1

Save hours of time and lots of money by using the Internet wisely when you plan your travel. You can shop for the best airline rates and even name your own price if you are flexible in your travel plans.

Several good books are available to help you use the Internet for your travel plans. Please check our web site at www.TTC.com for suggested books.

Focus on Dallas-Fort Worth

Although this is the world's second busiest airport, it is surprisingly easy to use. However, the transportation between terminals is slow.

LOVE FIELD
Love Field is a $10 to $15 taxi ride from downtown Dallas. The phone number is 214-555-6073.
Love Field is the hub of Western Airlines, which offers service within Texas, to many cities in the surrounding states, and, with stops, to destinations as far away as Chicago.

BETWEEN THE AIRPORT AND TOWN
It costs around $30 to get

Texas Tidbits

- To receive mail while traveling in Dallas, have it sent c/o General Delivery at the city's main post office.
- Most businesses open between 8 a.m. and 10 a.m. and close around 6 p.m. Many are also open on weekends.
- Banks operate weekdays from 9 a.m. until 2 or 3 p.m., and some are also open on Saturday mornings.
- Post offices are open weekdays from 8 a.m. to 5 p.m. and Saturday mornings.

's legal on on a hen he inter- such a itted. Of full e sure ing.

this three-wealthy tyle man-National

strict. It ck struc-ners and was often e 1970s.

Global Savings & Loan

Your Guide to Online Banking

Account	ATM Card	Check Writing	Monthly Fee
Regular Checking	None	Unlimited	$ 9.00
Interest Checking	Express Card	Unlimited	10.00
Basic Checking	Express Card	Unlimited	4.50
Student Checking	Express Card	Unlimited	3.00

Note: Fees may apply to telephone banking calls and the use of the ATM Express Card.

Designing Cover Pages

Goals

- Type at least 49wpm/5'/5e
- Design cover pages

A. Type 2 times.

A. WARMUP

```
1       Buzz told us that Flight #7864 got into Phoenix just      11
2   3 minutes before Vick's! This is quite remarkable when       22
3   you realize that we never planned for such a "coincidence."   34
    |  1  |  2  |  3  |  4  |  5  |  6  |  7  |  8  |  9  |  10 |  11 |  12
```

SKILLBUILDING

B. PROGRESSIVE PRACTICE: ALPHABET

If you are not using the GDP software, turn to page SB-7 and follow the directions for this activity.

C. DIAGNOSTIC PRACTICE: NUMBERS

If you are not using the GDP software, turn to page SB-5 and follow the directions for this activity.

Keyboarding Connection

Searching the Yellow Pages

Do you find the Yellow Pages of your phone directory handy? Try the Internet as an alternate source. Many of the Web's search engines have a Yellow Pages feature that is quite useful.

You can use the Yellow Pages feature to search for mailing addresses and phone numbers of businesses and organizations. The Yellow Pages link appears in most leading Internet search engines. These search engines may also provide a map of the location of the business or organization.

The Yellow Pages feature of a search engine is like having all the phone directories in the United States at your fingertips.

YOUR TURN Click the Yellow Pages feature on one of your favorite search engines. Search for a business in your city by name and then by category. Did you retrieve the address and phone number of the business using both search methods?

D. Take two 5-minute timed writings. Review your speed and errors.

Goal: At least 49wpm/5′/5e

D.   5-MINUTE TIMED WRITING

```
 4        Why do people choose a particular career? Your first    11
 5   instinct might likely be to say that people work to make     22
 6   money. That may be true, but extensive research has shown    34
 7   that many other factors are considered just as important     45
 8   and that these factors should be carefully considered when   57
 9   you are about to accept a new position.                      65
10        There are many rewards that a job can provide such as   76
11   a chance to be creative, or the chance to spend time with    88
12   people whose company you enjoy, or the feeling that you are 100
13   doing something useful for yourself or for your employer.   111
14   The quality of the work environment is also an important    123
15   consideration in choosing a career, as is the chance to     134
16   work closely with people on a daily basis.                  142
17        Obviously, your career should allow you to advance in  153
18   your field and to be competitive for promotions. You should 165
19   be able to see a clear line for advancement in your job and 177
20   be given a chance to demonstrate your abilities so that     189
21   your coworkers and supervisors recognize your strengths.    200
22   Parallel to these factors is the need for your job to give  212
23   you adequate challenges on a daily, continuing basis. If    223
24   your work is not challenging, boredom will set in, and you  235
25   might soon be looking for a change in your career.          245
     | 1 | 2 | 3 | 4 | 5 | 6 | 7 | 8 | 9 | 10 | 11 | 12
```

FORMATTING

Word Processing Manual

E.   WORD PROCESSING: WORD ART

Study Lesson 106 in your word processing manual. Complete all of the shaded steps while at your computer. Then format the jobs that follow.

DOCUMENT PROCESSING

Report 106-75

Cover Page

To ensure that your document is scored properly, insert 2 spaces at the beginning of the document.

1. Press the SPACE BAR 2 times and insert a picture related to vision or reading.
2. Drag and size the picture so that it looks similar to the one in the illustration on page 424.

3. Insert word art, about the size and in the same position as the one at the top of the illustration, with the words Preferred Optical Vision Plan in 2 lines as shown. Use the default font.

(Continued on next page)

4. Choose a style and color to coordinate with the picture.
5. Create a text box, about the size and in the same position as the one at the bottom of the illustration, to hold the directory information.
6. Remove the line around the text box, and change the fill to none.
7. Change to Arial Bold 20 point, center and type Directory of Participating Vision Care Specialists in 2 lines as shown in the illustration, and press ENTER 2 times.

8. Change to Arial 16 point, center, and type for all salaried employees of the San Francisco Community College District in 2 lines as shown in the illustration, and press ENTER 2 times.
9. Change to Arial 18 point, center, and type September 20--.
10. Change any of the font colors to coordinate with the picture as desired.

Preferred Optical

Vision Plan

Directory of
Participating Vision Care Specialists

for all salaried employees of the
San Francisco Community College District

September 20--

Arial Bold 20 pt.

Arial 16 pt.

Arial 18 pt.

Report 106-76

Cover Page

1. Press the SPACE BAR 2 times, and insert a picture related to dining.
2. Drag and size the picture so that it looks similar to the one in the illustration on page 425.
3. Insert word art, about the size and in the same position as the one at the top of the illustration, with the words Sonoma County's Dining Guide in 2 lines as shown.
4. Choose a style and color for the word art to coordinate with the picture, and use the default font.

5. Create a text box, about the size and in the same position as the one at the bottom of the illustration, to hold the bulleted list.
6. Remove the line around the text box, and change the fill to none.
7. Change to Arial Bold 24 point, and type the following list unformatted (without bullets):

    Fine Dining
    Midrange
    Bargain

8. Apply bullets to the list.

(Continued on next page)

9. Create a text box, about the size and in the same position as the one at the bottom of the illustration, to hold the date.
10. Add a line around the text box, and change the fill to a color that coordinates with the picture.

11. Change to Arial Bold Italic 26 point, and type Summer 20--.
12. Change any of the font colors to coordinate with the picture as desired.

Sonoma County's Dining Guide

Arial Bold 24 pt.

- **Fine Dining**
- **Midrange**
- **Bargain**

Arial Bold Italic 26 pt.

Summer 20--

Report 106-77

Cover Page

1. Create a cover page design of your own to be used as the insert for a view binder that holds information for one of your courses.
2. Insert at least one picture related to the subject of the course.

3. Insert at least one text box with a fill.
4. Insert some word art.
5. Change any of the font colors to coordinate with the picture or word art as desired.

Designing Announcements and Flyers

Goals

- Improve speed and accuracy
- Refine language arts skills in grammar
- Design announcements and flyers

A. Type 2 times.

A. WARMUP

```
1      Does Quentin know if 1/2 of the January order will be      11
2   ready? At 5:30 about 46% of the orders still hadn't been      22
3   mailed! Mr. Gray expects a very sizable loss this month.      34
    |  1  |  2  |  3  |  4  |  5  |  6  |  7  |  8  |  9  |  10  |  11  |  12
```

SKILLBUILDING

B. Take three 12-second timed writings on each line. The scale below the last line shows your wpm speed for a 12-second timed writing.

B. 12-SECOND SPEED SPRINTS

```
4   Rico will rush to tidy the big room that held the supplies.
5   Yale is a very fine school that has some very strict rules.
6   Helen will audit the books of one civic leader in the city.
7   The man had a name that was hard for the small girl to say.
    ' ' ' 5 ' ' ' 10 ' ' ' 15 ' ' ' 20 ' ' ' 25 ' ' ' 30 ' ' ' 35 ' ' ' 40 ' ' ' 45 ' ' ' 50 ' ' ' 55 ' ' ' 60
```

C. Type each sentence on a separate line by pressing ENTER after each sentence. Type 2 times.

C. TECHNIQUE PRACTICE: ENTER

```
8    Decorate the room. Attend the seminar. Go to the theater.
9    Watch the inauguration. Go to the rally. See the recital.
10   Run in the marathon. Bake the bread. Vacuum the bedrooms.
11   Visit the nursing home. Sell the ticket. Drive the truck.
```

D. DIAGNOSTIC PRACTICE: SYMBOLS AND PUNCTUATION

If you are not using the GDP software, turn to page SB-2 and follow the directions for this activity.

LANGUAGE ARTS

E. Study the rules at the right.

E. PRONOUNS

RULE ▶

nominative pronoun

Use nominative pronouns (such as *I*, *he*, *she*, *we*, *they*, and who) as subjects of a sentence or clause.

The programmer and <u>he</u> are reviewing the code.
Barb is a person <u>who</u> can do the job.

(Continued on next page)

Use objective pronouns (such as *me*, *him*, *her*, *us*, *them*, and *whom*) as objects of a verb, preposition, or infinitive.

The code was reviewed by the programmer and <u>him</u>.
Barb is the type of person <u>whom</u> we can trust.

Edit the sentences to correct any errors in the use of pronouns.

12 We hope they will take all of them to the concert tomorrow.
13 John gave the gift to she on Monday; her was very pleased.
14 If them do not hurry, Mary will not finish her work on time.
15 The book was proofread by her; the changes were made by he.
16 It is up to them to give us all the pages they read today.
17 Me cannot assure they that it will not rain for the picnic.

FORMATTING

Word Processing Manual

F. WORD PROCESSING: TABLE—MOVE

Study Lesson 107 in your word processing manual. Complete all of the shaded steps while at your computer. Then format the jobs that follow.

DOCUMENT PROCESSING

Report 107-78 ▶

Announcement

1. Change the left and right margins to 0.5 inch.
2. Press the SPACE BAR 2 times, and insert a picture associated with a large city.
3. Drag and size the picture so that it looks similar to the one in the illustration at the left and on page 428.
4. Create a text box, about the size and in the same position as the one at the top of the illustration, to hold the welcoming message.
5. Remove the line around the text box, and change the fill to none.
6. Change to Arial 28 point, center, and type The Hotel Cosmopolitan in 2 lines as shown in the illustration, and press ENTER 1 time.
7. Change to Arial 22 point, and center and type welcomes.
8. Insert word art, about the size and in the same position as the one at the top of the illustration, with the words NBEA Conference Attendees.
9. Drag and size the word art so that it looks similar to the word art shown in the illustration.

10. Change the word art font for readability if desired.
11. Choose a style and color for the word art to coordinate with the picture.
12. Insert a boxed table with 3 columns and 7 rows, and drag it into position as shown in the illustration.
13. Change to Times New Roman Bold 20 point, and type the centered column headings.
14. Change to Times New Roman 20 point, and type the left-aligned column entries.
15. Type the information in Column C in 2 lines as shown.
16. Merge the cells in Row 7, change to Times New Roman 16 point, and type the information as shown.
17. Automatically adjust the column width for all entries, and drag the table into position again.
18. Add a shading color to the first and last row to coordinate with the word art and picture.

(Continued on next page)

Event	Time	Location
President's Welcome	8:30-9:30 a.m.	Mezzanine Ballroom B
Internet Training	10-11:30 a.m.	First Floor Cityscape Room
NBEA Luncheon	12-1 p.m.	Mezzanine Grand Ballroom
Computer Workshops	1-3 p.m.	First Floor Rooms A, B, and D
Research Sessions*	3-5:30 p.m.	Third Floor Rooms 1, 3, and 5

nominative pronoun
nominative pronoun
objective pronoun
nominative and
objective pronouns

*President's Note: I encourage anyone who is interested to attend our research sessions this afternoon. Dr. Roy Phillips, who will be the facilitator, is excellent. Both of us are available to answer group questions during the session, or you may direct individual questions to either him or me after the session.

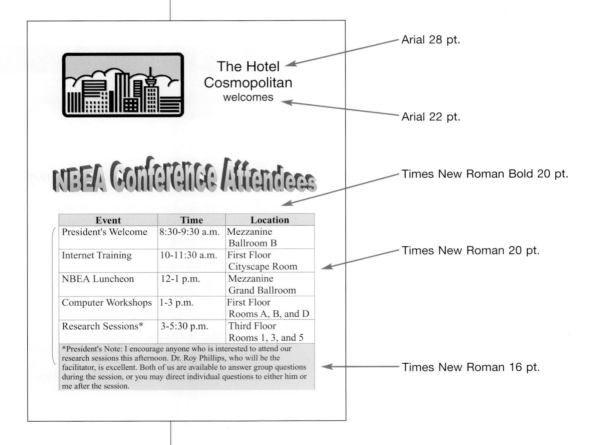

Arial 28 pt.

Arial 22 pt.

Times New Roman Bold 20 pt.

Times New Roman 20 pt.

Times New Roman 16 pt.

Report 107-79

Flyer

1. Press the SPACE BAR 2 times, and insert a picture associated with the summer season.
2. Drag and size the picture so that it looks similar to the one shown in the illustration on page 429.
3. Insert word art, about the size and in the same position as the one at the top of the illustration, with the words Summerset Homes.
4. Choose a style and color for the word art to coordinate with the picture.

(Continued on next page)

5. Create a text box, about the size and in the same position as the one in the middle of the illustration, to hold the message.
6. Remove the line around the text box, and change the fill to none.
7. Change to Arial 28 point; center and type Summerset Homes proudly invites you to the grand opening of our newest group of single-family homes! as shown in the illustration.
8. Create a text box, about the size and in the same position as the one at the bottom of the illustration, to hold the address information.
9. Remove the line around the text box, and add a fill using a color to coordinate with the word art and the fill.
10. Change to Arial 12 point; center and type as shown in the illustration:
    Summerset Homes
    520 Southwest Harbor Way
    Portland, OR 97201
    800-555-2649
    www.Summerset.com
11. Insert a star-shaped symbol between each item in the address block as shown in the illustration.
12. Insert 2 spaces before and after the star-shaped symbol.
13. Insert a boxed table with 3 columns and 5 rows, and drag it into position as shown in the illustration.
14. Change to Times New Roman 22 point, and type the column entries.
15. Automatically adjust the column width for all entries, and drag the table into position again.

Shadow Pines	1,235 sq. ft.	$209,990
Ocean View	1,495 sq. ft.	223,990
Country Meadow	1,759 sq. ft.	265,990
Desert Breeze	2,042 sq. ft.	295,990
Valley Oasis	2,537 sq. ft.	322,990

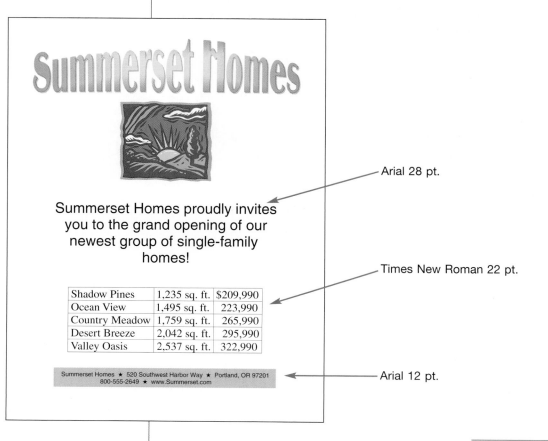

Summerset Homes

Summerset Homes proudly invites you to the grand opening of our newest group of single-family homes!

Shadow Pines	1,235 sq. ft.	$209,990
Ocean View	1,495 sq. ft.	223,990
Country Meadow	1,759 sq. ft.	265,990
Desert Breeze	2,042 sq. ft.	295,990
Valley Oasis	2,537 sq. ft.	322,990

Summerset Homes ★ 520 Southwest Harbor Way ★ Portland, OR 97201
800-555-2649 ★ www.Summerset.com

Arial 28 pt.

Times New Roman 22 pt.

Arial 12 pt.

1. Create an announcement or flyer design of your own for an upcoming event at work or on campus.
2. Press the SPACE BAR 2 times and insert at least one picture related to the topic of the announcement or flyer.
3. Insert at least one text box with a fill.
4. Insert some word art.
5. Apply color to your fonts to coordinate with the picture or word art.
6. Insert a table that contains information related to the topic of the flyer or announcement.

Designing Newsletters: A

Goals

- Type at least 49wpm/5′/5e
- Design newsletters

A. Type 2 times.

A. WARMUP

```
1      Does Pamela know if Region 29* (*Ventura) has met the    11
2  sales quota? Their exact target zone is just not clear;      22
3  they don't have to submit their totals until 4:30 on 5/7.    34
   |  1  |  2  |  3  |  4  |  5  |  6  |  7  |  8  |  9  |  10  |  11  |  12
```

SKILLBUILDING

B. PACED PRACTICE

If you are not using the GDP software, turn to page SB-14 and follow the directions for this activity.

Strategies for Career Success

Managing Business Phone Time

The average American spends an hour a day on the phone. Phone calls can be extremely distracting. Time is spent taking the call and following up after the call. You can take steps to reduce wasted time on the phone.

When you make an outgoing call, organize the topics you want to discuss. Have all the materials you need: pencils, paper, order forms, and so on. When you take an incoming call, answer it promptly. Identify yourself. It is common to answer the phone with your first and last name (for example, "Mary Smith speaking" or "Mary Smith").

Limit social conversation; it wastes time. Give concise answers to questions. At the end of the call, summarize the points made. End the conversation politely.

YOUR TURN Keep a log of your time on the phone for one day. What is your average conversation time? What can you do to reduce your average phone conversation time?

C. Take two 5-minute timed writings. Review your speed and errors.

Goal: At least 49wpm/5'/5e

C. 5-MINUTE TIMED WRITING

4	Purchasing a home is probably one of the most critical	11
5	financial decisions you will make in your lifetime. Dozens	23
6	of questions need to be answered when buying a home. For	34
7	example, how much of a down payment will you make and how	46
8	much of a monthly payment on your mortgage will you be able	58
9	to afford?	60
10	In addition to your mortgage payment, there are other	71
11	costs associated with buying a new home. The mortgage will	83
12	cover the principal and interest for your loan, but you	94
13	will also have homeowner's insurance and utilities to pay	106
14	such as water, sewer, electricity, and gas.	115
15	You may want to purchase a home through a real estate	126
16	agent, and it is important that you find out how much of a	137
17	commission will be charged for that service. When working	149
18	with a real estate agent, you need to let that person know	161
19	about the kind of community in which you would prefer to	172
20	live. Do you want to be close to schools, shopping centers,	184
21	and restaurants, or would you rather purchase a home in a	195
22	secluded neighborhood away from the noise and congestion of	207
23	a metropolitan city?	211
24	When you find a home that you like, look at it very	222
25	carefully to see if it is structurally well built, if you	234
26	like the floor plan, and if it is large enough for you.	245

| 1 | 2 | 3 | 4 | 5 | 6 | 7 | 8 | 9 | 10 | 11 | 12

FORMATTING

D. NEWSLETTER DESIGN

Newsletters are an excellent forum for communicating information on a wide range of subjects. A well-planned newsletter will employ all the basic principles of good design. However, because newsletters usually include information on a wide variety of topics, they are generally complex in their layout.

Most newsletters have the following elements in common: mastheads, main headings and subheadings, text arranged in flowing newspaper-column format using various column widths to add interest, text boxes to emphasize and summarize, pictures to draw readers' attention and interest to a topic, and a variety of borders and fills.

The design of a multipage newsletter must look consistent from one page to the next. This consistency provides unity to the newsletter design and is often achieved through the use of headers and footers.

Report 108-81

Newsletter

Reminder: You will finish the newsletter in Lessons 109 and 110.

Follow these steps to create the masthead and footer for the first page of the newsletter shown below.

1. Set all margins at 0.75 inch.
2. Create an open table with 2 columns and 2 rows. Drag the middle column border to the left so the first column is about 1.75 inches wide.
3. Right-align Column B.
4. In Column B, Row 1, change to Times New Roman Bold 48 point, and type `The Traveler's Connection` on two lines.
5. Press ENTER 1 time, change to Arial Bold 14 point, and type `A Newsletter From E-Travel.com`.
6. Move to Column A, Row 2, and type `Volume 9, Issue No. 5`.
7. Move to Column B, Row 2, and type `Spring 20--`.
8. Apply borders to the top and bottom of Row 2.
9. In Column A, Row 1, insert a picture associated with world travel.
10. Drag and size the picture so that it looks similar to the one shown in the illustration.
11. Insert a footer, and center and type `Page` followed by 1 space.
12. Insert a page number field and close the footer.

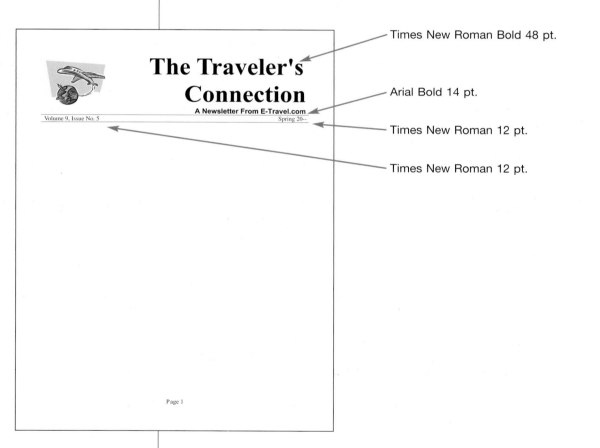

Times New Roman Bold 48 pt.

Arial Bold 14 pt.

Times New Roman 12 pt.

Times New Roman 12 pt.

Report 108-82

Newsletter

1. Create a newsletter masthead of your own related to travel and similar to the one in Report 108-81.

2. Use any picture that enhances the purpose of your travel newsletter.

Designing Newsletters: B

Goals

- Improve speed and accuracy
- Refine language arts skills in spelling
- Design newsletters

A. Type 2 times.

A. WARMUP

```
1        Approximately 90% of the weekly budget was just used      11
2   to buy equipment. A very sizable amount totaling $12,654       22
3   was spent on "necessities" as requested by the department!     34
    |  1  |  2  |  3  |  4  |  5  |  6  |  7  |  8  |  9  |  10  |  11  |  12
```

SKILLBUILDING

PPP PRETEST → PRACTICE → POSTTEST

PRETEST
Take a 1-minute timed writing. Review your speed and errors.

B. PRETEST: Alternate- and One-Hand Words

```
4        A great auditor is eager to spend a minimum of eighty     11
5   hours to amend a problem. If he assessed a penalty that        22
6   exceeded the usual fee, I reserve the right to correct it.     34
    |  1  |  2  |  3  |  4  |  5  |  6  |  7  |  8  |  9  |  10  |  11  |  12
```

PRACTICE
Speed Emphasis:
If you made no more than 1 error on the Pretest, type each *individual* line 2 times.
Accuracy Emphasis:
If you made 2 or more errors, type each *group* of lines (as though it were a paragraph) 2 times.

C. PRACTICE: Alternate-Hand Words

```
7   also amend maps thrown blame city problem panel formal down
8   snap rigid lens social visit with penalty right height half
9   chap usual such enrich shape dish auditor spend eighty kept
```

D. PRACTICE: One-Hand Words

```
10  was only great pupil regret uphill scatter homonym assessed
11  bed join water nylon target pompon savages minimum exceeded
12  age hook eager union teased limply reserve opinion attracts
```

POSTTEST
Repeat the Pretest timed writing and compare performance.

E. POSTTEST: Alternate- and One-Hand Words

F. SUSTAINED PRACTICE: NUMBERS AND SYMBOLS

F. Take a 1-minute timed writing on the first paragraph to establish your base speed. Then take four 1-minute timed writings on the remaining paragraphs. As soon as you equal or exceed your base speed on one paragraph, advance to the next, more difficult paragraph.

```
13      Shopping in the comfort and convenience of your own      11
14  living room has never been more popular than it is right     22
15  now. Shopping clubs abound on cable channels. You could      33
16  buy anything from exotic pets to computers by mail order.    45

17      Sometimes you can find discounts as high as 20% off      11
18  the retail price; for example, a printer that sells for      22
19  $565 might be discounted 20% and be sold for $452. You       33
20  should always investigate quality before buying anything.    44

21      Sometimes hidden charges are involved; for example,      11
22  a printer costing $475.50 that promises a discount of 12%    22
23  ($57.06) has a net price of $418.44. However, if charges     34
24  for shipping range from 12% to 15%, you did not save money.  45

25      You must also check for errors. Several errors have      11
26  been noted so far: Invoice #223, #789, #273, and #904 had    22
27  errors totaling $21.35, $43.44, $79.23, and $91.23 for a     34
28  grand total of $235.25. As always, let the buyer beware.     45
```

LANGUAGE ARTS

G. SPELLING

G. Type these frequently misspelled words, paying special attention to any spelling problems in each word.

```
29  operations health individual considered expenditures vendor
30  beginning internal pursuant president union written develop
31  hours enclosing situation function including standard shown
32  engineering payable suggested participants providing orders
33  toward nays total without paragraph meetings different vice
```

Edit the sentences to correct any misspellings.

```
34  The participants in the different meetings voted for hours.
35  The presdent of the union is working toward a resolution.
36  The health of each individal must be seriously considered.
37  Engineering has suggested providing orders for the vendor.
38  One expanditure has been written off as part of oparations.
39  He is inclosing the accounts payable record as shown today.
```

Report 109-83 ▶

Newsletter (continued)

> (!) Reminder: You will finish the newsletter in Lesson 110.

Open the file for Report 108-81 shown on page 433. Follow these steps to continue the newsletter as shown on page 437.

1. Move outside the table below Column A and press ENTER 2 times.
2. Insert File 109, and turn on automatic hyphenation.
3. Carefully place your insertion point in front of the second blank line under the masthead, and select all the newly inserted text including 1 blank line below the last line of text.
4. Create 3 columns with a line between columns.
5. Select the following headings in the newsletter, and change the font to Arial 24 point:

   A Few Tips for the Smart
      Traveler
   Planning Your Travel Online
   Focus on Dallas-Fort Worth

6. Select the following subheadings in the newsletter and bold them:

   THE AIRPORT
   LOVE FIELD
   BETWEEN THE AIRPORT AND TOWN

7. Place your insertion point in front of the second blank line under the masthead.
8. Insert a table with 1 column and 1 row.
9. Change to Arial 12 point, and type In This Issue:. Press ENTER 1 time.
10. Change to Times New Roman Italic 12 point, and type the following lines:

    A Few Tips for the Smart
       Traveler, Page 1
    Planning Your Travel
       Online, Page 1
    Focus on Dallas-Fort
       Worth, Page 2
    Texas Tidbits, Page 2
    Thistle Hill, Page 2

11. Add a shading color to the table to coordinate with the picture in the masthead.
12. Insert a picture in the space above each of the bulleted items in the first article on the first page of the newsletter. The pictures should be associated in some way with the topic in each of the bulleted items.
13. Drag and size the pictures so that they look similar to the ones shown in the illustration.
14. Place your insertion point in the blank line above the heading "Planning Your Online Travel," and apply a top border.
15. Place your insertion point in the blank line above the heading "Focus on Dallas-Fort Worth," and apply a top border.

(Continued on next page)

The Traveler's Connection

A Newsletter From E-Travel.com

Arial 12 pt.

Times New Roman Italic 12 pt.

Volume 9, Issue No. 5   Spring 20--

A Few Tips for the Smart Traveler

We all have visions of the perfect vacation. They usually include a beautiful hotel, a comfortable room, great food, and wonderful entertainment. Unfortunately, sometimes our vision doesn't exactly align itself with reality, and our dream has suddenly turned into a nightmare. You can avoid this situation if you will do some smart advance planning.

Here are some smart travel tips that can turn your dream vacation into a reality:

- Do your homework. Your best bet is to find out all you can about your destination before you do anything else. Find a good travel agent, do your own research on the Internet, and buy some good travel books on your destination in your favorite bookstore.

- Carry medications and other essentials with you. To avoid a disaster, carry everything you can't function without in the event that your luggage is lost. This would include medications, money, tickets, toiletries, visas, passports, eyeglasses, and anything else you can think of that is irreplaceable in the course of a day or two.

- Buy travel insurance. If you are taking an expensive vacation and are not completely sure you can make it, buying travel insurance is a wise expenditure. Many people today have children and aging parents whose needs are unpredictable.

- Confirm all reservations. Be sure that all your reservations including hotels, cars, and entertainment are confirmed and that you have the different confirmation numbers and phone numbers written down. Nothing can ruin a trip faster than finding out that you don't have a place to sleep or suitable transportation. You will find that if you take these tips to heart, your vacation will be just as wonderful as you imagined!

Arial 24 pt.

Planning Your Travel Online

The Internet has opened up a wealth of information that used to be the domain of individual travel agencies. If you have a computer and Internet access, you can make reservations, buy tickets, book entertainment packages, and do any number of other things.

Arial 24 pt.

Save hours of time and lots of money by using the Internet wisely when you plan your travel. You can shop for the best airline rates and even name your own price if you are flexible in your travel plans.

Several good books are available to help you use the Internet for your travel plans. Please check our Web site at www.TTC.com for suggested books.

Focus on Dallas-Fort Worth

This month's focus is on the Dallas-Fort Worth area.

THE AIRPORT
The Dallas-Fort Worth International Airport is 17 miles from the business districts of each town. The phone number is 214-555-8888.

Although this is the world's second busiest airport, it is surprisingly easy to use. However, the transportation between terminals is slow.

LOVE FIELD
Love Field is a $10 to $15 taxi ride from downtown Dallas. The phone number is 214-555-6073.

Love Field is the hub of Western Airlines, which offers service within Texas, to many cities in the surrounding states, and, with stops, to destinations as far away as Chicago.

BETWEEN THE AIRPORT AND TOWN
It costs around $30 to get to downtown Dallas by taxi from the Dallas-Fort Worth International Airport. It is about $25 to downtown Fort Worth.

Cheaper bus and van service is also available. Please check our Web site at www.TTC.com. for details.

Arial 24 pt.

1. Open the file for Report 108-81 with the newsletter masthead you created.

2. Follow the steps for Report 109-83, and then delete everything on the second page of the newsletter.

3. Change the information in the contents text box at the top of the first column, insert a picture at the end of the last column of the newsletter to balance the page, and move any pictures around as needed.

Designing Newsletters: C

Goals

- Type at least 49wpm/5′/5e
- Design newsletters

A. Type 2 times.

A. WARMUP

```
1        At exactly 8:30 a.m., Quigley & Co. will host a wide    11
2   variety of chat room meetings; send e-mail to chat@QC.com.   23
3   Organizational skills will be the topics in Rooms K5 or J6.  34
    |  1  |  2  |  3  |  4  |  5  |  6  |  7  |  8  |  9  |  10  |  11  |  12
```

SKILLBUILDING

B. MAP

Follow the GDP software directions for this exercise in improving keystroking accuracy.

Keyboarding Connection

Effective E-Mail Management

Are you bombarded with e-mail? Take a few simple steps to manage e-mail more efficiently and reduce wasted time.

Create separate accounts for receiving messages that require your direct attention. Keep your mailbox clean by deleting messages you no longer need. Create folders to organize messages you need to keep (for example, set up folders for separate projects).

If you receive numerous e-mail messages, consider purchasing an e-mail manager. E-mail manager programs help you manage multiple e-mail accounts, find messages using powerful search functions, and notify you when you receive a message from a specified person.

Keep backups of important files. Be cautious of e-mail from people you do not know. Check your e-mail on a regular basis to avoid buildup of messages.

YOUR TURN Review the current organization of your e-mail. List ways you can improve the management of your e-mail.

C. Take two 5-minute timed writings. Review your speed and errors.

Goal: At least 49wpm/5′/5e

C. 5-MINUTE TIMED WRITINGS

4	When the rate of unemployment is very low, jobs are	11
5	easier to find. Although you may find a job easily, what	22
6	can you do to make sure your job is one you will enjoy?	33
7	Here are some suggestions to assist you.	41
8	First, be certain you receive a job description when	52
9	you are hired. The job description should list all of the	64
10	requirements of the job and the details of what you will be	76
11	expected to do.	79
12	Second, you should receive some type of orientation to	90
13	your job and the company. During orientation, you will fill	102
14	out various tax forms, benefit forms, and insurance papers.	114
15	You may view a video that will help you learn more about	126
16	the company and available benefits.	133
17	Third, when you start your training, you should take	144
18	notes, pay attention, and ask questions. You should also	155
19	have your trainer check your work for a period of time to	167
20	be sure you are performing your duties correctly. If your	178
21	tasks are complex, you can break them down into smaller	189
22	parts so you can remember all aspects of your job.	200
23	Finally, when you know your job requirements, chart	210
24	your work each day. Concentrate on being part of the team.	222
25	Be zealous in striving to work beyond the expectations of	234
26	your supervisor. Then, you will achieve job satisfaction.	245

| 1 | 2 | 3 | 4 | 5 | 6 | 7 | 8 | 9 | 10 | 11 | 12 |

DOCUMENT PROCESSING

Report 110-85 ▶

Newsletter (continued)

Open the file for Report 109-83, shown on page 437. Follow these steps to finish creating the newsletter shown on pages 441 and 442.

1. Place your insertion point directly in front of the first blank line underneath the last line of text in the newsletter.
2. Insert File 110A.
3. Insert a picture in the space to the right of the heading "Focus on Dallas-Fort Worth" on the second page of the newsletter. The pictures should be associated with the concept of focusing on a subject or associated with Texas.

4. Drag and size the picture so that it looks similar to the one shown in the illustration on page 442.
5. Insert word art, about the size and in the same position as the word art at the top of the bulleted list on the second page of the newsletter, with the words Texas Tidbits.
6. Choose a style and color for the word art to coordinate with the newsletter.
7. Insert a picture at the bottom of the second page in the space to the left of the information on "Thistle Hill." The picture should be associated with the

(Continued on next page)

If your printer or computer memory is limited, try previewing the document before you print, and then print only 1 page at a time.

information about Thistle Hill or with Texas.

8. Drag and size the picture so that it looks similar to the one shown in the illustration.

9. Create a text box, about the size and in the same position as the one at the bottom of the newsletter, to hold the information about Thistle Hill.

10. Insert File 110B and adjust the size of the text box as needed.

11. Add a fill color or fill effect to the text box to coordinate with the picture to the left of the text box.

12. Create a text box, about the size and in the same position as the one at the bottom of the newsletter, to hold the information about tours.

13. Change to Times New Roman Bold 12 point, and center and type `For tour information, call 817-555-2663`.

14. Remove the lines around the text box, and change the fill to none.

15. The first page of the newsletter should look like the illustration below.

16. The second page of the newsletter should look like the illustration on page 442.

The Traveler's Connection

A Newsletter From E-Travel.com

Volume 9, Issue No. 5　　　　　　　　　　　Spring 20--

In This Issue:
A Few Tips for the Smart Traveler, Page 1
Planning Your Travel Online, Page 1
Focus on Dallas-Fort Worth, Page 2
Texas Tidbits, Page 2
Thistle Hill, Page 2

A Few Tips for the Smart Traveler

We all have visions of the perfect vacation. They usually include a beautiful hotel, a comfortable room, great food, and wonderful entertainment. Unfortunately, sometimes our vision doesn't exactly align itself with reality, and our dream has suddenly turned into a nightmare. You can avoid this situation if you will do some smart advance planning.

Here are some smart travel tips that can turn your dream vacation into a reality:

- Do your homework. Your best bet is to find out all you can about your desti-

nation before you do anything else. Find a good travel agent, do your own research on the Internet, and buy some good travel books on your destination in your favorite bookstore.

- Carry medications and other essentials with you. To avoid a disaster, carry everything you can't function without in the event that your luggage is lost. This would include medications, money, tickets, toiletries, visas, passports, eyeglasses, and anything else you can think of that is irreplaceable in the course of a day or two.

- Buy travel insurance. If you are taking an expensive vacation and are not completely sure you can make it, buying travel insurance is a wise expenditure. Many people today have children and aging parents whose needs are unpredictable.

- Confirm all reservations. Be sure that all your reservations including hotels, cars, and entertainment are confirmed and that you have the different confirmation numbers and phone numbers written down. Nothing can ruin a trip faster than finding out that you don't have a place to sleep or suitable transportation.

You will find that if you take these tips to heart, your vacation will be just as wonderful as you imagined!

Planning Your Travel Online

The Internet has opened up a wealth of information that used to be the domain of individual travel agencies. If you have a computer and Internet access, you can make reservations, buy tickets, book entertainment packages, and do any number of other things.

Page 1

(Continued on next page)

Save hours of time and lots of money by using the Internet wisely when you plan your travel. You can shop for the best airline rates and even name your own price if you are flexible in your travel plans.

Several good books are available to help you use the Internet for your travel plans. Please check our web site at www.TTC.com for suggested books.

Focus on Dallas-Fort Worth

This month's focus is on the Dallas-Fort Worth area.

THE AIRPORT

The Dallas-Fort Worth International Airport is 17 miles from the business districts of each town. The phone number is 214-555-8888.

For tour information, call 817-555-2663

Although this is the world's second busiest airport, it is surprisingly easy to use. However, the transportation between terminals is slow.

LOVE FIELD

Love Field is a $10 to $15 taxi ride from downtown Dallas. The phone number is 214-555-6073.

Love Field is the hub of Western Airlines, which offers service within Texas, to many cities in the surrounding states, and, with stops, to destinations as far away as Chicago.

BETWEEN THE AIRPORT AND TOWN

It costs around $30 to get to downtown Dallas by taxi from the Dallas-Fort Worth International Airport. It is about $25 to downtown Fort Worth.

Cheaper bus and van service is also available. Please check our Web site at www.TTC.com. for details.

Texas Tidbits

- To receive mail while traveling in Dallas, have it sent c/o General Delivery at the city's main post office.
- Most businesses open between 8 a.m. and 10 a.m. and close around 6 p.m. Many are also open on weekends.
- Banks operate weekdays from 9 a.m. until 2 or 3 p.m., and some are also open on Saturday mornings.
- Post offices are open weekdays from 8 a.m. to 5 p.m. and Saturday mornings.
- At traffic lights, it's legal to make a right turn on a red light except when there is a sign at the intersection stating that such a turn is *not* permitted. Of course, come to a full stop first and make sure no traffic is coming.

Thistle Hill

In 1903, cattle baron William T. Waggoner built his daughter this three-story mansion as a wedding present. The house was built in a wealthy neighborhood known as Quality Hill. This Georgian Revival-style mansion has been restored to its 1912 condition and is listed in the National Register.

It is located today on Pennsylvania Avenue near the hospital district. It cost about $38,000 when the nearly 11,000-square-foot, red brick structure was built back in 1903. The house was used for lavish dinners and parties to entertain many of Fort Worth's powerful and elite. It was often referred to as the "honeymoon cottage" and was restored in the 1970s.

Page 2

Times New Roman Bold 12 pt.

Report 110-86

Flyer

Progress and Proofreading Check

Documents designated as Proofreading Checks serve as a check of your proofreading skill. Your goal is to have zero typographical errors when the GDP software first scores the document.

1. Press the SPACE BAR 2 times, and insert a picture related to a globe.
2. Drag and size the picture so that it looks similar to the one shown in the illustration on page 443.
3. Insert word art, about the size and in the same position as the one at the top of the illustration, with the words Global Savings & Loan.
4. Choose a style and color for the word art to coordinate with the picture.
5. Create a text box with no lines or fill and about the size and in the same position as the one shown at the middle of the illustration.
6. Change to Times New Roman 48 point, and center and type Your Guide to Online Banking in 2 lines as shown.
7. Insert a boxed table with 4 columns and 6 rows, and drag it into position as shown in the illustration.

8. Change to Arial Bold 18 point, and type the one- and two-column headings in Row 1 aligned as shown.
9. Move to Row 2, change to Times New Roman 20 point, and type the left-aligned column entries as shown.
10. Right-align the information in Column D, and add spaces after the dollar sign to align the dollar sign just to the left of the widest entry below it.
11. Merge the cells in Row 6, change to Times New Roman 14 point, and type the information as shown.
12. Adjust the column widths manually as shown.
13. Add a shading color to the first and last row to coordinate with the word art and picture.

(Continued on next page)

↓1X Account	↓1X ATM Card	Check Writing	Monthly Fee
Regular Checking	None	Unlimited	$ 9.00
Interest Checking	Express Card	Unlimited	10.00
Basic Checking	Express Card	Unlimited	4.50
Student Checking	Express Card	Unlimited	3.00

Note: Fees may apply to telephone banking calls and the use of the ATM Express Card.

Global Savings & Loan

Your Guide
to Online Banking — Times New Roman 48 pt.

— Arial Bold 18 pt.

Account	ATM Card	Check Writing	Monthly Fee
Regular Checking	None	Unlimited	$ 9.00
Interest Checking	Express Card	Unlimited	10.00
Basic Checking	Express Card	Unlimited	4.50
Student Checking	Express Card	Unlimited	3.00
Note: Fees may apply to telephone banking calls and the use of the ATM Express Card.			

— Times New Roman 20 pt.

— Times New Roman 14 pt.

Unit 23

Designing Web Pages

In The Game
5779 Del Monte Drive
Santa Rosa, CA 95409
888-555-7897
email@InTheGame.com

Home | Contact Us

If there is any sporting good item or apparel item related to baseball and softball, soccer, track and field, or gymnastics that you can't find on our site, we want to hear from you.

E-Mail
Send us an e-mail message now at email@InTheGame.com

Call Us
Call us toll-free at 888-555-7897.

Snail Mail
If you prefer to hold our mail, write to us at the address below:
the Game
el Monte Drive
Rosa, CA

In The Game
5779 Del Monte Drive
Santa Rosa, CA 95409
888-555-7897
email@InTheGame.com

Home | Contact Us

Welcome to In The Game, your online supplier specializing in sporting goods for baseball and softball, soccer, track and field, and gymnastics. We can offer you quality p
to you fast!

Baseball and Softball
If you can't wait to play ball, you'll love
Our line of gear includes automated ba
machines, batting tees, and radar guns
jerseys, and T-shirts.

Soccer
If scoring goals is on the top of your li
place. We have all types of soccer equi

Track and Field
Is running your game? We have batons
puts, starting blocks, starting pistols,

Gymnastics
You'll flip for our line of clothing, fan w
and training aids are first quality.

The Virtual Assistant

901 South Rainbow, Suite 1
Las Vegas, Nevada 89145
888-555-3499
email@TVA.com

Home | Services | Fees | References

Do you need a skilled assistant who works tirelessly on your documents, doesn't need any office space, and gives your work that personal touch? The Virtual Assistant is a professional document processing and design service that will help create the professional image your business demands.

You don't get a second chance at a first impression. The graphics experts in our word processing and desktop publishing departments will make sure your documents look gorgeous. Our editors, who have completed a series of rigorous courses in business English and business communications, will make sure they are letter-perfect. Please browse around our site for details.

Word Processing
- Correspondence
- Reports
- Proposals
- Manuals

Desktop Publishing
- Newsletters
- Brochures
- Letterheads
- Resumes

Layout Editing
- In-House Styles
- Custom Styles
- Master Documents
- Table of Contents
- Indexes

Copy Editing
- Proofreading
- Technical Editing
- Grammar Checking
- Writing Style

Creating, Saving, and Viewing Web Pages

Goals

- Improve speed and accuracy
- Refine language arts skills in capitalization
- Create, save, and view Web pages

A. Type 2 times.

A. WARMUP

```
1        The taxes* were quickly adjusted upward by 20 percent    11
2    because of the improvements to her house (built in 1901).     23
3    A proposed law will not penalize good homeowners like this.   34
     |  1  |  2  |  3  |  4  |  5  |  6  |  7  |  8  |  9  |  10  |  11  |  12
```

SKILLBUILDING

B. Take three 12-second timed writings on each line. The scale below the last line shows your wpm speed for a 12-second timed writing.

B. 12-SECOND SPEED SPRINTS

```
4    Their home is on a lake that is just east of her old house.
5    He has an old boat that is in bad need of a good paint job.
6    He got so many fish that she gave some to the nice old man.
7    She was so nice that it was easy for him to help her drive.
     | | | | 5 | | | | 10 | | | | 15 | | | | 20 | | | | 25 | | | | 30 | | | | 35 | | | | 40 | | | | 45 | | | | 50 | | | | 55 | | | | 60
```

C. PROGRESSIVE PRACTICE: ALPHABET

If you are not using the GDP software, turn to page SB-7 and follow the directions for this activity.

D. PACED PRACTICE

If you are not using the GDP software, turn to page SB-14 and follow the directions for this activity.

E. BASIC PARTS OF A WEB PAGE

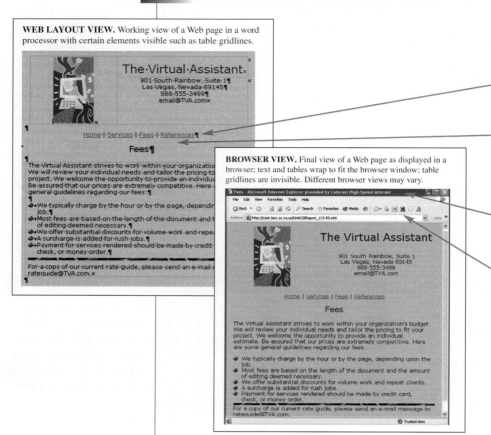

WEB LAYOUT VIEW. Working view of a Web page in a word processor with certain elements visible such as table gridlines.

BROWSER VIEW. Final view of a Web page as displayed in a browser; text and tables wrap to fit the browser window; table gridlines are invisible. Different browser views may vary.

LINK BAR. A group of hyperlinks used to navigate from one Web page to another in a Web site.

HYPERLINKS. These are clicked to move from one Web page to another or to move from one place on a page to another place.

TITLE BAR. Displays the title assigned to the Web page.

ADDRESS BAR. Displays the URL address for the Web page.

F. WEB SITE DESIGN GUIDELINES

Follow these guidelines to design effective Web sites:

- Plan appropriate, specific content first. Define the purpose of the site, and make a list of what visitors need to know.
- Organize the content into logical groups and subgroups, the way you would set up an outline in a report.
- Plan the main page (usually called a home page), which should identify the business and its services.
- Plan and test the site navigation. Hyperlinks help visitors jump from one spot or page to another.

- Plan the content and design details of specific pages, and use tables to position information.
- Design an appropriate, attractive visual theme with consistent design elements on each page to unify your site. Many programs come with a gallery of attractive themes with unified design elements and eye-catching color schemes.
- Use graphics to enhance your page, but use them sparingly because they increase download times.
- Use color to create a mood, attract attention, and categorize information.

Word Processing Manual

G. WEB PAGE—CREATING, SAVING, AND VIEWING

Study Lesson 111 in your word processing manual. Complete all of the shaded steps while at your computer. Then format the jobs that follow.

Report 111-87 ▶

Web Site

The projects in this unit must be completed in sequence in order for the steps to work correctly!

The file names assigned to the Web pages in this text are not typical. Most home pages are named either index.htm or default.html. The commercial server hosting a Web site should be contacted for any specific requirements for file names and extensions.

The Virtual Assistant Web site that starts in this lesson is continued through Lesson 115. Because each Web page builds upon a previous one, make certain that each Web page is correct before continuing to the next one. Follow these steps to create Report 111-87.htm, the home page of the Web site. Refer to the Web layout view of the home page on page 448 as needed. Note that hyphens are used in place of spaces in Web page file names so that the pages will display properly in a browser.

1. Save Report-111-87.doc as a Web page named Report-111-87.htm, and change the title to The Virtual Assistant.
2. Insert a centered, open table with 2 columns and 2 rows.
3. In Column B, Row 1, center and type The Virtual Assistant.
4. In Column B, Row 2, center and type these lines:

   901 South Rainbow, Suite 1
   Las Vegas, Nevada 89145
   888-555-3499
   email@TVA.com

5. Merge the cells in Column A, and insert a picture related to an office or business.

6. Resize the picture proportionally until it is about 2 inches wide, and center the picture.
7. Move the insertion point under the table, and press ENTER 1 time,
8. Type the following line centered, using the pipe symbol with 1 space before and after it as shown here. This line will be referred to as the link bar from now on.

   Home | Services | Fees | References

   Note: The pipe symbol is above the backslash symbol on most keyboards.
9. Press ENTER 2 times, and insert a centered, open table with 2 columns and 7 rows.
10. Merge the cells in Row 1, and type the information shown on page 448 in Row 1.
11. Move to Row 3, and continue typing the rest of the table as arranged on page 448, leaving Row 2 and Row 5 empty.
12. Save the page, view the Web page in a browser, and compare the browser view with the layout view in your word processor.

Do you need a skilled assistant who works tirelessly on your documents, doesn't need any office space, and gives your work that personal touch? The Virtual Assistant is a professional document processing and design service that will help create the professional image your business demands.

You don't get a second chance at a first impression. The graphics experts in our word processing and desktop publishing departments will make sure your documents look gorgeous. Our editors, who have completed a series of rigorous courses in business English and business communications, will make sure your documents are letter-perfect. Please browse around our site for details.

≡ organization

≡ course

Word Processing	Desktop Publishing
Correspondence	Newsletters
Reports	Brochures
Proposals	Letterheads
Manuals	Resumes
Layout Editing	Copy Editing
In-House Styles	Proofreading
Custom Styles	Technical Editing
Master Documents	Grammar Checking
Table of Contents	Writing Style
Indexes	

Reminder: You will finish building the Web site in Lessons 112 through 115.

(Continued on next page)

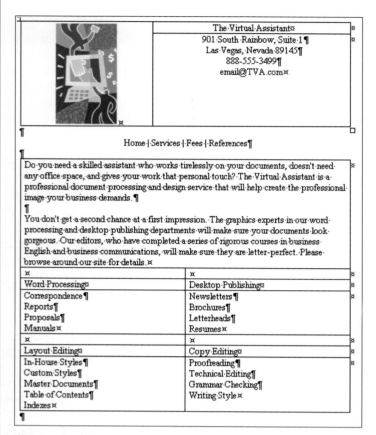

Web layout view of home page.

Report 111-88

Your Web Site

Plan and write the content for a Web site for a business of your own to include a home page and three related pages very similar to the Web pages in this unit. You may want to look ahead to the finished Web site on pages 465–466 for ideas. The Web site that starts in this lesson is continued through Lesson 114.

1. Save Report-111-88.doc as a Web page named Report-111-88.htm, and change the title to the name of the business.
2. Insert a centered, open table with 2 rows and 2 columns.
3. In Column B, Row 1, center and type the name of the Web site.
4. In Column B, Row 2, center and type the mailing address and e-mail address of the business.
5. Merge the cells in Column A, and insert a picture related to the business.
6. Resize and align the picture proportionally as needed.
7. Move the insertion point under the table, and press ENTER 1 time.

8. Type the following line centered using the pipe symbol with 1 space before and after it as shown here. This line will be referred to as the link bar from now on.

    Home | Services | Fees | References

    Note: The pipe symbol is above the backslash symbol on most keyboards.

9. Press ENTER 2 times, and insert a centered, open table with 2 columns and 7 rows.
10. Merge the cells in Row 1, and type the desired introductory information in the first row.
11. Move to Row 3, and continue typing the rest of the headings and information, as is done in Report 111-88, leaving Row 2 and Row 5 empty.
12. Save the page, view the Web page in a browser, and compare the browser view with the layout view in your word processor.

Creating More Web Pages

Goals

- Type at least 50wpm/5′/5e
- Create more Web pages

A. Type 2 times.

A. WARMUP

```
1      Missy examined these items: the #426 oil painting, a     11
2  Bowes & Elkjer porcelain vase, and the 86-piece collection   23
3  of glazed antique pitchers. There were 337 people present.   34
   |  1  |  2  |  3  |  4  |  5  |  6  |  7  |  8  |  9  |  10  |  11  |  12
```

SKILLBUILDING

B. PROGRESSIVE PRACTICE: NUMBERS

If you are not using the GDP software, turn to page SB-11 and follow the directions for this activity.

LANGUAGE ARTS

C. Study the rules at the right.

C. CAPITALIZATION

RULE ▶

≡ organization

Capitalize common organizational terms (such as *advertising department* and *finance committee*) only when they are the actual names of the units in the writer's own organization and when they are preceded by the word *the*.

The report from the Advertising Department is due today.

But: Our advertising department will submit its report today.

RULE ▶

≡ course

Capitalize the names of specific course titles but not the names of subjects or areas of study.

I have enrolled in Accounting 201 and will also take the marketing course.

Edit the sentences to correct any errors in capitalization.

```
8   The advertising department at their firm is excellent.
9   The Finance Committee here at Irwin will meet today.
10  I think I am going to pass keyboarding 1 with flying colors.
11  Their marketing department must approve the proposal first.
12  A class in Business Communications would be very helpful.
13  To take Math 102, you must have taken a beginning math course.
```

D. Take two 5-minute timed writings. Review your speed and errors.

Goal: At least 50wpm/5'/5e

D. 5-MINUTE TIMED WRITING

4	Employers want the people who work for them to have	11
5	many qualities of good character. Character is defined as a	23
6	distinctive feature of a person or thing. Character may be	34
7	what you are known for and may be why you remember someone	46
8	else. What are some of the traits you think of that are	57
9	linked with good character? A few traits might be respect,	69
10	honesty, trust, caring, leadership, attitude, tolerance,	81
11	fairness, and patience.	85
12	All people should have respect for themselves and for	96
13	others. If you respect people, you have a high regard for	108
14	the way they conduct themselves in all aspects of life.	119
15	However, before you can respect others, you need to have	131
16	respect for yourself.	135
17	Honesty and trustworthiness are similar traits. In	145
18	business dealings, people expect honesty and will admire	157
19	people who have this quality. They like to build business	168
20	relationships with companies whose employees are honest,	180
21	just, and trustworthy.	184
22	Your attitude is reflected in the way you act toward	195
23	other people or in the way you speak to them. You can make	207
24	great strides in advancing your career by taking a look at	219
25	the way you interact with people. You may want to take a	230
26	closer look at some character traits you want to improve.	242
27	Such improvements in life will amaze you.	250

| 1 | 2 | 3 | 4 | 5 | 6 | 7 | 8 | 9 | 10 | 11 | 12

Report 112-89 ▶

Web Site (continued)

Follow these steps to create a new services page for the Web site named Report-112-89.htm. Refer to the Web layout view of the Services page on page 452 as needed. Make the following changes to this report:

1. Change the title to Services.
2. Select and delete the table below the link bar.

3. Type Services centered on the second blank line below the link bar, and press ENTER 2 times.
4. Insert a centered open table with 1 cell.
5. Type the information below inside the table as shown in the Web layout view of the services page.
6. Save the page, and view the Web page in a browser.

Word Processing¶

We prepare documents with a professional look for correspondence of all types as well as reports, proposals, manuals, and so on.¶

Desktop Publishing¶

Our professional design specialists will create newsletters, brochures, letterheads, and other documents that are sure to capture your imagination.¶

Layout Editing¶

Our layout editors will transform your documents using in-house styles or custom styles. For your longer projects, they are experts at building master documents that include a cover page, table of contents, and index.¶

Copy Editing¶

Our copy editors will make sure that your document content is perfect. Proofreading, grammar, and writing style will all be checked so that your ideas are expressed clearly and effectively.

(Continued on next page)

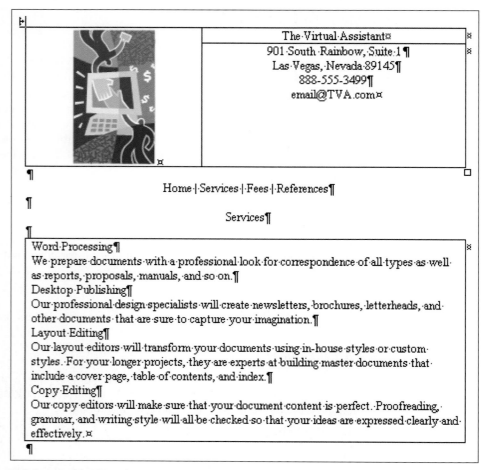

Web layout view of services page.

Report 112-90

Your Web Site (continued)

Follow these steps to create a new services page for your Web site named Report 112-90.htm similar to the Web layout view of the services page on this page. Make the following changes to this report:

1. Change the title to Services.
2. Select and delete the table below the link bar.

3. Type Services centered on the second blank line below the link bar, and press ENTER 2 times.
4. Create a centered open table with 1 cell.
5. Inside the table, type four headings followed by one or two sentences, each describing the services of your business.
6. Save the page, and view the Web page in a browser.

Creating Web Pages With Hyperlinks

Goals

- Improve speed and accuracy
- Refine language arts skills in composing
- Create Web pages with hyperlinks

A. Type 2 times.

A. WARMUP

1	Did you hear the excellent quartet of junior cadets?	11
2	Everybody in the crowd (estimated at over 500) applauded	22
3	"with gusto." The sizable crowd filled the 3/4-acre park.	34

| 1 | 2 | 3 | 4 | 5 | 6 | 7 | 8 | 9 | 10 | 11 | 12 |

SKILLBUILDING

B. DIAGNOSTIC PRACTICE: SYMBOLS AND PUNCTUATION

If you are not using the GDP software, turn to page SB-2 and follow the directions for this activity.

C. Type the columns 2 times. Press TAB to move from column to column.

C. TECHNIQUE PRACTICE: TAB KEY

4	T. Waters	L. Vigil	S. Zimmerly	D. Colwell	C. Foster
5	M. Goldbach	R. Hempker	G. Beckert	M. Kinsey	A. Lucero
6	C. Maclean	J. Nichols	I. Ohlsen	R. Parlee	S. Quale
7	J. Rondeau	G. Snowden	Y. Tokita	C. Upton	C. Vaughn

LANGUAGE ARTS

D. COMPOSING A PERSONAL-BUSINESS LETTER

Compose a two-paragraph personal-business letter that summarizes the content of the Web site design guidelines on page 446. Address the letter to your instructor; provide a suitable inside address and salutation for your letter. Also, provide a complimentary closing and sign the letter yourself.

In the letter, discuss the following:
Paragraph 1. Describe how to plan an effective Web site.
Paragraph 2. Describe how to design an effective Web site.

FORMATTING

E. HYPERLINKS

Hyperlinks are powerful navigational tools that are critical to the overall plan and design of a Web site. When clicked, they move a visitor from one page or one location on a page to another.

When you create a hyperlink, you must indicate the target. The hyperlink can point to the same page, to a different page, to another site, or perhaps to an e-mail address. You can assign a hyperlink to a word, a group of words, or a picture.

The presence of a text hyperlink is usually indicated by text that is underlined in a color different from that used on the rest of the words on the page. Also, the mouse pointer changes to a hand shape when hovering over a hyperlink.

Word
Processing
Manual

F. WEB PAGE—HYPERLINKS

Study Lesson 113 in your word processing manual. Complete all of the shaded steps while at your computer. Then format the jobs that follow.

DOCUMENT PROCESSING

Report 113-91

Web Site (continued)

Follow these steps to create a new fees page for the Web site named Report-113-91.htm. Refer to the Web layout view of the fees page on page 455 as needed. Make the following changes to this report:

1. Change the title to Fees.
2. Change Services to Fees on the second blank line below the link bar.
3. Move inside the table below "Services," and select and delete the information inside the table.
4. Type the information below inside the table as shown in the Web layout view of the Fees page.
5. Save the page, and view the Web page in a browser.

The Virtual Assistant strives to work within your organization's budget. We will review your individual needs and tailor the pricing to fit your project. We welcome the opportunity to provide an individual estimate. Be assured that our prices are extremely competitive. Here are some general guidelines regarding our fees:
¶
We typically charge by the hour or by the page, depending upon the job. ¶
Most fees are based on the length of the document and the amount of editing deemed necessary. ¶
We offer substantial discounts for volume work and repeat clients. ¶
A surcharge is added for rush jobs. ¶
Payment for services rendered should be made by credit card, check, or money order. ¶
¶
For a copy of our current rate guide, please send an e-mail message to rateguide@TVA.com. ¶

(Continued on next page)

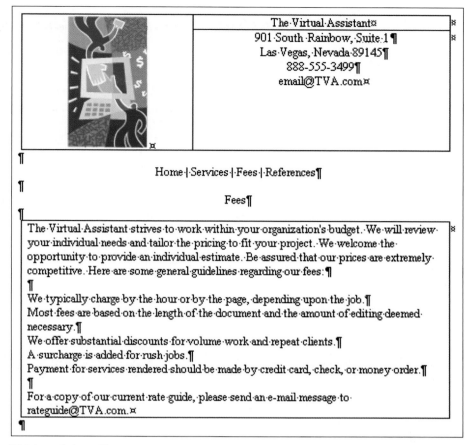

Web layout view of fees page.

Report 113-92

Web Site (continued)

Follow these steps to insert hyperlinks on the link bar for the fees page. Make the following changes to this report:

1. Insert three text hyperlinks for the first three words on the link bar as follows:

   Home links to Report-111-87.htm
   Services links to Report-112-89.htm
   Fees links to Report-113-92.htm

2. Manually open Report-111-87.htm (the home page) and Report-112-89.htm (the services page).

3. Insert three text hyperlinks for the first three words on the link bar for each page just as you did in step 1.

4. On Report-111-87.htm (the home page), insert four more text hyperlinks for each of the four headings on the home page ("Word Processing," "Desktop Publishing," "Layout Editing," and "Copy Editing") to link to the services page, Report-112-89.htm.

5. Save all pages, test all the hyperlinks, and edit any hyperlinks as needed.

(Continued on next page)

The·Virtual·Assistant¤
901·South·Rainbow,·Suite·1¶
Las·Vegas,·Nevada·89145¶
888-555-3499¶
email@TVA.com¤

Home·|·Services·|·Fees·|·References¶
¶
Fees¶

Web layout view of fees page with hyperlinks.

English·and·business·communications,·will·make·sure·they·are·letter-perfect.··Please·browse·around·our·site·for·details.¤	
¤	¤
Word·Processing¤	Desktop·Publishing¤
Correspondence¶	Newsletters¶
Reports¶	Brochures¶
Proposals¶	Letterheads¶
Manuals¤	Resumes¤
¤	¤
Layout·Editing¤	Copy·Editing¤
In-House·Styles¶	Proofreading¶
Custom·Styles¶	Technical·Editing¶
Master·Documents¶	Grammar·Checking¶
Table·of·Contents¶	Writing·Style¤
Indexes¤	

Web layout view of home page with hyperlinks.

Report 113-93

Your Web Site (continued)

Follow these steps to create a new page for your Web site named Report-113-93.htm similar to the Web layout view of the fees page on this page. Make the following changes to this report:

1. Change the title to Fees.
2. Change Services to Fees on the second blank line below the link bar.

3. Move inside the table below "Services," and select and delete the information inside the table.
4. Type content similar to the fees page on page 455.
5. Save the page, and view the Web page in a browser.

Report 113-94

Your Web Site (continued)

Follow these steps to insert hyperlinks on the link bar for the Fees page. Make the following changes to this report:

1. Insert three text hyperlinks for the first three words on the link bar as follows:

   Home links to Report-111-88.htm
   Services links to Report-112-90.htm
   Fees links to Report-113-94.htm

2. Manually open Report-111-88.htm (the home page) and Report-112-90.htm (the services page).

3. Insert three text hyperlinks for the first three words on the link bar for each page just as you did in step 2.
4. On Report-111-88.htm (the home page), insert four more text hyperlinks for each of the four headings on your home page to link to the services page, Report-112-90.htm.
5. Save all pages, test all the hyperlinks, and edit any hyperlinks as needed.

Creating More Web Pages With Hyperlinks

Goals

- Type at least 50wpm/5′/5e
- Create more Web pages with hyperlinks

A. Type 2 times.

A. WARMUP

```
1        This series* (*6 films, 28 minutes) by J. Zeller goes    11
2   beyond the "basics" of computers. Viewers keep requesting     23
3   an extension on the dates; this includes 3/2, 5/5, and 8/9.   34
    | 1 | 2 | 3 | 4 | 5 | 6 | 7 | 8 | 9 | 10 | 11 | 12
```

SKILLBUILDING

B. MAP

Follow the GDP software directions for this exercise in improving keystroking accuracy.

Keyboarding Connection

Using Hypertext

Do you know how to surf the Web? It's easy! The Web contains pages, which are blocks of text, visuals, sound, or animation. Hypertext is a format in which certain words in the text of a Web page are highlighted, underlined, or colored differently from the other words. These colored or highlighted words link to other pages on the Web.

When you point to a hyperlink and click the mouse button, the page connected to that word is displayed. Therefore, one page on the Web can link to many other pages. Hypertext pages do not have to be read in any specific order.

Hypertext enables you to connect and retrieve Web pages from computer networks worldwide. With hypertext, you can point and click or surf your way all over the Web.

YOUR TURN   Open a page on the Web. Surf the Web using the hyperlinks displayed on the page.

C. Take two 5-minute timed writings. Review your speed and errors

Goal: At least 50wpm/5'/5e

C. 5-MINUTE TIMED WRITING

4 Before you apply for jobs, you will want to do some	11
5 detective work. First, choose a business for which you want	23
6 to work and then use the Internet to find out about the	34
7 company. If you find a Web site for the business, then you	46
8 can learn all about the company, its hiring policies, the	57
9 job listings, and how to apply for a job opening.	67
10 When you are researching a company, you want to learn	78
11 about the history of the company. You may be able to find	90
12 out how stock analysts expect the company stock to perform	102
13 in the coming months if the company is publicly held.	112
14 When you find a job opening for which you know that	123
15 you want to apply, read carefully to see what type of work	135
16 experience and education the company requires for the job.	147
17 When you prepare your resume, emphasize your qualifications	159
18 based on the requirements listed for the job. If the person	171
19 who should receive job inquiries is not listed, contact the	183
20 company by phone or e-mail to get a name. Personalize your	194
21 cover letter and resume, if possible, for the company.	205
22 The information you find in your research will be	217
23 very helpful during the interview with a representative of	228
24 the company. Ask good questions and speak confidently about	240
25 the job. Emphasize how your skills would be valuable.	250

| 1 | 2 | 3 | 4 | 5 | 6 | 7 | 8 | 9 | 10 | 11 | 12

Report 114-95

Web Site (continued)

Follow these steps to create a new references page for the Web site named Report-114-95.htm. Refer the Web layout view of the references page on page 460 as needed. Make the following changes to this report:

1. Change the title to References.
2. Change Fees to References on the second blank line below the link bar.

3. Move inside the table below "References," and select and delete the information inside the table.
4. Type the information below inside the table as shown in the Web layout view of the references page.
5. Save the page, and view the Web page in a browser.

↓2X

I've been in a highly successful business for over 10 years and attribute much of that success to the skilled professionals at The Virtual Assistant. I am always confident that my work will go out error-free. They are top-notch professionals and can work for my team anytime! ↓2X

Mike Rashid
Network Engineer
Denver, Colorado ↓4X

The documents produced by The Virtual Assistant are impeccable! I can count on professional, reliable, competent, and efficient service without question. It is so easy to send documents back and forth via the Internet, and we all know that time is money. I highly recommend TVA for any of your word processing needs. ↓2X

Nancy Shipley
Attorney-at-Law
Chicago, Illinois ↓2X

(Continued on next page)

The·Virtual·Assistant¤

901·South·Rainbow,·Suite·1¶

Las·Vegas,·Nevada·89145¶

888-555-3499¶

email@TVA.com¤

Home·|·Services·|·Fees·|·References¶

References¶

I've·been·in·a·highly·successful·business·for·over·10·years·and·attribute·much·of·that· success·to·the·skilled·professionals·at·The·Virtual·Assistant.·I·am·always·confident·that· my·work·will·go·out·error-free.·They·are·top-notch·professionals·and·can·work·for·my· team·anytime!¶

Mike·Rashid¶

Network·Engineer¶

Denver,·Colorado¶

The·documents·produced·by·The·Virtual·Assistant·are·impeccable!·I·can·count·on· professional,·reliable,·competent,·and·efficient·service·without·question.·It·is·so·easy·to· send·documents·back·and·forth·via·the·Internet,·and·we·all·know·that·time·is·money.·I· highly·recommend·TVA·for·any·of·your·word·processing·needs.¶

Nancy·Shipley¶

Attorney·-·at·-·Law¶

Chicago,·Illinois¶

Web layout view of references page.

Report 114-96

Web Site (continued)

Follow these steps to insert any missing hyperlinks on the link bar for all pages. Make the following changes to this report:

1. Insert a text hyperlink for the last word on the link bar as follows:
   References links to Report-114-96.htm.

2. Manually open Report-111-87.htm (the home page), Report-112-89.htm (the services page), and Report-113-92.htm (the fees page).

3. Insert any missing text hyperlinks on the link bar for each page as needed.

4. Save all pages, test all the hyperlinks, and edit any hyperlinks as needed.

Report 114-97 ▶

Your Web Site (continued)

Follow these steps to create a new references page for your Web site named Report-114-97.htm similar to the Web layout view of the references page on page 460. Make the following changes to this report:

1. Change the title to References.
2. Change Fees to References on the second blank line below the link bar.

3. Move inside the table below "References," and select and delete the information inside the table.
4. Type the information for two references; follow the setup for the references page on page 460.
5. Save the page, and view the Web page in a browser.

Report 114-98 ▶

Your Web Site (continued)

Follow these steps to insert any missing hyperlinks on the link bar for all pages of your Web site. Make the following changes to this report:

1. Insert a text hyperlink for the last word on the link bar as follows:

   References links to Report-114-98.htm.

2. Manually open Report-111-88.htm (the home page), Report-112-90.htm (the services page), and Report-113-94.htm (the fees page).
3. Insert any missing text hyperlinks on the link bar for each page as needed.
4. Save all pages, test all the hyperlinks, and edit any hyperlinks as needed.

Formatting Web Pages

Goals

- Improve speed and accuracy
- Refine language arts skills in proofreading
- Format Web pages

A. Type 2 times.

A. WARMUP

```
1      Contact bxvacuum@clean.com to order the large-sized    11
2  grips. They were just lowered to $160 from $240 (a 33 1/3%  22
3  markdown). Jay's #55 quilts were reduced to $88 from $99.   34
        |  1  |  2  |  3  |  4  |  5  |  6  |  7  |  8  |  9  |  10  |  11  |  12
```

SKILLBUILDING

 **PRETEST → PRACTICE → POSTTEST**

PRETEST
Take a 1-minute timed writing. Review your speed and errors.

B. PRETEST: Common Letter Combinations

```
4      He did mention that they are sending a lawful taping    11
5  of the comedy format to a performing combo. A motion to     22
6  commit a useful option forced a fusion of forty persons.    33
        |  1  |  2  |  3  |  4  |  5  |  6  |  7  |  8  |  9  |  10  |  11  |  12
```

PRACTICE
Speed Emphasis:
If you made no more than 1 error on the Pretest, type each *individual* line twice.
Accuracy Emphasis:
If you made 3 or more errors, type each *group* of lines (as though it were a paragraph) 2 times.

C. PRACTICE: Word Beginnings

```
7  for forty forth format former forget forest forearm forbear
8  per peril perky period permit person peruse perform persist
9  com combo comic combat commit common combed compose complex
```

D. PRACTICE: Word Endings

```
10  ing doing mixing living filing taping sending biking hiding
11  ion onion nation lotion motion option mention fusion legion
12  ful awful useful joyful earful lawful helpful sinful armful
```

POSTTEST
Repeat the Pretest timed writing and compare performance.

E. POSTTEST: Common Letter Combinations

F. Take a 1-minute timed writing on the first paragraph to establish your base speed. Then take four 1-minute timed writings on the remaining paragraphs. As soon as you equal or exceed your base speed on one paragraph, advance to the next, more difficult paragraph.

F. SUSTAINED PRACTICE: CAPITALIZATION

13   Even though he was only about thirty years old, Jason   11
14 knew that it was not too soon to begin thinking about his   23
15 retirement. He soon found out that there were many things   34
16 involved in his plans for an early and long retirement.   45

17   Even without considering the uncertainty of social   10
18 security, Jason knew that he should plan his career moves   22
19 so that he would have a strong company retirement plan. He   34
20 realized that he should have an Individual Retirement Plan.   45

21   When he became aware that The Longman Company, the   10
22 firm that employed him, would match his contributions to a   22
23 supplemental retirement account, he began saving even more.   34
24 He used the Payroll Department funds from the Goplin Group.   46

25   He also learned that The Longman Company retirement   11
26 plan, his Individual Retirement Plan, and his supplemental   22
27 retirement account are all deferred savings. With those   33
28 tax-dollar savings, Jason bought New Venture Group mutuals.   45

LANGUAGE ARTS

G. Edit this paragraph to correct any typing or formatting errors.

G. PROOFREADING

29   The idea and practise of sharing risk originated in
30 antiquetry. Many years ago, Chinese merchants deviced an
31 injenious way of protecting themselves against the chance
32 of a financialy ruinous accadent in the dangerous river
33 along the trade routtes when they were delivring goods.

FORMATTING

H. MORE WEB SITE DESIGN GUIDELINES

Follow these guidelines to design effective Web sites:

- Experiment with the themes that come with most programs.
- If you use a theme, experiment with the embedded styles that can be applied to titles, headings, subheadings, and so on, for design consistency.
- Choose a consistent look for headings and subheadings, including font size, color, and alignment, for design unity.
- Use color to establish moods: black is somber; white is clean, organized, or sterile; bright colors are energetic but may be hard to read. Experiment and use your judgment.

I. WEB PAGE—DESIGN THEMES

Study Lesson 115 in your word processing manual. Complete all of the shaded steps while at your computer. Then format the jobs that follow.

DOCUMENT PROCESSING

Report 115-99

Web Site (continued)

Follow these steps to format the Web site.

1. Manually open Report-111-87.htm (the home page), Report-112-89.htm (the services page), Report-113-92.htm (the fees page), and Report-114-96.htm (the references page).

2. Apply a design theme to each page that coordinates with the picture at the top of each page. Remove any table borders as needed or if desired.

3. Move to each page, and apply a Heading 1 style to "The Virtual Assistant." Align the text and adjust the table as needed to position the picture and text attractively. Copy and paste the table from one page to the next if desired.

4. Move to the home page, and add a bullet to each item under each heading beginning with the heading "Word Processing."

5. Apply a Heading 3 style to each heading beginning with the heading "Word Processing."

6. Move to the services page, apply a Heading 2 style to "Services," center the line, and delete the blank line below the link bar.

7. Add a bullet to each sentence under each heading.

8. Apply a Heading 3 style to each heading beginning with "Word Processing."

9. Move to the fees page, apply a Heading 2 style to "Fees," center the line, and delete the blank line below the link bar.

10. Add a bullet to each sentence under the first paragraph except for the last sentence on the page.

11. Insert a horizontal line in the blank line after the last bulleted item.

12. Move to the references page, apply a Heading 2 style to "References," center the line, and delete the blank line below the link bar.

13. Place the insertion point in front of the first blank line in the table, and insert a horizontal line.

14. Place the insertion point in front of the second blank line between the references, and insert a horizontal line.

15. Place the insertion point in front of the second blank line under the last reference, and insert a horizontal line.

16. Change any styles, fonts, borders, or colors as desired.

17. Test all the hyperlinks, edit any hyperlinks as needed, and save all pages.

18. View your finished Web site in a browser.

Note: If you would like to format the Web site you created for your own business in Lessons 111–114, follow steps similar to those in Report 115-99.

Keyboarding Connection

Choosing a Different Home Page

You don't have to start at the same home page every time you use your browser. You can change the browser's home page to start at one of your favorite Web pages. Here's how to do it.

In Netscape, go to the chosen page and select Preferences from the Edit menu. Click the Navigator category in the Preferences dialog box. Click the Use Current Page button in the "home page" area. Choose Home Page in the "Navigator starts with" area. Click OK.

In Internet Explorer, from the chosen page select Internet Options from the Tools menu. Click the General tab, and then click the Use Current button in the "home page" area. Click OK.

YOUR TURN Using your browser, access a favorite Web page. Make it your browser's home page.

The Virtual Assistant

901 South Rainbow, Suite 1
Las Vegas, Nevada 89145
888-555-3499
email@TVA.com

Home | Services | Fees | References

Do you need a skilled assistant who works tirelessly on your documents, doesn't need any office space, and gives your work that personal touch? The Virtual Assistant is a professional document processing and design service that will help create the professional image your business demands.

You don't get a second chance at a first impression. The graphics experts in our word processing and desktop publishing departments will make sure your documents look gorgeous. Our editors, who have completed a series of rigorous courses in business English and business communications, will make sure they are letter-perfect. Please browse around our site for details.

Word Processing
- Correspondence
- Reports
- Proposals
- Manuals

Desktop Publishing
- Newsletters
- Brochures
- Letterheads
- Resumes

Layout Editing
- In-House Styles
- Custom Styles
- Master Documents
- Table of Contents
- Indexes

The Virtual Assistant

901 South Rainbow, Suite 1
Las Vegas, Nevada 89145
888-555-3499
email@TVA.com

Home | Services | Fees | References

Services

Word Processing
- We prepare documents with a professional look for correspondence of all types as well as reports, proposals, manuals, and so on.

Desktop Publishing
- Our professional design specialists will create newsletters, brochures, letterheads, and other documents that are sure to capture your imagination.

Layout Editing
- Our layout editors will transform your documents using in-house styles or custom styles. For your longer projects, they are experts at building master documents that include a cover page, table of contents, and index.

Copy Editing
- Our copy editors will make sure that your document content is perfect. Proofreading, grammar, and writing style will all be checked so that your ideas are expressed clearly and effectively.

(Continued on next page)

The Virtual Assistant

901 South Rainbow, Suite 1
Las Vegas, Nevada 89145
888-555-3499
email@TVA.com

Home | Services | Fees | References

Fees

The Virtual Assistant strives to work within your organization's budget. We will review your individual needs and tailor the pricing to fit your project. We welcome the opportunity to provide an individual estimate. Be assured that our prices are extremely competitive. Here are some general guidelines regarding our fees:

- We typically charge by the hour or by the page, depending upon the job.
- Most fees are based on the length of the document and the amount of editing deemed necessary.
- We offer substantial discounts for volume work and repeat clients.
- A surcharge is added for rush jobs.
- Payment for services rendered should be made by credit card, check, or money order.

For a copy of our current rate guide, please send an e-mail message to rateguide@TVA.com.

The Virtual Assistant

901 South Rainbow, Suite 1
Las Vegas, Nevada 89145
888-555-3499
email@TVA.com

Home | Services | Fees | References

References

I've been in a highly successful business for over 10 years and attribute much of that success to the skilled professionals at The Virtual Assistant. I am always confident that my work will go out error-free. They are top-notch professionals and can work for my team anytime!

Mike Rashid
Network Engineer
Denver, Colorado

The documents produced by The Virtual Assistant are impeccable! I can count on professional, reliable, competent, and efficient service without question. It is so easy to send documents back and forth via the Internet, and we all know that time is money. I highly recommend TVA for any of your word processing needs.

Nancy Shipley
Attorney-at-Law
Chicago, Illinois

Follow these steps to create the home page and Contact Us page for this Web site:

1. Change the title of Report-115-100A.htm to In The Game, Home.
2. Insert Home-115A.htm into the home page (Report-115-100A.htm).
3. Leave Report-115-100A.htm open, and create an additional new Web page named Report-115-100B; change the title to In The Game, Contact Us.
4. Insert the file Contact Us-115B.htm into Report-115-100B.htm.
5. Insert a picture related to sports in the open cell in Column A on the Contact Us page (Report-115-100B.htm).
6. Resize the picture proportionally until it is about 1 inch wide, and center the picture in the open cell in Column A on the Contact Us page.
7. Apply a design theme to the Contact Us page that coordinates with the picture.
8. Apply a Heading 1 style to "In The Game," and center the line on the Contact Us page.

9. Apply a Heading 3 style to the headings "E-Mail," "Call Us," and "Snail Mail" on the Contact Us page.
10. Select the table and the link bar at the top of the Contact Us page, copy it, move to the top of the home page, and paste it.
11. Apply the same design theme to the home page that you used on the Contact Us page.
12. Apply a Heading 3 style to the headings "Baseball and Softball," "Soccer, Track and Field," and "Gymnatics" on the home page.
13. Change any styles, fonts, borders, or colors as desired on both pages.
14. Insert text hyperlinks on the link bar of each page as follows:
    Home links to Report-115-100A.htm
    Contact Us links to Report-115-100B.htm
15. Test all the hyperlinks, edit any hyperlinks as needed, and save all pages.
16. View your finished Web site in a browser.

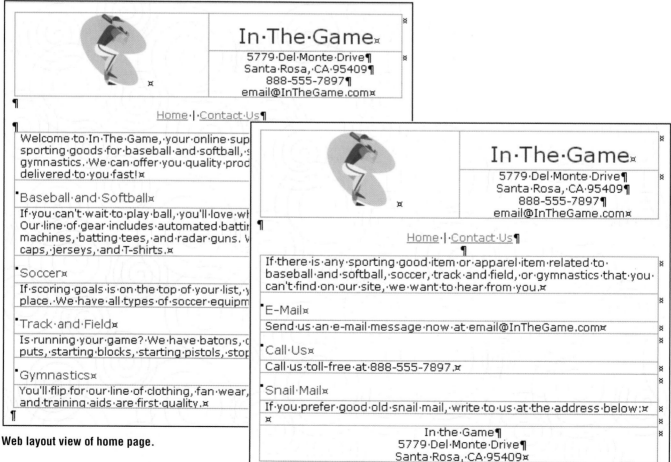

Web layout view of home page.

Web layout view of contact us page.

Unit 24

Skillbuilding and In-Basket Review

Suite Retreat

3539 Shell Basket Lane
Sanibel Island, Florida 33957
941-555-3422
email@SuiteRetreat.com

Home | Rates

Are you ready to experience a private beach retreat with warm waters,
_____ e skies? The personnel at Suite Retreat
_____ make sure your stay is a pleasurable one.

_____ on a private beach on the Gulf of Mexico
_____ ntry road. You will feel the soothing
_____ urroundings and charming cottage suites
_____ inding drive. Each suite is beautifully
_____ h marble baths and private whirlpools for
_____ for further details on our suites.

_____ le recreation during your stay, we have a
_____ e on the property:

_____ d tennis courts

_____ ning, you will find a small golf course and
_____ y walking distance about a half mile

All-City, Inc.
17 North Eighth Street   ◆   Columbia, MO 65201   ◆   800-555-9981   ◆   www.ACI.com

Insuring you at home a

Sports 'R Us
3939 Townsgate Drive
San Diego, CA 92130
www.SRU.com

In-Basket Review (Insurance)

Goals

- Type at least 50wpm/5′/5e
- Format documents used in the insurance industry

A. Type 2 times.

A. WARMUP

```
1      He realized that exactly 10% of the budget ($62,475)    11
2   was questionable. Several key people reviewed it; most of   22
3   them wanted to reject about 1/3 of the proposed line items!  34
    |  1  |  2  |  3  |  4  |  5  |  6  |  7  |  8  |  9  |  10  |  11  |  12
```

SKILLBUILDING

B. PROGRESSIVE PRACTICE: ALPHABET

If you are not using the GDP software, turn to page SB-7 and follow the directions for this activity.

Strategies for Career Success

Managing Group Conflict

Not all team members have the same opinion or approach to solving a problem. Before a group can reach an agreement, conflicts must be addressed and expressed openly. Follow these steps to manage group conflict.

Take everyone's feelings and opinions seriously. Don't be afraid to disagree. Offer and accept constructive criticism. Find points of agreement. When the group makes a decision, support it fully.

Be a good listener. Take notes, maintain eye contact, restate what you hear, and listen for the emotions behind the words. Try to view the situation through the other person's eyes. Don't jump to conclusions. Ask nonthreatening questions to clarify meaning, and listen without interrupting. Most group conflicts don't get resolved until everyone feels he or she has had a chance to be heard.

YOUR TURN When is the last time you had a conflict with a coworker? What did you do about it? What was the result?

C. Take two 5-minute timed writings. Review your speed and errors.

Goal: At least 50wpm/5'/5e

C. 5-MINUTE TIMED WRITING

4	Several factors should be considered before you buy a	11
5	new printer for your computer. First, decide how you will	23
6	use the new printer. If you plan to use the printer for	34
7	composing letters or reports, you may want to shop for an	45
8	ink jet printer that is reasonably priced and capable of	57
9	doing general tasks. If you are purchasing the printer for	69
10	office use, you may wish to shop for a printer that prints	80
11	documents more quickly and of exceptional quality. Finally,	92
12	if you plan to use a digital camera with the printer, you	104
13	will want a printer that is designed to print documents of	116
14	photo quality.	119
15	Resolution, speed, and paper handling are some other	130
16	factors you should consider when you purchase a printer.	141
17	Resolution refers to how sharp the image appears on the	152
18	paper. With printers producing a higher resolution, the	163
19	imaging gives you higher-quality output. You will see this	175
20	amazing difference in imaging when you compare some samples	187
21	of print from the other kinds of printers.	196
22	If you expect to print long documents, then you will	207
23	want to look for a reliable printer with a feed tray that	218
24	holds large amounts of paper. The more expensive printers	230
25	are usually faster printers. After assessing your printer	241
26	needs, you are ready to make your purchase.	250

| 1 | 2 | 3 | 4 | 5 | 6 | 7 | 8 | 9 | 10 | 11 | 12

DOCUMENT PROCESSING

Form 116-15

Letter Template

Use the first letter template in your word processing software.

Situation: Today is December 27, 20--. You are employed in the office of All-City, Inc., an insurance company in Columbia, Missouri. Offices are located at 17 North Eighth Street, Columbia, MO 65201, and their phone number is 800-555-9981. All City, Inc., handles auto, home, and life insurance coverage. The Web site address is www.ACI.com.

Mr. Greg Scher, executive vice president, has written the letter shown on page 471. You are to type it using a correspondence template. He prefers block-style letters with *Sincerely* as his complimentary closing and uses his title in the writer's identification. The letter should be addressed to Ms. Rosa Nunez, 731 Broad Street, Newark, NJ 07102, and you should use standard punctuation. This letter includes two enclosures. The company slogan is "Insuring you at home and around the world."

¶ Your recent letter was filled with excellent questions, Ms. Nunez, and I am more than happy to answer them for you.

¶ All City, Inc., handles auto, home, and life insurance coverage for you and your family. However, since you are primarily interested in auto insurance, I have enclosed a brochure with the details and a table with required minimum coverage for the states you mentioned.

¶ ACI's automobile policy combines both mandatory and optional coverages in one package. This policy can be tailored to meet your individual needs so that you end up with a policy that provides comprehensive protection. However, the best way for you to understand fully what we can offer you is to schedule a meeting at your convenience.

¶ Ms. Elena Ortega will be calling you in the next day or two to arrange an appointment after you have had a chance to review the enclosed materials. We also have an excellent Web site at ACI.com filled with helpful information. Again, thank you for your inquiry, Ms. Nunez.

Table 116-55

Boxed Table

The boxed table below is to be enclosed with the letter when it is sent to Ms. Nunez.

STATE MINIMUM COVERAGE REQUIREMENTS		
Minimum Limits	**State**	**Required Coverage**
25/50/10	NY	Bodily Injury and Property Damage Liability, Personal Injury Protection, Uninsured Motorist
15/30/5	NJ	Bodily Injury and Property Damage Liability, Personal Injury Protection, Uninsured Motorist
15/30/5	PA	Bodily Injury and Property Damage Liability, Medical Payments
20/40/10	CT	Bodily Injury and Property Damage Liability, Uninsured and Underinsured Motorist

Mr. Scher has sketched out a letterhead form, and he would like you to design the finished letterhead for All-City, Inc.

Insert a decorative image.

Identify our company, including our Web site.

Insert our company slogan with a border above it.

In-Basket Review (Hospitality)

Goals

- Improve speed and accuracy
- Refine language arts skills in word usage
- Format documents used in the hospitality industry

A. Type 2 times.

A. WARMUP

```
1        The executive meeting won't begin until 8:15; please    11
2    contact just the key people at zfnet@mail.com. Did Kay say   23
3    that quite a group* (*234) is expected by 9 o'clock today?   34
     |  1  |  2  |  3  |  4  |  5  |  6  |  7  |  8  |  9  | 10  | 11  | 12
```

SKILLBUILDING

B. Take three 12-second timed writings on each line. The scale below the last line shows your wpm speed for a 12-second timed writing.

B. 12-SECOND SPEED SPRINTS

```
4    Half of the space was going to be used for seven new desks.
5    She will soon know if all their goals have been met or not.
6    You must learn to focus on each one of your jobs every day.
7    The group will meet in the new suite that is down the hall.
     I I I 5 I I I 10 I I I 15 I I I 20 I I I 25 I I I 30 I I I 35 I I I 40 I I I 45 I I I 50 I I I 55 I I I 60
```

C. Type line 8. Then type lines 9–11 (as a paragraph), reading the words from right to left. Type 2 times.

C. TECHNIQUE PRACTICE: CONCENTRATION

```
8        When typing, always strive for complete concentration.
9    concentration. complete for strive always typing, When
10   errors. your on down cut may rate typing your in decrease A
11   errors. of number the reduce to rate reading your down Slow
```

D. DIAGNOSTIC PRACTICE: SYMBOLS AND PUNCTUATION

If you are not using the GDP software, turn to page SB-2 and follow the directions for this activity.

E. Study the rules at the right.

E. WORD USAGE

RULE ▶

accept/except

Accept means "to agree to"; *except* means "to leave out."
All employees <u>except</u> the maintenance staff should <u>accept</u> the agreement.

RULE ▶

affect/effect

Affect is most often used as a verb meaning "to influence"; *effect* is most often used as a noun meaning "result."
The ruling will <u>affect</u> our domestic operations but will have no <u>effect</u> on Asian operations.

RULE ▶

farther/further

Farther refers to distance; *further* refers to extent or degree.
The <u>farther</u> we drove, the <u>further</u> agitated he became.

RULE ▶

personal/personnel

Personal means "private"; *personnel* means "employees."
All <u>personnel</u> agreed not to use e-mail for <u>personal</u> business.

RULE ▶

principal/principle

Principal means "primary"; *principle* means "rule."
The <u>principle</u> of fairness is our <u>principal</u> means of dealing with customers.

Edit the sentences to correct any errors in word usage.

12 The company cannot accept any collect calls, except for his.
13 The affect of the speech was dramatic; everyone was affected.
14 Further discussion by office personal was not appropriate.
15 Comments made during any meeting should never be personal.
16 If the meeting is held any further away, no one will attend.
17 The principle reason for the decision was to save money.
18 Office ethics is a basic principle that should be practiced.
19 He cannot except the fact that the job was delegated to Jack.
20 Any further effects on office personnel will be evaluated.

DOCUMENT PROCESSING

Situation: You are employed at the office of Suite Retreat, a group of vacation cottage-style suites in Sanibel, Florida. The office and suites are located at 3539 Shell Basket Lane, Sanibel Island, FL 33957. The phone number is 941-555-3422, and the e-mail address is email@SuiteRetreat.com.

Ms. Maxwell, your boss, has asked you to redesign the Web site for Suite Retreat. She has written a description of Suite Retreat that she wants you to use in the home page. You should also include identifying information and a picture that will capture the feeling of a carefree beach vacation spot. The theme and styles you choose for the Web site should reflect the same image.

Begin by creating the home page as shown on page 476. Add the title Suite Retreat Home.

Report 117-101

Web Site

personal/personnel

affect/effect

personal/personnel

farther/further

 **Reference Manual**

Refer to page R-12C of the Reference Manual for a review of list formatting.

farther/further

¶ Are you ready to experience a private beach retreat with warm waters, endless white sand, and blue skies? The personnel at Suite Retreat are at your service and will make sure your stay is a pleasurable one.

¶ Suite Retreat is hidden away on a private beach on the Gulf of Mexico at the end of a secluded country road. You will feel the soothing effects of our lush, tropical surroundings and charming cottage suites the moment you enter our winding drive. Each suite is beautifully decorated and appointed with marble baths and private whirlpools for your personal use. Click here for further details on our suites.

¶ If you are interested in a little recreation during your stay, we have a variety of activities available on the property:

- Shuffleboard courts and tennis courts
- Bicycles and kayaks
- Swimming and shelling

¶ If you enjoy golf and fine dining, you will find a small golf course and excellent seafood within easy walking distance about a half mile farther down the beach.

Strategies for Career Success

What to Exclude From Your Resume

What items should you omit from your resume? Don't list salary demands. If the job posting requires a salary history, create a separate page listing the salaries for each position you've held. If the job posting wants your salary requirements, in the application letter state, "Salary expectation is in the range . . . ," and provide a range (usually a $5,000 range).

Exclude personal information such as race, gender, health status, age, marital status, religious preference, political preference, national origin, and physical characteristics (for example, height, weight). Do not provide your Social Security number or your photograph.

Exceptions to listing personal information do exist. For example, if you are applying for a job at a political party's headquarters and you are a member of that party, listing your party affiliation might be important to your potential employer.

YOUR TURN Review your resume. Have you included any personal information? If your answer is yes, does it serve a purpose for being in your resume?

Ms. Maxwell has asked you to continue building the Web site by making the following changes: Change the title to "Suite Retreat Rates." Add two hyperlinks to the link bar on both pages. The Home hyperlink should point to Report-117-101.htm, and the Rates hyperlink should point to Report-117-102.htm. Also add a hyperlink on the home page to the word *here* in the last sentence of the second paragraph to link to the Rates page. Apply the same theme and styles as used on the home page to the Rates page, and type the information as shown in the illustration below.

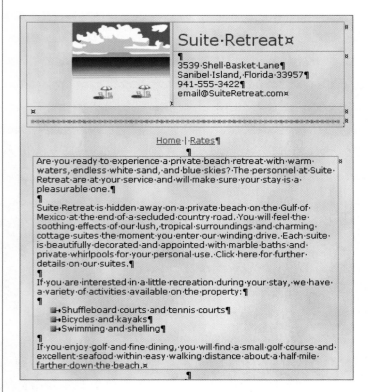

Home page.

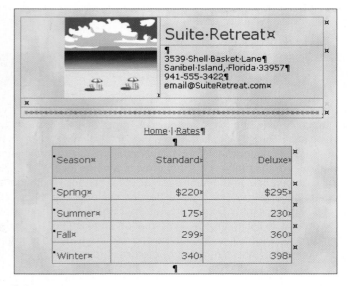

Rates page.

In-Basket Review (Retail)

Goals

- Type at least 50wpm/5'/5e
- To format documents used in the retail industry

A. Type 2 times.

A. WARMUP

```
1        Does Pamela know if Region 29* (*Ventura) has met the    11
2  sales quota? Their exact target zone is just not clear;        22
3  they don't have to submit their totals until 4:30 on 5/7.      34
   |  1  |  2  |  3  |  4  |  5  |  6  |  7  |  8  |  9  |  10  |  11  |  12
```

SKILLBUILDING

B. PACED PRACTICE

If you are not using the GDP software, turn to page SB-14 and follow the directions for this activity.

C. Take two 5-minute timed writings. Review your speed and errors.

Goal: At least 50wpm/5'/5e

C. 5-MINUTE TIMED WRITING

4	Job sharing is a current concept that many places are	11
5	using to keep valued workers. People are finding a wide	22
6	range of reasons for not wanting to work full time. Here	34
7	are some tips on how to approach your boss if you would	45
8	like to try job sharing.	50
9	First, check your company handbook for an authorized	61
10	policy regarding this concept. If there is no rule that	72
11	prohibits the concept, then try to enlist a coworker who	83
12	would like to job share and help you in writing a proposal	95
13	for job sharing where you work.	101
14	Next, define your needs and your goals. Develop a work	113
15	schedule that will meet all of your personal and monetary	124
16	needs. Be sure that you include enough time to get the work	136
17	done. If you want to work at your home on occasion, be sure	148
18	to state your desires. You might find it is often quite	159
19	helpful to maintain a journal of your job duties, noting	171
20	how much time is devoted to each task. Your plan should	182
21	also include details about the logistics of your proposal.	194
22	Decide how to cope with unexpected crisis situations.	205
23	Finally, time your presentation so there will be no	215
24	unnecessary interruptions. Be organized, persistent, and	227
25	professional in your presentation. Prepare to be successful	239
26	by compiling clearly defined ideas to support your plans.	250

| 1 | 2 | 3 | 4 | 5 | 6 | 7 | 8 | 9 | 10 | 11 | 12

DOCUMENT PROCESSING

Form ▶ 118-17

Memo Template

Use the first memo template in your word processing software.

Situation: Today is January 5, 20--. You are employed as an administrative assistant to Kelley O'Brian. Ms. O'Brian is vice president of marketing for Sports 'R Us, a retailer for sports equipment and clothing in San Diego, California, at 3939 Townsgate Drive, San Diego, CA 92130. The Web site is www.SRU.com.

The company is in the midst of launching a brand-new line of women's sportswear for the beach. Ms. O'Brian has written the memo below to Hitochi Morimoto, president of Sports 'R Us, with a copy to Barbara Warrick, vice president of sales. You are to type the memo, using a memo template. The subject of the memo is SRU Sunwear Ad Campaign.

(Continued on next page)

¶ I am pleased to tell you that we are in the final stages of our ad campaign to launch our newest line of women's beach sportswear named SRU Sunwear. We are just about to sign Cindy Bloom to serve as our spokesperson and featured model in our magazine ad campaign.

¶ I have scheduled a meeting for next week so that you can meet Cindy and see a representative sampling of our exciting new sportswear line. My staff members will also be ready with a presentation for our ad campaign, which will focus on the practicality and smart good looks of our newest beachwear. I have attached an agenda for your review.

¶ Our company has always been known for the value and quality of our sportswear. This line is based on a smaller emerging brand that will save our customers money while still maintaining the high quality they have come to expect. I look forward to our meeting next week.

Report 118-103

Agenda

Prepare the meeting agenda shown below. The agenda should be attached to the memo when it is sent to Mr. Morimoto. It should be titled SRU SUNWEAR AD CAMPAIGN. The meeting will be held on January 12, 20--, at 11 a.m.

Call to order
Approval of minutes of December 20 meeting
Introduction of Cindy Bloom
Progress report on the status of the ad campaign
Presentation of the ad campaign
Presentation of some samples from the new sportswear line
Announcements
Miscellaneous
Adjournment

Ms. O'Brian has sketched out a cover page for the ad campaign report and would like you to design the finished cover page for the SRU Sunwear line of beach apparel. The report will be distributed at the meeting.

Insert some word art with the name of our sportswear line.

Insert a picture related to our new line of beach sportswear.

Identify our company and our address, including our Web site.

In-Basket Review (Government)

Goals

- Improve speed and accuracy
- Refine language arts skills in spelling
- Format documents used in government work

A. Type 2 times.

A. WARMUP

```
1        Turner & Finch will charge us $10,234 to complete the    11
2   job. Do they realize that they quoted us an initial fee of    23
3   exactly $9,876? Kelly will call them very soon to verify.     34
    |  1  |  2  |  3  |  4  |  5  |  6  |  7  |  8  |  9  |  10  |  11  |  12
```

SKILLBUILDING

PPP PRETEST → PRACTICE → POSTTEST

PRETEST
Take a 1-minute timed writing. Review your speed and errors.

B. PRETEST: Close Reaches

```
4        Sadly, the same essay was used to oppose and deny the    11
5   phony felony charge. After the weapon was located in his      22
6   pocket, the jury was left to cast the joint ballot anyway.    34
    |  1  |  2  |  3  |  4  |  5  |  6  |  7  |  8  |  9  |  10  |  11  |  12
```

PRACTICE
Speed Emphasis:
If you made no more than 1 error on the Pretest, type each *individual* line 2 times.
Accuracy Emphasis:
If you made 2 or more errors, type each *group* of lines (as though it were a paragraph) 2 times.

C. PRACTICE: Adjacent Keys

```
7   po post spot pours vapor poker powder oppose weapon pockets
8   sa sash same usage essay sadly safety dosage sample sailing
9   oi oily join point voice doing choice boiled egoist loiters
```

D. PRACTICE: Conscecutive Fingers

```
10  ft left soft often after shift gifted crafts thrift uplifts
11  ny onyx deny nylon vinyl phony anyway skinny felony canyons
12  lo loss solo loser flood color locate floral ballot loaders
```

POSTTEST
Repeat the Pretest timed writing and compare performance.

E. POSTTEST: Close Reaches

F. SUSTAINED PRACTICE: PUNCTUATION

13	Have you ever noticed that a good laugh every now and	11
14	then really makes you feel better? Research has shown that	23
15	laughter can have a very healing effect on our bodies. It	34
16	is an excellent way to relieve tension and stress all over.	46
17	When you laugh, your heart beats faster, you breathe	11
18	deeper, and you exercise your lungs. When you laugh, your	22
19	body produces endorphins--a natural painkiller that gives	34
20	you a sense of euphoria that is very powerful and pleasant.	46
21	Someone said, "Laugh in the face of adversity." As it	11
22	happens, this is first-rate advice. It's a great way to	22
23	cope with life's trials and tribulations; it's also a good	34
24	way to raise other people's spirits and relieve tension.	45
25	Finding "humor" in any situation takes practice--try	11
26	to make it a full-time habit. We're all looking for ways	22
27	to relieve stress. Any exercise--jogging, tennis, biking,	34
28	swimming, or golfing--is a proven remedy for "the blues."	45

LANGUAGE ARTS

G. SPELLING

29 practice continue regular entitled course resolution assist
30 weeks preparation purposes referred communication potential
31 environmental specifications original contractor associated
32 principal systems client excellent estimated administration
33 responsibility mentioned utilized materials criteria campus

34 It is the responsability of the administration to assist.
35 The principle client prepared the excellent specifications.
36 He mentioned that the critiria for the decision were clear.
37 The contractor associated with the project referred them.
38 He estamated that the potential for resolution was great.
39 I was told that weeks of reguler practice were required.

Correspondence 119-99

Business Letter in Block Style

Highlighted words are spelling words from the language arts activities.

Situation: Today is November 4, 20--. Use this date in all documents as needed. You work as an administrative assistant for Ruth McBride. She is research director for Ride Share, a free government-funded commuter service in Chicago that informs people about commuting alternatives. For the purposes of this simulation, your name will be Roberto Duran. Your e-mail address is rduran@rideshare.net.

Ms. McBride has left the letter below in your in-basket to be sent to Mr. Jason Davis, executive director for Canadian CarShare, which is located at 1233 West Third Avenue, Vancouver, BC V6J 1K1 in Canada. When communicating with Cana-dian firms, use A4 metric-size paper and adhere to Canadian mailing guidelines.

Ms. McBride prefers a block-style letter with standard punctuation, uses *Sincerely* as the complimentary close, and likes her business title typed below her name in a letter closing. Add this post-script notation at the end of the letter:

> Any statistics you might choose to include on the environmental impact associated with car sharing in your Web site at http://www.carshare.ca would be very helpful.

¶ Ride Share is a government-funded commuter service whose mission is to inform our citizens about commuting alternatives in the Chicago area. My responsibility is to gather as many facts as possible regarding the regular practice of car sharing in Canada.

¶ As I understand this concept, a car share client could conceivably mix and match alternative modes of transportation and also have exclusive use of a reserved car for a fixed period of time. For example, a commuter could arrive at work on a train, pick up a reserved car at a nearby parking lot to run errands at lunch, return the car an hour later, and then continue home perhaps using a van pool or bus. The commuter would pay about 20 to 40 cents a kilometer along with some monthly membership fees.

¶ If you can tell me which cities have successfully utilized car sharing in Canada since it was first introduced and why, I can begin preparation for a proposal for a car sharing pilot project as a potential commuter alternative here in the Chicago area.

Open the file for Correspondence 119-99. Ms. McBride would like you to send the same letter to Mr. Frans Zimmerly, executive director of Europa CarShare at Siesmayerstrasse 23, 60323 Frankfurt, GERMANY. When communicating with German firms, use A4 metric-size paper and adhere to German mailing guidelines.

Find and replace all instances of "Canada" with "Germany." Add this postscript at the end of the letter:

Any statistics you might choose to fax to me at +1.800.555.5553 regarding the environmental impact associated with car sharing in Germany would be very helpful.

Prepare this e-mail message to be sent to Ms. McBride. Type the e-mail greeting, Hi, Ms. McBride:, and the body shown below in correct format. Type Roberto as the clos-ing and type this signature: Roberto Duran | E-Mail: rduran@rideshare.net | Phone: 773-555-0107. Save the e-mail message, but do not send it.

¶ I sent the two letters to the executive directors of CarShare as you requested. I will follow up in a week with phone calls and e-mail messages as follows:

¶ Mr. Jason Davis

+1.604.877.5555

jdavis@carshare.ubc.ca

¶ Mr. Frans Zimmerly

+49.30.20304-0

fzimmerly@carshare.de

¶ I found some statistics about car sharing that might be useful. Car sharing was first introduced in Quebec City in 1994 and now has about 1,200 users in six Canadian cities. About 90,000 car share commuters are located worldwide, with about half of them in Europe.

Keyboarding Connection

E-Mail Privacy

How private are your e-mail messages? Although there has been a lot of discussion about hacking and Internet security, e-mail may be more secure than your phone or postal mail. In fact, most new-generation e-mail programs have some kind of encryption built in.

It is not hackers who are the most likely to read your e-mail. It is anyone with access to your incoming mail server or your computer. If your computer and incoming server are at work, then you can assume that your supervisor can read your e-mail. In some companies, it is a normal practice to monitor employees' e-mail. Therefore, you should not send e-mail from work that you wouldn't want anyone there to read.

If you are serious about e-mail privacy, you may want to examine other encryption methods. Different products are available to ensure that your e-mail is read only by the intended recipient(s).

YOUR TURN Perform a keyword search, using a search engine (for example, www.altavista.com), for information on different products that are available to protect your e-mail privacy.

In-Basket Review (Manufacturing)

Goals

- Type at least 50wpm/5'/5e
- Format documents used in the manufacturing industry

A. Type 2 times.

A. WARMUP

```
 1        Order extra color cartridges very soon! G & K Supply     11
 2   just announced a 15% discount on orders for the following     22
 3   cartridges: QB728 and ZM 436* (*for the ink-jet printers).    34
     |  1  |  2  |  3  |  4  |  5  |  6  |  7  |  8  |  9  |  10  |  11  |  12
```

SKILLBUILDING

B. DIAGNOSTIC PRACTICE: NUMBERS

If you are not using the GDP software, turn to page SB-5 and follow the directions for this activity.

C. MAP

Follow the GDP software directions for this exercise in improving keystroking accuracy.

D. Take two 5-minute timed writings. Review your speed and errors.

Goal: At least 50wpm/5′/5e

D. 5-MINUTE TIMED WRITING

```
 4        With modern technology, it is possible to work at a      11
 5   job full time and never leave your house. You can set up a    22
 6   home office with a phone line, a facsimile, and a computer    34
 7   system. Before choosing to work at home, however, you will    46
 8   want to examine carefully your reasons for working at home.   58
 9        Some people think about working at home so they can      69
10   have more time to spend with their families. Other people    80
11   like to have more flexibility in their work schedule. They    92
12   are looking for the opportunity to enjoy a better quality    104
13   of life or to participate in other activities.              113
14        There are some factors to consider before you make     124
15   the decision to work at home. You will want to consider the 135
16   ultimate cost of benefits that you could give up if you     147
17   change your place of work. You will want to check with your 159
18   employer to see if you are entitled to paid vacation days   170
19   and health insurance or if you can make contributions to    182
20   your retirement plan. Another factor to consider is the     193
21   limited contact with peers.                                 198
22        Before making the ultimate decision to work at home,   209
23   develop some realistic expectations of how you will spend   221
24   each day. Although you can organize your work to fit your   232
25   schedule, you will find the real challenge is to determine  244
26   a routine that works for you.                               250
     |  1  |  2  |  3  |  4  |  5  |  6  |  7  |  8  |  9  |  10 |  11 |  12
```

DOCUMENT PROCESSING

Situation: Today is November 5, 20--. Use this date on all documents as needed. You work as an administrative assistant for Melanie Stone at MedPro Manufacturing, one of the largest medical diagnostic equipment manufacturers in the world. The home office is located in Arden, North Carolina, with branch offices located worldwide.

Your boss has left a business report in your in-basket for you to format and type. The title of the report is MedPro Manufacturing. The subtitle of the report is Vision, Innovation, and Partnership. Use the date after the subtitle.

(Continued on next page)

¶ Med Pro Manufacturing is 1 of the largest medical diagnostic equipment manufacturers in the world. We have been in business for almost eighty years and our company has a solid reputation for quality and reliability in all our manufacturing processes. We take great pride in our current state-of-the-art manufacturing facilities because we realize that doctors' reputations and patients' lives depend on the quality and reliability of our products and medical supplies.

VISION

¶ MedPro's vision for the New Millennium is to continue the manufacturing of circuit boards, light sources, fiber-optic light guides, and scanning engines. We have in place a stringent quality management process so that our customers are guaranteed a superior product at a competitive price. Because of these high standards, our company has attained the most current ISO Certification. We have reduced consistently our manufacturing cycles without sacrificing quality.

INNOVATION

¶ Everyone at MedPro from those on the manufacturing floor to those in the presidents office is committed to the continuation of the research and development of innovative products and high-tech manufacturing processes.

Products. Our electronic stethoscope system combined a revolutionary acoustic technology and teamed it with the power of a computer to produce extraordinary results in doctors offices. We specialize in innovative products for children. Our autorefractor has allowed optometrists and ophthalmologists to perform objective refraction on children that is more quickly and easily than ever before. We are committed to the continuous development of innovative products like these.

Manufacturing processes. Our fiber-optic light guides and scanning engines are 2 more examples of how MedPro is committed to innovation in the manufacturing process as well. Our computercontrolled manufacturing

(Continued on next page)

and CAD/ECAD equipment helps us to control precisely the manufacturing of all our medical equipment. These same innovative processes have helped us reduce our costs and reduce our manufacturing cycle.

PARTNERSHIP

¶ One of the most effective ways to ensure success is to develop partnerships with other innovative businesses that have the same commitment to high standards and are leaders in their respective fields. Our teamwork and collaboration with our partners have helped us to establish an international presence and reputation. Our website can be found at http://medpro.com, and it is filled with a wealth of information. All details of our products, services, employees, contact information, and so on, can be found there. We look forward to your business.

Correspondence 120-102

Business Letter in Block Style

Progress and Proofreading Check

Documents designated as Proofreading Checks serve as a check of your proofreading skill. Your goal is to have zero typographical errors when the GDP software first scores the document.

A letter that includes a table has also been left in your in-basket to be typed. The letter is to be sent to Mrs. Carmen Tamashiro, associate director for Medical Relief International, which is located at 3-5-1 Kanda Jinbo-cho, Chiyoda-ku Tokyo 101, JAPAN. The subject line is Relief Medical Supplies. When communicating with Japanese firms, use A4 metric-size paper and adhere to Japanese mailing guidelines.

Ms. Stone, public relations director, prefers a block-style letter with standard punctuation and likes to use a predesigned format for tables. She prefers *Sincerely* as the complimentary close, uses the company name in the closing, and likes her business title typed below her name in the closing. She does not use a courtesy title.

¶ Med Pro Manufacturing is happy to send our tenth shipment of relief medical supplies to be distributed as needed to the people of Japan who have been devastated by recent earthquakes and other natural disasters.

(Continued on next page)

¶ MedPro Manufacturing is happy to send our tenth shipment of relief medical supplies to be distributed as needed to the people of Japan who have been devastated by recent earthquakes and other natural disasters.

¶ Our previous shipments to Japan have amounted to well over $1 million worth of medical supplies such as antibiotics, surgical supplies, catheters, packs, crutches, splints, braces, and slings. MedPro Manufacturing usually sends medical goods and equipment exclusively; however, some of the earlier shipments have also included basic survival supplies. Our employees have helped us in our efforts to gather hundreds of tents, sleeping bags, blankets, flashlights, coats, socks, gloves, and all-weather apparel.

¶ Several international branches of our company would also like to offer their help if you need it. The table below includes all the pertinent information:

Address	E-Mail	Telephone
Marie Desaulnier 27, rue Pasteur 14390 Cabaurg FRANCE	medpro.com@email.fr	+33.1.64531515
Frank Liberman Mittlerer Pfad 9 D-70499 Stuttgart GERMANY	medpro.com@email.de	+49.711.8871624
Manny Yamamoto 16-13, 2-chome Hongo Tokyo 113-0033 JAPAN	medpro.com@email.jp	+81.3.38138841

¶ If I can offer you any further assistance or information, please don't hesitate to contact me at +1.704.555.8945.

Skills Assessment on Part 6

5-Minute Timed Writing

1	The potential to reach your career goals has never	10
2	been better. The person who will move forward in a career	22
3	is the one who will make the bold moves to follow his or	33
4	her dreams. He or she will have the required attributes of	45
5	initiative and motivation to put forth maximum efforts in	57
6	order to realize a fulfilling career.	64
7	If you want to get ahead in the highly competitive	75
8	business world today, you need a personal coach or mentor	86
9	who is experienced in motivating people who want to reach	98
10	their potential. You may be afraid to go after your dream	110
11	career because you are afraid of failure. Your personal	121
12	mentor will help you to minimize any problems you incur. He	133
13	or she will encourage you to strive for more.	142
14	When you decide to work with a qualified coach, you	153
15	are investing in yourself. You can trust your coach to help	165
16	you through this joyful process of expanding your horizons	176
17	until you reach your goal. When you think you have reached	188
18	your limit, your coach will make suggestions for additional	200
19	improvement. He or she will present the strategies you can	212
20	use to be successful. Your coach will guide you in making	224
21	the critical decisions for advancing your career. The final	236
22	decision to improve your skills and become successful is	247
23	yours, however.	250

| 1 | 2 | 3 | 4 | 5 | 6 | 7 | 8 | 9 | 10 | 11 | 12 |

Form ▶ Test 6-18

Memo Template

Select the first memo template listed in your word processing software.

To: Michael Lani, Human Resources Director │ **CC:** Armando Lopez, President │ **From:** Charlene Morimoto, Committee Chairperson │ **Date:** October 18, 20-- │ **Re:** Turkey Trot Fun Run Fund-Raiser

¶ It's time once again for our annual Turkey Trot Fun Run, in which all proceeds are donated to the Read-2-Learn literacy program for inner-city youth. Since 1980, our Read-2-Learn Committee has donated over $200,000 to this very worthy cause, and we have every intention of raising at least $8,000 in this Fun Run on Thanksgiving Day, but we need your help.

¶ As our director of human resources, you are in a unique position to help us raise funds. If you could encourage each of our employees to donate $20 to sponsor one runner in this event, we would easily meet our goals this year. Last year we had over 400 sponsored runners.

(Continued on next page)

¶ The Read-2-Learn program is specifically targeted at the inner-city elementary students in our neighborhood in their quest for basic literacy skills. Our business is located in a rich, multicultural urban neighborhood that is in desperate need of this type of program. I have attached a brochure that explains all details of this reading program and an event flyer. If you need additional copies, please let me know. Also, please visit our Web site at http://www.turkeytrot.org for further details.

¶ urs | Attachments

Report
Test 6-106

Web Page

1. Change the title of Report-Test-6-106.htm to Read-2-Learn.
2. Insert a centered, boxed table with 2 columns and 4 rows.
3. Type the information on page 494 and arrange it as shown below.
4. Insert a picture related to reading and size it approximately as shown. Apply a coordinated design theme.
5. Insert horizontal lines in Rows 2 and 4. Change any styles, fonts, or colors as desired.

Read-2-Learn

A Youth Literacy Program of the Los Angeles Public Library

Our mission is to provide instruction in the basic literacy skills of reading and writing for elementary school children. Read-2-Learn offers participants free tutoring and a variety of other support services. Our volunteer tutors have been trained and will be matched with students to provide optimal conditions for learning and practicing basic reading and writing skills. The learner's interests and needs are always considered first.

This literacy program is funded by the Los Angeles Public Library; government grants; special events; and contributions from corporations, foundations and individuals. Our services include the following:

- Free individualized tutoring
- A resource library including books, tapes, games, and manuals
- Basic computer literacy instruction
- Small group or one-on-one instruction for learners
- Ongoing evaluation and instructional support with a reading specialist
- Referrals to other literacy programs

(Continued on next page)

Read-2-Learn

A Youth Literacy Program of the Los Angeles Public Library

Our mission is to provide instruction in the basic literacy skills of reading and writing for elementary school children. Read-2-Learn offers participants free tutoring and a variety of other support services. Our volunteer tutors have been trained and will be matched with students to provide optimal conditions for learning and practicing basic reading and writing skills. The learner's interests and needs are always considered first.

This literacy program is funded by the Los Angeles Public Library; government grants; special events; and contributions from corporations, foundations, and individuals. Our services include the following:

- Free individualized tutoring
- A resource library including books, tapes, games, and manuals
- Basic computer literacy instruction
- Small group or one-on-one instruction for learners
- Ongoing evaluation and instructional support with a reading specialist
- Referrals to other literacy programs

**Report
Test 6-107**

Flyer

Press the SPACE BAR 2 times, and create the flyer as shown in the illustration.

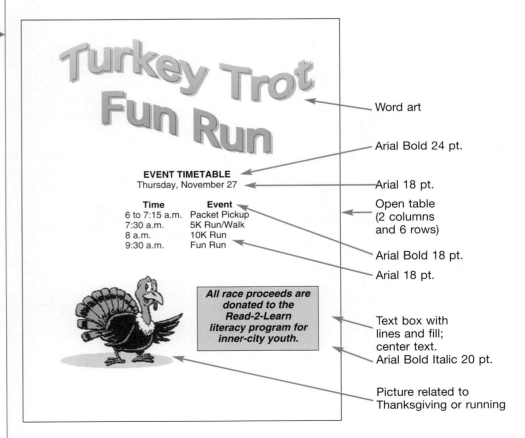

Word art

Arial Bold 24 pt.

Arial 18 pt.

Open table
(2 columns
and 6 rows)

Arial Bold 18 pt.

Arial 18 pt.

Text box with
lines and fill;
center text.

Arial Bold Italic 20 pt.

Picture related to
Thanksgiving or running

EVENT TIMETABLE
Thursday, November 27

Time	Event
6 to 7:15 a.m.	Packet Pickup
7:30 a.m.	5K Run/Walk
8 a.m.	10K Run
9:30 a.m.	Fun Run

All race proceeds are donated to the Read-2-Learn literacy program for inner-city youth.

(Continued on next page)

Type this information in the open table and text box as shown in the flyer illustration on page 494.

EVENT TIMETABLE
Thursday, November 27

Time	Event
6 to 7:15 a.m.	Packet Pickup
7:30 a.m.	5K Run/Walk
8 a.m.	10K Run
9:30 a.m.	Fun Run

All race proceeds are donated to the Read-2-Learn literacy program for inner-city youth.

SKILLBUILDING

Diagnostic Practice: Symbols and Punctuation

The Diagnostic Practice: Symbols and Punctuation program is designed to diagnose and then correct your keystroking errors. You may use this program at any time throughout the course after completing Lesson 19.

Directions

1. Type one of the three Pretest/Posttest paragraphs 1 time, pushing *moderately* for speed. Review your errors.
2. Note your results—the number of errors you made on each symbol or punctuation key. For example, if you typed *75&* for *75%*, you would count 1 error on the % key.
3. For any symbol or punctuation key on which you made 2 or more errors, type the corresponding drill lines 2 times. If you made only 1 error, type the drill line 1 time.
4. If you made no errors on the Pretest/Postest paragraph, type one set of the Practice: Symbols and Punctuation lines on page SB-4.
5. Finally, retype the same Pretest/Posttest, and compare your performance with your Pretest.

PRETEST/POSTTEST

Paragraph 1

```
Price & Joy stock closed @ 5 1/8 yesterday; it was up 13%
from yesterday. If we had sold our "high-demand" shares*
(*300 of them) before 3:30 p.m., we'd have made $15,000,
wouldn't we? Oh, well! I'll be in my office (#13C) crying.
```

Paragraph 2

```
The Time/CNN poll had the slate of Myers & Bassey ahead by
just 5%. Weren't you surprised? I was; after all, "they"*
(*meaning the crew) had ordered 60# of food @ $9.50 a pound
for a victory party at 3:30 p.m. today. What a sad mix-up!
```

Paragraph 3

```
Didn't my colleague* (*Elsa Jones-Salizar) send in $50 as a
10% deposit for reserving Room #5B on Friday and/or Monday?
Attached to her deposit was a note that said, "Call Tibby,
& me @ 10:30 a.m."; I was surprised. She sounded desperate!
```

PRACTICE: Individual Reaches

Ampersand

```
juj ju7j j7j j7&j j&&j j&&j juj ju7j j7j j7&j j&&j j&&j &&&
Alma & Bill & Carr & Dern & Epps & Farr & Gary & Horn & Ing
Jack & Kyle & Mann & Nash & Okum & Parr & Rand & Star & Tua
Uber & Vern & Will & Xang & Year & Zack & Sons & Bros & Inc
```

Apostrophe

```
;;; ;'; ;'; ';' ';' ''' Al's Bo's Di's it's Jo's Li's Moe's
you'd he'll she'd it'll she'll they'd aren't you're they're
we're we've we'll can't you've you'll hasn't didn't they've
she's don't isn't won't hadn't wasn't here's that's what'll
```

SKILLBUILDING

Asterisk	kik ki8k k8*k k8*k k**k k**k ki8k k8*k k8*k k**k k**k Note* Ames* Beck* Carr* Dern* Epps* Farr* Gary* Horn* Iago* Jack* Kyle* Mann* Nash* Okum* Parr* Rand* Star* Teri* Uber* Vern* Will* Xang* Year* Zack* Note* Star* Also* List* Text* Cite*
At Sign	sws sw2s s2@s s2@s s@s s@@s and sws sw2s s2@s s2@s s@s s@@s 138 @ 34 and 89 @ 104 and 18 @ 458 and 89 @ 10 and 18 @ 340 162 & 31 and 48 & 606 and 81 @ 923 and 69 @ 42 and 54 @ 128 277 @ 89 and 57 & 369 and 70 @ 434 and 50 @ 15 and 37 @ 512
Colon	;;; ;:; ;;; :;: ::: and :/: and :?: and :p: and :-: and ::: From: Name: City: Madam: 4:30 Bill to: Address: To: cc: PS: Date: Rank: Time: Dept.: 27:1 Subject: Time in: Hi: Re: Cf: Sirs: Ext.: Apt.: State: 1:00 Ship to: Acts 4:2 FY: ID: OS:
Comma	kkk k,k k,k and ,k, and ,i, and ,8, and I,I and K,K and ,,, Ava, ebb, lac, had, foe, elf, hug, ugh, poi, raj, ink, gal, bum, Ben, ago, cop, req, far, has, dot, tau, env, wow, sax, I am, you are, he is, we are, they are, Al, Ty, Hy, Jo, Ann
Diagonal	;;; ;/; /// and p/p and /p/ and 0/0 ;;; ;/; /// and p/p /// a/c c/o B/L ft/s ac/dc and/or he/she cad/cam due/dew 1/2005 I/O n/a B/S n/30 AM/FM ob/gyn on/off lay/lie fir/fur 2/2006 p/e m/f w/o km/h d/b/a ad/add to/too set/sit him/her 3/2007
Dollar Sign	frf fr4 f4f f$f f$f f$f $40 $44 $44 f$f f4f $ff $45 $54 $$$ $40 and $82 and $90 and $13 and $33 and $56 and $86 and $25 $214 plus $882 plus $900 plus $718 plus $910 plus $112 plus $1,937.53 plus $337.89 tax $3,985.43 minus $150.75 discount
Exclamation Mark	aqa aqla aq!a a!!a a!!a aqa aqla aq!a a!!a a!!a Go! Hi! Lo! Oh! Wow! Gas! Dig! Yes! Sit! Rats! Darn! Well! Drat! Shoot! So! Eat! Air! Out! Not! Aim! Whoa! Wait! Whee! Oops! Yahoo! No! Yea! Eek! Run! Boo! Buy! Look! Help! Duck! Alas! There!
Hyphen	;;; ;p; ;-; -;- --- and -;- and -;- and -/- and -:- and -P- add-on be-all F-stop H-bomb A-frame age-old all-day boo-boo how-to in-out jam-up log-in come-on cop-out end-all fade-in mix-up no-win say-so tie-up one-act pig-out rip-off T-shirt
Number/Pound	de3d de3#d d3#d d3#d d##d d##d #33 #33 #333 de3d de3#d d3#d 45# of #245 and 837# of #013 and 31# of #981 and 2# of #013 12# of #883 and 345# of #328 and 67# of #112 and 8# of #109 54# of #542 and 378# of #310 and 13# of #189 and 6# of #657
Parentheses	lo91 lo91 lo(1 lo(1 1((1 1((1 ;p0; ;p0; ;p); ;p); ;)); ;)); (a) (b) (c) (d) (e) (f) (g) (h) (i) (j) (k) (l) (m) (n) (o) (p) (q) (r) (s) (t) (u) (v) (w) (x) (y) (z) (1) (2) (3) (4) (5) (6) (7) (8) (9) (0) (@) (#) ($) (&) (*) (-) (;) (,) (:)

Percent

```
ftf ft5f f5f f5%f f%%f f%%f ftf ft5f f5f f5%f f%%f f%%f %%%
40% and 82% and 90% and 13% and 33% and 56% and 86% and 25%
21% and 48% and 82% and 90% and 70% and 18% and 91% and 10%
34.5% off 89% increase 12% credit 67% finished 10% discount
```

Period

```
1.1 ... and .1. and .o. and .9. and .(. and .O. and L.L ...
Jan. Feb. Mar. Apr. Jun. Jul. Aug. Sep. Oct. Nov. Dec. a.m.
Sun. Mon. Tue. Wed. Thu. Fri. Sat. Mrs. Esq. Mex. Can. D.C.
I am. I see. We do. He is. I can. Do not. Help me. Go slow.
```

Question Mark

```
;;; ;/; ;?; ??? ?;? and p?p and ?0? and ?)? and ?-? and ???
So? Who? What? Can I? Why not? Who does? Stop here? Is she?
Me? How? When? May I? Who, me? Says who? Do it now? For me?
Oh? Why? Am I? Do we? Am I up? How much? Who knows? Will I?
```

Quotation Mark

```
;'; ;"; ;"; ";" """ and ;'; ;"; ;"; ";" """ and ;"; ";" """
"Eat" "Sit" "Rest" "Stay" "Roll" "Hello" "Look" "Pet" "Dry"
"Yes" "Lie" "Halt" "Next" "Move" "Write" "Type" "Ink" "Sew"
"Beg" "See" "Walk" "Wave" "Stop" "Speak" "File" "Run" "Cry"
```

Semicolon

```
;;; ;;; and ;'; and ;"; and ;p; and ;-; and ;/; and ;?; ;;;
tea; ebb; Mac; mid; lie; arf; hug; nth; obi; Taj; ark; Hal;
dim; man; bio; hop; seq; our; Gus; let; you; Bev; row; lax;
do not cry; that is Liz; see to it; I am sad; we do; I can;
```

PRACTICE: SYMBOLS AND PUNCTUATION

```
Doe & Fry sued May & Ito; Ho & Fox sued Doe & Lee for M&Ms.
Ann's dad said he's happy she's out of school; she'd agree.
Yesterday* (*April 9), the rock star said **** right on TV.
E-mail them at glyden@sales.com to buy 3 @ $89 or 9 @ $250.

Hi, Ross: Place odds of 3:1 on the game at 10:30 and 11:15.
Tom gave Ava, Jo, Al, and Tyson a red, white, and blue car.
On 3/1/2008, he will receive a pension and/or a big buyout.
The $80 skirt was cut to $70 and then $55 for a $25 saving.

What! No ice! I'm mortified! Run, order some more. Quickly!
Jones-Lynch built an all-season add-on to her A-frame home.
Please order 500# of #684, 100# of #133, and 200# of #1341.
The answer is (a) 1, (b) 4, (c) 7, or (d) all of the above.

The car was cut 15% and then 25% for a final saving of 40%.
Mr. R. J. Dix ordered from L. L. Bean on Dec. 23 at 11 a.m.
Who? Me? Why me? Because I can type? Is that a good reason?
"Look," he said, "see that sign?" It says, "Beware of Dog."
Stop here; get out of your car; walk a foot; begin digging.
```

Diagnostic Practice: Numbers

The Diagnostic Practice: Numbers program is designed to diagnose and then correct your keystroking errors. You may use this program at any time throughout the course after completing Lesson 14.

Directions

1. Type one of the three Pretest/Posttest paragraphs 1 time, pushing *moderately* for speed. Review your errors.
2. Note your results—the number of errors you made on each key and your total number of errors. For example, if you type *24* for *25*, you would count 1 error on the number *5*.
3. For any number on which you made 2 or more errors, select the corresponding drill lines and type the drills 2 times. If you made only 1 error, type the drill 1 time.
4. If you made no errors on the Pretest/Posttest paragraph, type 1 set of the drills that contain all numbers on page SB-6.
5. Finally, retype the same Pretest/Posttest, and compare your performance with your Pretest.

PRETEST/POSTTEST

Paragraph 1

    The statement dated May 24, 2004, listed 56 clamps; 15 batteries; 169 hammers; 358 screwdrivers; 1,298 pliers; and 1,475 files. The invoice numbered 379 showed 387 hoes, 406 rakes, 92 lawn mowers, 63 tillers, and 807 more lawn items.

Paragraph 2

    My inventory records dated May 31, 2004, revealed that we had 458 pints; 1,069 quarts; and 8,774 gallons of paint. We had 2,953 brushes; 568 scrapers; 12,963 wallpaper rolls; 897 knives; 5,692 mixers; 480 ladders; and 371 step stools.

Paragraph 3

    Almost 179 hot meals were delivered to the 35 shut-ins in April, 169 in May, and 389 in June. Several workers had volunteered 7,564 hours in 2004; 9,348 hours in 2003; 5,468 in 2002; and 6,577 in 2001. About 80 people were involved.

PRACTICE: INDIVIDUAL REACHES

1 aq aq1 aq1qa 111 ants 101 aunts 131 apples 171 animals a1
They got 11 answers correct for the 11 questions in BE 121.
Those 11 adults loaded the 711 animals between 1 and 2 p.m.
All 111 agreed that 21 of those 31 are worthy of the honor.

2 sw sw2 sw2ws 222 sets 242 steps 226 salads 252 saddles s2
The 272 summer tourists saw the 22 soldiers and 32 sailors.
Your September 2 date was all right for 292 of 322 persons.
The 22 surgeons said 221 of those 225 operations went well.

3 de de3 de3ed 333 dots 303 drops 313 demons 393 dollars d3
Bus 333 departed at 3 p.m. with the 43 dentists and 5 boys.
She left 33 dolls and 73 decoys at 353 West Addison Street.
The 13 doctors helped some of the 33 druggists in Room 336.

4 fr fr4 fr4rf 444 fans 844 farms 444 fishes 644 fiddles f4
My 44 friends bought 84 farms and sold over 144 franchises.
She sold 44 fish and 440 beef dinners for $9.40 per dinner.
The 1954 Ford had only 40,434 fairly smooth miles by May 4.

5 fr fr5 fr5rf 555 furs 655 foxes 555 flares 455 fingers f5
They now own 155 restaurants, 45 food stores, and 55 farms.
They ordered 45, 55, 65, and 75 yards of that new material.
Flight 855 flew over Farmington at 5:50 p.m. on December 5.

6 jy jy6 jy6yj 666 jets 266 jeeps 666 jewels 866 jaguars j6
Purchase orders numbered 6667 and 6668 were sent yesterday.
Those 66 jazz players played for 46 juveniles in Room 6966.
The 6 judges reviewed the 66 journals on November 16 or 26.

7 ju ju7 ju7uj 777 jays 377 jokes 777 joists 577 juniors j7
The 17 jets carried 977 jocular passengers above 77 cities.
Those 277 jumping beans went to 77 junior scouts on May 17.
The 7 jockeys rode 77 jumpy horses between March 17 and 27.

8 ki ki8 ki8ik 888 keys 488 kites 888 knives 788 kittens k8
My 8 kennels housed 83 dogs, 28 kids, and 88 other animals.
The 18 kind ladies tied 88 knots in the 880 pieces of rope.
The 8 men saw 88 kelp bass, 38 kingfish, and 98 king crabs.

9 lo lo9 lo9ol 999 lads 599 larks 999 ladies 699 leaders 19
All 999 leaves fell from the 9 large oaks at 389 Largemont.
The 99 linemen put 399 large rolls of tape on for 19 games.
Those 99 lawyers put 899 legal-size sheets in the 19 limos.

0 ;p ;p0 ;p0p; 100 pens 900 pages 200 pandas 800 pencils ;0
There were 1,000 people who lived in the 300 private homes.
The 10 party stores are open from 1:00 p.m. until 9:00 p.m.
They edited 500 pages in 1 book and 1,000 pages in 2 books.

All numbers   ala s2s d3d f4f f5f j6j j7j k8k 191 ;0; Add 6 and 8 and 29.
The That 349-page script called for 10 actors and 18 actresses.
The check for $50 was sent to 705 Garfield Street, not 507.
The 14 researchers asked the 469 Californians 23 questions.

All numbers   ala s2s d3d f4f f5f j6j j7j k8k 191 ;0; Add 3 and 4 and 70.
They built 1,299 houses on the 345-acre site by the canyon.
Her research showed that gold was at 397 in September 2004.
For $868 extra, they bought 15 new books and 61 used books.

All numbers   ala s2s d3d f4f f5f j6j j7j k8k 191 ;0; Add 5 and 7 and 68.
A bank auditor arrived on May 26, 2004, and left on May 27.
The 4 owners open the stores from 9:30 a.m. until 6:00 p.m.
After 1,374 miles on the bus, she must then drive 185 more.

Progressive Practice: Alphabet

This skillbuilding routine contains a series of 30-second timed writings that range from 16wpm to 104wpm. The first time you use these timed writings, take a 1-minute timed writing on the Entry Timed Writing paragraph. Note your speed.

Select a passage that is 2wpm higher than your current speed. Then take six 30-second timed writings on the passage.

Your goal each time is to complete the passage within 30 seconds with no errors. When you have achieved your goal, move on to the next passage and repeat the procedure.

Entry Timed Writing

Bev was very lucky when she found extra quality in the home she was buying. She quietly told the builder that she was extremely satisfied with the work done on her new home. The builder said she can move into her new house next week.

| 1 | 2 | 3 | 4 | 5 | 6 | 7 | 8 | 9 | 10 | 11 | 12

11
23
35
47

16wpm

The author is the creator of a document.

18wpm

Open means to access a previously saved file.

20wpm

A byte represents one character to every computer.

22wpm

A mouse may be used when running Windows on a computer.

24wpm

Soft copy is text that is displayed on your computer screen.

26wpm

Memory is the part of the word processor that stores information.

28wpm

A menu is a list of choices to direct the operator through a function.

30wpm

A sheet feeder is a device that will insert sheets of paper into a printer.

32wpm

An icon is a small picture that illustrates a function or an object in software.

34wpm

A window is a rectangular area with borders that displays the contents of open files.

36wpm

To execute means to perform an action specified by an operator or by the computer program.

38wpm

Output is the result of a word processing operation. It can be either printed or magnetic form.

40wpm

Format refers to the physical features which affect the appearance and arrangement of your document.

42wpm — A font is a style of type of one size or kind which includes all letters, numbers, and punctuation marks.

44wpm — Ergonomics is the science of adapting working conditions or equipment to meet the physical needs of employees.

46wpm — Home position is the starting position of a document; it is typically the upper left corner of the display monitor.

48wpm — The mouse may be used to change the size of a window and to move a window to a different location on the display screen.

50wpm — An optical scanner is a device that can read text and enter it into a word processor without the need to type the data again.

52wpm — Hardware refers to the physical equipment used, such as the central processing unit, display screen, keyboard, printer, or drives.

54wpm — A peripheral device is any piece of equipment that will extend the capabilities of a computer system but is not required for operation.

56wpm — A split screen displays two or more different images at the same time; it can, for example, display two different pages of a legal document.

58wpm — When using Windows, it's possible to place several programs on a screen and to change the size of a window or to change its position on a screen.

60wpm — With the click of a mouse, one can use a button bar or a toolbar for fast access to features that are frequently applied when using a Windows program.

62wpm — An active window can be reduced to an icon when you use Windows, enabling you to double-click another icon to open a new window for formatting and editing.

64wpm — Turnaround time is the length of time needed for a document to be keyboarded, edited, proofread, corrected if required, printed, and returned to the originator.

66wpm — A local area network is a system that uses cable or another means to allow high-speed communication among many kinds of electronic equipment within particular areas.

68wpm — To search and replace means to direct the word processor to locate a character, word, or group of words wherever it occurs in the document and replace it with newer text.

SKILLBUILDING

70wpm
Indexing is the ability of a word processor to accumulate a list of words that appear in a document, including page numbers, and then print a revised list in alphabetic order.

72wpm
When a program needs information from you, a dialog box will appear on the desktop. Once the dialog box appears, you must identify the option you desire and then choose that option.

74wpm
A facsimile is an exact copy of a document, and it is also a process by which images, such as typed letters, graphs, and signatures, are scanned, transmitted, and then printed on paper.

76wpm
Compatibility refers to the ability of a computer to share information with another computer or to communicate with some other apparatus. It can be accomplished by using hardware or software.

78wpm
Some operators like to personalize their desktops when they use Windows by making various changes. For example, they can change their screen colors and the pointer so that they will have more fun.

80wpm
Wraparound is the ability of a word processor to move words from one line to another line and from one page to the next page as a result of inserting and deleting text or changing the size of margins.

82wpm
It is possible when using Windows to evaluate the contents of different directories on the screen at the very same time. You can then choose to copy or move a particular file from one directory to another.

84wpm
List processing is a capability of a word processor to keep lists of data that can be updated and sorted in alphabetic or numeric order. A list can also be added to any document that is stored in one's computer.

86wpm
A computer is a wondrous device, which accepts data that are input and then processes the data and produces output. The computer performs its work by using one or more stored programs, which provide the instructions.

88wpm
The configuration is the components that make up your word processing system. Most systems include the keyboard that is used for entering data, a central processing unit, at least one disk drive, a monitor, and a printer.

90wpm

Help for Windows can be used whenever you see a Help button in a dialog box or on a menu bar. Once you finish reading about a topic that you have selected, you will see a list of some related topics from which you can choose.

92wpm

When you want to look at the contents of two windows when using Windows, you will want to reduce the window size. Do this by pointing to a border or a corner of a window and dragging it until the window is the size that you want.

94wpm

Scrolling means to display a large quantity of text by rolling it horizontally or vertically past the display screen. As the text disappears from the top section of the monitor, new text will appear at the bottom section of the monitor.

96wpm

The Windows Print Manager is used to install and configure printers, join network printers, and monitor the printing of documents. Windows requires that a default printer be identified, but you can change the designation of it at any point.

98wpm

A stop code is a command that makes a printer pause while it is printing to permit an operator to insert text, change the font style, or change the kind of paper in the printer. To resume printing, the operator must use a special key or command.

100wpm

A computerized message system is a class of electronic mail that enables any operator to key a message on any computer terminal and have the message stored for later retrieval by the recipient, who can then display the message on his or her terminal.

102wpm

Many different graphics software programs have been brought on the market in recent years. These programs can be very powerful in helping with a business presentation. If there is any need to share data, using one of these programs could be quite helpful.

104wpm

Voice mail has become an essential service that many people in the business world use. This enables anyone who places a call to your phone to leave a message if you cannot answer it at that time. This special feature helps lots of workers to be more productive.

Progressive Practice: Numbers

This skillbuilding routine contains a series of 30-second timed writings that range from 16wpm to 80wpm. The first time you use these timed writings, take a 1-minute timed writing on the Entry Timed Writing paragraph. Note your speed.

Select a passage that is 4 to 6wpm *lower* than your current alphabetic speed. (The reason for selecting a lower speed goal is that sentences with numbers are more difficult to type.) Take six 30-second timed writings on the passage.

Your goal each time is to complete the passage within 30 seconds with no errors. When you have achieved your goal, move on to the next passage and repeat the procedure.

Entry Timed Writing

Their bags were filled with 10 sets of jars, 23 cookie	11
cutters, 4 baking pans, 6 coffee mugs, 25 plates, 9 dessert	23
plates, 7 soup bowls, 125 recipe cards, and 8 recipe boxes.	35
They delivered these 217 items to 20487 Mountain Boulevard.	47

| 1 | 2 | 3 | 4 | 5 | 6 | 7 | 8 | 9 | 10 | 11 | 12

16wpm
There were now 21 children in Room 2110.

18wpm
Fewer than 12 of the 121 boxes arrived today.

20wpm
Maybe 12 of the 21 applicants met all 15 criteria.

22wpm
There were 34 letters addressed to 434 West Cranbrooke.

24wpm
Jane reported that there were 434 freshmen and 43 transfers.

26wpm
The principal assigned 3 of those 4 students to Room 343 at noon.

28wpm
Only 1 or 2 of the 34 latest invoices were more than 1 page in length.

30wpm
They met 11 of the 12 players who received awards from 3 of the 4 trainers.

32wpm
Those 5 vans carried 46 passengers on the first trip and 65 on the next 3 trips.

34wpm
We first saw 3 and then 4 beautiful eagles on Route 65 at 5 a.m. on Tuesday, June 12.

36wpm
The 16 companies produced 51 of the 62 records that received awards for 3 of 4 categories.

38wpm
The 12 trucks hauled the 87 cows and 65 horses to the farm, which was about 21 miles northeast.

40wpm

She moved from 87 Bayview Drive to 657 Cole Street and then 3 blocks south to 412 Gulbranson Avenue.

42wpm

My 7 or 8 buyers ordered 7 dozen in sizes 5 and 6 after the 14 to 32 percent discounts had been bestowed.

44wpm

There were 34 men and 121 women waiting in line at the gates for the 65 to 87 tickets to the Cape Cod concert.

46wpm

Steve had listed 5 or 6 items on Purchase Order 241 when he saw that Purchase Requisition 87 contained 3 or 4 more.

48wpm

Your items numbered 278 will sell for about 90 percent of the value of the 16 items that have code numbers shown as 435.

50wpm

The managers stated that 98 of those 750 randomly selected new valves had about 264 defects, far exceeding the usual 31 norm.

52wpm

Half of the 625 volunteers received over 90 percent of the charity pledges. Approximately 83 of the 147 agencies will have funds.

54wpm

Merico hired 94 part-time workers to help the 378 full-time employees during the 62-day period when sales go up by 150 percent or more.

56wpm

Kaye only hit 1 for 4 in the first 29 games after an 8-game streak in which she batted 3 for 4. She then hit at a .570 average for 6 games.

58wpm

The mail carrier delivered 98 letters during the week to 734 Oak Street and also took 52 letters to 610 Faulkner Road as he returned on Route 58.

60wpm

Pat said that about 1 in 5 of the 379 swimmers had a chance of being among the top 20. The best 6 of those 48 divers will receive the 16 best awards.

62wpm

It rained from 3 to 6 inches, and 18 of those 20 farmers were fearful that 4 to 7 inches more would flood about 95 acres along 3 miles of the new Route 78.

64wpm

Those 7 sacks weighed 48 pounds, more than the 30 pounds that I had thought. All 24 believe the 92-pound bag is at least 15 or 16 pounds above its true weight.

66wpm

They bought 7 of the 8 options for 54 of the 63 vehicles last month. They now own over 120 dump trucks for use in 9 of the 15 new regions in the big 20-county area.

68wpm

Andy was 8 or 9 years old when they moved to 632 Glendale Street away from the 1700 block of Horseshoe Lane, which is about 45 miles directly west of Boca Raton, FL 33434.

70wpm

Doug had read 575 pages in the 760-page book by March 30; Darlene had read only 468 pages. Darlene has read 29 of those optional books since October 19, and Doug has read 18.

72wpm

That school district has 985 elementary students, 507 middle school students, and 463 high school students; the total of 1,955 is 54, or 2.84 percent, over last year's grand total.

74wpm

Attendance at last year's meeting was 10,835. The goal for this year is to have 11,764 people. This will enable us to plan for an increase of 929 participants, a rise of 8.57 percent.

76wpm

John's firm has 158 stores, located in 109 cities in the West. The company employs 3,540 males and 2,624 females, a total of 6,164 employees. About 4,750 of those employees work part-time.

78wpm

Memberships were as follows: 98 members in the Drama Guild, 90 members in Zeta Tau, 82 members in Theta Phi, 75 in the Bowling Club, and 136 in the Ski Club. This meant that 481 joined a group.

80wpm

The association had 684 members from the South, 830 members from the North, 1,023 members from the East, and 751 from the West. The total membership was 3,288; these numbers increased by 9.8 percent.

Paced Practice

The Paced Practice skillbuilding routine builds speed and accuracy in short, easy steps by using individualized goals and immediate feedback. You may use this program at any time after completing Lesson 9.

This section contains a series of 2-minute timed writings for speeds ranging from 16wpm to 96wpm. The first time you use these timed writings, take the 1-minute Entry Timed Writing.

Select a passage that is 2wpm higher than your current typing speed. Then use this two-stage practice pattern to achieve each speed goal: (1) concentrate on speed, and (2) work on accuracy.

Speed Goal. To determine your speed goal, take three 2-minute timed writings in total. Your goal each time is to complete the passage in 2 minutes without regard to errors. When you have achieved your speed goal, work on accuracy.

Accuracy Goal. To type accurately, you need to slow down—just a bit. Therefore, to reach your accuracy goal, drop back 2wpm from the previous passage. Take consecutive timed writings on this passage until you can complete the passage in 2 minutes with no more than 2 errors.

For example, if you achieved a speed goal of 54wpm, you should then work on an accuracy goal of 52wpm. When you have achieved 52wpm for accuracy, move up 4wpm (for example, to the 56-wpm passage) and work for speed again.

Entry Timed Writing

If you can dream it, you can live it. Follow your   10
heart. There are many careers, from the mundane to the   21
exotic to the sublime. Start your career planning now.   32
Prepare for the future by exploring your talents, skills,   44
and interests.   47

| 1 | 2 | 3 | 4 | 5 | 6 | 7 | 8 | 9 | 10 | 11 | 12 |

16wpm

Your future is now. Seize each day. After you have explored your personal interests, study the sixteen career clusters for a broad range of job possibilities.

18wpm

While exploring various job options, think about what a job means to you. A job can mean something you do simply to earn money or something you find more rewarding and challenging.

20wpm

If you have a job you enjoy, work means more than just receiving wages. It means using your talents, being among people with like interests, making a contribution, and gaining a sense of satisfaction.

22wpm

What is the difference between a job and a career? Think carefully. A job is work that people do for money. A career is a sequence of related jobs built on a foundation of interests, knowledge, training, and experiences.

24wpm

Learn more about the world of work by looking at the sixteen career clusters. Most jobs are included in one of the clusters that have been organized by the government. During your exploration of careers, list the clusters that interest you.

26wpm

Once you identify your career clusters of interest, look at the jobs within each cluster. Find out what skills and aptitudes are needed, what education and training are required, what the work environment is like, and what is the possibility for advancements.

28wpm

Use your career center and school or public libraries to research career choices. Search the Internet. Consult with professionals for another perspective of a specific career. As you gather information about career options, you may discover other interesting career possibilities.

30wpm

Gain insights into a career by becoming a volunteer, participating in an internship, or working a part-time or temporary job within a chosen field. You will become more familiar with a specific job while developing your skills. You'll gain valuable experience, whether you choose that career or not.

32wpm

Whichever path you choose, strive for a high level of pride in yourself and your work. Your image is affected by what you believe other people think of you as well as by how you view yourself. Evaluate your level of confidence in yourself. If you have self-doubts, begin to build up your self-confidence and self-esteem.

34wpm

Self-esteem is essential for a positive attitude, and a positive attitude is essential for success in the world of work. While you cannot control everything that happens at work, you can control how you react. Your attitude matters. Becoming more confident and cultivating positive thoughts can bring you power in your life and on the job.

36wpm

Several factors lead to success on the job. People who have studied the factors say that it is the personal traits that often determine who is promoted or who is not. One of the finest traits a person can possess is the trait of being likable. Being likable means a person is honest, courteous, loyal, thoughtful, pleasant, kind, and most assuredly, positive.

38wpm

If you are likable, probably you relate well with others. Your kindness serves you well in the workplace. Developing good interpersonal relationships with coworkers will make work more enjoyable. After all, think of all the hours you will spend together. By showing that you are willing to collaborate with your coworkers, most likely you will receive their cooperation in return.

40wpm

Cooperation begins on the first day of your new job. When you work for a company, you become part of the team. Meeting people and learning new skills can be exciting. For some people, however, any new situation can trigger anxiety. The best advice is to remain calm, do your job to the best of your ability, learn the workplace policies, be flexible, avoid being too critical, and always be positive.

42wpm

When you begin a new job, even if you have recently received your college diploma, chances are you will start at the bottom of the organizational chart. Each of us has to start somewhere. But don't despair. With hard work and determination, soon you will be climbing up the corporate ladder. If you are clever, you will embrace even the most tedious tasks, take everything in stride, and use every opportunity to learn.

44wpm

If you think learning is restricted to the confines of an academic institution, think again. You have plenty to learn on the job, even if it is a job for which you have been trained. As a new worker, you won't be expected to know everything. When necessary, do not hesitate to ask your employer questions. Learn all you can about your job and the company. Use the new information to enhance your job performance and to prepare for success.

46wpm

Begin every valuable workday by prioritizing all your tasks. Decide which tasks must be done immediately and which can wait. List the most important tasks first; then determine the order in which each task must be done. After you complete a task, triumphantly cross it off your priority list. Do not procrastinate; that is, don't put off work you should do. If a task needs to be done, do it. You will be on top of your task list if you use your time wisely.

48wpm

Prevent the telephone from controlling your time by learning to manage your business phone calls. Phone calls can be extremely distracting from necessary tasks. When making an outgoing call, organize the topics you want to discuss. Gather needed materials such as pencils, papers, and files. Set a time limit, and stick to business. Give concise answers, summarize the points discussed, and end the conversation politely. Efficient telephone usage will help you manage your time.

50wpm

As with anything, practice makes perfect, but along the way, we all make mistakes. The difference between the successful people and those who are less successful is not that the successful people make fewer mistakes. It's that they don't give up. Instead of letting mistakes bring them down, they use their mistakes as opportunities to grow. If you make a mistake, be patient with yourself. You might be able to fix your mistake. Look for more opportunities for success to be just around the corner.

52wpm

Be patient with yourself when handling problems and accepting criticism. Handling criticism gracefully and maturely may be a challenge. Still, it is vital in the workplace. Criticism presented in a way that can help you learn and grow is constructive criticism . When you see criticism as helpful, it's easier to handle. Believe it or not, there are some employees who welcome criticism. It teaches them better ways to succeed on the job. Strive to improve how you accept constructive criticism, and embrace your growth.

54wpm

People experience continuous growth during a career. Goal setting is a helpful tool along any career path. Some people believe that goals provide the motivation needed to get to the place they want to be. Setting goals encourages greater achievements. The higher we set our goals, the greater the effort we will need to reach these goals. Each time we reach a target or come closer to a goal, we see an increase in our confidence and our performance, leading to greater accomplishments. And the cycle continues to spiral onward and upward.

56wpm

One goal we should all strive for is punctuality. When employees are tardy or absent from the workplace, it costs the company money. If you are frequently tardy or absent, others have to do their own work and cover for you. If you are absent often, your peers will begin to resent you, causing everyone stress in the department. Being late and missing work can damage the relationship with your manager and have a negative effect on your career. To avoid these potential problems, develop a personal plan to assure that you arrive every day on time or early.

58wpm

Holding a job is a major part of being an adult. Some people begin their work careers as adolescents. From the beginning, various work habits are developed that are as crucial to success as the actual job skills and knowledge that a person brings to the job. What traits are expected of workers? What do employers look for when they evaluate their employees? Important personal traits include being confident, cooperative, positive, and dependable. If you are organized, enthusiastic, and understanding, you have many of the qualities that employers value most in their employees.

60wpm

Being dependable is a desirable trait. When a project must be completed by a specific time, a manager will be reassured to know that reliable workers are going to meet the deadline. Workers who are dependable learn to utilize their time to achieve maximum results. Dependable workers can always be counted on, have good attendance records, are well prepared, and arrive on time ready to work. If a company wants to meet its goals, it must have a team of responsible and dependable workers. You, your coworkers, your supervisors, and your managers are all team members, working to reach common goals.

62wpm

The ability to organize is an important quality for the employee who wishes to display good work habits. The worker should have the ability to plan the work that needs to be completed and then be able to execute the plan in a timely manner. An employer requires a competent worker to be well organized. If an office worker is efficient, he or she handles requests swiftly and deals with correspondence without delay. The organized worker does not allow work to accumulate on the desk. Also, the organized office worker returns all phone calls immediately and makes lists of the activities that need to be done each day.

64wpm

Efficiency is another work habit that is desired. An efficient worker completes a task quickly and begins work on the next project eagerly. He or she thinks about ways to save steps and time. For example, an efficient worker may plan a single trip to the copier with several copying jobs rather than multiple trips to do each separate job. Being efficient also means having the required supplies to successfully complete each job. An efficient employee zips along on each project, uses time wisely, and stays focused on the present task. With careful and thorough planning, a worker who is efficient can accomplish more tasks in less time.

66wpm

Cooperation is another ideal work habit. As previously mentioned, cooperation begins on the first day on the job. Cooperation is thinking of all team members when making a decision. A person who cooperates is willing to do what is necessary for the good of the whole group. For you to be a team player, it is essential that you take extra steps to cooperate. Cooperation may mean being a good sport if you are asked to do something you would rather not do. It may mean you have to correct a mistake made by another person in the office. If every employee has the interests of the company at heart and works well as a team player, then cooperation is at work.

68wpm

Enthusiasm is still another work trait that is eagerly sought after by employers. Being enthusiastic means that a person has lots of positive energy. This is reflected in actions toward your work, coworkers, and employer. It has been noted that eagerness can be catching. If workers show they are eager to attempt any project, they will not only achieve the highest praise but will also be considered for career advancement. How much enthusiasm do you show at the workplace? Do you encourage people or complain to people? There will always be plenty of good jobs for employees who are known to have a wealth of zeal and a positive approach to the projects that they are assigned.

70wpm

Understanding is also a preferred work habit for every excellent worker. In today's world, virtually all business includes both men and women of different religions, races, cultures, work ethic, abilities, aptitudes, and attitudes. You'll interact with various types of people as customers, coworkers, and owners. Treat everyone fairly, openly, and honestly. Any type of prejudice is hurtful, offensive, and unacceptable. Prejudice cannot be tolerated in the office. Each employee must try to understand and accept everyone's differences. Because so many diverse groups of people work side by side in the workplace, it is essential that all coworkers maintain a high degree of mutual understanding.

72wpm

It can be concluded that certain work habits or traits can play a major role in determining the success of an employee. Most managers would be quick to agree on the importance of these traits. It is most probable that these habits would be evaluated on performance appraisal forms. Promotions, pay increases, new responsibilities, and your future with the company may be based on these evaluations. You should request regular job performance evaluations even if your company does not conduct them. This feedback will improve your job performance and career development by helping you grow. If you continually look for ways to improve your work habits and skills, then you will enjoy success in the workplace and beyond.

74wpm

You can be certain that no matter where you work, you will use some form of computer technology. Almost every business is dependent upon computers. Companies use such devices as voice mail, fax machines, cellular phones, and electronic schedules. Technology helps to accomplish work quickly and efficiently. A result of this rapidly changing technology is globalization, which is the establishment of worldwide communication links between people. Our world is becoming a smaller, global village. We must expand our thinking beyond the office walls. We must become aware of what happens in other parts of the world. Those events may directly affect you and your workplace. The more you know, the more valuable you will become to the company.

76wpm

Technological advancements are affecting every aspect of our lives. For example, the advent of the Internet has changed how we receive and send information. It is the world's largest information network. The Internet is often called the information superhighway because it is a vast network of computers that connect people and resources worldwide. It is an exciting medium to help you access the latest information. You can even learn about companies by visiting their Web sites. Without any doubt, we are all globally connected, and information technology services support those necessary connections. This industry offers many different employment opportunities. Keep in mind that proficiency in keyboarding is beneficial in this field and in other fields.

78wpm

It is amazing to discover the many careers in which keyboarding skill is necessary today, and the use of the computer keyboard by executive chefs is a prime example. The chefs in major restaurants must prepare parts or all of the meals served while directing the work of a staff of chefs, cooks, and other kitchen staff. The computer has become a necessary tool for a variety of tasks, including tracking inventories of food supplies. By observing which items are favorites and which items are not requested, the chef can calculate food requirements, order food, and supervise the food purchases. Additionally, the computer has proven to be a very practical tool for such tasks as planning budgets, preparing purchase orders for vendors, creating menus, and printing out reports.

80wpm

Advanced technology has opened the doors to a wider variety of amazing new products and services to sell. It seems the more complex the products, the higher the price of the products, or the greater the sales commission, the stiffer the competition. Selling these technical products requires detailed product knowledge, good verbal skills, smooth sales rapport, and proficient keyboarding skills. Business favors people with special training. For example, a pharmacy company may prefer a person with knowledge in chemistry to sell its products. Selling is for people who thrive on challenges and changes in products and services. Sales is appealing to people who enjoy using their powers of persuasion to make the sales. The potential for good earnings is very high for the well-trained salesperson.

82wpm

As you travel about in your sales job or type a report at the office or create Friday night's pasta special for your five-star restaurant, always remember to put safety first. Accidents happen, but they don't have to happen regularly or to have such serious consequences. Accidents cost businesses billions of dollars annually in medical expenses, lost wages, and insurance claims. A part of your job is to make certain you're not one of the millions of people injured on the job every year. You may believe you work in a safe place, but accidents occur in all types of businesses. A few careless people cause most accidents, so ensure your safety on the job. Safety doesn't just happen. Safety is the result of the careful awareness of many people who plan and put into action a safety program that benefits everyone.

84wpm

In today's market, you need more than the necessary skill or the personal qualities described above to succeed in the workplace. Employers also expect their employees to have ethics. Ethics are the principles of conduct governing an individual or a group. Employees who work ethically do not lie, cheat, or steal. They are honest and fair in their dealings with others. Employees who act ethically build a good reputation for themselves and their company. They are known to be dependable and trustworthy. Unethical behavior can have a spiraling effect. A single act can do a lot of damage. Even if you haven't held a job yet, you have had experience with ethical problems. Life is full of many opportunities to behave ethically. Do the right thing when faced with a decision. The ethics you practice today will carry over to your workplace.

86wpm

Now that you know what is expected of you on the job, how do you make sure you will get the job? Almost everyone has experienced the interview process for a job. For some, the interview is a traumatic event, but it doesn't have to be stressful. Preparation is the key. Research the company with whom you are seeking employment. Formulate a list of questions. Your interview provides you the opportunity to interview the organization. Don't go empty-handed. Take a portfolio of items with you. Include copies of your resume with a list of three or more professional references, your academic transcript, and your certificates and licenses. Be sure to wear appropriate business attire. The outcome of the interview will be positive if you have enthusiasm for the job, match your qualifications to the company's needs, ask relevant questions, and listen clearly.

88wpm

How can you be the strongest candidate for the job? Be sure that your skills in reading, writing, mathematics, speaking, and listening are solid. These basic skills will help you listen well and communicate clearly, not only during a job interview, but also at your workplace. The exchange of information between senders and receivers is called communication. It doesn't matter which occupation you choose; you will spend most of your career using these basic skills to communicate with others. You will use the basic skills as tools to gain information, solve problems, and share ideas. You will use these skills to meet the needs of your customers. The majority of jobs available during the next decades will be in the industries that will require direct customer contacts. Your success will be based upon your ability to communicate effectively with customers and coworkers.

90wpm

Writing effectively can help you gain a competitive edge in your job search and throughout your career. Most of us have had occasion to write business letters whether to apply for a job, to comment on a product or service, or to place an order. Often it seems easy to sit and let our thoughts flow freely. In other cases, we seem to struggle to find the proper wording while trying to express our thoughts in exactly the right way. Writing skill can improve with practice. Implement the following principles to develop your writing skill. Try to use language that you would be comfortable using in person. Use words that are simple, direct, kind, confident, and professional. When possible, use words that emphasize the positive side. Remember to proofread your work. Well-organized thoughts and proper grammar, spelling, and punctuation show the reader that you care about the quality of your work.

92wpm

Listening is an essential skill of the communication process. It is crucial for learning, getting along, and forming relationships. Do you think you are an active or passive listener? Listening is not a passive activity. Conversely, active listening is hearing what is being said and interpreting its meaning. Active listening makes you a more effective communicator because you react to what you have heard. Study the following steps to increase your listening skills. Do not cut people off; let them develop their ideas before you speak. If a message is vague, write down your questions or comments, and wait for the entire presentation or discussion to be finished. Reduce personal and environmental distractions by focusing on the message. Keep an open mind. Be attentive and maintain eye contact whenever possible. By developing these basic communication skills, you will become more confident and more effective.

94wpm

Speaking is also a form of communication. In the world of work, speaking is an important way in which to share information. Regardless of whether you are speaking to an audience of one or one hundred, you will want to make sure that your listeners get your message. Be clear about your purpose, your audience, and your subject. A purpose is the overall goal or reason for speaking. An audience is anyone who receives information. The subject is the main topic or key idea. Research your subject. Using specific facts and examples will give you credibility. As you speak, be brief and direct. Progress logically from point to point. Speak slowly and pronounce clearly all your words. Do people understand what you say or ask you to repeat what you've said? Is the sound of your voice friendly and pleasant or shrill and off-putting? These factors influence how your message is received. A good idea is worthless if you can't communicate it.

96wpm

Developing a career is a process. You have looked at your interests, values, skills, aptitudes, and attitudes. Your exploration into the world of work has begun. The journey doesn't stop here, for the present is the perfect place to start thinking about the future. It's where you begin to take steps toward your goals. It's where you can really make a difference. As you set personal and career goals, remember the importance of small steps. Each step toward a personal goal or career goal is a small victory. That feeling of success encourages you to take other small steps. Each step builds onto the next. Continue exploring your personal world as well as the world you share with others. Expect the best as you go forward. Expect a happy life. Expect loving relationships. Expect success in life. Expect fulfilling and satisfying work in a job you truly love. Last but not least, expect that you have something special to offer the world, because you do.

Supplementary Timed Writings

**Supplementary
Timed Writing 1**

All problem solving, whether personal or academic, involves decision making. You make decisions in order to solve problems. On occasion, problems occur as a result of decisions you have made. For example, you may decide to smoke, but later in life, you face the problem of nicotine addiction. You may decide not to study mathematics and science because you think that they are too difficult. Because of this choice, many career opportunities will be closed to you. There is a consequence for every action. Do you see that events in your life do not just happen, but that they are the result of your choices and decisions?

How can you prepare your mind for problem solving? A positive attitude is a great start. Indeed, your attitude affects the way in which you solve a problem or make a decision. Approach your studies, such as science and math courses, with a positive and inquisitive attitude. Try to perceive academic problems as puzzles to solve rather than homework to avoid.

Critical thinking is a method of problem solving that involves decoding, analyzing, reasoning, evaluating, and processing information. It is fundamental for successful problem solving. Critical thinking is a willingness to explore, probe, question, and search for answers. Problems may not always be solved on the first try. Don't give up. Try, try again. Finding a solution takes sustained effort. Use critical thinking skills to achieve success in today's fast-paced and highly competitive world of business.

| 1 | 2 | 3 | 4 | 5 | 6 | 7 | 8 | 9 | 10 | 11 | 12

SKILLBUILDING

For many, the Internet is an important resource in 10
their private and professional lives. The Internet provides 22
quick access to countless Web sites that contain news, 33
products, games, entertainment, and many other types of 44
information. The Web pages on these sites can be designed, 56
authored, and posted by anyone, anywhere around the world. 68
Utilize critical thinking when reviewing all Web sites. 79

Just because something is stated on the radio, printed 90
in the newspaper, or shown on television doesn't mean that 102
it's true, real, accurate, or correct. This applies to 113
information found on the Internet as well. Don't fall into 125
the trap of believing that if it's on the Net, it must be 137
true. A wise user of the Internet thinks critically about 149
data found on the Net and evaluates this material before 160
using it. 162

When evaluating a new Web site, think about who, what, 173
how, when, and where. Who refers to the author of the Web 185
site. The author may be a business, an organization, or a 197
person. What refers to the validity of the data. Can this 209
data be verified by a reputable source? How refers to the 221
viewpoint of the author. Is the data presented without 232
prejudice? When refers to the time frame of the data. Is 244
this recent data? Where refers to the source of the data. 256
Is this data from an accurate source? By answering these 267
critical questions, you will learn more about the accuracy 279
and dependability of a Web site. As you surf the Net, be 290
very cautious. Anyone can publish on the Internet. 300

| 1 | 2 | 3 | 4 | 5 | 6 | 7 | 8 | 9 | 10 | 11 | 12

Supplementary Timed Writing 3

Office employees perform a variety of tasks during 10
their workday. These tasks vary from handling telephone 21
calls to forwarding personal messages, from sending short 33
e-mail messages to compiling complex office reports, and 44
from writing simple letters to assembling detailed letters 56
with tables, graphics, and imported data. Office workers 67
are a fundamental part of a company's structure. 77

The office worker uses critical thinking in order to 88
accomplish a wide array of daily tasks. Some of the tasks 100
are more urgent than other tasks and should be completed 111
first. Some tasks take only a short time, while others take 123
a lot more time. Some tasks demand a quick response, while 135
others may be taken up as time permits or even postponed 147
until the future. Some of the tasks require input from 158
coworkers or managers. Whether a job is simple or complex, 170
big or small, the office worker must decide what is to be 182
tackled first by determining the priority of each task. 193

When setting priorities, critical thinking skills are 204
essential. The office worker evaluates each aspect of the 216
task. It is a good idea to identify the size of the task, 228
determine its complexity, estimate its effort, judge its 239
importance, and set its deadline. Once the office worker 250
assesses each task that is to be finished within a certain 262
period of time, then the priority for completing all tasks 274
can be set. Critical thinking skills, if applied well, 285
can save the employer money or, if executed poorly, can 296
cost the employer. 300

| 1 | 2 | 3 | 4 | 5 | 6 | 7 | 8 | 9 | 10 | 11 | 12

Each day business managers make choices that keep 10
businesses running smoothly, skillfully, and profitably. 21
Each decision regarding staff, finances, operations, and 32
resources often needs to be quick and precise. To develop 44
sound decisions, managers must use critical thinking. They 56
gather all the essential facts so that they can make good, 68
well-informed choices. After making a decision, skilled 79
managers review their thinking process. Over time, they 90
refine their critical thinking skills. When they encounter 102
similar problems, they use their prior experiences to help 114
them solve problems with ease and in less time. 124

What type of decisions do you think managers make that 135
involve critical thinking? Human resources managers decide 147
whom to employ, what to pay a new employee, and where to 158
place a new worker. In addition, human resources managers 170
should be unbiased negotiators, resolving conflict between 182
other employees. Office managers purchase copy machines, 194
computers, software, and office supplies. Finance officers 206
prepare precise, timely financial statements. Top managers 218
control business policies, appoint mid-level managers, and 230
assess the success of the business. Plant supervisors set 242
schedules, gauge work quality, and evaluate workers. Sales 254
managers study all of the new sales trends, as well as 265
provide sales training and promotion materials. 275

Most managers use critical thinking to make wise, well- 286
thought-out decisions. They carefully check their facts, 297
analyze these facts, and make a final judgment based upon 309
these facts. They should also be able to clearly discern 320
fact from fiction. Through trial and error, managers learn 332
their own ways of solving problems and finding the most 343
effective and creative solutions. 350

| 1 | 2 | 3 | 4 | 5 | 6 | 7 | 8 | 9 | 10 | 11 | 12

**Supplementary
Timed Writing 5**

In most classes, teachers want students to analyze 10
situations, draw conclusions, and solve problems. Each 21
of these tasks requires students to use thinking skills. 32
How do students acquire these skills? What is the process 44
students follow to develop thinking skills? 53

During the early years of life, children learn words 63
and then combine these words into sentences. From there, 74
they learn to declare ideas, share thoughts, and express 85
feelings. Students learn numbers and simple math concepts. 97
They may learn to read musical notes, to keep rhythm, to 108
sing songs, and to recognize many popular and classical 119
pieces of music. Students learn colors, identify shapes, 130
and begin drawing. During the early years, students learn 142
the basic problem-solving models. 149

One way to solve problems and apply thinking skills 159
is to use the scientific approach. This approach requires 171
the student to state the problem to be solved, gather all 183
the facts about the problem, analyze the problem, and pose 195
viable solutions. Throughout this process, teachers ask 206
questions that force students to expand their thinking 217
skills. Teachers may ask questions such as these: Did you 229
clearly state the problem? Did you get all the facts? Did 241
you get the facts from the right place? Did you assume 252
anything? Did you pose other possible solutions? Did you 263
keep an open mind to all solutions? Did you let your bias 275
come into play? Did you listen to others who might have 286
insights? Did you dig deep enough? Does the solution make 298
sense to you? 301

This simple four-step process for solving problems 311
gives students a model to use for school, for work, and 322
for life. While the process may not be used to solve every 334
problem, it does provide a starting point to begin using 345
critical thinking skills. 350

| 1 | 2 | 3 | 4 | 5 | 6 | 7 | 8 | 9 | 10 | 11 | 12

Supplementary Timed Writing 6

A major goal for nearly all educators is to teach critical thinking skills to a class. Critical thinking, which is the process of reasonably or logically deciding what to do or believe, involves the ability to compare and contrast, resolve problems, make decisions, analyze and evaluate, and combine and transfer knowledge. These skills benefit the student who eventually becomes a part of the workforce. Whether someone is in a corporate setting, is in a small business, or is self-employed, the environment of today is highly competitive and skilled employees are in great demand.

One factor in achieving success in the workforce is having the ability to deal with the varied demands of the fast-paced business world. Required skills are insightful decision making, creative problem solving, and earnest communication among diverse groups. These groups could be employees, management, employers, investors, customers, or clients.

In school, we learn the details of critical thinking. This knowledge extends far beyond the boundaries of the classroom. It lasts a lifetime. We use critical thinking throughout our daily lives. We constantly analyze and evaluate music, movies, conversations, fashion, magazine or newspaper articles, and television programs. We all had experience using critical thinking skills before we even knew what they were. So keep on learning, growing, and experimenting. The classroom is the perfect setting for exploration. Take this opportunity to see how others solve problems, give each other feedback, and try out new ideas in a safe environment.

A person who has learned critical thinking skills is equipped with the essential skills for achieving success in today's workforce. There are always new goals to reach.

| 1 | 2 | 3 | 4 | 5 | 6 | 7 | 8 | 9 | 10 | 11 | 12 |

Supplementary Timed Writing 7

Use your unique creativity when applying critical | 10
thinking skills. One of the first steps in unlocking your | 22
creativity is to realize that you have control over your | 33
thinking; it doesn't control you. Creativity is using new | 45
or different methods to solve problems. Many inventions | 56
involved a breakthrough in traditional thinking, and the | 67
result was an amazing experience. For example, Einstein | 78
broke with tradition by trying lots of obscure formulas | 89
that changed scientific thought. Your attitude can form | 100
mental blocks that keep you from being creative. When you | 112
free your mind, the rest will follow. | 120

Do your best to unleash your mind's innate creativity. | 131
Turn problems into puzzles. When you think of a task as a | 143
puzzle, a challenge, or a game instead of a difficult | 154
problem, you open your mind and encourage your creative | 165
side to operate. Creative ideas often come when you are | 176
having fun and are involved in an unrelated activity. | 187
You will find that when your defenses are down, your brain | 199
is relaxed and your subconscious is alive; then creative | 210
thoughts can flow. | 214

Habit often restricts you from trying new approaches | 225
to problem solving. Remember, there is usually more than | 237
one solution. Empty your mind of the idea of only one way | 249
of looking at a problem and strive to see situations in a | 261
fresh, new way. How many times have you told yourself that | 273
you must follow the rules and perform tasks in a certain | 284
way? If you want to be creative, look at things in a new | 295
way, break the pattern, explore new options, and challenge | 307
the rules. If you are facing a difficult problem and can't | 319
seem to find a solution, take a quick walk or relax for | 330
a few minutes; then go back to the problem renewed. When | 341
working on homework or taking a test, always work the | 352
easiest problems first. Success builds success. | 362

A sense of humor is key to being creative. Silly and | 373
irrelevant ideas can lead to inventive solutions. Humor | 384
generates ideas, puts you in a creative state of mind, | 395
and makes work exciting! | 400

| 1 | 2 | 3 | 4 | 5 | 6 | 7 | 8 | 9 | 10 | 11 | 12

SKILLBUILDING

Keyboarding is a popular business course for many students. The major objectives of a keyboarding course are to develop touch control of the keyboard and proper typing techniques, build basic speed and accuracy, and provide practice in applying those basic skills to the formatting of letters, reports, tables, memos, and other kinds of personal and business communications. In the early part of a keyboarding course, students learn to stroke by touch using specific techniques. They learn to hit the keys in a quick and accurate way. After the keys are learned and practiced, students move into producing documents of all sizes and types for personal and vocational use.

When you first learn keyboarding, there are certain parameters, guidelines, and exercises to follow. There are rules intended to help you learn and eventually master the keyboard. Creating documents requires students to apply critical thinking. What format or layout should be used? What font and font size would be best? Are all the words spelled correctly? Does the document look neat? Are the figures accurate? Are punctuation and grammar correct?

There is a lot to learn in the world of keyboarding. Be persistent, patient, and gentle with yourself. Allow failure in class and on the job; that's how we learn. It's okay to admit mistakes. Mistakes are stepping-stones for growth and creativity. Being creative has a lot to do with risk taking and courage. It takes courage to explore new ways of thinking and to risk looking different, being silly and impractical, and even being wrong. Your path to creativity is such a vital component of your critical thinking skills. Allow your creative thoughts to flow freely when producing each of your keyboarding tasks.

Keyboarding skill and personal creativity are valuable attributes for life and on the job. The worker who can see situations and problems in a fresh way, reason logically, explore options, and come up with inventive ideas is sure to be a valuable employee.

| 1 | 2 | 3 | 4 | 5 | 6 | 7 | 8 | 9 | 10 | 11 | 12 |

**Supplementary
Timed Writing 9**

One of the most important decisions we all have to
face is choosing a career. The possibilities can appear
overwhelming. Fear not! Your critical thinking skills will
save you! Start your career planning today. Begin with
self-assessment. What are your interests? Do you enjoy
working indoors or outdoors? Do you prefer working with
numbers or with words? Are you the independent type or
would you rather work with a group? What are your favorite
academic studies? Think about these questions and then
create a list of your interests, skills, aptitudes, and
values. What you discover about yourself will help you in
finding the career that is right for you.

After you have explored your personal interests, look
at the sixteen career clusters for a wide range of job
prospects. Most jobs are included in one of these clusters
that have been organized by the government. During your
exploration, make a note of the clusters that interest you
and investigate these clusters.

Gather as much information as possible by using all
available resources. Scan the Help Wanted section in the
major Sunday newspapers for job descriptions and salaries.
Search the Net. The Internet provides electronic access to
worldwide job listings. If you want to know more about a
specific company, access its home page. Go to your college
placement office. Sign up for interviews with companies
that visit your campus. Visit your local school or county
library and ask the reference librarian for occupational
handbooks. Talk with people in your field of interest to
ask questions and get advice. Attend chapter meetings of
professional organizations to network with people working
in your chosen profession. Volunteer, intern, or work a
part-time or temporary job within your career choice for
valuable, first-hand insight. Taking an initiative in your
job search will pay off.

A career search requires the use of critical thinking
skills. These skills will help you to choose the career
that will match your skills and talents.

| 1 | 2 | 3 | 4 | 5 | 6 | 7 | 8 | 9 | 10 | 11 | 12 |

Ten-Key Numeric Keypad

Goal

- To control the ten-key numeric keypad keys.

Some computer keyboards have a separate ten-key numeric keypad located to the right of the alphanumeric keyboard. The arrangement of the keypad enables you to type numbers more rapidly than you can when using the top row of the alphanumeric keyboard.

To input numbers using the ten-key numeric keypad, you must activate the Num Lock (Numeric Lock) key. Usually, an indicator light signals that the Num Lock is activated.

On the keypad, 4, 5, and 6 are the home keys. Place your fingers on the keypad home row as follows:

- First finger (J finger) on 4
- Second finger (K finger) on 5
- Third finger (L finger) on 6

The keypad keys are controlled as follows:

- First finger controls 1, 4, and 7
- Second finger controls 2, 5, and 8
- Third finger controls 3, 6, 9, and decimal point

- Right thumb controls 0
- Fourth finger controls ENTER

Since different computers have different arrangements of ten-key numeric keypads, study the arrangement of your keypad. The illustration shows the most common arrangement. If your keypad is arranged differently from the one shown in the illustration, check with your instructor for the correct placement of your fingers on the keypad.

NEW KEYS

A. Use the first finger to control the 4 key, the second finger to control the 5 key, and the third finger to control the 6 key.

Keep your eyes on the copy.

Before beginning, check to be sure the Num Lock key is activated.

Type the first column from top to bottom. Next, type the second column; then type the third column. Press ENTER after typing the final digit of each number.

A. THE 4 , 5 , AND 6 KEYS

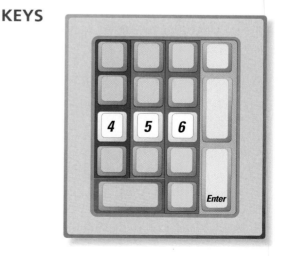

444	456	454
555	654	464
666	445	546
455	446	564
466	554	654
544	556	645
566	664	666
644	665	555
655	456	444
456	654	456

B. Use the 4 finger to control the 7 key, the 5 finger to control the 8 key, and the 6 finger to control the 9 key.

Keep your eyes on the copy.

Press ENTER after typing the final digit of each number.

B. THE 7, 8, AND 9 KEYS

474	585	696
747	858	969
774	885	996
447	558	669
744	855	966
477	588	699
444	555	666
747	858	969
774	885	996
747	858	969

C. Use the 4 finger to control the 1 key, the 5 finger to control the 2 key, and the 6 finger to control the 3 key.

Keep your eyes on the copy.

Press ENTER after typing the final digit of each number.

C. THE 1, 2, AND 3 KEYS

444	555	666
111	222	333
144	225	336
441	552	663
144	255	366
411	522	633
444	555	666
414	525	636
141	252	363
411	525	636

D. Use the right thumb to control the 0 key.

Keep your eyes on the copy.

Press ENTER after typing the final digit of each number.

D. THE *0* KEY

404	470	502
505	580	603
606	690	140
707	410	250
808	520	360
909	630	701
101	407	802
202	508	903
303	609	405
505	401	506

E. Use the 6 finger to control the decimal key.

Keep your eyes on the copy.

Press ENTER after typing the final digit of each number.

E. THE . KEY

4.5	7.8	1.2
6.5	9.8	3.2
4.4	7.7	1.1
4.4	7.7	1.1
5.5	8.8	2.2
5.5	8.8	2.2
6.6	9.9	3.3
6.5	9.9	3.3
4.5	7.8	1.2
6.5	8.9	1.3

McGraw-Hill/Irwin and the GDP author team would like to acknowledge the participants of the 2004 Focus Group for their efforts in making the 10th edition the best it can be:

Special thanks goes to Ken Baker for his work as the tech editor on GDP.

Kim Aylett
Branford Hall Career Institute
Southington, CT

Ken Baker
Sinclair Community College
Dayton, OH

Lenette Baker
Valencia Community College
Orlando, FL

Joyce Crawford
Central Piedmont Community College
Charlotte, NC

Martha Gwatney
Northern Virginia Community College
Annandale, VA

Marijean Harmonis
Community College of Philadelphia
Philadelphia, PA

Mary Hedberg
Johnson County Community College
Overland Park, KS

Kay Ono
Leeward Community College
Pearl City, HI

Marcia Polanis
Forsyth Tech Community College
Winston-Salem, NC